INTRODUCTION TO SOCIOLOGY

Catherine Court
B.A., M.Ed.

TUDOR

© C. Court 1997, revised edition 1999

First published in Great Britain by Tudor Business Publishing Limited.

A CIP catalogue for this book is available from the British Library

ISBN 1 872807 02 X

The right of Catherine Court to be identified as the author
of this work has been asserted by her in accordance with the
Copyright, Designs and Patents Act 1988.

Typeset by Deltatype Ltd, Birkenhead, Merseyside
Printed and Bound in Great Britain by
Athenaeum Press Ltd, Newcastle upon Tyne.

Introduction to Sociology

ACKNOWLEDGEMENTS

The author thanks the following for granting permission to reproduce photographs in this book:

    Mary Evans Picture Library
    Photofusion
    W & S Associates

The author would also like to thank the Associated Examining Board for granting permission to reproduce 'A' level examination questions.

    Every effort has been made to obtain necessary permission with reference to copyright material. The publishers apologize if inadvertently any sources remain unacknowledged and will be glad to make the necessary arrangements at the earliest opportunity.

For Alexander and Helena

CONTENTS

INTRODUCTION

"Nothing is permanent except change." (Aristotle).

Change is a constant feature of all societies, shaping the culture and politics of people's lives. Sociology is the study of this change – past, present and future – enabling us to understand our social world.

This book provides an accessible introduction to the basic principles of sociology. The chapters mirror the AS and 'A' level topics in the AEB syllabus. In particular, recent topics such as culture, and sex and gender have been included in this text. The book is written in a clear and concise way, to enable students to understand theoretical perspectives and to appreciate the empirical evidence underlying them. Excessive use of sociological theory is avoided in order to make the subject suitable as both an introductory text and a revision aid.

A checklist of essential terms is included at the end of each chapter to aid understanding and revision. Self-assessment questions following each chapter enable students to test their knowledge of the subject matter, and may be useful for tutors to set as homework. Where appropriate, AEB 'A' level questions are included at the end of certain chapters.

Introduction to Sociology is a text which covers the requirements for 'A' level courses and will prove valuable to undergraduates approaching the subject for the first time. It will also be of benefit to BTEC, access, nursing, and social work students.

Catherine Court

CHAPTER ONE

THE SOCIOLOGICAL PERSPECTIVE

LEARNING OBJECTIVES

ON COMPLETION OF THIS CHAPTER THE STUDENT SHOULD BE ABLE TO:

1 DEFINE SOCIOLOGY
2 UNDERSTAND HOW SOCIOLOGY EMERGED AS A DISCIPLINE
3 EXPLAIN THE MAIN SOCIOLOGICAL PERSPECTIVES: FUNCTIONALIST, CONFLICT, INTERPRETIVE
4 IDENTIFY ALTERNATIVE THEORIES OF SOCIETY

Sociology as a subject

The word sociology comes from the Latin word socius meaning people, and the Greek word logos, meaning the study of. It can be defined as: the scientific and systematic study of the organisation of societies, including the structure and functions of their institutions, and the behaviour of people within these groups.

Reasons for emergence

Before the eighteenth century, religion had provided the framework for explaining society. During the 1800s classical humanism) represented by Hobbes, Locke, Rousseau, Voltaire) replaced religion in the period known as the 'Age of Enlightenment'. The nineteenth century witnessed the industrial revolution, scientific developments, and the urge to develop a scientific and systematic study of social phenomena. Auguste Comte (1798–1857), a French social philosopher, wanted to develop a scientific approach to studying objective facts about the social world. He described this view as positivism, and is credited with defining sociology as a discipline.

The growth of sociology as a subject throughout the nineteenth century occurred through the work of three main sociologists: Emile Durkheim (1858–1917), Karl Marx (1818–1883), and Max Weber (1864–1920). These three men contributed to the expansion and diversification of the subject and had a great influence on subsequent

People in society

sociologists. Due to these factors they are, along with Auguste Comte, often referred to as the 'Founding Fathers' of the subject.

The sociological perspective

Sociology is best understood as a subject which is made up of a number of separate though interrelated approaches. These sociological perspectives are simply different ways of trying to understand the social world. There is no one single set of terms or concepts or theories; there is more than one way of studying society and interpreting the findings.

There are three major perspectives or views of society, each with their own body of theory and particular methods of studying society. They are: the functionalist perspective, the conflict perspective, and the interpretive perspective.

The functionalist perspective

The functionalist perspective has its origins in nineteenth century attempts to explain society by using models or analogies against which to compare society. One major analogy which emerged during the nineteenth century was the human body or

biological organism model. Although the analogy of the human body has been known and used for many centuries, great discoveries in biology and in particular Darwin's theory of evolution, renewed interest in the biological analogy. The British sociologist Herbert Spencer (1820–1903) was one of the most important proponents of the biological analogy. Spencer pointed out that when discussing the 'evolution' of human societies he was referring to super organic evolution which is a form of evolutionary change over and above that which applies to biological organisms. Thus, both biological organisms and human societies share a number of similarities: they grow in size; as they grow there is a differentiation of internal elements; this differentiation of structure is accompanied by a differentiation of function; the individual parts can survive and function in spite of damage to the organism or the society.

The work of the **social pathologists** went much further than Spencer in its biological analogy. Social pathology was based on seeing society as an organism, with a preoccupation with classifying the ills of society. A 'healthy' society is seen as good and desirable, whereas 'sickness' is undesirable and bad, with the ultimate cause of sickness and 'social problems' being socialisation failure.

The biological analogy is very limiting as a theory. It tells us little about how society actually operates, with evolution occurring as a result of adaptation to the physical environment. But this assumes that if the environment never changes then society will remain the same. Also, evolutionary change is slow, and cannot account for the rapid and revolutionary change which can occur in societies. Finally, this analogy takes no account of social stratification or class conflict within society.

Mechanical analogies of society also have a long history. In the seventeenth century social mechanics likened society to an astronomical system where the elements were human beings attracted and repulsed in a similar way to the planets and stars. In more recent times the mechanical analogy has compared society to the internal combustion engine or to a watch, where the different 'bits' inside them combine together to make the machine work. An even more modern mechanical analogy of society is the cybernetic model, or the notion of a self-regulating machine, for example a thermostat. Using this model to examine society, it could be argued that when crime and delinquency reach a certain (unacceptable) level, society reacts by voting extra financial resources to the police, social workers, housing redevelopment projects. This neutralises the perceived threat to the overall stability of the society, and returns the whole social structure to its steady state. Thus an equilibrium is maintained. However, in the cybernetic model no attempt is made to examine who decides the 'maximum/minimum' temperatures acceptable to society, and who intitiates state intervention. There is also no attempt to evaluate the effects of the intervention.

EMILE DURKHEIM

One of the most renowned early functionalists was Emile Durkheim, the first professor of sociology (at the Sorbonne University, Paris). This 'founding father' of the subject attempted to outline a scientific theory of society which could be applied to any society at any point in history.

Durkheim's theory stated that society has a reality or existence of its own, over and above the individuals who comprise it. Durkheim believed that all the members of society are controlled by 'social facts' such as common values, norms, morals and laws which have an existence of their own. These social facts are passed on from one generation to the next, and guide peoples' behaviour. Durkheim's views of society constantly stress the importance of the whole of society rather than its individual constituent members. He used the term social solidarity to describe the way in which societies continue and persist, despite changes in individual members. In order to maintain social solidarity society must have a collective conscience, which is a social fact referring to a set of norms and customs which are obeyed by the majority of people. The existence of a collective conscience further supports the functionalist view that the whole of society is always greater than its parts.

Durkheim's views constantly stress the importance of the integration of individuals into a community. This integration is achieved partly through the occupations which people hold (the division of labour), and partly through the collective conscience. If this integration is threatened to the extent that peoples' values and beliefs begin to break down, for example in wars, then a condition known as anomie can arise within a society. Individuals themselves do not 'have' anomie; rather, it is a condition of society which can subsequently affect individuals.

TALCOTT PARSONS

The American sociologist Talcott Parsons (1902–1979) further developed the functionalist view by concentrating on what he called **structural functionalism**, which refers to human action which is structured around norms, roles, and institutions, all of which are functional or necessary for the continuance of society.

Parsons had a model of society as a functioning system made up of many interlocking sub-systems which in turn are made up of interconnecting parts. Examples of sub-systems include the education sub-system, the economic sub-system, the political sub-system, etc. Thus, the economic sub-system needs the education sub-system to supply it with skilled workers. Society is the point at which all these sub-systems combine to create a structure which is able to support the total social needs of the population.

Another important element of Parsons' theory of society is the emphasis he puts on a society's equilibrium. Thus, a society is in a state of perfect equilibrium if there is no conflict; everyone knows what is expected of an individual in any role; and these expectations are met with the appropriate responses from others in society. Obviously this cannot be achieved in practice, but it is assumed that society is always striving to achieve it. Parsons argues that the two key processes for attaining this theoretical state of equilibrium are socialisation and social control.

One of the biggest criticisms levelled against Parsons is concerned with the inability of the equilibrium view to explain social change: in a society with perfect equilibrium there would be no incentive to innovate or change the status quo, hence social change would not develop.

ROBERT MERTON

Another significant American sociologist who modified the functionalist approach was Robert Merton (b.1910). He made a distinction between **manifest functions** and **latent functions**. Manifest functions are those which are recognised and intended by the individuals involved: for example, a manifest function of schools is to impart knowledge. Latent functions are the unintended and unrecognised consequences of social behaviour: for example, a latent function of schools is to maintain social control by occupying the time of young people.

Merton also used the term **dysfunction** to refer to the way in which certain types of behaviour can have a detrimental effect on society: for example, the increase in lone parent families over the past twenty years has put enormous financial and social pressures on most western societies.

REVIEW OF FUNCTIONALISM

As a sociological perspective, functionalism does have some advantages in its analysis of society. Thus, it enables society to be seen as a totality with the interconnections between its structures and sub-systems. It emphasises the importance of society's influence over the behaviour of individuals in society, in particular stressing the importance of socialisation and social control.

However, functionalism does raise some problems for the study of society, particularly in its assumption that society is almost a being in itself which thinks and functions. This all embracing view of society leads to the assumption that all individuals in society share the same values, resulting in overall consensus. This may be true in small scale societies, but it is doubtful if it exists in large scale industrial ones. Equilibrium theory, and the emphasis on passive socialisation, makes it difficult for functionalism to explain social change. Finally, if everything in society serves a function which is necessary for the maintenance of the social structure then functionalism would defend the status quo: for example, poverty serves vital functions in society such as the maintenance of work incentives.

The conflict perspective

This view of society also has its origins in the nineteenth century, and is largely based on the writings of Karl Marx (1818–1883), although many sociologists writing this century have modified his views to incorporate the changes which have occurred in modern industrial societies.

KARL MARX

Marx was born in Germany of Jewish background, and his early work was strongly influenced by Hegelian philosophy which took the view that ideas are produced by individuals, and the material world can thus be changed by changing ideas. Marx became one of the Young Hegelians who criticised Hegel's work, believing that our ideas are derived from, and reflect, the material world. Upon moving to Paris, Marx was influenced by French socialism, and in 1848 he was the co-author, with Frederick Engels, of the 'Communist Manifesto'. Shortly after, Marx moved to London, where the ongoing industrial revolution and his study of English economics resulted in the publication of his major work 'Capital' in the 1860s. The word **Marxism** refers to the system of the theories and teachings of Marx, in close collaboration with Engels, leading to the development of a scientific and coherent conception of the world and the changes taking place within it.

Just like Comte and Spencer, Marx envisaged society as an entire system of interconnected institutions. He also believed that the scientific study of societies was thus a science of social systems. This whole view of society is called **macro-sociological**, in contrast to social action or interpretive theories which are **micro-sociological** because they are concerned with the behaviour of individuals in small groups.

The role of the economic system in society is crucial to an understanding of Marx's theories. He believed that the material or economic base of a society was critical in determining the social relations of a society. Thus the substructure of a society refers to the productive forces or technology of the society. This substrucure determines what form the social institutions (for example, family, education, government) will take and what kind of religious beliefs will develop. The social institutions and the beliefs created by the substructure are known as the superstructure.

By tracing societies throughout history Marx was able to demonstrate how all societies developed through a number of stages, each of which corresponds to an economic system with its own distinctive substructure and superstructure. This development took place via a process called dialetical materialism, which is a struggle of opposites caused by man's development of the material world. Hence, Marx identified five distinct types of society, based on different productive forces, with each type of society undergoing revolutionary change before it evolved into the next type. Marx concentrated his work mainly on the fifth stage, capitalism, with his model of society based on the conviction that society was a changing process and that the form it assumed was the outcome of conflicts.

REVIEW OF THE CONFLICT PERSPECTIVE

Marx established the foundations of the conflict perspective, using historical and comparative references to apply his model to all kinds of society. However, his process of historical materialism, whereby history can predict the future, with capitalism leading to conflicts and ultimately socialism, has not been fulfilled. According to Karl Popper, Marx's theory suffers from historicism because a law which does not accurately predict the future must also be wrong when applied to the past.

Marx is also often accused of being an economic determinist because of his insistence that changes in the economic base of society cause changes in the social structure. Individuals can and do change their situation independently of economic forces.

Since Marx's death in the late nineteenth century many American and European sociologists have used his ideas to develop theories concerning the origin and nature of conflicts within society. In particular, they have used the existence of conflicts to explain social stratification and the continuance of inequalities within society.

The social action or interpretive perspective

In common with the conflict perspective, the social action or interpretive perspective emphasises the active role of individuals in society. However, it is micro-sociological, because its main concern is the behaviour of individuals, concentrating on the social interaction between human beings and the way in which people continually construct and contribute to the existence of their social world.

MAX WEBER

The German philosospher and sociologist Max Weber (1864–1920) was the first to develop a theory of social action which was concerned with the meanings people have for their actions. Weber was interested in what things meant and how people made sense of their lives and actions, and those of others.

In social interaction with others, individuals attempt to understand the meanings for others' behaviour. On the basis of these meanings new actions and decisions are made or constructed. Thus, for Weber, people are in a continual process of constructing social reality or negotiating answers and actions based on an understanding of other peoples' behaviour.

All actions have both intended and unintended consequences. In the study of religion sociologists would ask 'What does religion mean for the individuals involved?' However, religion may have different meanings for Catholics, Jews, Baptists, etc. For many religions the intended purpose of church attendance is to worship God, but the unintended consequence may be to further social connections.

Weber noted that individuals are free to choose their actions and roles, such as career and parenthood. Whereas functionalists would argue that people are constrained by social forces into acting out roles, interpretive sociologists argue that people can step out of roles, or change them, or abandon them completely.

Social action theory presents what is described as a **dramaturgical** view of society, where society is seen as a stage upon which people act out roles in a continual drama of life. This approach is particularly evident in the work of the American sociologist Erving Goffman. Functionalists also see society as a stage, but there is no choice in the roles which are given out to people and, if anyone tries to change them or steps out of them, they are punished and coerced back into their allotted parts.

Since Weber's first account of the perspective, social action theory has developed along several different routes this century.

SYMBOLIC INTERACTIONISM

This branch of social action theory emerged in the 1920s and 1930s from the work of a group of American philosophers (W.I. Thomas and G.H. Mead being the most important). This theory has as its basis the idea that symbols and gestures provide the means by which humans interact with each other and their environment. Social life can only continue if the meanings of symbols such as smiling, waving and talking are largely shared by all members of society. Symbolic interactionism is also useful in explaining how the process of labelling takes place in society, and in particular how less able children in schools, juvenile delinquents, and drug takers are labelled by, respectively, teachers, law enforcement agencies, and the general public. The work of Howard Becker on the process by which certain people are labelled as deviants is a good example of the application of interactionist ideas.

PHENOMENOLOGY

This is another area of interpretive sociology, predominantly derived from the work of American sociologists such as Alfred Schutz. This view emphasises the process by which people interpret objects or 'phenomena' in the social world, for example, the meanings people give to concepts such as time and distance, and objects such as furniture, clothing, cars. Schutz was interested in the way in which 'strangers' (for example, immigrants) perceive the social world in a different way to non-strangers (that is, natives), because of their unfamiliarity with the cultural environment.

ETHNOMETHODOLOGY

This area of interpretive sociology attempts to describe how individuals make sense of the same social situation. Different individuals can experience the same situation and yet give a contradictory account of it: for example, witnesses at an accident, or even students in a sociology class! The term was originally coined by the American Harold Garfinkel, who stressed the importance of understanding the methods and rules used by people to make sense of society. Taken to an extreme, however, the theory implies that it is impossible to really understand human behaviour, as each individual has his or her own particular perception of a situation which can never be experienced in the same way by someone else.

REVIEW OF THE SOCIAL ACTION PERSPECTIVE

Social action or interpretive sociology emphasises the human nature of society, seeing it as the result of the construction of active human beings. It uncovers the social processes by which the mind, the self, actions and meanings are created and unfold as individuals interact with other individuals and groups in society. Contrary to the functionalist view, social action theory allows for conflicts of meanings and actions, and explains social change.

The major criticism of this perspective is that it is almost entirely subjective in that it concentrates on individual action and meaning, and ignores the objective nature of the world into which the individual is born. In ignoring the objective nature of society, social action must also ignore the process of socialisation, and the culture which is passed on to the next generation. This perspective presumes that individuals can be free and complete people without any process of social learning taking place to influence their thoughts and deeds. Social action theory also ignores the class nature of society, and the fact that individuals are born into a social class which has meanings for the individuals concerned. The theory allows for social change, but does not account for the difficulties which individuals and groups have in trying to alter social structure.

CONCLUSION

The three major sociological perspectives outlined above are not exhaustive. It is possible to identify other theories, which are largely derived from one of the three major views. **Humanist sociology** (derived from the interpretive perspective) relies on a concern for social justice and an emphasis on the active role of people in achieving social change. **Feminist sociology** (a combination of the interpretive and conflict approaches) has emerged in the past twenty years as a response to the importance which gender carries within the social structure, and a rejection of the functionalist world view as western, white, middle class and male. **Reductionist theories** are attempts to explain social facts by reference to biology or individual behaviour, and have their roots in theories based on social evolution. Thus, **sociobiology** is the study of the inheritance of genetically determined behaviours such as intelligence and aggression. **Social exchange theory** is an economic model of cost and benefit to explain people's behaviours, whereby people act in a way which brings the most benefits at the least cost.

Finally, the American sociologist C.W. Mills (1916–1962) argued that everyone is capable of seeing society from different viewpoints, or using what he described as the 'sociological imagination' in their daily lives. Most people are able to see the social world in terms of the social forces which are at play, rather than purely from an individual viewpoint. For example, unemployment can be seen through the eyes of the unemployed person and the effects it has on that individual and his/her family (what Mills calls 'personal troubles'). On the other hand, unemployment can be viewed in a wider context and its causes and consequences seen as beyond a person's control (what Mills calls 'public issues'). Hence, the subject of sociology is one which many people can relate to via events in their own lives, but using theoretical perspectives to help them to understand and interpret their social world.

CHECK YOUR UNDERSTANDING

After reading this chapter you should now be able to define the following terms.

1 Sociology
2 Founding Father
3 Positivism
4 Social evolution
5 Social pathology
6 Social structure
7 Functionalism
8 Structural-functionalism
9 Manifest function
10 Latent function
11 Dysfunction
12 Materialism
13 Social relations of production
14 Macro-sociology
15 Micro-sociology
16 Social action
17 Symbolic interaction
18 Phenomenology
19 Ethnomethodology
20 The 'sociological imagination'

SELF-ASSESSMENT QUESTIONS

1 Why is sociology made up of a number of different perspectives?
2 Why do sociologists use analogies to study society?
3 How useful is the biological analogy?
4 What contribution does social pathology make to functionalism?
5 What does Durkheim mean by 'social facts'?
6 Why is Parsons' equilibrium theory inadequate as an explanation for human behaviour?
7 Why was the economic system important in Marx's theory of society?
8 How has Marx's theory been criticised?
9 Describe Max Weber's view of social action.
10 What does the 'dramaturgical view' contribute to interpretive sociology?
11 What is the major criticism of the interpretive perspective?
12 What other ways of 'seeing the social world' have emerged from the three major perspectives?

'A' LEVEL SOCIOLOGY ESSAY QUESTIONS

1   Outline and evaluate the Marxist view that an understanding of conflict between competing groups is essential to explanations of social change (November, 1992).

2   Assess the claim made by interactionists that the social world has to be explained in terms of the meanings that actors give to their actions (Summer, 1994).

CHAPTER TWO

THE RESEARCH PROCESS

Learning Objectives

ON COMPLETION OF THIS CHAPTER THE STUDENT SHOULD BE ABLE TO:

1 APPRECIATE THE CONNECTION BETWEEN SOCIOLOGY AND SCIENCE
2 HAVE AN UNDERSTANDING OF THE NATURE OF SCIENCE AND SCIENTIFIC RESEARCH
3 DEFINE OBJECTIVITY AND UNDERSTAND ITS ROLE IN THE RESEARCH PROCESS
4 DESCRIBE THE MAIN SAMPLING TECHNIQUES AND THEIR ADVANTAGES AND DISADVANTAGES
5 EXPLAIN THE METHODS OF DATA COLLECTION USED IN SOCIOLOGY, AND UNDERSTAND THEIR ADVANTAGES AND LIMITATIONS
6 INDICATE HOW THEORETICAL PERSPECTIVES IN SOCIOLOGY ARE OFTEN LINKED TO PARTICULAR RESEARCH TECHNIQUES

Sociology and science

August Comte argued that sociology should be based on the methodology of the natural sciences, resulting in a 'positive science of society' which would reveal the laws governing human behaviour. This approach is known as **positivism**. Comte insisted that only directly observable 'facts' were acceptable in the study of society. These facts could then be measured or quantified and used to develop theories based on cause and effect relationships.

Emile Durkheim in 'The Rules of Sociological Method' (1895) developed this approach to argue that sociology is the study of social facts which must be regarded as 'things'. These social facts refer to any form of behaviour which has an existence of its own, independent of its effects on individuals in society. Thus, institutions, beliefs, and values can all be regarded as social facts and treated in the same way as objects and events in the natural world. Durkheim saw society as an autonomous reality, existing outside the individual. Society is thus formed by a collective conscience – the shared norms and values which exist as part of our individual identity as well as having a reality outside of us.

In his study entitled 'Suicide' (1897) Durkheim sets out to investigate the phenomenon sociologically by demonstrating that suicide is caused by the social factors belonging to society, rather than the alternative explanations such as climate, race, heredity, etc. which were prevalent at the time of his writing. He believed that success in explaining suicide by social causes would add weight to his goal of establishing sociology as a scientific and academically respectable discipline with its own subject matter – the social world. (For further discussion of Durkheim's study of suicide see pp. 142–145)

The approach which Durkheim used for gathering data, describing, classifying and analysing social facts, and using this material to generate theories, is known as an **inductive approach**. The opposite of this is a **deductive approach**, which begins with a theory and then uses appropriate data to test that theory. This latter view is the one taken by Karl Popper in 'The Logic of Scientific Discovery' (1959) who argues that the test of whether a theory or law is scientific depends on whether it can be falsified. The statement 'All swans are white', for example, is easily falsified when a black swan is seen, even if a single non-white swan is not observed in a lifetime. The point is that the proposition contains the possibility of being falsified, and is therefore scientific. Thus, according to Popper, sociological theories such as Marx's theory of history are unscientific because they are subjective and can never be proved wrong. However, he believes that some theories of human behaviour are open to the possibility of falsification, but it is difficult to apply this to society where it is impossible to limit and control human variables.

The question of whether the social sciences in general, and sociology in particular, *are* sciences therefore depends entirely on the definition of science. If a very narrow view is taken in defining science, in so far as it models itself on natural science, then sociology and the other social sciences can never be truly 'scientific'.

THE COMMON SCIENTIFIC METHOD

The 'Founding Fathers' (Comte, Durkheim) believed that a science of society was possible in so far as the social sciences could follow the Scientific Method. The similarity between the natural sciences and the social sciences thus lies in their Common Scientific Method based on positivist principles such as:

1 identifying an area or problem to study;
2 developing a hypothesis and suitable research questions;
3 selecting appropriate methods to study the area;
4 collecting relevant data;
5 analysing the data;
6 reporting the findings and conclusions;
7 making the results open to public accountability and to criticism and testing by other researchers.

The nature of science

The claim of sociology to be a science, on a par with the natural sciences, raises a number of issues concerning the whole concept of what 'science' is. Thus, it is necessary to examine the conditions under which modern, natural science is produced, and the extent to which natural science is objective, detached, and value-free, all of which are seen as the hallmarks of 'real science'.

Scientific development and research

Within the last fifty years scientific development and research has become a highly organised social activity, involving ever increasing numbers of scientific workers and huge sums of money and resources. As J. Ravetz argues in his book 'Scientific Knowledge and its Social Problems' (1971), there has been an increasing 'industrialisation of science'.

This expansion of the scientific industry has been documented by Leslie Sklair in 'Organised Knowledge' (1973) where he describes how science can be divided into two categories, namely big science and little science.

Big science is where scientists work in large scale organisations, in teams requiring a high degree of bureaucratisation. According to Sklair: 'They often handle large sums of money, and they are often responsible for complex and expensive premises and equipment'.

Little science is described as Sklair as 'the lone scientist working industriously by himself with his own materials and apparatus' who is 'largely, but not entirely, a thing of the past'. Ravetz refers to the lone scientist as the 'scientific craftsman'.

Money and resources for scientific research come from three main sources: the government, private industry and charitable foundations. Most scientific research in Britain is funded by the government, which therefore has a great deal of power in deciding how and what research will take place. As Sklair points out: 'Science, and especially big science, does not just happen, it is directed. Thus businessmen, civil servants, and politicians, and not scientists, far less the public, decide how science will progress. They do so by deciding how much of their resources they are willing to pour into the selected areas of big science.'

Natural science is clearly neither value-free nor detached from the social world. Science is a social activity which is controlled and directed by powerful groups and by the state, so that 'in most, if not all situations where science and politics meet, science advises and politics decides' (Sklair). Thus the value of natural science to the powerful groups lies in its usefulness to provide reliable data which permits future prediction and increased control over the natural world. For the natural scientists who work in big science there are the material rewards of prestige and status, and funds for large scale research.

Those who fund natural science research decide, for their own purposes and aims, what types of research are most useful to them. So, too, with those sociologists who argue that society is no different from nature. Their research is selected by funding organisations in terms of its usefulness in solving their 'problems'. Thus their research is into 'problems': public opinion, voting behaviour, advertising and consumer attitudes, personnel work, etc. Such research means that the research findings will not be critical of the funding organisations, even if the findings are critical.

For many social scientists the growth of big science has meant the channelling of large sums of money into 'useful science' which can produce practical solutions to the funding groups' problems. The problem for social scientists is that of convincing the government, businessmen, and foundation workers of the 'usefulness' of their research before they receive any funds. Also, some social scientists have seen the professional status, prestige, and superior facilities that big science has brought to the natural scientists. Thus they have sought to argue that sociology can be useful, can predict, and can even lead to 'mastery of the social world'. In other words it is similar to natural science. From this view the functionalists and positivists argue that the social world, and the relationships of human beings, are not different from the natural world and its animate and inanimate objects. They argue that human beings act in predictable ways, so that if we use the methods of natural science, such as statistics and laboratory experiments, this will provide us with the data to predict future behaviour, which can then be planned and controlled. As P. Lazarsfeld in 'The Language of Social Research' (1955) wrote: 'The purpose of social science is the prediction and control of human behaviour.' What Lazarsfeld does not mention is, after sociology has collected the 'useful data' and made its predictions, which groups will do the controlling and social engineering. Surely it will be those groups who funded such 'useful' research in the beginning.

Objectivity

Objectivity is the lack of personal values and bias in one's work – that is, the sociologist attempts not to take sides. The sociologist tries to be neutral, value-free and detached by trying to keep philosophical views, political allegiances, religious beliefs, social preferences, and personal feelings from in any way influencing work or social research. Science as a social institution, with values and theoretical judgments, has been a subject of study since Comte, Durkheim, and Marx claimed that the natural sciences were free from social influences. However, Thomas Kuhn in 'The Structure of Scientific Revolutions' (1962) dismisses the notion that science is merely a collection of theories, methods, and factual findings. Instead, he suggests that scientists and sociologists make use of paradigms or particular perspectives about their area of study which influence the direction and nature of their research. Scientists and sociologists are strongly committed to these paradigms, which are taught to new researchers as part of their socialisation into an academic culture. Kuhn argues that scientific paradigms change at given periods of history and are superceded by new ones. Kuhn refers to the incompatability between paradigms as 'incommensurability', and the emergence and establishment of a new paradigm constitutes what Kuhn calls a 'scientific revolution'. This revolution is complete when the scientific community in the particular field becomes committed to it wholeheartedly. Kuhn, therefore, does not see science as a rational activity, but recognises the social character of science which affects the conditions under which scientific knowledge is produced.

Functionalists such as Robert Merton provide examples of how science is influenced by cultural and material conditions. Merton argues that there is a 'scientific ethos' comprised of certain norms, values and rules, which institutionalise science and control the production of knowledge. This notion of scientists conforming to a set of norms regulating their work has been challenged by a number of writers. M. Polanyi in 'Personal Knowledge' (1958) argues that beliefs operate in all scientific knowledge, although not in an obvious way. He claims that the ideology of 'objectivism' is used by scientists to screen the social and cultural factors influencing the production of scientific knowledge. Similar to Kuhn's 'paradigmatic science', Polanyi argues how every belief system is sustained by: a circularity of ideas or constant reinforcement; subsidiary explanations for problematic results; and a refusal to consider any rival explanations of phenomena.

Sociology is not exempt from these issues as it is a body of knowledge which is socially produced, reflecting the personal values of individual sociologists as well as the economic, political, and social contexts within which their ideas and theories are formulated.

The controversy about value-judgements in science started at the beginning of the twentieth century when Max Weber stated that they had no place in sociology. He argued that sociology should only deal with the facts. Thus, if sociology is to be accepted as 'scientific', then it must be as objective and 'value-free' as the natural sciences are supposed to be.

Opponents of Weber's view argue that values have a place in sociology, and furthermore that values are unavoidable. Thus to choose to be value-free is itself an expression of certain values. That scientific research necessarily involves values can be shown by the example of many nuclear physicists who, having worked on the first atomic bomb and seen its military use and effects on Hiroshima, later refused to continue any more research on nuclear weapons for the US Army and government. As Alvin Gouldner in 'The Myth of a Value-Free Sociology' (1975) comments: 'Before Hiroshima physicists also talked of a value-free science; they too vowed to make no value-judgements.'

In his paper 'Whose Side Are We On' (1967), Howard Becker argues that values cannot be avoided. Thus he writes: 'To have values, or not to have values, the question is always with us. When sociologists undertake to study problems that have relevance to the world we live in, they find themselves caught in a cross-fire. Some tell them not to take sides, to be neutral and do research that is technically correct and value-free. Others tell them that their work is shallow and useless if it does not express a deep commitment to a value position.' Becker argues that since sociologists cannot be neutral, then they cannot avoid taking sides in research. Therefore the key question is, 'Whose side are we on?' and 'Whose side do we take in social research?' Most sociologists, when conducting their research, only take into account the views of officials, such as teachers, doctors, police, etc. They only accept the 'officials' view', and are therefore taking sides no matter how 'neutral' they may claim to be. Becker further argues that since we can never avoid taking sides, we can never have a balanced picture. We need to take into account the views of all the groups involved.

A solution to the problem of bias is that when a sociologist studies a group he/she must state that they are interested only in that particular group. Becker argues that we must be aware of the bias and state openly the bias in the final report, thus seeking to lessen its effects on the research and the results. J. Madge in 'The Tools of Social Science' (1969) summarises the value-free position thus: 'Value-free social science is unattainable, but bias is less dangerous if fully exposed.'

Sampling techniques

It is often impractical and financially prohibitive to study the whole population for a sociological study. Thus the sociologist will select a cross-section, or small sub-group which is representative of the larger population. This cross-section is known as a representative sample. There are a number of ways in which samples can be taken, with varying degrees of representativeness.

Random sampling is the most basic form of sampling where the sociologist starts with a sampling frame or an up-to-date list of the people under investigation. From the sampling frame the sample is chosen at random, with each member of the population having an equal chance of being selected. This method has the advantage of being

Filling in a questionnaire face-to-face with the interviewer

quick, easy and cheap to do. However, the main disadvantage is that the same type of people may be selected by chance, for example all young males or all smokers, which would make the sample unrepresentative.

Systematic random sampling is where people are selected from the sampling frame in a systematic way, for example by taking every 2nd, 5th, or 12th name from the list. The main problem with this method is that if the sampling frame is organised systematically then it can lead to an unrepresentative sample, for example a list of children which alternates between males and females would result in an all female sample if every 2nd name was chosen and a girl was second on the list.

Quota sampling is where the population to be studied is divided into chosen categories, such as age, sex, occupation, social class, etc. The interviewer selects a quota or number from each group, and picks people in public places or door-to-door until the quotas are filled. Quota sampling is often used for opinion polls and market research. This method is quick, cheap and simple to do. It ensures a more representative sample, but suffers from interviewer bias in the choice of prospective interviewees.

Stratified sampling is where the population is divided into groups or strata according to certain characteristics, and each stratum is then sampled by random. This method maintains the representativeness of the sample and avoids the problem of bias caused by interviewer selection. By using proportional stratified sampling it is possible to increase the representativeness of the sample by ensuring that the groups in the sample are in the same proportion as they are found in the total population under study. However, stratified samples can only be taken if researchers have sufficient information on the stratas to be able to take appropriate samples.

Cluster sampling is where the population is divided into a large number of groups, called clusters, and a sample is taken among the clusters. It is frequently used in social surveys to cut down the cost of gathering data, by reducing expenses such as listing costs and travel costs involved in interviewing.

Multi-stage sampling is where samples are selected from clusters several times over, for example a random sample of census tracts may be selected, then within each tract a random sample of streets could be taken. The interviewer might be instructed to select every 4th house within the streets chosen, and to interview every 2nd adult within each of these households.

The main disadvantage with both cluster and multi-stage sampling is that the clusters selected may not be representative of the whole population. Obviously, it is advisable to select as many clusters as possible to increase the representativeness of the final sample.

Multi-phase sampling is where certain questions are confined to a fraction of the sample, and general information is gained from the total sample. This can save time and money, and provide a wide range of information.

Snowball sampling is where the researchers may have difficulty in locating suitable subjects for the survey, for example criminals, drug addicts, the mentally ill. One way to obtain such groups may be to find one individual who fits the criteria, and then ask that person if they know anyone else, and so on until the required number is obtained. The obvious advantage is that a list can be found where one did not exist beforehand. However, the sample is unlikely to be representative because it is not random and relies on personal contacts.

Volunteer sampling provides an alternative means of generating a sample, where adverts, leaflets, radio, TV are used to announce the survey and requests are made for volunteers. This method shares the same advantages and disadvantages as snowballing.

The research design

Sociological investigations use a range of empirical methods in order to study society. Empiricism is the act of experiencing something with one's senses, that is, obtaining information directly or indirectly from the social world, rather than relying on speculation and imagination. Sociologists usually prefer to use a variety of research methods such as interviews and observation, to make sure of collecting reliable and valid data. N. Denzin in 'The Research Act in Sociology' (1970) calls this research procedure 'triangulating' the data collection. The set of selected empirical methods is referred to as the research design. The major methods employed in social research are:

1 The collection of new material (primary data collection) by questionnaires, interviews, observation, longitudinal studies, and experiments.
2 The analysis of existing material (secondary data collection), by utilising statistical data, historical and contemporary material.

The methods of conducting sociological research are often categorised as either **quantitative** or **qualitative**. The former includes methods which result in largely statistical data (for example, social surveys, questionnaires, and stuctured interviews). The latter includes methods which produce descriptive data (for example, unstructured interviews, participant and non-participant observation).

When sociologists carry out research projects they may cause problems for, or even do harm to, the people they study. This makes it necessary for sociologists to consider the ethical implications of their research. Social research may, on rare occasions, cause physical harm, for example studies of competition or conflict may lead to hostile or aggressive behaviour. Psychological harm to participants may occur when questioning them about sensitive issues such as crime, sexuality and mental illness. Finally, ethical considerations surrounding confidentiality and consent may occur when people are observed without being informed, or are misinformed about the nature of the study.

Methods of data collection

The research method most commonly associated with sociology is the social survey. This is a method of collecting information from a sample of people by means of questionnaires or interviews.

QUESTIONNAIRES

Questionnaires or formal recording schedules are used for collecting factual data or for questioning opinions and attitudes on particular issues. The first step in questionnaire design is to define the problems and theoretical questions to be tackled, deciding what topics to cover. This usually involves a review of existing research in the field. It is essential to design a questionnaire that has a clear layout, good printing, and instructions which are understood by the respondent. The researcher should aim to ask questions only from people likely to be able to give meaningful answers. Several other key issues must be borne in mind: the willingness to complete the questionnaire; the accuracy or reliability of the answers and the validity or relevance of the answers. It is important that the questions are: phrased in simple, everyday language; unambiguous; use neutral terms; not too personalised or embarrassing; and cover the correct time span for behaviour.

The only solution to all these difficulties is to have pre-tests (checks on small isolated problems of design), and eventually pilot surveys which are small scale models of the main survey based on a small group which is representative of the larger sample. It is during these stages that problems of wording, question order, and types of question should be decided. Types of questions include the following.

Pre-coded questions, where the respondent has a fixed number of answers to choose from. These questions are sometimes called multiple choice questions.

Open-ended questions, where the respondent is free to answer at length on a subject.

Classification questions, which enable the researcher to categorise the sample, for example by age, sex, race, occupation, income group.

Factual or knowledge questions, which are used to assess the respondents' understanding of a topic.

Motivation questions, which help to reveal the reasons for particular actions or beliefs.

Opinion questions, which can be used to determine a respondent's views on a specific subject.

Postal questionnaires are a relatively cheap method of finding out facts from a large number of people dispersed over a wide area. The main advantage of this method is the avoidance of interviewer bias, or the influence of the interviewer on the interviewee's responses. The major disadvantage is that non-response rates tend to be high in comparison with other methods of data collection. Therefore, attractively designed questionnaires that are short, easy to complete, simple to return, sponsored by a group with prestige, and presented with an incentive to return, such as a free gift, are likely to be the most successful.

An example of low response rate is provided by D. Wedderburn, 'Workplace Inequality' (1970) where she used postal questionnaires in her study of working conditions for different occupational grades in large firms. She achieved a response rate of 55% from over 880 firms sampled. Certain characteristics, however, were shared by those who replied, which were not shared by the sample population who failed to reply, for example geographical, industrial and size distribution.

INTERVIEWS

Interviews use questionnaire schedules as well as 'free discussion' in order to obtain information. There are several types of interview.

Mass or structured interviews are brief, formal interviews in which the wording of the questions and the order in which they are asked is fixed and defined, which means that precise answers are required. This format may produce quantitative as well as qualitative data, and reduces the effect of interviewer bias.

Focused or unstructured interviews are those where the topic is chosen by the interviewer, but the reply is free or open. This means that the interviewer is able to rephrase questions, can prompt the interviewee, and give encouragement where necessary. Although this method can yield a large amount of qualitative data it is very prone to interviewer bias.

Non-directive or unstructured interviews allow the respondents to talk freely and at length on any subject which they choose. Obviously interviewer bias is a problem, and also a lot of irrelevant information may be collected if the interviewees are not directed towards particular topics.

There are a number of common problems which affect all three types of interview:

Interviewer bias or interviewer effect arises from the ways in which the social interaction between the interviewer and interviewee may influence the reactions and replies of the respondents. Factual questions may be answered accurately, but replies to questions on attitudes or opinions may reflect either what the respondent thinks the interviewer wishes to hear, or what he/she thinks would be a widely acceptable opinion. A number of British and American studies have indicated that the greater the status difference between interviewer and respondent, the less likely it is that the respondents are willing to express their true feelings. M. Schofield, in researching for 'The Sexual Behaviour of Young People' (1968) had to be very careful choosing his interviewers, because questions on premarital intercourse may vary according to the interviewer. Similarly J Allan Williams Jr in 'Interviewer – Respondent Interaction' (1971) found that black Americans in the 1960s who were questioned on civil rights demonstrations were more likely to approve of such action if the interviewer was black rather than white. Interviewer effects may be partly offset by using 'interpenetrating samples' where each of several interviewers with different personal characteristics are allocated interviews at random in each of the areas to be surveyed. In a large and complex investigation of couples in the US, P. Blumstein and P. Schwartz, 'American Couples' (1983), used two interviewers so that partners could be interviewed separately as well as together, helping to ensure the maximum amount of depth, yet reducing interviewer interference. The role in which the interviewer is cast by the respondent, and the respondent's attitude towards the role may affect replies. E.Bott in 'Family and Social Network' (1968) found herself cast in the different roles of scientific investigator, friend of the family, and therapist.

Household replies refers to situations where responses may vary depending on which member of the household actually replies, so bias may be introduced if a particular member of all households is always interviewed, for example husband or wife. In J. Tunstall's 'The Fishermen' (1962) men who were interviewed in the presence of their wives often underestimated the amount of money spent on beer compared to their figures in separate interviews. In addition, the timing of interviews must be carefully considered because daytime interviews exclude all those who work during the day, whereas evening interviews exclude those working night shifts.

Misinterpretation of answers by the interviewers can affect the results. One way of avoiding this may be to record the interviews so that transcripts can be reviewed later. Tape recording was used by J. and E. Newsom in 'Patterns of Infant Care' (1963) who found that people did not feel self-conscious in the presence of a recorder, and the interviews could be replayed many times to obtain the relevant data.

Administrative errors can occur in recording the responses, especially with pre-coded questions. Clerical mistakes can also arise if the questionnaire schedule is long, or the time available to interviewer or respondent is short, and answers are inaccurately noted.

OBSERVATION

Observation is a fact of everyday life, whether it involves observing other people and their actions, or being the subject of someone else's observation. This casual observation is, however, unstructured and not conducted according to rules. The observation which sociologists use as a method of investigation is structured and disciplined, and conducted according to certain rules. Thus the sociologist 'sees' actions and activities which the casual observer either ignores or misses because of not knowing who or what to select for observation.

Non-participant observation is where the observer is not involved in the group being watched, and where the group is unaware that it is being observed. The observer merely tries to watch what others are doing, and may not even know the group or the individuals involved. The sociologist is interested in observing behaviour and attitudes; he or she is not concerned with the meaning or the motivation behind the actions or behaviour, but only with how the group or individuals behave. There are two kinds of non-participant observation. Simple observation is usually confined to public places and involves observation of physical movements and gestures, speech patterns and dialects, language, looks and glances, and physical distances between people. In contrast mechanical observation can be conducted in both public and private places, and may include the use of various aids: cameras, binoculars, telescopes, listening devices, cassette recorders, etc.

Non-participant methods of observation do have certain problems, for example simple observation is limited to public places, and much of the observation does not take account of the meanings or intentions underlying behaviour. Also, many of the methods of mechanical observation are illegal in many countries, and there are ethical considerations regarding privacy and confidentiality.

Participant observation is one of the main research methods used in ethnography, which is the study of the way of life of a group of people. Cultural anthropologists apply the method of participant observation or fieldwork to small, technologically simple societies. Anthropologists would then describe such a culture in an ethnography. Sociologists would use participant observation to study a category of people or a particular setting, and present their results as a case study. Participant observation as a method of collecting information involves three main stages: entry, or gaining access or sponsorship to the group under study; in position, or the time spent collecting the data from the group under study; exit, when the researcher completes the project and has to leave the social group or community under study. Questions arise as to the objectivity of participant observation because the researcher is interacting with the data being studied. It is unavoidable that the researcher will be regarded as a participant, and consequently it is difficult not to 'take sides' whilst doing such research.

Studies using participant observation as a method have a long history, and one of the earliest in sociology is included in the work of C. Booth, 'Life and Labour of the People in London' (1904). Booth was studying the extent to which poverty existed in the city, and he spent many years at the end of the nineteenth century observing the conditions in which people were living. For some of the time he rented accommodation in the poorer parts of the city and noted the patterns of life in the streets around his lodgings.

Many occupational studies in the 1960s used participant observation, for example H. Becker, 'The Boys in White' on student doctors and W. Westley, 'Violence and the Police'. Two American studies of police behaviour have used participant observation as the primary research method. Both studies were conducted by female sociologists, which is important since males and male values tend to predominate in the police world. J. Hunt 'Police Accounts of Normal Force' (1985) set out to overcome the (mostly) male resistance of the police officers by changing her perceived identity and adopting a 'combat personality' which gave her acceptance into the police culture. S. Martin, 'Breaking and Entering: Policewomen on Patrol' (1982) studied the Washington DC police, and revealed some of the problems that women encounter when they become police officers.

Participant observation is frequently used to study deviant and sexuals groups where access to information is often restricted. In L. Humphreys 'The Tearoom Trade' (1975) the author secretly observed the homosexual behaviour of men in public toilets (called 'tearooms' by those who frequent them). Humphreys took the role of 'watch-queen' or a lookout who signals those engaged in homosexual acts that a stranger or police officer is approaching. Only a few of the men he studied were aware of his true identity, and although Humphreys took care to protect the identities of the men under observation, he was violating ethical standards of social research.

Studies of deviant groups are often criticised for their biased nature, for example H. Becker, 'Outsiders' (1966) which tends to be rather sympathetic to groups such as drug takers. Similarly, J. Young, 'The Drugtakers' (1972) on drug sub-cultures in London and N. Polsky, 'Hustlers, Beats and Others (1971) on pool room hustling, may give a rather glamorous view of these activities.

The issue of participation in the group's activites creates moral and political decisions for the researcher. L. Festinger et al, 'When Prophecy Fails' (1964) involved the researchers feigning religious beliefs in order to study sects. J. Patrick, 'A Glasgow Gang Observed' (1973) used disguised observation to study gang actions but found he was required to participate in similar behaviour. One way of resolving the issue of participation is to obtain sponsorship into the group. A good example of this is provided by W. Whyte, 'Street Corner Society' (1955) which researched an Italian American gang in Boston over a three year period in the 1930s. To gain access and acceptance into the 'Cornerville' neighbourhood Whyte befriended 'Doc' as a key informant, and thus obtained 'insider status' in the group. This enabled Whyte to research the group 'from the inside out', but also meant that he began to see himself as a group member rather than as an objective social researcher. It is also possible to change status during the research. J. Roth, 'Timetables: Structuring the Passage of Time in Hospital Treatment and Other Careers' (1963) initially studied the hospital where he was confined with TB as an 'insider'. However, after his recovery he continued doing the same research by studying other hospitals as an 'outsider'.

In some instances identity may be partly revealed, for example E. Goffman, 'Asylums' (1961) where Goffman revealed himself to the principal of the mental institution where he was studying the patients. Goffman also conducted a study of gambling behaviour in 'Where the Action Is' (1967) when he trained as a croupier so that he could work at the gaming tables of Nevada casinos. He remained, though, a sociologist first and a casino employee second.

The range of problems which occur with participant observation as a method of data collection can be summarised as follows.

1. Difficulties may occur when entering the group, being accepted by the people, and remaining within the group.
2. The observer may become too emotionally involved with the people in the group which can lead to biased reporting.
3. The researcher's presence in the group changes the situation and the behaviour of the people under study.
4. The results obtained from studying one group of people are not typical of another similar group; the study cannot be replicated.
5. If the true identity of the researcher is known to the group this may affect their

behaviour; similarly, if the observer's identity is hidden then this may also affect the results.

6. The group under investigation can control what the observer sees and hears.
7. Participant observation is a very time consuming method as some researchers spend years with their subjects.
8. This method can be expensive if a lot of time and/or travel is involved.
9. Researchers may be in physical danger in some instances of observation.
10. Recording data during participant observation is a problem as notebooks and recording devices can be obtrusive. Trying to remember events later on is very unreliable and may lead to biased accounts.

LONGITUDINAL STUDIES

Longitudinal studies are used to investigate a large sample of people over many years, or even possibly over their whole lives. These studies may be retrospective, that is, they trace the events in people's lives back through time (for example, a study of people who died of lung cancer may involve tracing their medical records to see if they smoked) or they may be prospective, which involves following people in their present and future lives. In Britain the first major longitudinal study was started in 1947 by the Population Investigation Committee on every child born in the first week of March, 1946. The same sample was used by J.W.B. Douglas in 'The Home and the School' (1964) to follow the children's educational careers. Other significant longitudinal studies include the National Child Development Study, based on 17,000 children born in the first week of March, 1958, and the Newson Studies which started in 1963.

The advantages of longitudinal studies are that events are recorded as they happen which reduces bias and unreliability of memory; it is possible to return to the sample for further or follow-up information; and a large, representative sample covering regional and social class variations can be constructed.

The main problem with this method is the cost of continuing the research, as the human resources needed to conduct the survey are large, in addition to the travel costs involved, and the time needed to analyse the results. Another major difficulty is that over a period of time the sample reduces in size due to death, emigration, lack of co-operation, moving house, etc. This sample attrition will result in a smaller, but more importantly, a less representative sample. Another disadvantage of this type of survey is that much of the data may be of little or no value, and therefore selection of data is of crucial importance. Furthermore, some of the interviewers used may be untrained, for example teachers, health visitors, social workers, and this may create biased recording of the interviews.

EXPERIMENTS

Experiments are usually associated with the natural sciences and take place in laboratory settings. They are typically devised to test a specific hypothesis or a relationship between facts or variables. Successful experiments depend on careful control of all the factors that might affect what is being measured. In social science experiments have to be conducted 'in the field' or in actual social situations where phenomena that could never be artificially created in a laboratory can be observed, for example schools, factories, hospitals, prisons. However, the inability to control the field environment means that hypotheses are typically more general in sociology than they might be in a laboratory. It is also difficult to replicate field experiments because of their individualistic nature.

Attempts to create laboratory experiments in social science have, however, been made. P. Zimbardo, 'Pathology of Imprisonment' (1972), used the basement of the psychology building at Stanford University to create an artificial prison ('Stanford County Prison') to test the hypothesis that the character of prison itself, and not the personalities of prisoners and guards, is the cause of prison violence. Using volunteers selected from newspaper advertisements, Zimbardo 'imprisoned' half of the subjects and used the other half to take on the role of 'guards'. Although the experiment was designed to last two weeks, Zimbardo had to call a halt to the research before the end of the first week as abusive, degrading and violent behaviour spread amongst the 'prisoners' and the 'guards'. Zimbardo's hypothesis was supported by his research, but more importantly his study illustrates the ethical dilemmas surrounding such attempts to re-create social situations in artificial settings.

One of the major problems with field experiments is that subjects may change their behaviour if they are aware of being part of a research project. This is often known as the 'Hawthorne Effect', after a classic experiment by Elton Mayo in the 1930s at the Hawthorne factory of the Western Electric Co. near Chicago. Mayo was studying workers' productivity by changing lighting, heating, break times, etc. Mayo found that productivity rates increased even when conditions were made less favourable for the workers. After a period of time the researchers realised that the workers were working harder simply because they knew that they were being studied.

SECONDARY SOURCES OF DATA COLLECTION

These are 'second hand' sources of material which may be used by the sociologist to review a subject area, to prove a hypothesis, or to provide background material for a research project.

Official statistics are collected mainly by government organisations: census data, registration of births, deaths, and marriages, figures on crime, unemployment, poverty, etc. Such large and wide ranging sources of information cannot easily be obtained by sociologists so they are of great use to social researchers. The main advantage of official statistics is that they are generally reliable, since repeated applications of the same techniques of collecting data produce the same result. However, official statistics are not always valid, that is, they do not measure what they are supposed to: crime statistics reliably measure criminal acts but are not valid because many crimes go unrecorded. A technique must be reliable if it is to be valid, though a reliable measure is not necessarily a valid one. The use of official statistics by sociologists is described in detail in Chapter 10.

Historical records/documents are used to make comparisons with past societies. J.A. Banks, 'Prosperity and Parenthood' (1957), used this method to examine the relationship between middle class standards of living and family limitations in Victorian England. He used official government reports as well as letters, newspapers, pamphlets, etc. to illustrate that the reduction in middle class family size had more to do with economic considerations than other factors. The main problem with this method is that the material is created for purposes other than sociological analysis, which means that it is not always in a suitable format for use by social researchers.

Contemporary records and personal documents share the same problems as historical documents, and may be particularly subject to bias, for example, personal diaries.

Content analysis is the systematic analysis and description of the content of communication media, such as television, radio, newspapers, magazines, books, etc. Researchers might use this type of method to obtain data on political views and attitudes, news reporting techniques, and propaganda messages transmitted via the media.

Existing research which has been conducted by other social scientists may be used to help formulate or test hypotheses, be used as a comparison, or be added to and improved upon.

The comparative method dominated sociology in the nineteenth and early twentieth centuries as a means of comparing similarities and differences between societies. Durkheim was a major proponent of this method, as he believed that sociological theories should be testable and, as experimenting with whole societies was impossible, the comparative method should be used as a method of quasi-experimental or indirect experiment.

As already noted in the section on experiments, the experimental method in sociology is inappropriate as the sociologist cannot hold social conditions or variables constant. Thus sociologists attempt to compare societies where certain phenomena are similar or different. In the method of agreement sociologists will compare two or more examples of a phenomenon which are different in all respects but one, for example Western Europe and Japan both became feudal despite being vastly different societies. The method of difference compares two or more examples of a phenomenon which are similar in all respects but one: although Western Europe, China and India were basically economically similar in the nineteenth century the Protestant ethic was only present in Western Europe and thus encouraged the development of capitalism in these countries first.

Theoretical perspectives and research techniques

Most sociologists use whatever research techniques suit their purpose, often using a variety of methods in the course of a single piece of research. It is often assumed that quantitative methods are used by sociologists holding a functionalist or conflict perspective, and interpretive sociologists are frequently associated with qualitative techniques.

Both conflict and consensus approaches fall within the structuralist perspective and are concerned with analysing 'whole' societies or social systems. The social world is seen as one which can be understood and explained by the use of the research strategies of the natural sciences. By adopting the objective, detached and rational strategy of the natural sciences the structuralists aim to develop a body of scientific knowledge of laws and theories to explain the social world. In contrast to this emphasis on law-like behaviour and quantifying features of social life, the interpretive view emphasises 'man as an active social being', who gives meanings to the social world. Sociologists who hold the interpretive view tend to favour qualitative methods such as participant observation and unstructured interviews, where there are no explicit hypotheses, small samples, and the results focus on behaviour and attitudes rather than statistical data.

Thus, there are substantial links between the theoretical perspectives and the various research methods. The interdependence of theoretical and research issues means that assumptions about the nature of the social world lead to certain research strategies and data being used. It is not always possible to compartmentalise sociological perspectives and methods, and many sociologists still use whatever method suits their purpose, irrespective of their theoretical standpoint. However, by making research decisions and choices the sociologist is also making theoretical statements about how the social world can be analysed and understood.

CHECK YOUR UNDERSTANDING

After reading this chapter you should now be able to define the following terms.

1   Positivism
2   Social facts
3   Collective conscience
4   Inductive theory
5   Deductive theory
6   Scientific theory
7   Big Science
8   Little Science
9   Objectivity
10 Paradigms
11 Scientific ethos
12 Value-judgements
13 Representative sample
14 Random sample
15 Systematic random sampling
16 Quota sampling
17 Stratified sampling
18 Cluster sampling
19 Snowball sampling
20 Empiricism
21 The research design
22 Primary data collection
23 Secondary data collection
24 Quantitative data
25 Qualitative data
26 Social survey
27 Questionnaires
28 Pilot surveys
29 Interviews
30 Interviewer bias
31 Participant observation

32 Ethnography
33 Longitudinal studies
34 Sample attrition
35 Field experiments
36 The Hawthorne Effect
37 Official statistics
38 Reliability
39 Validity
40 Comparative method

SELF-ASSESSMENT QUESTIONS

1 What is the 'scientific method' adopted by both natural and social scientists?
2 Define 'objectivity'.
3 How have value-judgements affected the development and practice of sociology?
4 How does the choice of sampling method affect the representative nature of the sample?
5 Describe the three types of interviews.
6 Explain the problems caused by interviewer bias.
7 Discuss the main problems of participant observation.
8 Why might the experimental method be termed 'positivist'?
9 How could the use of the comparative method be used to justify the claim of sociology to be scientific?.
10 Why would interpretive sociologists tend to use participant observation?

'A' LEVEL SOCIOLOGY ESSAY QUESTIONS

1 Critically evaluate the usefulness of questionnaires to sociological research (AEB, Nov. 1992).
2 Outline and assess the advantages and disadvantages of primary and secondary data as sources of information in sociological research (AEB, summer, 1994).
3 Evaluate the ways in which scientific thinking and methods have influenced sociological research (AEB, summer, 1995).

CHAPTER THREE

CULTURE

LEARNING OBJECTIVES

ON COMPLETION OF THIS CHAPTER THE STUDENT SHOULD BE ABLE
TO:

1 UNDERSTAND THE MEANING OF CULTURE AND ITS MAIN
   COMPONENTS
2 EXPLAIN THE NATURE OF CULTURAL DIVERSITY
3 COMPREHEND THE THEORETICAL ANALYSIS OF CULTURE

Culture and its main components

The sociological definition of culture is much broader than the 'common-sense' one
which refers to art, theatre, literature, etc. In sociology culture is the total way of life of a
society, or the entire range of material objects, ideas and attitudes that the people within
a society have created and adopted for carrying out collective life. This includes
language, symbols, knowledge and beliefs, values and norms.

The material culture of a society refers to the objects and tools that are used in some
way by the members of a particular society, for example houses, cars, clothes,
machinery, etc. Material culture reflects not only a society's cultural values, but also its
technology. Modern industrialised societies often judge cultures with simple technology
as less advanced. However, while our technology has produced labour saving devices
and advances in medical care, it has also contributed to the creation of nuclear weapons
and holes in the ozone layer. Technological advances can result in the material culture
outstripping the non-material elements. Thus the development of automation can make
existing work practices inappropriate for the new technological conditions. This
situation where some parts of a cultural system change more rapidly than others is
called **cultural lag**.
Cultural transmission is the way in which values, attitudes and language are passed
down from one generation to another, and the process by which individuals learn their
culture is called **socialisation**.

Symbols refer to anything that carries a particular meaning for members of a culture:
it is the way in which cultural communication occurs via message carriers. Language is a

Modern industrial society

most important symbol, as are clothes, gestures, and signs such as morse code. The meaning conveyed by the symbol is dependent on the culture concerned: different languages use different words to mean the same thing. Similarly, an action or object with important symbolic meaning within one culture may have a very different or no meaning at all in another. For example, a cricket bat in England symbolises sport, whereas in other cultures it may indicate a weapon. The act of sunbathing in western cultures is unknown in many pre-industrial societies. Gestures also have different meanings according to culture: the 'A-Okay' symbol of thumb and forefinger in a circle is an insulting sign in Greece and Turkey.

Semiotics is the study of signs and symbols and is a discipline in its own right founded by the French cultural critic Roland Barthes. He concludes that every human phenomena has a symbolic meaning, sometimes **overt**, for example the authority conveyed by a teacher's desk, and sometimes **covert**, for example the male power relationships indicated when men open doors for women. Symbols also change over time and between cultures: fur coats used to be associated with wealth and success, but more recently they are regarded as symbols of the inhumane treatment of animals.

Language is a system of symbols with structured meanings which allow members of a society to communicate with each other. All cultures have a spoken, if not a written, language and it is the most important medium for cultural transmission. The significance of language in shaping our reality and our world can be seen in many ways. The Eskimos have twenty specific words for snow according to texture, rate of fall, dampness, etc. which reflects the importance of the weather in that particular culture. Differences in the use of language between cultures can be summarised by the Sapir-Whorf hypothesis, which states that 'we know the world only in terms of our language'. Thus, humans do not describe the same reality with the words they use. It also implies that language develops as society progresses. Technological advances in computing have led to a whole new language: ram, CD rom, internet, etc.

Values are standards or attitudes of desirability within a culture, such as rightness, honesty, respect for life. It also refers to personal values such as political and moral beliefs, attitudes to education, work, marriage, etc. Value inconsistency can occur when values differ because of certain criteria, for example sex, age, race, religion. It can also arise when there is conflict between society's expected values and an individual's personal values, for example society's views of femininity/masculinity and an individual's sexual orientation. Value conflict arises where there are differences between policy and practice, for example equal opportunities and personal experience of discrimination.

Norms are sets of rules that guide people's behaviour within a society. They may be formal, as in the laws of the land and rules and regulations of clubs and organisations. Alternatively, they may be informal, such as custom, tradition, and convention, for example behaviour in libraries, classrooms, restaurants, etc. Norms may be proscriptive or forms of behaviour which people should not participate in, such as stealing. Or they may be prescriptive and state what people must do, for example observe certain forms of behaviour in church. A system of rewards and punishments or **sanctions** are used to persuade people to conform to normative behaviour. Sanctions may be imposed formally, for example a certificate for passing an exam or a fine for speeding, and informally, for example verbal praise from a teacher or a parent sending a child to its room. Sanctions form an important part of a culture's system of social control, encouraging conformity to social norms.

Mores is a term first described by W.G. Sumner 'Folkways' (1959) to refer to norms that have great moral significance, and often relate to respect for people and property. They can be proscriptive, such as taboos concerning sexual relations with children, or prescriptive, such as wearing clothes in public places. There are strong legal and social sanctions for violating mores.

Folkways were also defined by Sumner, and refer to norms that have little moral significance. Folkways are more concerned with the courtesies and manners of society which govern day to day conduct, for example eating habits, dress codes, general etiquette. Violations of folkways result in only minor penalties, for example social opprobrium.

Cultural diversity

A society's culture is not consistent, but varies according to geographical region, religion, race, class, age, etc. There is thus a need to appreciate the wide ranging nature of cultural patterns.

Sub-cultures refer to aspects of cultural life which differ from the dominant or mainstream culture in some distinctive way, for example teenagers, Jews, Jehovah's Witnesses, homosexuals, aristocracy, etc. Sub-cultures frequently have their own broken 'language', dress codes, values, etc. A recent example of a culture based on ethnicity is the former Yugoslavia, which now comprises a number of republics, such as Serbia, Croatia and Bosnia, each with their own language, religion, and cultural values. Even occupations constitute sub-cultures as they often exhibit distinctive features according to hours of work, value systems, specific language/terminology.

Counterultures or contracultures describe cultural patterns or sub-cultures which are strongly opposed to the dominant culture. Counterultures represent cultural differences within a society which question the morality or values of the mainstream culture. Many counterultures are linked to youth, and the term was widely used to describe the 1960s life styles of the hippie movement. Other counterultures reflect political disaffection, such as anti-war groups during the Vietnam conflict in the US and the IRA in Northern Ireland. Counterultures develop not only different principles and values, but often a distinctive 'uniform' or appearance, for example long hair and bright clothes or 'camouflage' outfits.

Ethnocentrism occurs when people judge other cultures by the standard of their own culture. Our understanding of the social world is so bound up in our cultural understandings that to some extent ethnocentrism is inevitable. An alternative view to this biased evaluation of unfamiliar cultures is **cultural relativism** or the practice of judging a culture by its own standards. This requires an understanding of the norms and values of an alternative culture, as well as an ability to 'see' the world through the eyes of peoples with a different perspective of society.

Theoretical analysis of culture

Culture enables people to understand their world and their role(s) within it. However, it is also a subject of study for sociologists and anthropologists who will view the nature of culture from several different perspectives.

Structural-functional analysis sees society in terms of a stable system of integrated parts devised to meet various human needs. These parts or **cultural traits** become engrained within the individual's own way of feeling and thinking, and internalised so that the individual becomes part of a given culture. The structural-functional approach suggests that all cultures have at least some traits in common because all cultures are created by human beings. The term '**cultural universals**' refers to those traits which are found in every culture of the world. G. Murdock, 'Social Structure' (1965) compared hundreds of different cultures and found many general traits common to all, such as birth, marriage and funeral rites of passage, language, customs, humour.

The notion of society based on a value consensus was described by Durkheim with his idea of a 'collective conscience' or moral consensus within society. T. Parsons, 'The Social System' (1964) further developed this idea to create a model of society as a social system based on four sub-systems (economic, political, kinship, and community). Value consensus is maintained via the institutions and roles within the four sub-systems, for example the family and school convey values of loyalty, respect, conformity to laws and norms.

The main limitation of the structural-functional analysis is its emphasis on consensus and the dominant cultural patterns at the expense of cultural diversity. There is a tendency to ignore cultural differences within and between societies, particularly those differences that arise from social inequality. It also places much emphasis on cultural stability and underplays cultural change.

Social conflict analysis also stresses the importance of values in maintaining cohesion in society. Conflict structuralists such as L. Althusser and P. Bourdieu emphasise the capacity of society to mould people into conformity and reproduce itself through generations. The conflict view argues that societies are not unified and based on consensus, but are divided and split by cultural divisions. The conflict approach asks questions about how certain values dominate within a society and are linked with social inequality. Marx argued that the working class were socialised to accept the dominant ideology (the ideas and values of the rich and powerful) in order to legitimise inequality. From the conflict view the existence of sub-cultures based on class, wealth, race, gender, etc. are critical to an understanding of the existence and perpetuation of social inequality.

The interpretive analysis of culture uses symbolic interactionism to understand the nature of culture. Thus, the importance and use of language is critical in this approach, as well as the meaning of phrases and terms, and the context within which behaviour takes place. Research in this area has included the work of A. Schutz, 'The Stranger' (1964) who demonstrated how immigrants or 'strangers' perceive the social world in a different way to natives or 'non-strangers' who are familiar with the cultural environment. H. Garfinkel, 'Studies in Ethnomethodology' (1967) stressed the importance of understanding the methods and rules used by people to make sense of society, for example the act of sunbathing is a distinctive western phenomenon, which to many tribal or primitive societies may be interpreted as a religious ceremony or a punishment.

Sociobiology is another theory concerned with culture, which originates from nineteenth century relationships between biology and sociology. Rivalry between the two disciplines over the nature of human behaviour persisted up until the middle of this century when sociologists had effectively demonstrated that culture rather than biology was the major influence on people's lives. Within the last twenty years, however, new ideas have attempted to link human behaviour to aspects of biological evolution. This has led to the development of sociobiology, which seeks to explain cultural patterns as the product, at least in part, of biological causes, for example the male and female roles of child rearing are seen as being related to biological functions of sex. Similarly, different reproductive strategies lead to different cultural attitudes regarding sexual behaviour. The danger with the sociobiological view is that it can be used to justify inequalities if, for example, it is believed that intelligence is genetically determined according to sex and race. It is impossible to ignore sex-linked differences, but it is doubtful that biological forces will ever be shown to totally determine human behaviour, as the latter is learned within a system of culture. Biological forces are also subject to change, for example methods of birth control have enabled sex and reproduction to be separated.

Finally, it should not be assumed that humans are prisoners of their culture, but the role of culture in allowing people to shape, create and reorganise their social world, leading to cultural diversity and change, should be recognised.

CHECK YOUR UNDERSTANDING

After reading this chapter you should now be able to define the following terms.

1 Culture
2 Material culture
3 Cultural lag
4 Cultural transmission
5 Values
6 Value inconsistency
7 Norms
8 Sanctions
9 Mores
10 Folkways
11 Sub-culture
12 Ethnocentrism
13 Cultural universals
14 Cultural traits
15 Sociobiology

SELF-ASSESSMENT QUESTIONS

1 How does the material culture of a society influence people's lifestyles?
2 How can sanctions be used to ensure conformity to social norms?
3 Give examples of the ways in which language shapes our social world.
4 Explain the difference between sub-cultures and countercultures.
5 Describe the differences between the structural-functional and social conflict views of culture.

CHAPTER FOUR

SOCIALISATION

Learning Objectives

On completion of this chapter the student should be able to:

1 Understand the nature of the socialisation process
2 Define the main agents of socialisation, and appreciate their influence on the development of identity
3 Appreciate the theoretical perspectives on socialisation

The nature of the socialisation process

Socialisation is the process by which individuals learn the culture of their society, and behave in a socially acceptable manner. Socialisation is significant for society's cultural continuity as well as for the development of individual characteristics and personality. Socialisation is a lifelong process which occurs early in life in infancy and childhood via primary socialisation by 'significant others' such as parents, siblings, other relatives and care givers. Secondary socialisation occurs when children begin to interact with 'generalised others' outside their immediate family circle, for example friends and teachers at schools, youth and community organisations, etc. Socialisation continues throughout life as people move in and out of jobs, relationships, communities, and organisations.

The importance of socialisation is best illustrated by the existence of feral (or wild) children who have avoided the process, and thus have a limited amount of human cultural influence. Some of these cases include children who were allegedly found living in the wild with animals, for example the 'Wild Boy of Aveyron' and the 'Wolf Children of Bengal'. The latter case involved two young girls aged eight and two who were found in India living with wolves. The girls were brought to an orphanage where even after several years they continued to display animal-like behaviour such as walking on all fours, eating food off the floor, playing with the dogs, and howling. These and other cases of children reared by animals are not as reliable as documented examples of children who have been neglected or isolated from human contact. K. Davis, 'Extreme Social Isolation of a Child' (1940) describes the stories of Anna and Isabelle who were both born illegitimately in rural areas of the US in the 1930s. Due to their stigmatised condition they were isolated from human contact and given minimal attention. Anna

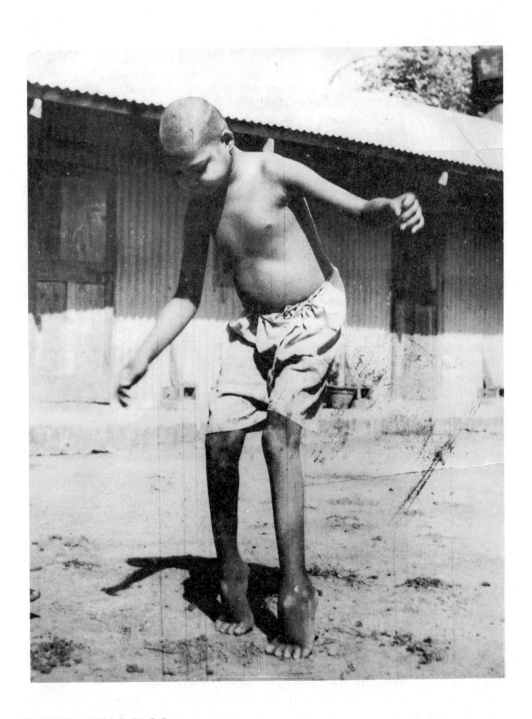

The 'Wolf boy of Allahabad' in India

lived with her mother and grandfather, but was consigned to an attic room and fed just enough milk to keep her alive. When Anna was discovered at five years old she was strapped to a chair, dressed in rags, and physically emaciated. She showed no signs of human communication and it was initially believed that she was blind and deaf. Isabelle was a child with a similar background, but with a deaf mute mother and no male living in close proximity. As a consequence she too was lacking communication skills, and was afraid of male figures when she was first taken into care. These cases amply demonstrate the importance of human contact for human beings to become human.

NATURE V/S NURTURE

Charles Darwin's work on the theory of evolution in the mid-nineteenth century influenced people to apply his ideas to the understanding of human behaviour. 'Naturalists' claimed that all human behaviour was instinctive or part of the 'nature' of the human species. By the end of the nineteenth century this view was quite firmly entrenched, with the notion that some people are 'born criminals' or that females are inherently more emotional than males. This view was also used to explain variations between societies, based on biological rather than cultural differences, for example European and N. American cultures were regarded as somehow more 'biologically evolved' than less technologically advanced ones.

By the beginning of the twentieth century naturalistic explanations of behaviour were being challenged by many psychologists. J. Watson, 'Behaviorism' (1930) argued that human behaviour was not instinctive but learned within a social environment. **Behaviourism**, as this theory was known, also rejected the notion that cultural variations reflected evolutionary differences. Watson was convinced that nurture or learning was far more influential than nature in determining behaviour. This view gradually gathered supporting evidence, notably from anthropologists who demonstrated that cultural patterns were highly variable, even among similar technological societies. M. Mead, 'Sex and Temperament in Three Primitive Societies' (1963) provided evidence to show that differences are due to conditioning or socialisation, especially in early childhood, and that the conditioning is culturally determined.

Nurture theory does not totally exclude a role for biology in determining human behaviour. Obviously heredity is important for physical features which can influence personality. Also, research on twins, for example T. Bouchard's twin studies on the transmission of intelligence, and recent attempts at gene mapping have indicated that many forms of behaviour may have a significant biological input. However, it must be remembered that the development of genetically inherited characteristics ultimately depends on the prevailing cultural conditions. Nature and nurture are thus inseparable.

Agents of socialisation

These are major social institutions which have an important role to play in the socialisation process. They include family, friends, school, workplace, mass media.

The family is central to the process of cultural transmission. Children acquire attitudes, interests, values, beliefs, etc. predominantly from their parents. The family group provides the child with a social position within society in terms of class, race, religion, etc. These family aspects of social identity eventually become part of the child's own social identity. The influence of the family on class values has been amply demonstrated in a number of studies covering the UK, USA, Italy, Taiwan, Poland and

Japan conducted by M.L. Kohn, 'Class and Conformity – a Study in Values' (1977). Research in Britain by J. and E. Newson, 'Four Years Old in an Urban Community' (1970) has produced similar results to Kohn's study, indicating that parents at different levels of the class structure have different values that they communicate. The major findings are that middle and upper class parents tend to value autonomy, self-direction, creativity, and long-term gratification. In contrast, working class parents tend to promote conformity to rules, respect for authority, and short-term hedonism. The Newsons also found differences in class attitudes to punishment, with the middle class favouring verbal disciplining compared to the physical punishments preferred by the working class. Socialisation thus has a role to play in contributing to the perpetuation of the existing class structure as it influences expectations, occupational choice, marriage partners, etc.

Schools are a significant area of socialisation as children come into contact with unfamiliar people and new experiences. Contact with peers who share similar interests, social position and age is increased. The importance of anticipatory socialisation or social learning directed at gaining a desired position, such as club membership, is enhanced. At the same time interaction with children from different social backgrounds reinforces children's own identities. The main purpose of school is to impart knowledge and skills. However, beyond this formal curriculum children also learn the hidden curriculum cultural values such as competitiveness, success, team work, discipline, and culturally approved sex roles in terms of behaviour and subject choices. Schools contribute to the perpetuation of social inequality by linking gender and social class to the extent and type of education that children receive, a theme developed in Chapter 8.

The socialisation process which occurs in organisations and workplace settings varies according to the type and nature of the institution. In military establishments intense training programmes lead to high levels of direct socialisation. In many organisations the norms and values of the workplace may be imparted in an informal way by colleagues. Socialisation in **total institutions** where people live and work in the same place has been well documented by E. Goffman, 'Asylums' (1961), illustrating how new members have to 'unlearn' old norms and values and be resocialised into new ones.

The role of the mass media in the socialisation process, in particular the increase in television viewing hours over the past twenty years, has led to a number of studies concerning the influence of television on children. The two main topics of research are violence and the media, and the presentation of male and female roles in the media. Stereotyping of male/female roles is covered in Chapter 5, and research on violence and the media is evaluated in Chapter 18. The influence of television programmes such as 'soaps' and chat shows on people's attitudes and cultural stereotypes is difficult to measure, but the ease of availability and the one-way process that characterises television makes its power difficult to ignore.

Theoretical analysis of socialisation

In a similar way to culture, socialisation can be viewed from three different perspectives.

Structural-functionalists tend to see socialisation as the critical process by which individuals learn to conform to society's expectations in a collective way. For example males and females are socialised into roles which are best suited to the capitalist nature of society: women take care of children and the home, and men go out to work (T.Parsons and R.F. Bales, 'Family, Socialization and Interactive Process' (1955)). For Parsons primary socialisation is crucial in moulding the child's personality to fit the needs of the society. However, this view of socialisation assumes that all families socialise their children into the same collective norms and values, and does not take account of negative aspects of socialisation which may occur in some families.

An interpretive analysis of socialisation argues that through symbols children acquire an understanding of themselves and others. C.H. Cooley, 'Human Nature and the Social Order' (1902), emphasised the social nature of the self with his concept of the 'looking glass self'. Essentially, every child develops a self-image that reflects how others respond to him/her. Thus, a person's self-concept is based on the responses and reactions of others. Individuals also have an active role to play by anticipating other people's actions or 'taking the role of the other'.

Another significant contributor to the interpretive model of socialisation is G.H. Mead, 'Mind, Self and Society' (1934), which describes how children arrive at a point where they are concerned about how others in society will respond to their behaviour. This process of 'other awareness' marks the culmination of a developmental period when the 'I' part of the self is joined by the 'me' part, thus balancing the active and passive roles of the self. Although the interpretive approach contributes enormously to our understanding of the socialisation process, its emphasis on micro issues means that it tends to ignore questions about who defines the roles within society and the consequences for individuals for displaying certain behaviour.

A conflict perspective on socialisation argues that class membership does not just depend on occupation or wealth, but also the way in which values, attitudes, and beliefs characterise class identification. For example, J. Tunstall, 'The Fishermen' (1962) and N. Dennis, P. Henriques, C. Slaughter, 'Coal is Our Life' (1956) both found that families living in small isolated areas with one major industry tended to have traditional sex roles, and also spent their leisure time in distinctive ways. The class socialisation found within families from affluent or skilled working-class backgrounds has been documented by J. Goldthorpe and D. Lockwood, 'The Affluent Worker' (1968). The values which are found in middle class families have been described by C. Bell, 'Middle Class Families' (1968). Different class perspectives are also to be seen in attitudes towards education, where the middle class practise deferred gratification (the delay of immediate pleasure for future rewards) and the working class tend more towards short term hedonism (immediate rewards).

The conflict view helps to explain the perpetuation of social inequalities, but the classes are not always so different in their values, and there may be greater areas of common culture than there are variations.

Socialisation and freedom of choice

Although society has a powerful effect on our outward behaviour and our innermost feelings, it must not be assumed that people are merely puppets responding to society's wishes. The puppet analogy of society has been termed the 'oversocialised' conception of the human being by D. Wrong, in 'The Oversocialised Conception of Man' (1961). We must remember that we are biological as well as social beings, and we can never be entirely shaped by our society. The power of society is such that it can act on humans, but human spontaneity and creativity also causes humans to act on society. According to P. Berger, 'Invitation to Sociology' (1963), people reflect, evaluate, and act to change society. Thus, sociology may help us to understand how we are moved to behave in particular ways, but as humans we retain the freedom to decide our modes of behaviour.

CHECK YOUR UNDERSTANDING

After reading this chapter you should now be able to define the following terms.

1 Socialisation
2 Primary socialisation
3 Secondary socialisation
4 Feral children
5 Nature v nurture
6 Behaviourism
7 Agents of socialisation
8 Anticipatory socialisation
9 Total institutions
10 Looking glass self
11 Deferred gratification
12 Short-term hedonism

SELF-ASSESSMENT QUESTIONS

1 How do primary and secondary socialisation contribute to the socialisation process?
2 What can the existence of feral children tell us about the significance of the socialisation process?
3 Summarise the nature v nurture debate.
4 How do agents of socialisation affect behaviour?
5 Explain how sociological perspectives have different interpretations of the relevance of socialisation.

CHAPTER FIVE

SEX AND GENDER

LEARNING OBJECTIVES

ON COMPLETION OF THIS CHAPTER THE STUDENT SHOULD BE ABLE
TO:

1 DISTINGUISH BETWEEN DEFINITIONS OF SEX AND GENDER
2 PROVIDE CROSS-CULTURAL EVIDENCE FOR GENDER DIFFERENCES
3 DESCRIBE FEMINISM AND THE WOMEN'S MOVEMENT
4 GIVE AN ACCOUNT OF THE POSITION OF WOMEN IN SOCIETY
5 SUMMARISE THE EVIDENCE ON SEX AND GENDER STEREOTYPING
6 EVALUATE THEORIES OF GENDER DIFFERENTIATION

Sex and gender

The terms sex and gender are frequently used interchangeably in everyday life, but increasingly sociologists have come to make use of a distinction between the two words. Sex is generally used to describe the biological differences between women and men (those based on anatomy, physiology, chromosomes, hormones), and leads to the definition of people as either male or female. Gender, however, is used to indicate the social and cultural differences, including personality, which exist between women and men, and lead to the attribution of characteristics known as femininity and masculinity. Gender is thus socially constructed rather than biologically determined.

However, distinctions between male/female, masculine/feminine are not as clear cut as appears, for example the connection between a person's sex and their choice of leisure activity or their style of clothing is not easily explained. Confusion about the use of the terms exists even among sociologists, who often use the term sex roles when gender roles are actually being written or talked about. Sociological research on sex roles or gender roles tends to concentrate on the different ways in which women and men are expected to behave, in a general manner, as well as in relation to their roles as parents, workers, spouses, etc.

Sex and gender are interrelated with a third aspect of human behaviour – **sexuality**. Although sexuality is mostly seen in biological terms (physical attraction and arousal) there are also social and cultural aspects of sexuality, such as the context within which people meet, talk, and form relationships, the clothes they wear, etc. The whole process conforms to certain cultural expectations rather than purely biological urges. The biological and cultural aspects of sexuality vary between different cultures as well as within a culture over a period of time. Society sets norms and passes laws concerning sexual behaviour: the age of consent for sexual intercourse, the legality of homosexual behaviour, adultery, incest, etc. Thus, sexuality depends on biological differences as well as on expectations of behaviour based on gender.

Cross-cultural comparisons

Cross-cultural research from anthropologists has shown that gender roles do not automatically follow from biological differences. In particular the western connection between female/feminine and male/masculine is not always present in many societies.

M. Mead, 'Sex and Temperament in Three Different Societies' (1935) based on research in New Guinea found that the Arapesh made little distinction between the gender roles of men and women, with both sexes exhibiting gentle and submissive behaviour (what we would define as feminine). The Mundugamor people showed few distinctions between the sexes, but in general all the members of the society expressed rough, aggressive and competitive personalities (our notion of masculine behaviour). Finally, the Tchambuli people expressed the reverse of western gender roles, with the women taking on the heavy manual work and shaving their heads, while the men looked after the children and adorned themselves with jewellery.

Other cross-cultural evidence of differing gender roles comes from Y. and R.F. Murphy, 'Women of the Forest' (1974) which studies the Munderucú, a remote Indian population living in the Amazonian region of Brazil. This group of people are hunters and gatherers, being largely self-sufficient. The Murphys found that there was a strict division of labour along gender lines, where the men hunted, made major decisions, and held religious power. In contrast the women were the gatherers, childcare providers, and were essentially passive in decision and power-making roles. However, the women's perception of their role was one of opposition rather than oppression. The women did not feel inferior or regard the males as superior; they accepted that their roles were different, but equally important.

The presence of overlapping gender roles has been documented by M.K. Rosaldo and L. Lamphere (eds.), 'Woman, Culture and Society' (1974) in their study of the Kung, hunters and gatherers in the Kalahari region of Africa. There is some degree of division of labour by gender, but it is not strict, and there is considerable overlap in hunting and gathering as both activities are seen as important. This overlap in economic activities carries over into other areas of life, such as childcare, and there appears to be little differentiation in the socialisation patterns of males and females. Further evidence of society's power to create gender differences is found in studies of collective settlements in Israel called kibbutzim. Here, the values of social equality are practised via shared work tasks, communal property, shared domestic tasks and childcare responsibilities, and joint decision making. Children are raised apart from their parents in separate dormitories, and appear to have little interest in sexual relations and few gender differences. The extent of the social equality to be found in kibbutzim has been challenged by L. Tiger and J. Shepherd, 'Women in the Kibbutz' (1975) which found that subtle but persistent biological characteristics may undermine gender equality.

Comparative cultural studies do indicate the widespread nature of the division of labour along gender lines. However, there are considerable differences as to the actual tasks which are labelled as female or male. Generally, there are more tasks which are male-specific than those which are strictly female. Men's work is usually associated with higher rewards and status, and it is rare to find a society where the work of men is regarded as unimportant or trivial. Men are more likely to occupy positions of power and influence related to politics, industry and religion than women. There are no existing reliable accounts of fully functioning matriarchies, though there are instances of societies where women occupy positions of influence within the kinship group or as individuals. However, these tend to be more limited and restricted in scope than those which are allocated to men.

Comparative studies are useful in illustrating the variety of ways in which societies create gender differences and practise gender roles. These studies indicate that gender roles are too variable to be considered a simple expression of the biological categories of sex.

Feminism and the women's movement

A universal pattern in all societies is some degree of **patriarchy**, which is a form of social organisation in which males dominate females. This universal tendency towards patriarchy is based on **sexism**, or the belief that one sex is innately superior to the other. Patriarchy is thus based on the belief that males are naturally superior to females and therefore rightly dominate them.

Patriarchy in technologically simple societies reflects biological differences of sex. Pregnancy and childbirth restrict women's lives in these societies, while men's greater strength allows them to dominate in economic activities. However, in industrial societies advanced technology reduces the significance of the biological differences between females and males, for example choice in pregnancy, labour saving devices in the home, industrial machinery to reduce the need for muscle power, etc. In spite of these advances, patriarchy in industrial societies persists; thus, there must be social and cultural reasons for its continuance. Its persistence, in spite of equal opportunities legislation in most Western nations, and the fact that no society has eradicated patriarchy, does not mean that patriarchy is inevitable. As gender is a social construct it is subject to change, but the engrained nature of gender roles makes the eradication of patriarchy difficult to achieve. S. Goldberg, 'The Inevitability of Patriarchy (1974) argues that biological differences generate different behaviours in the sexes, making the complete removal of patriarchy difficult, if not impossible to attain.

Feminism emerged as a response to patriarchy, and broadly refers to support for social equality of the sexes, leading to opposition to patriarchy and sexism. What is described as the 'first wave' of feminism occured between 1890 and 1920, and was characterised in Britain by the Suffragette Movement, whose main aim was political. This movement was led primarily by middle-class women such as the Pankhursts, who benefited most from it, and did little to improve the social, economic, or occupational working conditions of working-class women.

The 'second wave' of feminism emerged in the 1960s in the United States as part of the larger, radical movements of the mid and late '60s such as the civil rights organisations and Vietnam anti-war groups. As J. Mitchell, 'Woman's Estate' (1971) describes, these other political organisations provided the impetus for women to develop their own movement, with their own philosophy, which would be independent of the traditional stereotypes which were still prevalent in other radical movements. In Britain the Women's Liberation Movement was less influenced by pre-existing radical movements than it was by the labour movement and class conflicts such as the 1968 strike at Fords in Dagenham which involved working-class women unionists. According to D. Bouchier, 'The Feminist Challenge' (1983), women were starting to compare their inferior position in society with that of the whole working class. There were other differences between the British and the American movements: the more moderate American feminists created a national group to represent them (the National Organisation of Women) whereas British feminism has relied on grassroots groups or women working through existing leftwing political organisations. Although the Americans have always had a strong radical feminist strand, represented by such authors as S. Firestone, 'The Dialectic of Sex' (1972) and K. Millett 'Sexual Politics' (1970), they have never expressed the socialist/Marxist perspective of many British feminists such as A. Coote and B. Campbell, 'Sweet Freedom' (1982) and A. Oakley, 'Housewife' (1974).

J.Dale and P.Foster, 'Feminists and State Welfare' (1986) have suggested that the first wave of feminism concentrated on what they call 'public rights' such as legal and political equality, represented by a national, hierarchical organisation. In contrast, the second wave is characterised by many small and informal groups which concentrate on 'private issues' such as motherhood, family, and personal identity.

There appears to be no agreement about the aims of the women's liberation movement, either in Britain or in the United States. However, it is possible to identify 'types' of feminism which reflect the whole spectrum of feminist concerns from the liberal to the most radical.

Liberal feminism is essentially concerned with the achievement of equal opportunities legislation, which in Britain was gained via the Equal Opportunities Act, 1970, the Sex Discrimination Act, 1975, and the creation of the Equal Opportunities Commission. Critics of this brand of feminism would argue that, despite the legislation, inequalities still remain, and changes in the law alone will not result in sexual equality.

Radical feminism accepts that there are natural biological differences between the sexes, but does not accept the inevitability of male domination. They view society as an arena of sexual oppression or conflict, and rather than concentrating on equal rights have emphasised inequalities in sex, relationships, and childcare. Radical feminists support the notion of separatism, where men and women live in different social worlds, breaking the tie between women and reproduction, and permitting women to achieve both economic independence and sexual freedom.

Marxist/socialist feminism gives priority to the significance of class as a factor in social inequality. Socialism and feminism are inextricably linked according to this view, and only with the abolition of capitalism will women be able to experience social equality. This perspective assumes that equality will follow naturally from socialism, which has not proved to be the case in countries which claim to have become socialist. Feminists would argue that only with the development of 'pure' or true socialism will equality for women be achieved.

Black feminism concentrates on the twin inequalities of sexism and racism, and the special interests and problems of women from minority groups. One of the disadvantages of this approach is that it further fragments the women's movement into smaller groups with their own particular aims, which reduces the impact which a larger, national movement could have.

Post-feminism is the term used to refer to developments in the women's movement which have occurred during the 1980s and 1990s. Over this period the number of internal divisions and disagreements over the aims of the movement have become even more pronounced, and have been discussed by J.Mitchell and A.Oakley (eds.) 'What is Feminism?' (1986).

Many women are now reacting against feminism in the belief that the real battles have been won with the passing of equal opportunities legislation. However, S.Faludui, 'Backlash' (1992) argues that sexual equality is an illusion, and that despite equal opportunities laws, social inequalities and female stereotypes are still pervasive throughout society, for example negative images of career women in the media.

B.Friedan, 'The Second Stage' (1983) argues that it was initially necessary for women to attack conventional values of motherhood, family roles, gender role stereotyping, etc., but it is now necessary for women to stop criticising all aspects of society which affect women and develop positive ideas about what feminism actually stands *for*, rather than what it is against.

Feminists thus need to balance the values they wish to maintain with the rights and changes they desire to see in society.

Women in society

The extent to which gender is deeply rooted in society and the persistence of patriarchy is largely due to variations in power between the sexes, the division of labour between males and females, and the expectations attached to gender roles.

GENDER AND THE FAMILY

Children quickly learn that males and females are different, as gender is incorporated into personal identity, and children learn to act according to cultural expectations of masculine and feminine behaviour. Thus, boys are socialised into behaving in a rational, assertive, analytical, and dominant way, while girls are expected to be emotional, submissive, weak, and deferential. This gender role reinforcement is conducted in a direct manner, with parents teaching specific skills, as well as in an indirect way by children modelling themselves on their same sex parent.

J.Bernard, 'The Female World' (1981) has described how females and males enter different worlds within one society, with girls socialised into a 'pink world' of Barbie dolls, dresses, and playing 'house', and boys growing up in a 'blue world' of action toys, casual clothes, and war games. Parental attitudes are largely instrumental in determining these roles, and even at the level of touching, lifting, and playing with children parents are instilling behavioural expectations. N.Henley, 'Body Politics – Power, Sex, and Non-Verbal Communication' (1977) has shown that in adult life the extent to which males and females touch, whether they sit or stand in certain situations and the power and authority that this conveys are forms of behaviour which are directly related to childhood socialisation patterns.

GENDER AND THE PEER GROUP

The influence of the peer group on gender roles can be seen in the reactions of adolescents to sexuality, as well as in the different criminal activities which are committed by the sexes. S.Lees, 'Losing Out: Sexuality and Adolescent Girls' (1986) has shown how peer group behaviour in girls is carefully controlled so that they avoid being labelled as 'slags' or 'tarts'. Appearance and manner is important if a girl is to be viewed by her peer group as 'nice'. In terms of criminality A.Campbell, 'Girl Delinquents'

Sex and gender: children at play

(1981) found that shoplifting (the most common crime amongst females) is not just opportunistic, but is based on the perceived need to 'look good', which requires certain clothes and possessions.

GENDER AND EDUCATION

The educational system reinforces gender roles via the reading schemes which are in operation in schools, through the stereotypes which teachers hold of the sexes, and also by means of the 'hidden curriculum' (the often unconscious ways in which boys are treated with higher status and the subtle pressures which may be used to encourage girls to pursue certain subjects and careers). S.Sharpe, 'Just Like a Girl – How Girls Learn to Be Women' (1976) has described the way in which socialising agencies within the school tend to promote particular gender roles, for example by providing reading books which perpetuate gender stereotypes in which females have a largely domestic role. R.Deem, 'Schooling for Women's Work' (1980) found that males and females are encouraged to study different subjects, to the extent that the subjects become 'gendered': science is for boys and childcare is for girls. In relation to the hidden curriculum, D.Spender, 'Invisible Women: the Schooling Scandal' (1982) discovered that in most schools there was a dominance of the male view of the world, whether this was in the presentation of subject material (male explorers, male artists, etc.) or in the preoccupation with male achievements within the school. M.Stanworth, 'Gender and Schooling' (1983) observed gender relations between teachers and pupils in 'A' level classes, and found that questions from boys were more likely to be answered before those from girls, and teachers spent more time in conversation with boys than they did with girls. The relative achievement of girls compared with boys in schools will be discussed in Chapter 8.

GENDER AND EMPLOYMENT

Sex segregation occurs in employment, where certain occupations are filled primarily by women, and other jobs are reserved for men. This is the product of both restriction and of choice. J.Martin and C.Roberts, 'Women and Employment' (1984) argue that employment is 'gendered', and the attitude that 'a woman's place is in the home' was actually supported by most married women, who regarded their 'real' job as the care of the home and the children. Despite increased 'feminisation' of the workforce since the 1950s, men and women continue to occupy different positions in the labour market. Women are over-represented in part-time work (due to domestic and childcare responsibilites) and predominate in 'domestic' type occupations, such as teaching, caring, cleaning, catering, etc.

Although there may be an absence of overt discrimination (due to anti-discriminatory laws), there nevertheless exists institutional sexism which keeps women in low-paid and low-status jobs. This institutional sexism operates through the day-to-day rules, policies and practices of institutions that result in the discriminatory treatment of women, for example, machinery which is designed for men, inadequate childcare facilities, lack of promotion opportunities, etc.

Horizontal segregation occurs when men and women are found in different sorts of industries and occupations: women are under-represented in the construction industry and over-represented in the service industries.

Vertical segregation is when women and men are found at different job levels within an industry or occupation. Women tend to be over-represented at the lower levels and under-represented at the higher echelons (sometimes called the 'glass ceiling' – women can see where they want to go but cannot get there).

Inequality in employment opportunities based on sex-typing may, however, be changing. R.Crompton and K.Sanderson, 'Gendered Jobs and Social Change' (1990) believe that with the decline in traditional male industries, an increase in educational opportunities for females, and continued enforcement of anti-discriminatory laws there may be a convergence in the jobs which men and women do. The role of women in the workplace will be developed and discussed further in Chapter 15.

GENDER AND THE MASS MEDIA

Up until the 1980s the roles of females and males in television and the cinema were fairly stereotypical: men were the heroes, who took charge and gave orders, and the women were the submissive sex objects who did as they were told. Since the '80s it appears that more responsible, interesting and assertive roles have been given to women, such as the detective series 'Cagney and Lacey' and the film 'Alien' with Ripley, the female heroine. Children's television has been traditionally male–dominated, but recently that too has shown fewer stereotypical portraits of the sexes.

Advertising in the media also tends to promote gender role stereotyping, with women appearing overwhelmingly in adverts for cleaning, food, and domestic appliances, whereas men promote banking, car sales, and provide authoritative voice-overs. E.Goffman, 'Gender Advertisements' (1979) studied magazine and newspaper adverts and found that men were photographed to appear taller (implying male superiority) whereas women were presented lying down or seated on the floor. The expressions and gestures of the men exuded an air of competence and authority, whereas women were portrayed in child-like poses of innocence and naivety

In Britain, research by A. McRobbie in B.Waites, T.Bennett, and G.Martin (eds.) 'Popular Culture: Past and Present' (1982) has shown that teenage magazines such as *Jackie* promote images of girls who are out to attract boys and please them, with little reference to other interests which girl readers may have, such as future careers or hobbies. It is assumed that young females are only interested in pursuing romantic relationships.

Sex and gender stereotyping

A stereotype represents a belief that a certain group of people has a particular set of personal characteristics, which may serve as a justification for social inequality. Stereotypes exist in a social and not a personal sense, because they are based on the shared meanings and understandings of the culture within which they are expressed. Gender stereotypes represent general ideas about what most people consider to be typically masculine or feminine behaviour. O.Hartnett, 'The Sex Role System' (1978) describes how societies tend to attribute certain characteristcs to the sexes which in turn results in the gender roles being allocated sets of behaviour and attitudes. This 'sex role system' assigns men and women particular personality traits, (women are emotional, men are rational) and also encourages a division of labour based on these personality types, for example women are caring, therefore nursing is an appropriate job for them.

Female stereotypes predominate in the advertising industry. P.Maymay and R.Simpson, 'Sex Roles' (1981) studied women's activities in commercials, and found that they tend to participate in three key roles: maternal, housekeeping, and aesthetic (beauty and hygiene). Women's magazines also promote what has been called the 'culture of femininity'. M.Ferguson, 'Forever Feminine: Women' Magazines and the Cult of Femininity' (1983) discovered that the bulk of magazines catering for the 15+ age range emphasised the roles of wife, mother and beautifier. The articles and advertisements complemented and reinforced each other. However, the actual effectiveness and influence of such messages is difficult to evaluate. Women may identify with the images and stereotypes presented, or they may view them as fantasy or merely enjoy them for pleasure.

The argument that female stereotyping constantly encourages women to look their best is a common one. N.Wolf, 'The Beauty Myth' (1990) found that girls and women are pressured to worry about their looks, and to make themselves physically attractive to men. Some feminists have mixed feelings about the presentation of women. J.Radcliffe Richards, 'The Sceptical Feminist' (1982) claims that women should look their best and value their appearance for themselves.

Gender role labelling regarding 'reputations' is another area of debate. As already noted in the previous section on women in society, S.Lees, 'Losing Out' (1986) has described the importance of reputations to women and girls. Labels of 'slut', 'tart', etc. are attached to females who are too free with boys, yet they are seen as 'frigid' if they refuse to go out with particular boys or men. There operates a double standard in gender role stereotyping, with boys and men frequently labelled as 'studs' for their sexual prowess.

Even girls are guilty of perpetuating this standard for they frequently use the abusive terms themselves. However, there are indications that these attitudes may be changing. S.Lees, 'Sugar and Spice' (1993) found that some girls were beginning to question the labels, and are not as passive in their acceptance of such stereotyping. A.McRobbie, 'Feminism and Youth Culture' (1991) also saw a change from her previous research on teenage magazines, finding that the articles presented a more self-aware and less dependent image of females, with less emphasis on 'looking for a mate', and more information on careers.

It is important to remember that gender stereotypes also affect men, who tend to be missing from most gender studies. The way masculininty affects men's attitudes and behaviour is equally as important as female gender role stereotyping. There is an increasing recognition that gender studies should be widened to take account of the male perspective. Thus, a number of studies have emerged in the 1990s which concentrate on male gender roles, for example J.Hearn and D.Morgan, 'Men, Masculinities and Social Theory' (1990), M.Maynard, 'The Re-Shaping of Sociology' (1990), and D.Morgan, 'Discovering Men' (1990). However, all these studies tend to concentrate on what men are, or the social construction of masculinity, such as the development of the 'New Man', rather than on what men actually do in society, and the power that they have.

Both women and men are trapped by the stereotypes which society projects of them. The growth of 'male' gender studies may help to dispel the radical feminist images of all men as rapists or wife-beaters, just as groups within the women's movement have achieved the removal of many traditional female stereotypes.

Theories of gender differentiation

BIOLOGICAL EXPLANATIONS

Biological explanations of gender differentiation essentially argue that, because of the biological fact that women have offspring and men do not, women are naturally 'different' since their role as mothers necessitates a prolonged period of dependence by the human infant. It is important though to distinguish the biological facts of pregnancy and childbirth from motherhood as a social institution. As already indicated in cross-cultural studies, different societies approach childcare in various ways, depending on social arrangements and institutions. It is perhaps interesting to note that during the two world wars in Britain childcare was assumed by the state so that the female population was free to work in male occupations. This indicates that it is society, and not biology, which creates gender differences.

The belief that gender roles are linked to genetically-inherited forms of behaviour is associated with **sociobiology**, or the theory that humans have made evolutionary adaptations in order to survive. E.O. Wilson, 'On Human Nature' (1976) explains differences in male/female sexual behaviour in this way. Thus, promiscuity in men is 'natural' because the intention is to produce as many offspring as possible to ensure survival of the genetic line. Females, on the other hand, are far more circumspect in their sexual encounters because they can only bear a limited number of children, and therefore choose a mate who will support and remain with them.

S.Goldberg, 'Male Dominance' (1979) argues that male dominance is found in every known society, and is caused by the naturally higher levels of the hormone testosterone found in men. He believes that it is testosterone which drives men to become more competitive and power-seeking than women. He claims that results of studies of societies such as the Tchambuli in New Guinea, which appear to have submissive males, are based on flawed research.

It cannot be denied that women and men are genetically and hormonally different, but it is far from proven that these inherent characteristics are the basis of our societal gender roles.

PSYCHOLOGICAL EXPLANATIONS

These explanations are very similar to biological theories, in that they see gender differences as 'natural'. These differences appear in such areas as intelligence, spatial skills, creative ability, and personality characteristics. Early psychological testing found a large number of differences between women and men in the aforementioned categories. However, more recent and reliable testing has reduced these differences to two or three significant findings such as spatial ability and measures of aggression. It must be remembered that these are tendencies rather than absolute differences, and there remains far more overlap between the sexes in attitudes and abilities.

SOCIOLOGICAL EXPLANATIONS

A **structural-functional analysis** of gender differences concentrates on the functional contribution which gender differences make to the overall stability of society. In hunting and gathering societies superior male strength became associated with notions of masculinity, and allowed men to dominate women. With ineffective birth control it was inevitable that women's lives revolved around the home and children (seen as feminine activities). It is easy to see how, in technologically simple societies, the biological facts and the cultural facts of gender are closely linked. Over generations these ideas and attitudes become institutionalised, despite changes which make them inappropriate. For example, in industrial societies reliable birth control and labour-saving devices have provided women with potentially greater opportunities, but entrenched attitudes have made change slow.

T.Parsons, 'The Social System' (1951) believes that traditional gender differences contribute to social integration in society. Thus, gender defines a complementary set of roles that links males and females into family units which support the operation of society. The female role is one of internal cohesion or emotional support of the family combined with child-rearing. Males are decision makers and breadwinners. Via the socialisation process the instrumental male role and the expressive female role are transmitted to the next generation. Society enforces these roles through various means of social control such as internal guilt and external shame.

The major problem with the structural-functional analysis is that it assumes a singular, united, common vision of society that is shared by everyone. J.Z. Giele, 'Gender and Sex Roles' (1988) criticises this view for its reinforcement of the status quo and the way in which it ignores the personal conflicts and social costs which are produced by rigid traditional gender roles.

A social conflict analysis of gender differences uses an historical approach in order to understand how society has developed specific roles for men and women. F.Engels, 'The Origin of the Family, Private Property and the State' (1902) has related the issue of gender stratification to the formation of social classes. The surplus of food in horticultural and agrarian societes led to social classes based on the idea of private property, which led to the superiority of male power over female power. The surplus wealth derived from this private property made men concerned with obtaining heirs in order to pass down this property. The problem was solved with the establishment of monogamous marriage and the family unit, which ensured heirs, while at the same time tying women's lives to the home and the children. Capitalism intensified this male domination as men moved to work in the factories and women became capitalist consumers.

This theory helps to explain the origins of patriarchy, and the way in which gender promotes social conflict in a capitalist society, with women in a subjugated position and men gaining substantial economic and social advantages. However, this perspective does tend to ignore the extent to which males and females live together co-operatively without social conflict, and without male domination. Also, the assertion that capitalism is the basis of gender stratification is not entirely true, as many socialist economic systems also have patriarchal systems in operation.

CHECK YOUR UNDERSTANDING

After reading this chapter you should now be able to define the following terms.

1 Sex
2 Gender
3 Femininity
4 Masculinity
5 Patriarchy
6 Sexism
7 Feminism
8 Women's Liberation Movement
9 Liberal feminism
10 Radical feminism
11 Marxist/socialist feminism
12 Black feminism
13 Post-feminism
14 Institutional sexism

15   'The glass ceiling'
16   Stereotype
17   Gender stereotype
18   Sex role system
19   Sociobiology
20   Instrumental/expressive roles

SELF-ASSESSMENT QUESTIONS

1   What is the difference between the terms sex and gender?
2   How do cross-cultural examples of gender role differences illustrate the social nature of such roles?
3   What is feminism and how successful is it?
4   Summarise the evidence which indicates the prevalence of women's gender roles in modern society.
5   How does stereotyping reinforce male and female gender roles?
6   Assess the relative merits of the structural-functionalist and social conflict views of gender differentiation.

CHAPTER SIX

SOCIAL ORGANISATION

LEARNING OBJECTIVES

ON COMPLETION OF THIS CHAPTER THE STUDENT SHOULD BE ABLE TO:

1 UNDERSTAND THE NATURE OF SOCIAL STRUCTURE
2 EXPLAIN THE IMPORTANCE OF STATUS AND ROLE IN DEFINING PEOPLE'S IDENTITIES
3 DEFINE AN ORGANISATION, AND CLASSIFY ORGANISATIONS BY TYPE
4 EXPLAIN WEBER'S WORK ON ORGANISATIONS AND BUREAUCRACY
5 ASSESS OTHER SOCIOLOGICAL THEORIES OF ORGANISATIONS
6 DESCRIBE THE RELATIONSHIP BETWEEN BUREAUCRACY AND DEMOCRACY
7 EVALUATE SCIENTIFIC MANAGEMENT AND HUMAN RELATIONS THEORIES OF ORGANISATIONS
8 DESCRIBE THE NATURE OF POSTMODERN ORGANISATIONS

Social structure

Society is a social world which is shaped by its level of technological development, its economic system, and its particular culture. As described in Chapter 4, individuals become human only when they are socialised into the social system. Although our behaviour is shaped by society, individuals still maintain autonomy and interact in a positive way with their environment. A social structure is, however, necessary in order for people to make sense of their world and of particular social situations. The social structure is comprised of regular patterns of social interaction and persistent social relationships, which can be observed at any level from one-to-one interaction, through groups and organisations, to entire societies.

Social groups consist of at least two or more people who identify with one another and have a distinctive pattern of interaction, for example couples, families, friends, churches, businesses, social clubs. Groups have been categorised by C.H. Cooley, 'Social Organization' (1962) according to the degree and intensity of social interaction.

A primary group is small, with close relationships, longevity, and substantial influence on its members. Examples of such groups include family, close friends, and possibly small, enduring neighbourhoods. A **secondary group** is larger, with impersonal relationships, and is based on a specific interest or activity, for example people who work together in an office or factory, students in a class, people in a trade union. These groups are less influential than primary groups, but are seen as a significant means of achieving a particular goal (goal orientation). Generally, secondary relationships become more relevant in industrialised societies, whereas primary relationships dominate in pre-industrial communities. It is possible to distinguish other types of groups, such as **peer groups**, where the members share common interests, social position or age (for example teenagers, teachers, footballers), **ethnic groups**, which are based on shared culture (for example Jews, Asians, Welsh), and **racial groups**, which consist of groups of people with specific biological characteristics (for example caucasoid, negroid, mongoloid).

The groups which people belong to are structured by society to form social institutions, such as schools, families, companies, political parties, etc. These social institutions are organised into social systems, for example schools, colleges, universities are all parts of the education system. In turn, all the systems within a society-education, kinship, political, economic-form a coherent social structure. It is important, however, that this rather mechanistic view of society does not ignore the individual and the ways in which he/she participates within the groups and creates and moulds the institutions and systems.

The social structure within a society is not fixed, but changes over time, although major systems (class, economic, political) retain some level of persistence. The social structure itself can only guide, rather than rigidly determine human behaviour: society may create the statuses and roles, but it is individuals who act them out.

Status and role

Status refers to a recognised social position which an individual occupies within society. Every status which a person holds has attached to it certain rights, duties and expectations which are widely recognised within the society. The statuses which people occupy affect the interaction between individuals. The statuses of doctor and patient are clearly defined, and determine the type of interaction which occurs in a medical consultation. In family settings people occupy statuses of father, mother, son, daughter, which in turn create relationships between individuals. Status thus defines our position in relation to society and in relation to other individuals. The term 'status set' refers to all the statuses which a particular person holds at a specific time. For example, a woman is a mother to her children, a daughter to her parents, a teacher to her pupils, and a friend to other women and men. Status sets may be complex, and they are also changeable as people move in and out of jobs, pass through life stages, and take on new interests and activities.

Status is either ascribed or achieved. An **ascribed status** is one where social position is fixed at birth or assumed as part of the life stage process, for example sex, age, race, royalty. Ascribed statuses such as female, teenager, negro, and prince are ones which the individual has little or no choice over. In contrast, an **achieved status** is a social position which is chosen by the individual and reflects an achievement or measure of ability, for example sociology student, athlete, parent, lawyer. The two forms of status are, however, linked, as ascription affects achievement: children from middle-class backgrounds are more likely to become professionals, whereas disadvantaged children are more likely to 'achieve' positions connected with poverty or crime.

A role refers to expected patterns of behaviour which are attached to a particular status. Thus, teacher status has certain rights and obligations attached to it, but the ways in which the teacher performs these activities is described as a role. People occupy a status and perform a role, often according to society's role expectations. Therefore, teachers are expected to impart knowledge, maintain discipline, and encourage social development, but the manner and style in which they do this is related to the teacher's own personality and individual 'performance'. E. Goffman, 'The Presentation of Self in Everyday Life' (1959) calls this social interaction a theatrical or dramaturgical performance because of the ways in which people present themselves in terms of their clothing, social settings, appearance, etc. People occupy many statuses at one time – called a status set – and therefore perform a range of multiple roles. R. Merton, 'Social Theory and Social Structure' (1968) calls the number of roles attached to a single status set a role set.

The relationship between the status set and the role set is illustrated below. Role sets are like the pillars of a bridge supporting the status set. Under the stress of role conflict it can be seen how one or more of the 'pillars' of the bridge may be under strain, and threaten the whole edifice.

Status Set	Teacher		Mother		Wife		Friend
	Teaching Role		Maternal Role		Conjugal Role		Confidante Role
Role Sets	Socialisation Role		PTA Role		Domestic Role		Social Role
	Colleague Role		Nurse Role		Hostess Role		Emotional Support Role

Role conflict refers to a situation in which a person who holds a position is confronted with conflicting or contradictory expectations so that compliance with one role makes performance of another difficult. There are three major forms of role conflict.

1. Role overload occurs when an individual in a role is confronted with a large number of expectations and finds it difficult, if not impossible, to satisfy all of them in a given time period, for example in high-status occupations and professions.

2. Inter-role conflict occurs when the expectations attached to one role are in conflict with the expectations of another role, for example working wives combining job and family roles.

3. Inter-sender role conflict occurs when two or more people have conflicting expectations of a person in a given role, for example lower level supervisors are caught between the demands of management and the demands of workers.

Resolving role conflict involves setting priorities for tasks, or compartmentalising areas of life so that roles linked to one status are performed in one place for part of the day, and other roles connected to other statuses are given other time allocations.

The social interaction connected with status and role illustrates the active part which individuals play in the social organisation of their societies. Although we are influenced by the groups and organisations in which we live, work and play, as individuals we shape our roles and generally conduct our behaviour with a large degree of personal freedom.

Definition and classification of organisations

A century ago most social life occurred in small social groups such as the family, friends, workplaces. Today, people's lives revolve more around formal organisations, large secondary groups that are formally organised to achieve specific goals. The large size, impersonal nature, and formal atmosphere in these organisations are designed to accomplish specific tasks rather than meet personal needs.

The growth of organisations is related to the increasingly specialised division of labour, which generates systems of rules and hierarchies of authority designed to pursue specific goals. Modern industrial societies are thus organisational societies where people attend schools, are employed by companies, join trade unions, etc. Work, leisure, sickness and religion are all conducted in organisations which have clearly defined goals, in contrast to primary social units such as the family and peer group, which are more diffuse in their goals. Organisations thus have the following characteristics:

1. They consist of a large number of people.
2. There is a formal division of labour and co-ordination of people's activities.
3. They are formed to achieve a specific goal.
4. They have a hierarchical authority structure.
5. There is a set body of rules and procedures.

In summary, an organisation can be defined as the rational co-ordination of the activities of a large number of people for the achievement of a specific goal through the division of labour, and with a hierarchy of authority and prescribed rules.

CLASSIFICATION OF ORGANISATIONS

Organisations can be classified in a variety of ways. A. Etzioni, 'A Comparative Analysis of Complex Organisations' (1975) has identified three types of organisation based on how members relate to the organisation.

Normative organisations, where the goal is to pursue a morally worthwhile cause, for personal satisfaction or for social prestige, but usually no monetary reward is given to members. Normative organisations are sometimes called voluntary associations. Examples are WRVS, PTA, political parties, religious organisations.

Coercive organisations, where the goal is to maintain order, and people are usually compulsorily detained in these organisations. Members are thus forced to join coercive organisations as a form of punishment (prisons) or for treatment (psychiatric hospitals). These organisations usually have distinctive features such as locked doors, barred windows, and security personnel.

Utilitarian organisations, where the goal is to generate profits for the owners and income in the form of salaries for the employees. Most people choose to join a utilitarian organisation in order to make a living. Although people have the freedom to leave, they have less freedom than people in normative organisations, for they need to remain in paid employment.

From different viewpoints it is possible that a formal organisation may fall into all of these categories. A prison is a coercive organisation to an inmate, a utilitarian organisation to a prison officer, and a normative organisation to a part-time volunteer visitor.

P. Blau and W. Scott, 'Formal Organisations' (1962) have classified organisations according to who the 'prime beneficiary' is, or who benefits most from the organisation. They have identified four types of organisation corresponding to different prime beneficiaries.

Mutual benefit associations, where the members of the organisation are the main beneficiaries, for example a trade union.

Business concerns, where the owners benefit most from the organisation.

Service organisations, where the clients in the organisation benefit the most from the activities, for example building societies.

Commonweal organisations, are organisations where the public mainly benefit, for example libraries.

T. Parsons, 'Structure and Process in Modern Societies' (1960) has grouped organisations according to their overall purpose in society:

Organisations with production goals, that is, they exist to make consumer goods, for example Unilever.

Organisations with political goals, for example, the Conservative Party.

Organisations with integrative goals, which help to resolve conflicts within society, for example the legal system.

Organisations concerned with 'pattern maintenance' or the transmission of knowledge and values, for example schools.

Max Weber, organisations and bureaucracy

Max Weber's work on bureaucracy and organisations has to be viewed in the context of his general theory of social action. He believed that, in order to explain human action, it was necessary to understand the meanings which lie behind human behaviour. Weber outlined three types of social action, which correspond to three types of authority, each resulting in a particular form of organisational structure.

Traditional action is based on custom and tradition, and corresponds to traditional authority derived from custom and loyalty, for example the power of kings in feudal Europe. The authority is legitimised by inherited status and personal affection. The organisational structure deriving from traditional authority consists of a **hierarchy** of people dependent on those above them, whose position in the structure is related to the level of ownership of land.

Charismatic action (or affective action) is based on personal attraction to an individual held in very high esteem, and corresponds to charismatic authority. The authority is legitimated by the special qualities of the leader, who uses personal attraction to evoke devotion and loyalty, for example Jesus, Napoleon, Hitler. The organisational structure resulting from charismatic authority has no legal rules and no fixed hierarchy of officials. The crucial importance of the leader in charismatic authority means that after the death of the key figure the movement must adapt to either traditional or rational authority if it is to survive. Christianity is no longer directly based on the charisma of Jesus, but has become 'routinised' in terms of both traditional and rational authority.

Rational action is based on the clear identification of a specific goal, and the selection of the most appropriate means of attaining it. The rational authority deriving from this form of action is based on the acceptance of a set of impersonal rules. The legitimacy is provided by the professional qualifications and competence of the people within the organisation, for example civil servants, managers, administrators. The organisational structure of rational authority is **bureaucracy**, a hierarchical organisation which is rationally designed to co-ordinate the work of individuals in order to achieve administrative tasks and organisational goals. Weber saw the expression of bureaucracy in state administration, education, business, etc., and predicted that this organisational structure would become the dominant form in modern industrial societies.

WEBER'S IDEAL TYPE BUREAUCRACY

An 'ideal type' represents a pure form which is not expected to exist in reality. In practice it is only possible to approximate to an ideal type. The characteristics of Weber's ideal type bureaucracy are as follows:

1. The staff members are personally free, observing only the impersonal duties of their offices.
2. They are organised in a clearly defined hierarchy of offices.
3. The functions of the offices are clearly specified.
4. The office is filled by an individual on the basis of a free contractual relationship. Thus, in practice, there is free selection of office holders.
5. Candidates for office are selected on the basis of technical qualifications. In the

The headquarters of the European Union in Brussels – an example of modern rational organisation

most rational case this is tested by examination, or guaranteed by diplomas certifying technical training, or both. People are appointed, not elected.

6. Office holders are remunerated by fixed salaries in money, with a right to pensions. The salary scale is primarily graded according to rank in the hierarchy. The official is always free to resign, and under certain circumstances his or her position may also be terminated.

7. The official's post is his or her sole, or major, occupation.

8. The official's occupation constitutes a career. There is a system of promotion according to seniority or achievement, or both. Promotion is dependent upon the judgement of superiors.

9. The official may appropriate neither the post nor the resources that accompany it. Thus the official is entirely separated from the ownership of the means of the administration.

10. The official is subject to strict systematic discipline and control in the conduct of the office. The discharge of duties is to proceed impartially and without bias.

These characteristics can be summarised into six key elements.

1. Specialisation
2. Hierarchy of officials
3. Rules and regulations
4. Technical competence
5. Impersonality
6. Formal, written communication.

Weber was aware that bureaucracies suffered from a number of inefficiencies or dysfunctions.

1. The strict control of officials restricted to their specialised tasks means that individuals often have little awareness of the relationship between their jobs and the organisation as a whole.
2. As bureaucrats are trained to follow rules and orders, in times of crisis they would be unable to adapt to rapidly changing situations.
3. The uniformity of bureaucratic procedures reduces spontaneity, creativity, and individual initiative, leading to what Weber called 'specialists without spirit'.
4. In a capitalist society the emphasis on responding to rules and regulations means that bureaucrats may be pressured to respond in a particular way. Weber advocated strong parliamentary control, particularly of the state bureaucracy, in order to avoid these problems.
5. The technical superiority of bureaucracy may increase democratic control, but it also 'dehumanises' society by constraining free will.
6. The rationality of bureaucracy can lead to people becoming trapped in an 'iron cage' of uniformity, making people disenchanted and reduced to 'man machines'.

Other sociological theories of organisations

Much of the later research on organisations has questioned the notion that Weber's ideal type bureaucracy is the most efficient way of realising organisational goals. Critics have attempted to show how certain aspects of the ideal type bureaucracy may in practice reduce organisational efficiency.

R. Merton, 'Social Theory and Social Structure' (1949) has argued that one of the main problems with bureaucracies is that they have a tendency to create a 'bureaucratic personality', which is characterised by conformity, inflexibility, and a lack of initiative and innovation.

A. Gouldner, 'Patterns of Industrial Bureaucracy' (1954) was interested in situations where bureaucratic forms of organisation might be inappropriate. He studied a gypsum plant in the USA to examine the social processes which lead to variations in degrees of bureaucratisation. Gouldner found that there was a significant difference in the degree of bureaucratisation between the gypsum mine and the factory making wall-boards from the gypsum. The two parts of the plant varied in division of labour, emphasis on rules, hierarchy of authority, and relationships between workers and supervisors. He found that the factory was considerably more bureaucratic, with the hierarchy of authority, the division of labour, official rules, and impersonality more widespread and developed. The difference between the two areas of the plant was explained by the nature of the work in both places. Thus, the miners had to operate with a more flexible system of rules, and make decisions in response to unplanned incidents such as cave-ins. In contrast, the workers in the factory followed a standard routine, with no opportunities to diverge from the clearly defined pattern of rules. Part of Gouldner's study examined the effects of a new manager at the plant, who attempted to impose a strongly bureaucratic system throughout the site. The miners opposed the increasing bureaucratisation, showing how work-group solidarity can resist bureaucracy when it is not compatible with non-routine, informal organisational structures.

T. Burns and G. Stalker, 'The Management of Innovation' (1966) supported Gouldner's findings from their study of twenty Scottish and English firms, mainly in the electronics industry. To illustrate the variations in bureaucratisation, Burns and Stalker identified two ideal types of organisation which they called **mechanistic** and **organic**. The firms in their research covered both of these types, with the mechanistic form similar to Weber's model of bureaucracy. By comparison, organic organisations are characterised by flexibility and consultation rather than by a rigid hierarchy and direct commands. An emphasis on organisational goals instead of pursuing set tasks, and the presence of overlapping occupational roles, are to be found in organic organisations. Burns and Stalker argue that mechanistic models are best suited to stable conditions, and organic systems to changing conditions. Although the electronics firms in the study were faced with unstable conditions (for example non-standardised products, changes in technology, market fluctuations), only some of them had developed an organic system. Burns and Stalker attribute this reluctance to adopt the organic model to a lack of commitment by management, the fear of loss of authority and autonomy, and personal ambition which prevents the exchange of information.

P. Blau, 'The Dynamics of Bureaucracy' (1963) disputes Weber's claim that any deviation from his ideal type will result in administrative inefficiency. Instead, Blau maintains that in some circumstances the opposite may be true, and organisations may function more efficiently when workers adapt, bend, or even break the rules. To prove his point, Blau used two examples: the American Federal Law Enforcement Agency (the FBI) and a state employment agency. In the study of federal agents working in one of nine district agencies based in Washington DC, Blau found that consultation between agents on cases was not officially approved practice. Confidentiality meant that cases could only be discussed with supervisors, but agents felt that frequent consultation might be interpreted as incompetence, and thus refrained from discussing cases with their superiors. To overcome these limitations on communication the agents contravened official rules and sought advice and guidance from each other. Blau claims that this pooling of information and experience served to increase the agents' efficiency, indicating that unofficial practices which are prohibited by official regulations can often lead to greater efficiency. Blau's study of interviewers in a state employment agency showed how official rules and procedures did not maximise efficiency, whereas informal group and norms resulted in higher productivity.

The theories outlined above use a **'systems' approach** to the study of organisations, which is based on the idea that an organisation can be viewed like a machine which has evolved from a simple to a complex form over time. This functional analysis tends to concentrate on the formal structure and functions of the organisation.

In contrast to this approach, the **'interpretive' view** is based on an analysis of the interactions of the members of the organisation, and starts from the view that the organisation consists of groups of people who interact with each other in a variety of ways. Consequently, the aims, methods, and goals of the organisation will fluctuate and change according to the relationships of those who are involved in it and who come into contact with it. There is thus a two-way effect between the organisational structure and the individuals who comprise it. D. Silverman, 'The Theory of Organisations' (1970) describes how roles within organisations are not fixed, but are constantly being negotiated as new situations arise. Thus, role expectations may change, and new meanings may be given to roles over time.

E. Goffman, 'Asylums' (1968) was the first major study of a single organisation from an interactionist perspective. Goffman spent a year in the late 1950s observing interaction in a mental hospital in Washington DC, with the aim of understanding the meanings given to the experience by the patients. He was particularly concerned with how the patient's self-concept was changed or modified by the time spent in the institution. In addition to his observations (based on his work as a member of staff) Goffman widened his study to include all organisations where people live and work within an organisation – described as a **'total institution'**. Examples of total institutions include prisons, ships, boarding schools, army barracks, monasteries, etc. Goffman described how individuals are 'mortified' or have their sense of self stripped away by organisational procedures such as public showering, haircuts, the wearing of a uniform, etc. Other humiliations such as lack of personal privacy contribute to their degradation. The responses of individuals or 'inmates' (as Goffman called them) to their situation is also described by Goffman to show how various 'adaptations' to the environment take place, for example withdrawal, intransigence, 'playing it cool', etc.

A. Strauss et al, 'The Hospital and its Negotiated Order' (1963) used an interpretive approach in their research into two psychiatric hospitals, and found that there were no clear-cut rules defining how staff and patients should behave. Furthermore, the goals of the organisations were not clearly defined, but open to considerable interpretation and negotiation. Overall, the goal of improving mental health and returning patients to the community was upheld, but the achievement of this goal involved a continuing process of negotiation and re-negotiation over treatment plans, privileges, time spans, etc. This concept of 'negotiated order' can equally be applied to companies, educational institutions, and government agencies.

D. Zimmerman, 'The Practicalities of Rule Use' (1971) studied the work of a Bureau of Public Assistance in the USA. In order to provide financial aid for the needy, applicants were interviewed by a caseworker before financial support was given. Officially, receptionists were supposed to allocate applicants to each caseworker in turn, but when a caseworker took longer than usual with someone, the receptionist would divert the clients to another worker to keep the line moving. This violation of official procedure illustrates how group norms can be used to modify the rules yet still achieve the goals of the organisation (in this case to ensure that all applicants were seen within a reasonable amount of time).

The main problem with the interpretive analysis of organisations is the over concentration and emphasis which is placed on small group dynamics at the expense of seeing the overall position of the organisation within society. For Marxists, this would mean looking at the role of the organisation within a capitalist economy.

Marx himself made little reference to bureaucracy in his work, except for seeing state bureaucracy as an instrument of class oppression and control by the bourgeoisie. After the class revolution, administrators would be elected and made accountable to the people, thus ceasing to be a means of control.

In practice, after the Bolshevik Revolution in 1917 Lenin believed that the state was in a 'transitional phase', where a bureaucracy was still necessary. However, once true communism was established, administrative tasks would be simplified so that virtually anyone could perform them, and they would be minimal anyway. This idea did not materialise as it soon became apparent that skilled administrative specialists were essential in a complex modern state. In fact, the Communist Party itself became a huge and centralised bureaucracy under Stalin, concentrating power in the hands of the leader.

Marxist and conflict perspectives of organisations concentrate on the influence which the profit-making nature of these organisations have on individuals. H. Braverman,

'Labour and Monopoly Capital: The Degradation of Work in the Twentieth Century' (1973) presents a Marxist theory of organisations and argues that capitalist employers and managers aim to control the workers in order to exploit their labour more effectively, and thus to increase their profits.

One way in which this is done is by the 'deskilling process' where jobs are designed and planned by managers and workers carry out pre-designed tasks. Deskilling also involves the replacement of many job tasks by machines, leaving the workers with little or no work to do. Braverman believes that managers frequently claim to be using human relations style management, where employees are involved in the decision-making process, but in reality there is little real concern for the workers or their opinions. However, it is possible that workers can resist deskilling, and in some companies there may be genuine efforts to involve the workforce in decision-making. C. Littler, 'The Development of the Labour Process in Capitalist Societies' (1982) studied employment practices in nineteenth-century Britain and the US, and found that employers often used other means apart from deskilling to control the workers, for example subcontracting. A. Friedman, 'Industry and Labour: Class Struggle and Work and Monopoly Capitalism' (1977) described the emergence of new forms of capitalist control such as responsible autonomy, which appear to give workers control over their tasks, and at the same time encourage identification with the company's goals. In practice Friedman argues that the workers control themselves for the employers.

The Marxist/conflict analysis summarised above does not offer any suggestions for how organisations may be run so that they can benefit all the members. It only offers the creation of a socialist society as a solution to workers oppression, but this has already proved to be ineffective.

THE DEBATE WITH WEBER

By the 1960s it was apparent to most organisational theorists that there was no single ideal type of bureaocracy as Weber had envisaged. Instead, bureaucracy appeared to be one part of a continuum, with highly bureaucratic jobs at one end (for example assembly line or routine clerical work), and at the other end professional occupations which seemed to have problems operating to set rules.

A realisation grew that different forms of organisation may be suited to different environmental contexts. From the 1960s onwards studies began to move away from the case study approach exemplified by Gouldner and Blau, towards comparative studies using quantitative data. One of the most influential of these is the so-called Aston studies of D. Pugh et al, 'Writers on Organisations' (1987) which classified and compared organisations, using four main factors which distinguish various types of organisation.

1. Structuring of activities, for example how formalised or standardised tasks are.
2. Concentration of authority, for example is it centralised or are people autonomous?
3. Line management, for example is communication direct or indirect?
4. The relative size of support staff, for example clerical/administrative help

Based on quantitative measurements for factors one and two above, the Aston studies derived a classification of four main types of bureaucracy.

Full bureaucracies, which were similar in nature to Weber's ideal type.

Workflow bureaucracies, which were highly structured, but authority was more decentralised than in a full bureaucracy.

Personnel bureaucracies, which had less structured activities but bureaucratic relationships.

Implicitly structured organisations, which were less structured and the workers largely autonomous.

The work of the Aston Group produced very similar findings to those of Burns and Stalker, with their mechanistic and organic organisations. The Aston Group have called these different responses of organisations an aspect of **contingency theory**, because many contingencies or different circumstances have to be taken into account when deciding the best structure for a particular organisation. Organisational structures thus vary in accordance with varying environments.

The methodology of the Aston studies is rather over-statistical, and may not take into account the views of all the workers, particularly as most of the data was collected from management sources, and may reflect a distinctive view of the organisation. The contingency theory makes little reference to the conflict which exists within organisations, especially as changes in the organisation may be as a result of the conflicts, rather than responses to the environment.

Bureaucracy and democracy

Marxist hopes for truly democratic organisations are dismissed as illusions by the Italian sociologist Roberto Michels (1876–1936). In his book 'Political Parties' (1911) Michels studied European socialist parties and trade unions, with particular emphasis on the German Socialist Party. These organisations were committed to the overthrow of the capitalist state and the creation of a socialist society. They claimed to be organised on democratic principles, directly representing the interests and wishes of their members. Michels argued that as direct democracy is, in practice, impossible, representative democracy must be established in order to carry out the wishes of the rank and file. However, the creation of a bureaucratic administration inevitably results in a specialised division of labour and a hierarchical structure, whereby decisions are increasingly taken by executive committees rather than by the rank and file. Thus, the very organisation which was created to represent its members ends up by largely excluding them from participation and decision-making. Michels argued that organisations inevitably produce oligarchy, that is rule by a small elite. This is known as the 'iron law of oligarchy'. In the particular case of the German Socialist Party, its commitment to the overthrow of capitalism was pushed into the background, as leaders were reluctant to take any action which might endanger their position. Michels predicted that a proletarian revolution and the establishment of a socialist society would result in a **dictatorship**, where the power would be concentrated in the hands of a group of leaders.

Michels made sweeping generalisations based on an examination of particular cases. He asserted that organisations inevitably result in the exclusion of the majority from participation in decision-making and in domination by a self-interested **oligarchy**. However, S.M. Lipset, M. Trow, and J. Coleman, 'Union Democracy' (1956) examined the organisational structure of the International Typographical Union (ITU), which they claim provides an exception to the iron law of oligarchy. The ITU, a craft printers union, is unique among American unions in that it contains two parties, which provides a constant check on the party in power, and serves to generate alternative policies to those of the existing leadership. Frequent elections and a two-party system mean that the rank and file can actually determine union policy. In addition, many decisions such as basic changes in union regulations and increases in officials' salaries are put to a referendum. For these reasons Lipset et al claim that the ITU is a democratic organisation. There is a high degree of participation by the rank and file who have the power to effect real changes in union policy, and to control the activities of their leaders. However, the ITU is a unique case. Only a combination of exceptional factors has produced its particular organisational structure. Lipset et al are pessimistic about the potential for democracy in organisations in general, as the average trade union member is not particularly involved in his job, and largely pre-occupied with home, family and leisure. They also have reservations about the effectiveness of representative democracy. They note how top union officials have steadily increased their salaries above those of the rank and file, and argue that many union leaders adopt policies to further their own political ambitions. Also, it is difficult for groups within a union to take action which is disapproved of by the leadership. Lipset et al conclude that without internal democracy, members of unions and organisations in general are largely forced to put their faith in the leadership. Representative democracy may result, but so might a self-interested oligarchy which pursues policies contrary to the interests of the membership. Lipset et al maintain that members' interests would be more likely to be represented if internal democracy along the lines of the ITU were built into the organisational structure of trade unions.

A somewhat different perspective on the question of democracy and organisations is provided by P. Selznick, 'TVA and the Grass Roots' (1966), in his study of the Tennessee Valley Authority. Like Michels, he studied an organisation which claimed to be democratic and showed how this claim was frustrated in practice. Selznick adopts a functionalist approach arguing that organisations have basic needs, the most fundamental of which is the need for survival. If the goal of democracy threatens the existence of the organisation, the goal will be likely to be displaced in order to ensure the organisation's survival. In his study of the Tennessee Valley Authority (created in 1933 as part of Roosevelt's 'New Deal' policy to combat poverty) Selznick found that the TVA's 'grass roots' policy stated that local people should enter into a partnership with the organisation for the development of their region. Giving many examples, Selznick argued that, far from representing the interests of the public, the TVA ended up serving 'the established farm leadership' rather than the impoverished, mainly black, tenant farmers. Thus, by working through the larger and more powerful interest groups and institutions, it merely reinforced the existing power structure.

Selznick's research suggests that as long as there are major power differentials within the clientele of the organisation, popular representation and participation in the decisions of the organisation will not be possible. Since, in order to survive, an organisation must co-operate with powerful interests, it will tend to represent them. While admitting that his conclusions are pessimistic, Selznick does not suggest that the democratic ideal is not worth striving for.

British studies of the relationship between bureaucracy and democracy tend to support Michels' thesis. J. Goldstein, 'The Government of a British Trade Union' (1952) studied the Transport and General Workers Union, and found that few members exercised their right to vote in elections or attended branch meetings. Decisions at local and national level were taken by a small number of active members. M. Jackson, 'Trade Unions' (1988) has found similar tendencies in other British trade unions.

An exception to this, however, is the work of H.A. Clegg, 'General Union' (1954) who found that ordinary members of the General and Municipal Workers Union often defeated motions which were proposed by the executive. It appears that the potential for democracy in trade unions often depends on local autonomy and strong local membership.

In conclusion, although Michels accepted that organisation was essential to democracy, he recognised that the bureaucratic structure inevitably produced oligarchical control, which ends democracy. He concluded that 'Who says organisation, says oligarchy.'

Scientific management and human relations

Other theoretical approaches in the sociology of organisations have been more concerned with organisational efficiency, and underpinned by 'management science'. These ideas sometimes reflect research which is described as being in 'the managerial tradition'.

Scientific management is an organisational theory concerning the ways in which management can encourage increased production from their workers. This theory argues that by using monetary incentives and varying the working conditions the employer can increase productivity. The theory of scientific management originated in the work of F.W. Taylor, 'The Principles of Scientific Management' (1911), who believed that there was 'one best way' of performing any work task. Management could use scientific principles in order to discover the most cost-effective and productive method of work. The scientific principles resulted in the development of 'time and motion studies' by which to measure the best way of achieving a task. The two aims of scientific management are thus to increase efficiency and output, and to end employer/employee conflict by finding the most suitable working conditions (based on 'scientific studies').

The main criticism of scientific management is from the Marxist perspective, which argues that the methods of scientific management will result in exploitation of workers, with increased output used for the benefit of the owners of capital, often at the expense of redundant workers.

Another criticism, from an interpretive viewpoint, is that Taylor assumed that people's primary motivation for work is economic, and that all workers will therefore respond positively to financial incentives. Taylor emphasised the individuality of the workers, rather than seeing them as members of social groups, where there would be considerable influence by the informal work group on individuals' behaviour.

The human relations school in contrast, emphasises the significance of group norms on individual behaviour and thus on levels of production. This was first recognised by E. Mayo, 'Human Relations of an Industrial Production' (1946) when he conducted the Hawthorne Studies at the Hawthorne Plant of the Western Electric Company in Chicago in 1927–32. Mayo's work was based on a series of experiments designed to investigate the relationship between working conditions and productivity. Mayo found that there was no consistent relationship between productivity and variables such as heating, lighting, rest periods, and financial incentives. However, he did find that workers' attitudes and group norms were important in setting the level of production. Thus, workers established a work rate to suit themselves, not management, and used group pressure to maintain a constant level of output. Thus, the social needs of acceptance, status within the group, and a sense of loyalty, were found to be more important than financial rewards.

In criticism, it could be argued that the Hawthorne Studies are not typical of every work situation. Indeed, T. Nichols and H. Beynon, 'Living with Capitalism: Class Relations and the Modern Factory' (1977) found in their study of a British chemical plant, where management had introduced a human relations style approach, the workers still retained a largely instrumental (working for money only) approach to activities. Furthermore, the human relations school also assumes, like scientific management, that there is little, or no, employer/employee conflict.

Postmodern organisations

It has been suggested that organisations in the last twenty years have moved away from the rigid techniques of mass production associated with Henry Ford's car assembly line. This has given rise to the term Post-Fordism, to refer to those organisations which have increased their flexibility and decentralised their bureaucracies.

M.J. Piore, 'Perspectives on Labour Market Flexibility' (1986) argues that most capitalist countries have now entered a post-Ford era, with much work organised according to the principles of 'flexible specialisation'. These methods have been adopted predominantly in Japan, where their economic success has led other capitalist countries to follow the same model. W. Ouchi, 'Theory 2: How American Business can meet the Japanese Challenge' (1981) has described five distinctions between formal organisations in Japan and their counterparts in Western industrial societies, describing the Japanese system thus:

Hiring and advancement: people are often recruited in groups, rather than individually, in order to promote corporate identity.

Lifetime security: jobs are intended to be for life within the company, thus there is strong, mutual loyalty between employer and employee.

Holistic involvement: social and recreational activities are provided for all staff, and sometimes housing too.

Non-specialised training: employees are trained in all aspects of the operation to increase levels of flexibility.

Collective decision-making: involving the employees increases economic equality between management and workers. Most companies have semi-autonomous working groups or 'quality circles'.

Although British companies do not appear to share all of the above characteristics, there does seem to be a trend towards greater flexibility. D. Clutterbuck, 'New Patterns of Work', (1985) describes how British Telecom is organised into divisions, with each division operated as an autonomous profit centre. Therefore, responsibility for decision-making and profitability has been passed down to the lower levels of the organisation.

S. Clegg, 'Modern and Postmodern Organisations' (1992) uses the term postmodern to refer to new types of organisations which differ significantly from the Ford model. In addition to greater employee autonomy, he emphasises the importance of flexibility and the breaking down of the rigid specialisation of workers which are characteristic of traditional Fordism. However, the importance of culture in this transition should not be underestimated. Japanese organisations have changed because they have transferred elements of their culture such as collective identity and social solidarity to business corporations. In countries where these aspects of culture are not as strong, or indeed are non-existent, organisational change may not be quite as successful.

CHECK YOUR UNDERSTANDING

After reading this chapter you should now be able to define the following terms.

1 Social structure
2 Social group
3 Social institution
4 Social system
5 Status
6 Ascribed status
7 Achieved status
8 Status set
9 Role
10 Role set
11 Role conflict
12 Organisation
13 Normative organisations
14 Coercive organisations
15 Utilitarian organisations
16 Traditional authority
17 Charismatic authority
18 Rational authority
19 Bureaucracy
20 Ideal type
21 Mechanistic organisations
22 Organic organisations
23 Total institution
24 Negotiated order
25 Contingency theory
26 Oligarchy
27 Scientific management
28 Human relations
29 Post-Fordism
30 Postmodern organisations

SELF-ASSESSMENT QUESTIONS

1 Describe the importance of social groups in the social structure.
2 How do status and role differ?
3 In what ways can organisations be classified?
4 Why is Weber's ideal type bureaucracy unworkable in practice?
5 How do mechanistic and organic organisations differ?
6 What is the 'iron law of oligarchy'?
7 To what extent is scientific management theory functionalist, and the human relations approach interactionist?
8 How do postmodern organisations differ from Fordist techniques of mass production?

'A' LEVEL SOCIOLOGY ESSAY QUESTIONS

1 Using examples, critically discuss interactionist explanations of the actions of people in organisations (AEB, summer, 1995).
2 Explain and evaluate the different approaches of functionalists and interactionists to the study of organisations (AEB, summer, 1992).
3 Evaluate Braverman's claim that work is deskilled not only to reduce labour costs but also to achieve managerial control over workers (AEB, summer, 1992).
4 Evaluate the claim made by some sociologists that organisations are inevitably undemocratic (AEB, summer, 1995).

CHAPTER SEVEN

THE FAMILY

LEARNING OBJECTIVES

ON COMPLETION OF THIS CHAPTER THE STUDENT SHOULD BE ABLE TO:

1 UNDERSTAND THE NATURE OF FAMILY STRUCTURE
2 DESCRIBE THE EFFECTS OF INDUSTRIALISATION ON FAMILY LIFE
3 DISCUSS THE NATURE OF MARRIAGE AND DIVORCE
4 SUMMARISE GENDER ROLES WITHIN THE FAMILY
5 EVALUATE THE MAIN THEORETICAL APPROACHES TO THE STUDY OF FAMILY LIFE

Family structure

THE UNIVERSAL FAMILY

The social anthropologist G.P. Murdock, 'Social Structure' (1949) compared 250 societies, from small hunting ones to large industrial ones. Although there were wide variations in the kinship relationships of these societies, he claimed that some form of family existed in every society, and concluded that the family is a universal institution (that is, a social group related by blood, marriage, or adoption, who share a common residence, co-operate economically, and rear children). Murdock saw the **nuclear family** of parent(s) and child(ren) as the basic unit around which all family systems are organised. The nuclear family may exist as a unit by itself, or as part of a larger kinship group, or extended family, which includes relatives beyond the immediate nuclear family, for example three generations under one roof.

Murdock believes that the family is universal because it performs four essential functions without which society could not survive:

Sexual: the regulation of sexual behaviour.

Reproductive: the creation of new generations.

Economic: a consumer unit, which shares resources and co-operates in tasks.

Educational: the socialisation of children into the culture of society.

The question of whether the family is universal depends to a large extent on the definition of a family. One of the most thorough and elaborate attempts to define a family can be found in the cross-cultural work of W.N. Stephens, 'The Family in Cross-Cultural Perspective' (1963). In addition to marriage, or a social contract similar to marriage, Stephens identifies three other concepts which are crucial to the definition of a family. These are: reciprocal economic obligations, common residence, and the rights and duties of parenthood. Essentially these four conditions mirror the four functions proposed by Murdock. However, Stephens critically analyses his definition by using empirical evidence to show the existence of groups of people who might approximate the criteria, but fall short of all the attributes. Thus, common-law spouses, single parent families, stable homosexual relationships, and communes, may conform to some of the definitional criteria, but do not 'fit' the sociological and lay views of the family.

Stephens' work is supported by F. Edholm, 'The Unnatural Family' (1982) who argues that many anthropologists, including Murdock, interpret kinship groups in other societies from an ethnocentric viewpoint (in terms of their own culture), and therefore look for universal similarities.

FAMILY DIVERSITY

Human societies demonstrate an enormous diversity in family and kinship groupings, suggesting that Murdock's concept of a universal family is one which is difficult to uphold. Some examples which appear to contradict his definition include the following.

The Nayar family system. The Nayar people of Kerala in Southern India are a family system which existed prior to British rule in 1792 which resulted in their change. They have been studied by K. Gough, 'Is the Family Universal? – the Nayar Case' in N. Bell and E. Vogel (eds.) 'A Modern Introduction to the Family' (1960). Gough found that young girls in this society married several males at a group ceremony, then returned home alone to be raised by their mother and grandmother. The Nayar household was headed by the grandmother, with sons spending some time at home before leaving to become warriors. The men would become 'visiting husbands' to their brides, but would not actually live with them. The household was thus centred primarily around the females, and polyandry (one woman having several husbands at a time) was practised because of the frequent male absenteeism and low male life expectancy. Thus, Gough argues that family systems tend to adapt to external environments. She describes the family as an 'adaptive institution'. According to Murdock's definition the Nayar would not constitute a family because there is no lifelong union of one husband and one wife, the biological parents do not have sole responsibility for socialisation of their children, and the economic function is provided by an essentially female population.

The New World black family. This is another example which does not fulfil Murdock's definition, because it does not have at least one spouse of each sex. Black family units in the islands of the West Indies, parts of Central America, and the USA, often consist only of a woman and her dependent children, and sometimes her mother. Possible explanations which have been put forward for the existence of these female-headed or matrifocal families include: the influence of traditional West African family life where polygyny (one man having many wives at the same time) is common; historical explanations related to slavery and the separation of families: and poverty, which often results in desertion by the husband.

The Israeli Kibbutz. This is another exception to Murdock's concept of a universal nuclear family. Only about four percent of Israelis actually live in kibbutzim. Here, the collective values of the whole community are emphasised, contrary to the individual economic co-operation of Murdock's type of family. The kibbutz case does not satisfy the criteria of common residence and the rights and duties of parenthood, for in order to release women from child-rearing their offspring are raised apart from their parents in special 'children's houses'. Parents and children see each other for a few hours each day, but essentially spend their lives apart. Women are therefore free to work and enjoy leisure on the same terms as men. Although many kibbutzim are now not so rigid in their application of this arrangement, they still do illustrate the existence of alternative institutions for child-rearing. B. Bettelheim, 'The Children of the Dream' (1971) has provided a detailed description of this type of family overleaf.

The commune movement. Communes were particularly prevalent in the late 1960s, and refer to a form of collective living where a number of nuclear families live together. They are often self-sufficient, and some of them practise communist principles in respect of property. Thus, in terms of Murdock's definition, they are not operating as single economic units, and there is shared parenting instead of biological responsibility for child-rearing. Geographical mobility has, however, meant that communes have remained a minority form of family living, tending to be more popular with single parent families where mutual co-operation is often of most benefit. A detailed review of 67 communes can be found in P. Abrams and A. McCullogh, 'Communes, Sociology, and Society' (1976).

The strict definition of the universal family as proposed by Murdock does not hold true in practice. Instead, it is preferable to regard the functions of the family as universal in some form or another. There is thus no such group as the 'conventional' family, as family structures vary according to a range of dimensions, some of which are summarised in the table overleaf.

Industrialisation and family life

There is a generally held assumption that the industrial revolution changed the structure of the family from extended to nuclear, destroying kinship relations in the process. The belief is that the **extended family** tends to reinforce family ties, and without it the nuclear family unit is less tied to a geographical area. T. Parsons, 'The Social System' (1951) maintains that the nuclear family is better 'suited' to the 'demands' of an industrial society than is the extended family, and therefore the isolated nuclear family is the typical family structure to be found in modern industrial society. However, the assumption that there were more extended families in pre-industrial times, and that nuclear families are better 'suited' to industrialism, has been questioned.

There is evidence to show that classic extended families characteristic of peasant societies, where there is a close-knit community in which relatives and neighbours rely on each other, have persisted into modern industrial societies: C.M. Arensburg and S.T. Kimball, 'Family and Community in Ireland' (1940). There is also substantial historical evidence which suggests that there were just as many nuclear family units in pre-industrial Europe as there are today. J. Goody, 'Evolution of the Family' in P. Laslett and R. Wall (eds.) 'Household and Family in Past Time' (1972) questions the general assumption that there is a gradual development in all human societies from patterns of extended kinship to nuclear family units. His comparative analysis of the relationship between the family and the 'domestic group' in a large number of societies shows that units of production were everywhere relatively small, kin-based units. W. Goode, 'World Revolution and Family Patterns' (1963) supports Goody, while P. Laslett, 'The World We Have Lost' (1965) and M. Anderson (ed.), 'Sociology of the Modern Family' (1971) provide empirical evidence to demonstrate that the proportion of extended families in pre-industrial England has been over-estimated. In fact, the extended family

Variations of Family Structure

--- Inheritance ---

Patrilineal
Descent comes from father's family.
Inherits from and owes allegiance to that family.

Matrilineal
Descent comes from mother's family.
Inherits and owes allegiance to that family.

Bilineal
Descent equal from both sides of family.
Inherits from and owes allegiance to both families.

--- Habitation ---

Patrilocal
Couple live with male's family.

Matrilocal
Couple live with female's family.

Neolocal
Couple start own household.

--- Authority ---

Patriarchy
Male, usually eldest, holds authority.

Matriarchy
Female, usually eldest, holds authority.

Egalitarian
Males and females have equal authority.

--- Number of Partners ---

Monogamy
One partner at one time.

Polygamy
More than one partner at one time.

Polygyny
One man, more than one wife at one time.

Polyandry
One woman, more than one husband at one time.

was more common at the peak of industrialisation, when there was a need for reliance in the absence of a welfare state, not before or after, and is not a characteristic of pre-industrial European rural society. Kinship ties were probably stronger pre-industrially, as in rural areas most people shared the same occupational experience, relations lived close by, and family could be seen frequently.

It appears that industrialisation may have changed the nature of kinship relationships, rather than the structure of the family itself. Anderson's research on the working-class in Preston, Lancashire found that these families were more likely to be dependent on kin for financial support and accommodation at the peak of the industrial revolution. In contrast, middle- and upper-class families in Victorian England regarded kinship as significant for property inheritance and also for the social influence which family connections could bring.

THE WORK OF M. YOUNG AND P. WILLMOTT

M. Young and P. Willmott, 'Family and Kinship in East London' (1962) illustrated the existence of extended family networks in Bethnal Green in traditional working-class communities in the 1950s. They suggested, however, that there was a trend away from these mutual support systems in favour of what they call the '**privatised nuclear family**'. Thus, in Bethnal Green, mothers and daughters had a very close relationship, and men worked in similar occupations (dockers, printers, market traders) often helping each other find work. Young and Willmott described how the Bethnal Green families were rehoused to Greenleigh, a new council estate in Essex about 30 miles away. Once there, the families became more 'privatised', or home-centred, and based on the nuclear, rather than the extended, family. Another characteristic was that the strong female relationships reduced in intensity, and wives became more dependent on their husbands for domestic help and companionship. Leisure time in Bethnal Green had largely consisted of the men drinking in the local pub, and the women visiting neighbours and relatives. In Greenleigh, leisure interests became more home-centred, and included gardening, watching television, and playing with the children. Privatisation for most women in Greenleigh was often interpreted as isolation rather than togetherness, as they lost their daily support network of close relatives and friends. This trend has been supported by the 1960s Luton study of J. Goldthorpe and D. Lockwood, 'The Affluent Worker' (1969).

M. Young and P. Willmott, 'The Symmetrical Family' (1975) is an account of changes in family life using their earlier research, historical evidence, and data from a survey in the London area in the early 1970s ('Family and Class in a London Suburb'). Using all this information they argue that the family in Britain has developed through three key stages:

Stage 1 – The pre-industrial family. This is characterised by a family which is organised around its economic function as a production unit, for example agriculture and cottage industries. In these families work and home life is not separated, so that many work and domestic activities are not clearly defined between men and women.

Stage 2 – The early industrial family. These are families which are heavily influenced by industrialisation and the creation of production units outside the home. Thus, in these families men go out to work while women are confined to the home and domestic tasks. This stage is characterised by kinship networks created largely by women in order to provide a mutual support system.

Stage 3 – The privatised nuclear family. According to Young and Willmott these families first emerged amongst the middle class, and then gradually spread to the working class during the late 1950s and early 1960s. They are nuclear, with few kinship relations, home-centred, and symmetrical. The concept of symmetricality did not imply that men and women shared the same roles, but that women were starting to take on work roles and careers outside the home, while men were becoming more involved in domestic activities. The notion that this type of family began in the middle class and filtered down to the working class is described by Young and Willmott as 'stratified diffusion'. In fact, the process of stratified diffusion could, according to the authors, result in the creation of a 4th stage, where the upper-class family model could be mirrored by the middle class. These families would have asymmetrical roles, where the husbands would be totally immersed in work, and the wives would lead a separate social and domestic life.

CRITICISMS OF YOUNG AND WILLMOTT

Their idea of the family moving through stages as industrialisation progresses assumes that there are no conflicts between the family and the effects of the industrial process. The emphasis on change as being positive also ignores the dysfunctions which industrial change may bring.

The concept of stratified diffusion implies that the working class always follow the model set by the middle class. This is not always so, and J. Goldthorpe and D. Lockwood, 'The Affluent Worker' (1969) found that the affluent or privatised workers in their study maintained a distinctive working-class outlook on life.

The idea of symmetricality may not hold true for the majority of families. Many studies have shown that, although women are becoming more involved in the world of work, the commitment made by men in the domestic and childcare field is still very limited: A. Oakley, 'The Sociology of Housework' (1974).

Young and Willmott may have underestimated the continuing importance of the extended family, even for the privatised families. With modern telecommunications and quick and reliable transport, the extended family still maintains regular contact and provides financial and emotional support (see below).

Families in modern industrialised societies

KINSHIP TIES

Despite the onset of industrialisation, there is extensive evidence to illustrate that the extended family continued, and continues, to be of significant importance in people's lives. R. Rosser and C. Harris, 'The Family and Social Change' (1965) found in their research into families in Swansea that most of them retained a modified or reduced form of extended family. The term **'modified extended family'** (first used by E. Litwak) refers to a geographically dispersed family which maintains contact using cars for transportation and telephones for communication. Similarly, C. Bell, 'Middle Class Families' (1968) found that close kin, although separated because of geographical and occupational mobility, continued to maintain contact with relatives via telephoning, letter writing and visits. Even for affluent workers in privatised families the extended family still remains important, as demonstrated by F. Devine, 'Affluent Workers Revisited: Privatism and the Working Class' (1992).

Queen Victoria with some of her extended family

FAMILY DIVERSITY

The belief that there is one single type of family structure in modern industrialised society is still upheld by some sections of society, despite extensive evidence to the contrary. E. Leach, 'A Runaway World?' (1967) argues that the concept of a '**cereal packet family**', consisting of a husband and wife with two or three children in a nuclear family, is heavily promoted by politicians and by the advertising industry. This is in spite of the fact that such families number less than 25% of households in Britain today. The impression given is that the 'cereal packet family' is the norm, and that any other variation is a deviant form. However, it is apparent that this conventional model family is no longer, or indeed never has been, the most common form of family. R.N. Rapport, M.P. Fogarty and R. Rapport (eds.), 'Families in Britain' (1982) have identified five distinctive elements of family diversity in Britain:

Organisational diversity refers to variations in structure, kinship network, household type, and division of labour between spouses. Examples of such families include the conventional nuclear, single parent, dual career, and reconstituted (formed after divorce and remarriage). The latter is the fastest growing group in society and, like the others, does not fit neatly into the 'cereal packet' format.

Cultural diversity refers to families which have different lifestyles due to ethnic origins and/or religious beliefs, for example Chinese, Asian, West Indian, Jews, Catholics, etc.

Class diversity. Differences in families exist according to class background, for example middle-class and working-class socialisation patterns and conjugal role relationships.

Life cycle diversity. Family life varies according to a person's position in the life cycle, for example single person, married person, parent, widow(er), etc.

'Cohort' diversity refers to family differences arising out of the periods at which the family has passed through different stages of the family life cycle, for example families whose children entered the labour market in the 1980s may experience increased dependency from these children due to high unemployment

In addition to the above it is possible to identify other areas of diversity, such as locality and family type. Certain areas of Britain are more likely to house certain family types, 'Geriatric wards' in coastal areas are more likely to attract elderly retired people, whereas older declining industrial areas are probably going to retain many traditional working class families.

Even with the range of family diversity outlined above, the basic features of family life such as marriage and procreation have remained static. R. Chester, 'The Rise of the Neo-Conventional Family' (1985) argues that the biggest change in family life has been the increase in the number of married women working. He thus proposes the use of the term '**neo-conventional family**' to describe modern day families, which are the same as traditional nuclear families, but more women are going out to work.

Marriage and divorce

MARRIAGE

Marriage rates have increased this century up to 1971, then shown a decline, with a growing number of remarriages from 1971, as indicated below.

Year	Marriages	Remarriages (as of all marriages)
1961	340,000	14%
1971	369,000	20%
1990	241,000	36%

(Adapted from *Social Trends*, 1994)

During the period 1979–91 there was also an increase in the cohabitation rates for non-married women, up from 11% to 23%, according to the *General Household Survey*, 1991. A reflection of this trend has been a parallel rise in the number of births outside marriage, from one in twenty between 1900 and 1960 to one in three in 1992 (*Social Trends*, 1994).

Many feminists have argued that cohabitation and illegitimate births are often a prelude to marriage, and are simply an indication of the growing independence of women and a lack of satisfaction with patriarchal marriage. R. Fletcher. 'The Shaking of the Foundations: Family and Society' (1988) argues that the increase in cohabitation and illegitimate births is not necessarily a sign of instability, as most couples are in conventional, but non-married relationships. In fact, cohabitation rates were just as common in the last century, and viewed then as a threat to the family Rev. A. Mearns, 'The Bitter Cry of Outcast London' (1883) condemned the common practice of couples living together out of wedlock in London's East End.

The increase in remarriage rates over the past twenty years indicates a trend towards serial monogamy, or marriage/divorce/remarriage, where couples change relationships more frequently than in the past, but still strive to maintain close dyadic or one-to-one bonds.

Marital breakdown

The breakdown of marital relationships can be measured in three ways.
1. Divorce
2. Separation
3. 'Empty-shell' marriages.

DIVORCE

Divorce statistics do not indicate anything about either the happiness of marriage or its stability. They represent only those people who, for one reason or another, have decided to seek legal recognition of the termination of the marriage. Divorce is defined as the dissolution of a marriage in the eyes of civil law by application of a divorce suit to the divorce court. The two parties are then free to re-marry if they so wish. Divorce figures can be presented in three ways:
  i. the actual number of divorces or decrees absolute granted each year;
 ii. the number of applications or petitions for divorce each year;
iii. the divorce rate, or the number of divorces per 1,000 married couples per year.

The divorce statistics are to a large extent a reflection of the ease and availability of divorce. Changes in divorce legislation over the past 130 years have made divorce easier and cheaper for people to obtain. The relevant laws affecting access to divorce are summarised below.

1857 Matrimonial Causes Act established the first divorce court (previously divorce was by Act of Parliament only), and granted husbands only the right to divorce, on the grounds of adultery or cruelty.

1878 Matrimonial Causes Act introduced maintenance for ex-wives, and also permitted women to divorce their husbands, but they had to prove both cruelty and adultery.

1923 Matrimonial Causes Act said that husbands and wives both had to prove either adultery or cruelty to obtain divorce.

1937 Herbert Act widened the grounds for divorce to include, in addition to adultery and cruelty, desertion, insanity, and mental cruelty.

1949 Legal Aid and Advice Act enabled the cost of divorce, in certain circumstances, to be borne by legal aid, thus widening the availability of divorce.

1969 Divorce Law Reform Act abandoned 'the matrimonial offence' concept, and the sole grounds for divorce became the 'irretrievable breakdown' of marriage, which could be demonstrated by using the existing grounds or one of the two new grounds (non-cohabitation for two years if both parties consent to the divorce, and five years non-cohabitation if one party objects to the divorce).

1984 Matrimonial Causes Act ended the ex-wife's automatic right to maintenance, and permitted divorce after one year of marriage rather than three.

1995 Lord Mackay's White Paper proposes to remove the need to prove 'fault' in a marriage, for example adultery, unreasonable behaviour, desertion. It also suggests that couples should be compelled to spend a year in mediation, encouraging them to negotiate their own settlements. Finally, the White Paper proposes that England and Wales follow the Scottish example, and require courts to take pension rights into account when splitting assets.

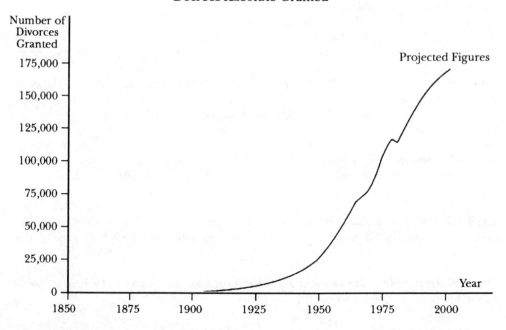

Decrees Absolute Granted

Taking the number of decrees absolute granted as the measurement for divorce, the increase in divorce parallels the changes in legislation, as can be seen from the graph on page 78.

SEPARATION

In countries where divorce is illegal, such as the Republic of Ireland, couples may express their marital dissatisfaction by taking out a legal separation. It is difficult to obtain reliable figures on the numbers of separations, as only legal separation orders are recorded. Couples who decide to 'unofficially' separate will not be counted. Although couples have always separated, especially when divorce was difficult to obtain, it does seem that couples are now more likely to seek formal legal separation orders than they were in the past.

'EMPTY-SHELL' MARRIAGES

These are existing marriages where people live together in name only, but essentially lead separate lives. It is obviously difficult, if not impossible, to measure or estimate the number of such marriages. However, it is probably likely that there are less 'empty-shell' marriages today than in the past, as divorce is easier to obtain, and the stigma surrounding divorce is less than it was.

EXPLANATIONS FOR MARITAL BREAKDOWN

Changes in divorce legislation have obviously contributed to the increased rates of divorce. Other factors which are significant in marital breakdown are as follow.

Changing expectations of marriage and family life. With less support from the extended family there may be more pressure on couples to derive all their needs from each other. According to R. Fletcher, 'The Family and Marriage in Britain' (1966) this has led to higher marital expectations within the relationship, and if these are not satisfied then couples will seek to end their relationship.

Changes in women's social position. Personal expectations of women have greatly increased this century, due to job opportunities, equal rights and more independence. Currently, three-quarters of divorce petitions originate from women, which may indicate that greater independence for women outside the family environment may create conflicts within the marriage. N. Hart, 'When Marriage Ends – A Study in Status Passage,' (1976) shows that many women experience conflict between work/career roles and domestic/childcare responsibilities. Increased divorce, initiated by women, may mean that women are expecting more from the marital relationship, and are dissatisfied with attempting to combine the two roles.

Changing religious and social values. Religious tolerance of divorce, and a decline in the significance of religion in people's lives, may mean that divorce has become more widely acceptable. B. Wilson, 'Religion in a Secular Society' (1966) argues that the secularisation process (or decline in the significance of religion in society) means that less stigma is now attached to divorce and divorcees. Even for those who do marry, less than half choose religious ceremonies, although some have little choice as they are remarrying, and certain religions do not condone second marriages.

Changes in living environments. City areas have higher divorce rates than rural areas, which might be related to loose family networks, less social control over personal behaviour, and generally more conflict and stress in urban life.

Demographic changes. Life expectancy has increased from the late 40s at the turn of the century to the late 70s today. This means that couples who marry in their twenties could potentially be married for forty or fifty years, whereas a century ago this would have been extremely rare. To expect couples to remain together for such a long period in a monogamous relationship may be too stressful, and thus result in higher levels of marital breakdown.

The age at which couples marry is a risk factor for marital breakdown. Thus, partners who marry under the age of twenty-one are more likely to get divorced than those who are older on marriage. Young marital age brings with it financial problems, difficulties with accommodation and perhaps pregnancy and childbirth.

It appears that there is no single or universalistic cause to explain the increasing divorce rate and high levels of marital breakdown in modern industrial societies. Thus, a multi-causal approach must be adopted in order to explain the problem.

Gender roles within the family

The nature of gender roles within the family will vary according to the historical conditions prevailing at the time, and will also change in response to social conditions and the economic requirements of the society.

INFLUENCE OF INDUSTRIALISATION

Prior to industrialisation, women played an important and complementary role to that of men in agricultural and cottage industries. This changed with the industial revolution, and A. Oakley, 'Housewife' (1974) has described how industrialisation brought men, women and children together in factories and mines as individual wage earners rather than as economic family units. However, between 1814 and 1914 married women were largely excluded from paid employment, with Factory and Education Acts helping to encourage the belief that 'a woman's place is in the home'. This exclusion of married women from the workforce helped to create the role of housewife as the primary role for married women. This was, though, largely restricted to middle-class women, as working-class wives had to work out of financial necessity. Throughout the nineteenth century there was a growing economic dependence of women and children on men, leading to increasing female dependency. For the women who did work, employment was limited to domestic service or unskilled manual work. This helped to initiate the concept of the family wage, where the husband's wage was regarded as sufficient to support his wife and children, leaving women free to perform the housewife role, and maybe work for pin money.

However, with the demand for female employment during the two world wars, and the social and legal changes affecting women this century, the growth in paid employment of married women has been significant, with over two-thirds now employed outside the home. Although half of these female workers are part-time, the jobs which women now hold cover a wide range of professional and manual areas, and the income which women earn is no longer regarded as pin money, but is essential to the family budget.

DEMOGRAPHIC INFLUENCES

Up until the 1860s women of all social classes tended to have large families, with an average of five or six surviving children. From the 1870s onwards, middle-class women began to reduce their family size, and by the principle of stratified diffusion, so did the working class. Thus, by the 1930s the average number of children per woman was two or three. This has remained steady until the present day, with a slight decline to less than two in the 1990s.

The reduced number of years which women now spend in pregnancy and childbirth means that their working lives outside the home have become increasingly more important, and their domestic role has diminished. Increasing life expectancy this century has also given women a much longer period after childbearing in which to plan and pursue a career.

CHANGING SOCIAL AND LEGAL POSITION OF WOMEN

Within Victorian society women were second-class citizens, denied the same legal, political, economic, and social rights enjoyed by many men. There existed no repectable alternative to marriage for women: it was either marriage, work on starvation wages, spinsterhood, or prostitution. For working-class women, 'work' meant extremely long hours on very low wages in a factory or sweatshop. For women a little higher up the social scale, work meant employment as a governess, or giving music or drawing lessons to the children of the wealthy. The position of spinsters was no better and they were regarded with contempt as 'surplus women'.

The emancipation of women, and their changing social position from that of a second-class citizen to one of equality, was a very slow process, which began in the 1850s and is still taking place today. Rather than listing the numerous Acts from the 1850s onwards, the importance of these legal changes is summarised below.

1. Legislation concerning property rights and divorce gradually stripped the husband of his power over his wife, children and the family property.
2. The divorce legislation widened the grounds upon which the wife could divorce or separate from her husband, and also permitted her to claim financial assistance from him.
3. In legal terms marriage began to be seen as a partnership based on legal equality over property and children. No longer was the husband the legal master and the wife the legal servant.
4. The activities of the women's suffrage movement eventually helped to gain the vote for women in 1928.
5. Educational institutions were gradually opened up to women, allowing them to obtain degrees, and from 1919 onwards enter the major professions.
6. The equal opportunities legislation of the 1970s promotes equal pay, aims to prevent sex discrimination and provides maternity benefits for pregnant women.

CHANGES IN CONJUGAL ROLES

The social emancipation of women, and their increasing equality with men in the wider society, has necessarily had its effects on marriage, and on role relationships in marriage. The social position of women in Victorian society and the early twentieth century was essentially that of a second-class citizen, and this was reflected within almost all marriages. Throughout this period and up to the 1950s, marriage was patriarchal, with authority and dominance held by the husband. The traditional role of the husband was, and was expected to be, 'the breadwinner', strong and aggressive outside the home, and dominant within it. The traditional role of the wife was, and was expected to be, 'the homemaker', submissive to husband and men in general. Work within the marriage was divided into 'men's work' and 'women's work', with husbands making financial and other major decisions, while wives were relegated to domestic and childcare tasks. E.Bott, 'Family and Social Network' (1957) identified two types of conjugal or marital roles:

Segregated or traditional conjugal roles, where the husband and wife lead largely separate social lives, and have clearly defined roles within the family.

Joint or companionate conjugal roles, where husband and wife share responsibilites, decision-making, and leisure activities, and roles are less sharply differentiated.

Examples of segregated conjugal role relationships are described by J.Tunstall, 'The Fisherman' (1962), N.Dennis, P.Henriques, and C.Slaughter, 'Coal is Our Life' (1956), and M.Young and P.Willmott, 'Family and Kinship in East London' (1962). The families described resided in small, isolated villages and towns, often with one major primary industry (fishing, mining, docks), and were predominantly working-class. The segregated conjugal role relationships common in such areas had already begun to disappear amongst the middle class, and the trend was spreading to the working-class. The major factors which were responsible for the gradual shift away from segregated roles to joint or companionate roles were as follows:

1. The changing social position of women in society.
2. The breakdown of the extended kinship network in the working class, due to social mobility.
3. The isolation of the nuclear family, in all classes, due to rehousing and redevelopment, resulting in the greater interdependence of couples.
4. Slum clearance programmes, with the consequent destruction of old working-class communities, has broken down the traditional patterns of role socialisation which were important for the continuation of the segregated role model.

Evidence for the transition from segregated to joint conjugal roles in working-class marriages can be found in M.Young and P.Willmott, 'Family and Kinship in East London' (1962), H.Gavron, 'The Captive Wife' (1966), and J. and E. Newson, 'Patterns of Infant Care' (1963). Although there is still some division of labour and role segregation, marriage in the now isolated (or privatised) nuclear family is far more of a partnership, with the husband becoming more 'home-centred'.

For middle-class and skilled working-class marriages, the change to joint roles has developed much more quickly. Empirical evidence can be found in J.Goldthorpe and D.Lockwood, 'The Affluent Worker' (1968), G.Gorer, 'Sex and Marriage in England Today' (1971), and M.Young and P.Willmott, The Symmetrical Family (1975). A particular development in joint marriages is the **dual-career family**, where husband and wife both have full-time careers, share the domestic work and childcare, and spend their leisure time together: R.R. Rapport, 'Dual-career Families' (1971) and 'Dual-career Families Re-examined' (1976). More recent studies such as S.Edgell, 'Middle Class Couples' (1980) found that wives were responsible for decision-making in areas which were considered by the couple to be unimportant, such as food purchases, buying children's clothes, and household decoration. In contrast, husbands made 'important' decisions, for example, car and house purchases.

Although segregated roles are associated with traditional working-class couples and joint roles are more common amongst middle-class couples, there is no clear connection between social class and conjugal roles. 'Issues of Social Trends' throughout the 1980s and '90s continue to show the household division of labour by marital status as largely segregated, irrespective of class. J.Pahl, 'Money and Marriage' (1989) found that the control of finances in marriage was by a variety of financial arrangements, regardless of social class, but in most cases men were the main beneficiaries. J.Martin and C.Roberts, 'Women and Employment: A Lifetime Perspective' (1984) interviewed nearly 6,000 women of all classes, and found that the majority of all the women did most of the housework, even when they worked. Women often carried the double burden of housework/childcare and paid employment. Roles in middle- and upper-class families can often be segregated, especially when wives are expected to support their husbands in their jobs by entertaining clients, acting as unpaid secretaries, and giving up their own promotion prospects in favour of their husband's career advancement.

It is very difficult to actually measure conjugal roles, particularly as decision-making depends on a range of factors such as career opportunities, presence of children, and individual personalities. As men tend to work for longer hours outside the home it may be that women automatically take on more domestic and childcare roles. It is also difficult to measure the time spent in various activities as some tasks are discrete, for example mowing the grass, while others are more complex, for example being 'on call' for a baby. Individuals often choose the tasks they do because they enjoy them, rather than because they are fitting into prescribed conjugal roles.

Theoretical perspectives on the family

THE FUNCTIONALIST APPROACH

The functionalist view tends to regard the family as universal, and holds the belief that the nuclear family is 'fitted' to the needs of modern industrial societies. T. Parsons and R.F. Bales, 'Family, Socialisation and Interaction Process' (1955) argue that increasing specialisation in industrial societies has led to functional differentiation, whereby many of the functions of the pre-industrial family have been taken over by specialised institutions, such as social services, health services. However, they maintain that there are two functions of the family which are 'basic and irreducible', or always present. These are **primary socialisation**, and the **stabilisation of adult personalities**. Based on small group work, Parsons and Bales reveal that all small groups have leaders and followers, and it is possible to distinguish between **instrumental leaders** (concerned with getting the job done), and **expressive leaders** (concerned with group cohesiveness). By applying these ideas to the family group it is possible to present the roles of its members as follows (see figure on p. 84).

Here, family roles are clearly defined, with parents as leaders and children as followers. Segregated gender roles are seen as natural and inevitable, with fathers having an instrumental leader role (work, decision-making) and mothers having an expressive leader role (housework and childrearing). The children are socialised by their parents into their appropriate gender roles. Parsons sees these roles as given or ascribed, and assumes acceptance of them by the individuals involved. He states that demands for equality by women may create 'role strains' for them, and paid employment for women

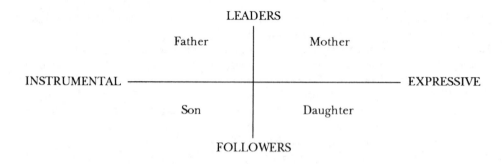

must always be secondary to their ascribed, expressive role. Some criticisms which can be levelled against Parsons include the following:

1. His conclusions are based on a small sample of middle-class American families in the 1950s, and ignores family diversity based on class, ethnicity, region, etc.
2. Parsons assumes that everyone benefits from the nuclear family, which is seen to suit capitalism rather than individual needs. Also, some men might have expressive roles and some women might take on instrumental roles.
3. Parsons does not explain the effects of industrialisation and social change on male/female roles.
4. A.Oakley 'Housewife' (1974) shows how anthropological evidence does not sustain Parsons' argument that women have always played the expressive role.
5. Parsons does not explain how housework (part of the wife's role) can be regarded as expressive, when it involves such instrumental tasks as shopping, cleaning, cooking, washing, etc.
6. Parsons emphasises the positive aspects of family life at the expense of the dysfunctions which might occur in families who fail to live up to role expectations, for example divorce, child abuse, single parents.

E.F. Vogel and N.W. Bell, 'The Emotionally Disturbed Child as the Family Scapegoat' (1968) is a functionalist analysis of a small number of American families which does point out the negative aspects of family life. They argue that conflicts between parents often result in projection on the child, who is used as an emotional scapegoat by the parents to relieve their tension. This might take the form of criticising a child for all the characteristics disliked in the spouse. For the child, this process is dysfunctional and he/she becomes emotionally disturbed. However, as a result of the child being used as the scapegoat the parents' relationship improves, and the family becomes unified. Although critical of these aspects of family life, Vogel and Bell still reflect the functionalist view that family life must be maintained at every cost, in this case at the expense of the child's emotions.

E.Leach, 'A Runaway World?' (1967) has a more critical view of family life in industrial society than Vogel and Bell. He compares the supportive network of family relationships in pre-industrial societies to the isolation of nuclear families in industrial societies. Leach regards the lack of emotional support from kin and community as a dangerous consequence of industrialisation, resulting in an intensification of emotional stress within the nuclear family unit. He compares the nuclear family to 'an overloaded electrical circuit' where the demands made on the members are so great that 'fuses blow'. In direct opposition to the functionalist view Leach does not regard the preservation of family life as vital at any cost to the individual members' emotional health.

Most of the discussion concerning the 'problems of family life' is derived from the functionalist view, and in particular from the ideas of the **social pathologists**. Thus, the functionalist perspective argues that the family is no longer capable or willing to carry out its functions, and the family as a system is breaking up, breaking down, or is becoming increasingly disorganised and unstable. From the social pathology view the family is seen as being 'sick' or 'ill'. Both of these sets of arguments are generally agreed on the view that 'the end of the nuclear family is nigh' unless something is done to halt the decline. Thus, there exists a situation where the rates of divorce, abortion, delinquency, illegitimacy, and other such 'problems' of the family are used to create what S. Cohen, 'Folk Devils and Moral Panics' (1973) terms a **'moral panic'** and a general belief that family life is disintegrating. These ideas concerning the family under threat and a moral decline in society are popular with a branch of the Conservative Party called the 'New Right'. They hark back to a 'golden age' when the family was supposedly stable and organised, and demand a return to 'traditional family values'. By introducing certain restrictions on social security benefits, for example for single parents, the New Right hope to prompt a return to 'traditional family life'. This 'victim-blaming' approach can often be used to justify a lack of childcare provision and poor job opportunities. Despite the fact that the perception of the 'cereal packet norm' is inaccurate, it is still upheld by the New Right as the model of family life which society should be aiming to achieve.

THE MARXIST APPROACH

A Marxist view of family life must be seen in the context of Marx's theory of **stratification**. Thus, the family is part of the superstructure of society, and therefore serves the needs of, and helps to maintain the infrastructure or economic system of society. Marx himself wrote very little on family life, but his collaborator F. Engels, 'The Origins of the Family, Private Property, and the State' (1902) used a Marxist analysis to explain the historical development of the capitalist family. In pre-industrial societies men and women worked alongside each other, and housework was not distinguished from any other kind of work. Marriage was an economic/productive contract based on a working relationship. In the sixteenth and seventeenth centuries the emergence of commodity production, for example weaving, carpentry, cobbling, caused a division of labour to occur between men and women, with the men going out to work. The distinction between **domestic labour** (unpaid housework) and **wage labour** (paid work outside the home) became more apparent as capitalism increased. The nature of male/female relationships also changed. Monogamy became the most efficient means of ensuring the transmission of private property through inheritance, resulting in the 'reification' of women; that is, women were regarded as objects on pedestals to be worshipped. Thus, in the nineteenth century, the ideal of family life was one based on individual attraction, united by love, and representing a sanctuary for men from the pressures of work. Marx likened the relationship to that of the bourgeoisie and the proletariat, with men representing the bourgeoisie, owning women as private property, and women as the proletariat, owning nothing and having no legal or political rights. Marx saw the industrial revolution as a great opportunity for women to enter the productive sphere. He further predicted that capitalism would provide a whole range of new labour-saving devices allowing women to enter the workforce and develop, along with men, a proletarian consciousness. The conflict Marx noted between work at home (domestic labour) and commodity production (wage labour) would be resolved with the onset of a socialist society and the abolition of private property, where child-rearing would be designated to state nurseries, thus giving women complete freedom to work on an equal basis with men.

Marxist-feminist theories have used a Marxist analysis to illustrate how the capitalist system oppresses women, and how the patriarchal family structure is the major obstacle to female emancipation. Women's domestic labour role serves the needs of capitalism and prevents gender equality in employment, where women are often used as a cheap, 'reserve army' of labour. J.J. Mitchell, 'Woman's Estate' (1971) argues that women need to be free from their domestic responsibilites by passing on their roles to other agencies, such as childcare. This would be the only way to create greater equality between the sexes and remove the obstacles to gender equality in the labour market. Further views on the patriarchal family are described in Chapter 5. There are a number of criticisms of the Marxist view, as follows:

1. A. Oakley, 'Housewife' (1974) criticises the view that there was no division of labour in pre-industrial societies. Anthropological and historical evidence reveals that women had most responsibility for childrearing.
2. The Marxist view can be criticised for **economic determinism**, the belief that the family responds to, and is determined by changes in the economic structure of society. This ignores the diversity both within and between capitalist societies.
3. There is no evidence that collective child-rearing scheme such as the kibbutz are healthier for children or that they totally free women for work. The nuclear family remains the most effective institution for primary socialisation.
4. Capitalism has not allowed women to take an important part in the process of production. The state has circumscribed employment for women in service industries, textiles, clothing, catering, etc., with low pay and poor working conditions.
5. Marxists ignore the positive aspects of family life, and the fact that many people are satisfied with their domestic situation. Attacks on the family by radical feminists may encourage dissent and lead to social problems such as divorce and single parenthood.

The Marxist approach is valid in the sense that it reminds us that the family is not a 'natural' institution, but is socially constructed and moulded by society. It thus gives an explanation of 'deviant' family groups in that they are responding to changes in society, so that instead of the family becoming unstable and disorganised it is simply changing and reorganising.

AN INTERPRETIVE APPROACH

This view emphasises the meaning of the family for the individuals involved, rather than its relationship to the wider society. It is thus concerned with examining the roles of individual members, how they experience family life, and how they affect other people within the family. Examples of this approach include P. Berger and H. Kellner, 'Marriage and the Construction of Reality' in M. Anderson (ed.) in 'Sociology of the Family (1980) which describes how individual family members construct their own reality of family life, often keeping family relationships for intimate and self-realisation purposes, with public relationships maintained at an impersonal level.

The socialisation process within the family is frequently described from this perspective, in particular noting that it is a two-way process, with children socialising their parents as much as they are undergoing socialisation from their mothers and fathers (see K.C. Backett, 'Images of Parenthood' in M. Anderson (ed.) 'Sociology of the Family' (1980)).

The major criticism of this perspective is that it is too insular, and ignores the wider social structure within which the family exists. By not taking account of the social structure it disregards the influence of power relations within society in the family. However, D. Clark, 'Constituting the Marital World: A Qualitative Perspective' (1991) identifies four types of marriage which illustrate how the interaction between the couples is influenced by the economic structure. These include 'establishing marriages', which are focused on planning and saving money and 'struggling marriages', which revolve around financial difficulties and problems with housing or unemployment. Thus, the interpretive approach can provide an insight into relationships within the family, and is also capable of showing how external influences can affect interaction.

CHECK YOUR UNDERSTANDING

After reading this chapter you should now be able to define the following terms.

1   Nuclear family
2   Extended family
3   Polyandry
4   Polygyny
5   Matrifocal
6   Patriarchal
7   Kibbutz
8   Privatised nuclear family
9   Symmetrical family
10   Stratified diffusion
11   Asymmetrical roles
12   Modified extended family
13   'Cereal packet' family
14   Neo-conventional family
15   Serial monogamy
16   Divorce
17   Separation
18   'Empty-shell' marriages
19   Female dependency
20   Segregated conjugal roles
21   Joint conjugal roles
22   Dual-career family

23 Functional differentiation
24 Instrumental leaders
25 Expressive leaders
26 Dysfunctions
27 Moral panic
28 'New Right'
29 Domestic labour
30 Wage labour

SELF-ASSESSMENT QUESTIONS

1 How accurate is it to claim that there is a 'universal family'?
2 Describe some of the variations in family structure.
3 How has industrialisation changed kinship relations rather than family structure?
4 What is the symmetrical family?
5 How diverse is modern family life?
6 Summarise the trends in marriage this century.
7 What are the main reasons for marital breakdown?
8 How has industrialisation influenced gender roles?
9 What are the causes of the change from segregated to joint conjugal roles?
10 How do the functionalist and Marxist views of the family differ?

CHAPTER EIGHT

EDUCATION

ON COMPLETION OF THIS CHAPTER THE STUDENT SHOULD BE ABLE
TO:

1 REVIEW THE HISTORY OF EDUCATION, INCLUDING THE KEY
  PIECES OF LEGISLATION FROM THE NINETEENTH CENTURY TO
  THE PRESENT DAY

2 DESCRIBE THE RELATIONSHIP BETWEEN SOCIAL CLASS AND
  EDUCATIONAL ACHIEVEMENT

3 DESCRIBE THE RELATIONSHIP BETWEEN GENDER AND
  EDUCATIONAL ACHIEVEMENT

4 DESCRIBE THE RELATIONSHIP BETWEEN ETHNICITY AND
  EDUCATIONAL ACHIEVEMENT

5 EXPLAIN AND EVALUATE THE MAIN SOCIOLOGICAL THEORIES OF
  EDUCATION

History of education

The history of education necessarily reflects the political and educational philosophies of
the period under discussion. Hence, the establishment of state education in the late
nineteenth century was a response to the industrial competition posed by Germany and
the USA. A literate and numerate workforce was required to enhance the progress of
industrialisation, but at the same time there was a fear amongst politicians that universal
education might ignite the masses and lead to revolution – 'knowledge is power'. More
recent developments in the mid-twentieth century reflected a concern with the
promotion of equality of opportunity and social cohesiveness. In the last twenty years
the area of vocational education has dominated many educational debates, along with
the issue of greater independence for schools and colleges.

Prior to state involvement in education in the 1870s, upper-class children (boys)
attended public schools to be prepared for university and public office; middle-class
children (again, predominantly boys) went to grammar schools to prepare for the
professions; and church and charity schools were available for working-class children

to be drilled in the three Rs. The most important laws regarding the history of state education in England and Wales are as follows.

1870 Forster's Education Act established a national system of elementary schools alongside the existing church schools. This education, from five years to ten years, was not free, and attendance was not compulsory.

1880 Mundella's Education Act made elementary education up to the age of ten years compulsory.

1902 Balfour's Education Act established local education authorities, and empowered them to provide some secondary education in secondary grammar schools (academic bias) and in central schools (industrial bias). The school leaving age was raised to thirteen, and 25% free scholarship places were allocated to post-elementary education.

1918 Fisher's Education Act made education up to the age of fourteen years free and compulsory.

1944 Butler's Education Act completely reorganised the educational system in England and Wales into three distinct areas: primary, secondary, and further. The most controversial part of the Act was the secondary tripartite system of schools, which allocated children to one of three schools based on the results of an exam (the eleven-plus).

The 1972 Education Act raised the school leaving age to sixteen years.

The 1988 Education Reform Act established a national curriculum for all state schools in England and Wales, combined with a national system of testing and assessment at 'key stages' (seven, eleven, fourteen and sixteen). The Act also reduced the role of the local education authorities, giving greater control to the schools and the governing body. Under the Act, city technology colleges and grant maintained schools were established, independent of local authority control.

The most significant post-war changes have occurred as a result of the 1944 and 1988 Acts. Up to 1944 there were essentially three types of school: elementary schools for the working class, grammar schools for the middle class, and public schools for the upper class. The aim of the 1944 Act was to create a national unified system of education, which would break down social class barriers. Three tiers of education were introduced: primary (two to eleven years), secondary (eleven to fifteen-plus), and further (post school leaving age). The Act greatly increased the responsibilities and duties of the Minister of Education, local education authorities, and parents. More importantly, it laid down the legal basis for a system in which all children, regardless of their parents' social and financial status, would have access to schools providing 'such variety of instruction as may be desirable in view of their different ages, abilities, and aptitudes'.

The most important section of the new educational system was the secondary tier, known as the **tripartite system**. The basic assumption behind the tripartite system was that it was possible to catergorise children into 'academic', 'technical', or 'practical', according to their abilities, and that provision of a particular type of schooling should be made accordingly. The school to which children were allocated was decided on the basis of their results in the 'eleven-plus' examination, involving tests in English and

Children in a state primary school

Maths in the last year of primary school. Children who passed the exam were allocated a place in grammar schools or in technical schools, while those who failed were sent to secondary modern schools. In practice few technical schools were built, so the system became a bipartite one with the children who passed the eleven-plus exam going to grammar schools to pursue an academic curriculum, and those who failed going to secondary modern schools to follow a more practical-based curriculum.

Compared to the educational provision in existence before the second world war the tripartite system did give greater educational opportunity to a wider range of children, particularly those from the working class. It also enabled a larger number of all children to obtain an academic education and go on to university, thus increasing social mobility. However, the tripartite system also attracted the following criticisms:

1. The method of selection at eleven was unfair and possibly inaccurate, as intelligence is not 'fixed' at eleven years, and many children are late developers or poor examinees.
2. A disproportionately larger number of middle-class children gained grammar school places due to parental socialisation, which helped them to perform better in the eleven-plus exam because of language skills, help with homework, etc.

3. The concept of '**parity of esteem**', whereby the three schools were supposed to be 'equal but different' was not achieved. Local education authorities often provided better facilities for grammar schools than for their secondary moderns, which did not have sixth forms. Also, the exam structure in the schools was different, with grammar schools preparing pupils for 'O' and 'A' levels from 1951 onwards, whereas secondary modern schools only started CSE exams from 1965.
4. The sharp division of children into 'academic' or 'practical' types assumed that children could not benefit from a diverse range of educational subjects.

The tripartite system was not regarded as successful in achieving the aim of equal educational opportunity. Criticisms of the system led to the Labour Government's policy in 1965 to introduce the **comprehensive school**, in an attempt to eliminate the social inequalities of the tripartite system.

The common feature of all comprehensive systems is that children of wide-ranging abilities attend the same secondary school at the age of eleven. Some comprehensive schools stream, band or test their pupils by general ability or subject ability, while others have little academic division (they are mixed ability). At present, nearly 90% of secondary school pupils attend comprehensive schools, with the remainder at grammar or secondary modern schools, or in private education. The absence of an exam at eleven, greater social and physical resources, social integration, an 'open sixth form', and less wastage of talent are some of the advantages of the comprehensive system. In spite of overcoming some of the problems of the tripartite system, comprehensive schools also attract a number of criticisms.

1. During the late 1960s and 1970s many comprehensive schools had very large numbers of pupils (up to 2,000), which was distressing for younger children who felt lost in the school. Split sites were also common, and transportation between them proved difficult and time-wasting.
2. It has been argued that more able pupils are held back in comprehensive schools, and do not achieve their full potential. However, long-term evidence from the National Child Development Study on 16,000 children born in March, 1958 found that bright children do just as well in comprehensives as they do in grammar schools. They also found that lower-ability pupils generally achieve better results in comprehensives than they do in secondary modern schools.
3. Critics of the comprehensive system believe that standards in these schools are lower than in the tripartite system, with the dilution of the grammar school stream. Evidence of exam results over the past two decades does not, however, bear this out.
4. The breakdown of social barriers which comprehensives were supposed to have achieved has not materialised, particularly as there are still grammar schools in the country and an independent sector of education. These grammar and private schools tend to 'cream off' the brighter pupils, leading to lower-ability, and predominantly working-class children in the comprehensives. In mixed class comprehensives it still appears that middle-class children prevail in the higher streams, largely as a result of class socialisation. Thus, the extent to which comprehensives can overcome class barriers is limited, as they have no control over the family background of their pupils.

It is not possible to have a truly national, comprehensive system of education whilst there is still an **independent sector** of education, with over 2,000 schools. These schools are financially self-supporting, most of them having been established through endowments by individuals or organisations such as the Church. About 200 of these are

Public school boys at Harrow

the public schools such as Eton, Harrow, Rugby, etc., which, while charging fees, act in the 'public' interest by not seeking to be profit-making. Essentially they are fee-charging, financially independent, single sex, and residential. The greater portion of the private sector is made up of **direct grant schools**, which are largely single sex grammar schools which lie between the state and the independent sector, for although they have their own governing bodies and charge fees, they are eligible for government grants. These grants are paid on condition that the local education authority could take up a certain number of places at the school, with the LEA paying the fees for the children winning such scholarships. In the 1976 Education Act the Labour Government required these schools to make a choice between entering the maintained state sector or becoming completely independent. However, under the 1980 Education Act the Conservative Government introduced the **Assisted Places Scheme**, in order to bridge the gap between the state and the independent sector. Thus, parents can be given financial help with the cost of tuition fees at certain independent schools. It is difficult to assess, however, which type of children are benefiting from the scheme. Although over 30,000 children are in the scheme, many of them are middle-class children who would have gone to a private school anyway, and their parents are simply receiving a helping hand with the fees.

The independent sector of education is often considered to be the only route into the top professions and most powerful positions in the country. In a study of elites at Cambridge, A. Giddens, 'An Anatomy of the Ruling Class' (1979) found that over 80% of Anglican bishops, principal judges, and army officers above the rank of major-general came from public school backgrounds, as did 60% of chief secretaries in the civil service, and 76% of Conservative MPs between 1951 and 1970 (in contrast to only 26% of Labour MPs over the same period). Although the Labour Government in the 1960s considered the abolition of the independent sector, they felt it would be anti-democratic to do so, for it would restrict parents' freedom of choice in the education of their children.

Whereas the 1944 Act reflected Labour Party philosophy of equal opportunity, the 1988 Education Reform Act embodied Conservative Party philosophy which viewed education as a market place, involving competition, diversity, and parental choice. Schools were obliged to publish National Curriculum test results and external exam results so that league tables of school results could be made available to the public. The league tables can, however, be misleading, as they do not take into account the pupil intake, the catchment area of the school, or the social environment of the school.

The **National Curriculum**, introduced under the 1988 Act, only applies to state schools, and lays down a curriculum for five to sixteen year olds in core subjects (English, maths, science) and seven other subjects. Core subjects are compulsory up to the age of sixteen, increasing equal opportunity for girls, who were often encouraged to drop science several years earlier. The testing of children at the ages of seven, eleven, fourteen, and sixteen may help to achieve standardisation between schools, but may also lead to schools streaming pupils on the basis of their test results, suggesting a return to eleven-plus style selection.

The other main initiative was the introduction of the 1988 Act **grant-maintained schools**, which are schools that have opted out of local authority control, and are financed directly by central government. These schools are self-governing, with headteachers and governors employing staff, deciding on curriculum matters, and managing their own budgets. At the present time, only about 15% of secondary schools have become grant-maintained and about two per cent of primary schools.

The 1988 Act also established city technology colleges (CTCs) for post-eleven education, which in addition to following the National Curriculum put great emphasis on maths, science, and technology. The fifteen CTCs are funded partly by industry and partly by the Department of Education.

Over the past twenty years there has been an increasing move towards developing vocationally relevant education, or what is known as **'new vocationalism'**. The impetus for the need to link education more directly to the world of work was the high levels of youth unemployment in the mid-1970s. This led to the creation of a number of vocational initiatives such as YTS (Youth Training Scheme), CPVE (Certificate in Pre-Vocational Education), and TVEI (Technical and Vocational Education Initiative). All of these schemes combined various amounts of work experience with time spent in the classroom.

In 1973 the Manpower Services Commission was set up to develop youth training in the 1970s, in particular the YOPs (Youth Opportunities Schemes) which started in 1978 and involved a six month work placement with one or two days a week in college. The YOPs were renamed YTS (Youth Training Schemes) in 1983 and were extended to one year placements, which became two years in 1986. Since the 1990s the work of the Manpower Services Commission has passed to the TECs (Training and Enterprise Councils).

In order to streamline qualifications and standardise the various awarding bodies the NCVQ (National Council for Vocational Qualifications) was created in 1986 to establish NVQs (National Vocational Qualifications) in various occupational areas, for example business, hairdressing, catering, health and social care. The introduction of vocational educational qualifications followed in 1992 with GNVQs (General National Vocational Qualifications), which are academically based courses in broad occupational areas such as health and social care, business, leisure and tourism, etc. The idea of combining some form of training with education has attracted a number of criticisms.

K. Roberts et al, 'What are Britain's 16–19 Year Olds Learning?' (1989) found that most young people were more interested in finding full-time jobs than going on short-term training schemes which often do not lead to employment. Many of the teenagers he interviewed felt that training was a poor substitute for a job.

D. Finn, 'Training Without Jobs' (1984) argues that the real purpose of training schemes is to reduce the unemployment figures and depress wages, as employers are more likely to employ a one or two year 'cheap' YTS trainee than a full-time 'expensive' employee.

The quality and relevance of the training which is given is often questioned. P. Cohen, 'Against the new vocationalism' in I. Bates et al, 'Schooling for the Dole?' (1984) found that many trainees were given menial tasks to do, watched other employees or ran errands, received little direct job training and learnt no specific occupational skills. In addition, the education received on most YTS courses tends to concentrate on social and life skills rather than on specific job skills.

The ability to obtain employment after a training scheme is often unrelated to the course followed. P. Ainley, 'Vocational Education and Training' (1990) showed that schemes varied in their ability to offer access to employment. He classifies schemes into four types: those that guarantee employment in large companies; schemes that lead to jobs in areas of demand; small shop schemes which offer some chances of employment; and schemes which merely provide cheap labour for employers and offer little chance of a job.

In many ways the division between academic education and vocational education is reminiscent of the tripartite system, in that academic courses such as 'A' levels are seen as being more valid and giving greater access to higher education and the professions than vocational courses such as GNVQs. There have been currently moves by the government to enhance the status of vocational education. The 1996 Dearing Review suggested changing the name of GNVQs to 'applied A levels' to encourage parity of esteem with traditional 'A' levels. Another suggestion to bridge the gap between the academic and the vocational is the proposed introduction of a single diploma which would list a combination of qualifications such as 'A' levels and GNVQ units. It remains to be seen whether these proposals are implemented and, if so, how successful they will be.

Social class and educational achievement

Despite the 1944 Education Act and the claim of 'equal opportunity for all', government reports such as Crowther 1959, Newsom 1963 and Plowden 1967, and a number of sociological studies in the 1960s such as J.W.B. Douglas, 'The Home and the School' (1964) and B. Jackson and D. Marsden, 'Education and the Working Class' (1966) showed that working-class children were not achieving as well in the education system as middle-class children. In the 1960s the child of a middle-class father was six times more likely to go to university than the child of a manual worker. Since it started in 1971 the General Household Survey has consistently showed that the higher the social class the greater the number and higher the level of qualifications. Longitudinal evidence has also been produced by the Oxford Social Mobility Studies in A.H. Halsey et al, 'Origins and Destinations: Family, Class and Education in Modern Britain' (1980) leading to the '1:2:4 Rule of Relative Hope', which states that whatever chance the son of an unskilled worker has of obtaining a non-manual job, the son of a skilled worker has twice the chance, and the son of a non-manual worker has four times the chance.

Attempts by sociologists to explain differential educational achievement between the social classes has generally focused on three areas: the child's home background; factors within the school situation itself; and the unequal nature of the society in which the educational system operates.

HOME BACKGROUND

The influence of home background on a child's future educational achievement can be seen in a number of areas. The social class that a child is born into will affect all of the child's life chances in many ways. Thus, social class factors reflect themselves in the family's wealth, level of income, parents' occupation, neighbourhood and housing, as well as the class values and view of society imparted to the child through primary socialisation.

Studies on **family size** have indicated that children from small families in all social classes tend, on average, to perform better at school than children from large families. A large family is not only more likely to be financially constrained and be unable to pay for educational facilities in the home, but also parents are unable to give as much attention to any of five or six children as they could with one or two. Family size increases in social classes 3, 4, and 5 (the working class), but even in families of the same size, middle-class children have more financial backing.

The significance of **birth order** varies with social class. Thus, it appears to matter much more to be an eldest child in a working-class family than in a middle-class one. Generally though, first born children receive more initial attention, and may benefit more from greater financial support.

The provision of **home facilities** will be largely influenced by family income and family size. Thus, the larger the family, the less the accommodation and the greater the overcrowding. Lower income groups with large families tend to congregate in 'twilight zones' or inner city areas which, as the Plowden Report (1969) noted, lack gardens, play areas and parks. Also, the ability to provide books, toys, educational visits and holidays is restricted in larger families and lower family incomes: J.W.B. Douglas, 'The Home and the School' (1964).

The importance of **language development** in primary socialisation, and the social variations which exist, has been closely studied by B. Bernstein, 'Social Class and Linguistic Development: A Theory of Social Learning' (1961). He argues that the two major social classes use two very different language codes. The middle class use a formal language or an elaborated code (for example 'My Mother taught me how to read'), while the working class use a public language or a restricted code ('Me Ma learnt me to read'). Bernstein does not argue that one code is better or worse than the other, but he does argue that the middle-class child is at a distinct advantage in that the elaborated code acquired at home is the same code used in school by teachers and in exams. Thus the middle-class child and the school 'speak the same language', whereas the working-class child is clearly at a disadvantage at school since his code is completely different from that used in schools.

The notion that working-class children speak a sub-standard form of English has been criticised by W. Labov, 'The Logic of Non-Standard English' (1973) who argues that it is not merely 'poor English' which these children speak, but a complete non-logical form of language in its own right. However, the divide between elaborated and restricted codes is very difficult to measure, and most children from all classes speak a mixture of both. It is the code which is used in schools and is understood more easily by the middle class which makes the difference in achievement.

The parents' own educational experiences are a major factor in the formation of their attitudes and expectations towards their children's education. Those parents who achieved 'success' in the education system will have high expectations that their own children will succeed, and those who 'failed' in the system will have low expectations of their children. Parental attitudes regarding the link between education and employment can also influence children's achievement. Thus, it is said that middle-class parents encourage in their children 'long-term gratification', that is to make sacrifices in time, money and pleasure now in order to do well at school and achieve the high rewards of a good job. Working-class parents preach 'short-term hedonism' or enjoying oneself now and leaving school at the first opportunity in order to make money and enjoy life. The recent large increases in youth unemployment, and the increased numbers staying on after the statutory leaving age, may indicate a change in these attitudes, with working-class parents seeing the future benefits of education for their children.

The belief that the culture of the working class is in some way 'deficient' or lacking in such areas as attitudes to education, language and child-rearing patterns led to a number of programmes of **compensatory education** in the late 1960s. The most well known of these measures were the Educational Priority Areas (EPAs) established in 1969 in Liverpool, Bradford, London, Dundee and Birmingham, and designed to give greater resources to improve the areas and the schools (mainly pre-school education). The EPAs were abolished in 1971, as it was felt that they were not achieving any recognisable improvements. E. Midwinter, who headed the Liverpool EPA, believed that compensatory education concentrated too much on children and schools, and not enough on enlisting the support of the home. He favoured community schools to link parents and the schools.

B. Bernstein, 'Education Cannot Compensate for Society' (1970), is one of the most prominent critics of compensatory education. He attacks the labelling of children in schools, which he sees as the real problem, and sees compensatory education as a process which directs attention away from the internal operation of the schools. His view is supported by W. Labov, 'The Logic of Non-Standard English' (1973), who criticises the way in which compensatory education blames the family, particularly in accusing the working class of 'verbal deprivation'. In response to the views of Bernstein and Labov, A.H. Halsey, 'Education Can Compensate' (1980) argues that British programmes have not been given a fair chance to prove that positive discrimination can work. He argues that much larger amounts of finance need to be pumped into policies, and quotes American evidence to support his view that success depends to a large extent on resources.

SCHOOL FACTORS

The importance of home factors on the child's school progress should not distract attention away from the equally important role of the school on the child's achievement. Most of the 'school' factors depend on the extent to which the school and the education system are largely middle-class institutions staffed by middle-class teachers expressing middle-class values and expectations. Such institutions are necessarily biased in favour of middle-class children, enabling them to achieve success and add to their initial advantages, while operating against working-class children, and further decreasing their chances of achievement. Some specific criticisms levelled against schools and teachers are described below.

Selection through streaming is widely used in both primary and secondary schools to separate children into different classes according to their 'supposed' ability. Sociological research into the effects of streaming has found that it can have profound effects on a child's educational achievement. J.W.B. Douglas, 'The Home and the School' (1964) found that once children had been selected by the eleven-plus exam their IQ scores changed, with the IQ of secondary grammar school pupils increasing by a few points on average, and the IQ of secondary modern pupils falling by a few points. The greatest decline in IQ score was by children from manual backgrounds who had higher test scores to start off with, but on entry to secondary modern school began to deteriorate. W. Taylor, 'The Secondary Modern School' (1963) believes that the lack of academic atmosphere in secondary modern schools and their lowly position in the educational and social structure is responsible for this decline in ability. In non-streamed junior schools B. Jackson, 'Streaming, An Educational System in Miniature' (1964) found that bright children were not held back in any way, and less able children seemed to benefit from mixed-ability groups. However, J. Barker-Lunn, 'Streaming in the Junior School' (1970) found that there was little difference in academic performance between streamed and non-streamed junior schools, but that streaming can affect the emotional and social development of the average or less able child.

The self-fulfilling prophecy is the process whereby once a child has been streamed, the teachers' expectations of the child's future progress will be largely influenced by the stream, rather than by the behaviour of any individual child within that stream. The teacher then communicates his/her expectations or 'prophecies' to the child, treating the child in such a way as to make the predictions come true. In their study 'Pygmalion in the Classroom' (1968) B. Rosenthal and L. Jacobsen tested the positive self-fulfilling prophecy, when children improve as the result of a prediction that they will do so. Based on intelligence tests given to pupils in an American elementary school who were randomly allocated to streams, they found that pupils in the top stream progressed much more quickly than those in the lower streams. Although this study has since been criticised for its methodology and for the ethical issues which it raises, it still indicates the effects which teachers' expectations can have on pupils' performance.

The effects of expectations and streaming on the child's achievement have also been described by J.W.B. Douglas, 'The Home and the School' (1964), where he provides evidence of both a positive and a negative self-fulfilling prophecy as a direct result of streaming. Thus, within the top streams a positive self-fulfilling prophecy is operating for the middle-class child, while in the lower streams a powerful negative self-fulfilling prophecy is operating on the working-class child.

Differential treatment between streams arises because of the different expectations resulting from selection and the working of the self-fulfilling prophecy. Thus, the 'C' and 'D' streams are often given the poorest accommodation, their teachers are less experienced, and there is a high turnover of staff. The opposite is true of the staff and facilities given to the 'A' and 'B' streams. The creation of two sub-cultures within the school as a direct result of streaming, continual selection, and home background, has been demonstrated by D. Hargreaves, 'Social Relations in a Secondary School' (1967). Posing as an English teacher, Hargreaves found two distinct sub-cultures at 'Lumley' school. Firstly, the academic sub-culture, made up of the 'A' and 'B' stream pupils who accepted the school's values and aims, were 'good pupils' who sought to 'please teacher', and who gained the rewards and successes that the school offered. Secondly, the delinquescent sub-culture, made up of pupils from the 'C' and 'D' streams who were rejected and labelled as 'failures' by the school, and who, after being continually deprived of any possibility of academic rewards from the school reacted in turn by rejecting the school and its values. These pupils sought success in the peer group by taking on adult roles, such as drinking, smoking, fighting, and sexual experimentation, thereby gaining group approval. These two sub-cultures, by being based on streams, were also reflections of social class. Later sociologists have criticised Hargreaves for being too simplistic in seeing just two sub-cultures within the school. P. Woods, 'The Divided School' (1979) also conducted a study on a secondary modern school, and he identified eight 'modes of adaptation' or ways of dealing with school life. It is rather rigid to assume, as Hargreaves did, that pupils all conform along class lines, and that teachers will automatically take the side of middle-class pupils.

School ethos has been found to be important in terms of pupils' attendance, academic achievement, behaviour in school, and juvenile delinquency rates outside school. The importance of 'good schools' was noted by J.W.B. Douglas, 'The Home and the School' (1968), and was empirically tested by M. Rutter, 'Fifteen Thousand Hours' (1979). Although Rutter's study has been criticised for its methodology and uncritical acceptance of gender, class, and racial divisions, it did attempt to examine the effects of school organisation and structure on ability levels.

SOCIETAL FACTORS

For many sociologists, to view education in isolation from the class structure is impossible, since the education system mirrors society in its class differences. In particular, the definition of 'classroom knowledge' has to be seen in terms of the nature and distribution of power in society as a whole. Thus, certain groups in society have the power to define what is seen as acceptable 'knowledge' in the education system. As these groups tend to be the dominant, middle-class groups, schooling will obviously favour their children, rather than those of the working class. R. Boudon, 'Education, Opportunity and Social Inequality' (1974) argues that middle-class and working-class children start their educational careers from different positions in the class structure (**positional theory**). Family and societal pressure is then put on the child to maintain his/her position in the class structure.

P. Bourdieu, 'Cultural Reproduction and Social Reproduction' (1973) presents a Marxian perspective on working-class problems of under-achievement. He argues that the function of schools is '**cultural reproduction**', which involves the transmission of only the dominant culture in society, which he calls 'cultural capital'. Success in school depends on the extent to which pupils can 'tap' into this cultural capital. Middle-class pupils have an overwhelming advantage as they have already been socialised into the dominant culture by their parents. As a consequence, success is achieved by middle-class children, and social inequality is reproduced in the education system.

M.F.D. Young (ed.), 'Knowledge and Control' (1971) supports Bourdieu's ideas, and attempts to question the nature of knowledge itself. As knowledge cannot be objectively evaluated or assessed, it is impossible to state that one form of knowledge is superior to any other form. The way in which certain knowledge comes to be regarded as superior is by people in power defining it as such. Therefore, all knowledge is equally valid, but its treatment is not. This view is called '**cultural relativism**'.

N. Keddie, 'Tinker, Tailor . . . The Myth of Cultural Deprivation' (1973) also uses a form of structural-interactionism to show how cultural reproduction occurs in the classroom through the labelling process. She argues that intelligent working-class children are often mis-labelled, and rejects the implication that working-class culture is inferior – the myth of '**cultural deprivation**'. Keddie supports the idea of a culturally differentiated curriculum, where the education system teaches working-class culture, rather than repressing it.

Gender and educational achievement

During the latter part of the nineteenth century when state education was first introduced, the main concern of educationalists was to encourage girls to attend schools in preference to entering domestic service or other employment. Once girls were established in schools there did not seem to be any reason why attention should focus on their achievements. However, since the 1944 Education Act there has been a growing concern with gender differences in the curriculum, differences in examination results between the sexes, and issues of discrimination against girls throughout the education system.

CURRICULUM ISSUES

The commencement of state education for girls at the end of the nineteenth century meant an extension of their domestic role, for girls were expected to study laundry, needlework and housework in addition to the three Rs. The 1902 Act exacerbated this, with the introduction of single sex schools and gender specific subjects, making cookery and needlework compulsory for girls only. Boys were made to study woodwork. This gender-segregated curriculum persisted up to and after the 1944 Education Act, although many of the comprehensive schools attempted to break down the division and allow girls to study 'boys' subjects' and boys to take up domestic subjects if they wished. However, it is only with the 1988 Education Reform Act and the introduction of the National Curriculum that boys and girls will study the same subjects up to fourteen, with science being compulsory for all up to the age of sixteen. This may help to reverse the trend whereby subject choices tend to be along gender lines, with girls predominantly choosing languages, social sciences and domestic subjects, and boys still more heavily represented in the hard sciences and technology. Research, though, shows that particularly in science this may prove difficult to achieve.

A. Kelly, 'Science for Girls' (1987) argues that science continues to be packaged in such a way to appeal more to boys than to girls: few girls are shown in serious poses in science books; the examples used to demonstrate phenomena are often male-oriented, such as the use of motorbikes to illustrate gravitational forces. Kelly found that in science lessons boys usually dominate by grabbing the apparatus first and pushing to the front of the class to observe the teacher's experiments. It is perhaps not surprising therefore that engineering, technology and physical science courses in higher education continue to be filled largely by males.

Examination results between the sexes also indicate variations. Evidence from *Social Trends* shows that girls consistently outperform boys overall, with girls gaining more GCSE passes and one 'A' level. However, boys do slightly better at achieving more than one 'A' level.

DISCRIMINATION

Discrimination against girls and women in the education system dates back to the nineteenth century, with degrees not being granted to women until 1877, and a segregated curriculum present in elementary and secondary schools. Under the 1944 Education Act the eleven-plus exam revealed that girls scored higher marks than boys on average, which would effectively lead to more girls going to grammar schools. In order to redress this 'imbalance', girls' scores were adjusted to ensure that equal numbers of boys and girls went to grammar school. This resulted in boys being awarded more places than they merited.

Research into classroom interaction has illustrated a number of areas where gender inequality is found. D. Spender, 'Invisible Women: The Schooling Scandal' (1983) shows how the content of the curriculum, the attitudes and expectations of the teachers, and social relations in the classroom all reinforce gender inequality. For example, she found that boys receive more 'teacher time' than girls, who frequently appear 'invisible' in the classroom. Boys also get away with more disruptive behaviour than girls, and often have their work marked higher, particularly in science subjects. M. Stanworth, 'Gender and Schooling' (1983) supported the above findings with her research into a further education college, where she found that girls learn to be 'second best'. J. French, 'Gender in the Classroom' (1986) tries to explain why boys receive this attention. Her observation of infant schools showed that a two-way process of interaction operates: boys are more problematic and disruptive, therefore they receive more attention. This continues on through secondary school, with boys demanding and receiving the most attention.

Although there are methodological problems with the above studies, in that they are small-scale pieces of research which are difficult to replicate, the observations and interviews still reveal a useful insight into discrimination in the classroom.

There are a number of ways of explaining gender inequality in education.

Biological explanations concentrate on the belief that women are inherently less intelligent than men. Physically though, girls mature earlier than boys and do better in the early years of education up to the age of eleven. Biology does not explain why girls then fall behind, come back to achieve better GCSE results at sixteen, yet fail to maintain this success at 'A' level.

Patriarchal ideology, or the belief that women are inferior to men, has also been proposed as an explanation for gender inequality. The socialisation process ensures that boys receive more attention and more financial support than girls. Girls are encouraged to believe that women are unsuited to 'men's work' and to the competitive nature of business. Criticisms of this view tend to concentrate on the way in which the myths and stereotypes created by men are used to maintain power over women.

Socialisation patterns of boys and girls can help to explain gender differences in education. S. Sharpe, 'Just Like A Girl' (1976) found that the biggest priority in many girls' lives was still marriage and family life, rather than the pursuit of a career. Many girls also tended to view women's occupational roles as limited to low-status and poorly-paid jobs such as office work, teaching, nursing, shop assistants, hairdressing, etc. Ten years on, S. Lees, 'Losing Out' (1986) conducted interviews and discussions with 100 fifteen to sixteen year olds from various class and ethnic groups, and found that the majority still saw their future in terms of domesticity, either as a full-time role or combined with a job. These girls were already combining school life with domestic chores (unlike their brothers), and did not envisage this pattern changing in the future.

Ethnicity and educational achievement

Evidence on the relationship between ethnicity and examination results is difficult to obtain as the Department of Education does not publish statistics on exam results by ethnic groups. Thus, figures have to be taken from government reports, independent surveys, and research organisations. All the available evidence shows the general trend that ethnic groups achieve poorer examination results than other members of the population. It is difficult to compare the information from these various sources as they use different sample sizes, different survey locations, a variety of ethnic classifications, and a number of types and levels of exams.

The most well-known source of evidence comes from the Swann Report, 'Education For All' (1985), a government report to examine the education of ethnic minorities in Britain. Based on a survey of five education authorities the Swann Report found that Asians do almost as well as whites or 'others', although Bangladeshis do particularly badly. The average performance of West Indians, however, was worse than that of whites, with only one percent going to university. Other studies have supported these findings, with West Indians having a higher than expected number of pupils in lower streams and in special schools. Variations in educational attainment between ethnic groups may not, however, be caused by ethnicity itself, but may be due to a number of interplaying factors as indicated below.

SOCIAL CLASS AND ETHNICITY

As already indicated earlier in this chapter, social class is a significant factor in educational achievement. The Swann Report found that as much as 50% of underachievement by West Indian children might be attributable to socio-economic factors. However, the local authorities featured in the Swann Report had a high ethnic concentration, and the class position of West Indians was therefore likely to be lower than that of West Indians living in largely white areas who had achieved middle-class status. Further evidence to indicate that social class may be more significant than ethnicity comes from D. Smith and S. Tomlinson, 'The School Effect' (1989), a study of over 70,000 children in multi-ethnic comprehensives which revealed that ethnicity did not influence exam entry. The results of school tests and social class background were more influential in determining exam entry. Thus, middle-class children from all ethnic groups with a particular reading score were more likely to be placed on higher level courses than working-class children with the same score.

SCHOOL INFLUENCE

The organisation and ethos of the school appear to be important factors in determining the success of all children. D. Smith and S. Tomlinson, 'The School Effect' (1989) found that different secondary schools achieved different results with children of similar background and ability. The progress and achievement of ethnic minorities depended in many cases on the individual school itself.

CULTURE

It is often suggested that the high percentage of single parent families and the large numbers of working women in West Indian households lead to a lack of cohesion and less stimulation for the children. In contrast, Asian families appear to be more motivated, with higher parental aspirations. These stereotypes might conceal other factors such as finance, the schools themselves, and racial discrimination. The Swann Report found that IQ scores of West Indians and Asians were not significantly different when socio-economic factors were taken into account.

RACISM

The Swann Report found little overt racism by teachers, although there was much covert or unintentional racism operating through the use of reading materials and language used in the classroom. In many cases a negative image of ethnic minorities was unconsciously promoted. C. Wright, 'School Processes – An Ethnographic Study' in J. Eggleston et al (eds.), Education For Some (1986) used classroom observation in inner-city primary schools to show that teachers perceive and treat ethnic minority children differently from white children. Asians and West Indians were excluded from discussions, and frequently seen as disobedient and aggressive, with poor expectations. Secondary school research by D. Gillborn, 'Race, Ethnicity and Education: Teaching and Learning in Multi-Ethnic Schools' (1990) echoed Wright's findings, with West Indian children the most frequently reported for misbehaviour.

Although both of these studies are small-scale and qualitative, they are the type of research which is more likely to find instances of racism than large-scale quantitative surveys where respondents may be reluctant to admit to racist attitudes. Racism in schools is difficult to measure, particularly as teachers' attitudes may not necessarily be reflected in classroom interaction. Also, pupils do not always automatically accept the negative stereotypes which are accorded them, and may have higher self-images than others think.

Explanations for the low educational attainment of ethnic minorities are to found in a combination of all of the above. The Swann Report concluded that racial discrimination inside and outside school combined with social deprivation were the main causative factors. The role and influence of cultural factors are difficult to evaluate, particularly as many ethnic minorities are reluctant to pursue these areas because of the self-blame attached to them.

Theories of education

THE FUNCTIONALIST THEORY

Functionalists regard the major function of education as the transmission of society's value system. At the turn of the century Durkheim was emphasising the importance of secondary socialisation in ensuring the individual's commitment to the social group, and hence to the creation of social solidarity. The teaching of national history in particular, Durkheim insisted, helped to forge this group unity – not so far removed from the National Curriculum's emphasis on British historical events and perceptions. In the 1950s Talcott Parsons reiterated Durkheim's views, and developed his ideas on the link between the division of labour and the teaching of specialised skills. Schools provide a link between the ascribed roles of the family and the achieved roles of the wider society, ensuring selection into occupational roles. Thus, Parsons believes that schools operate on meritocratic principles (open competition), resulting in role allocation to appropriate occupations. This concept of the most talented people being allocated to the most important and highly rewarded positions in society was developed in detail in the 1960s by K. Davis and W.E. Moore (see Chapter 9 for a full explanation and criticisms).

The functionalist view of the education system assumes that there is only one set of values to transmit, and these values are those of the ruling class or elite. The existence of different value systems and the notion that these might be transmitted by schools is ignored. Meritocratic principles do not appear to operate in schools, otherwise all social classes would achieve good results. Instead, schools reinforce class positions rather than offering everyone opportunities for advancement. School success is frequently based on class advantages rather than on ability or merit.

THE MARXIST THEORY

Marxists also believe that education socialises children, but they are highly critical of how this process which P. Bourdieu calls 'cultural reproduction', takes place, and into what values young people are socialised. L. Althusser presents an analysis of education in terms of a Marxist perspective. He argues that in order for the ruling class to survive and prosper, the 'reproduction of labour power' must take place, by reproducing the skills necessary for an efficient labour force, and by socialising such a workforce into accepting their role in society. Althusser argues that physical force cannot be used to achieve this goal, therefore education, religion, and the mass media ('Ideological State Apparatuses') must use the process of socialisation to create the submissive, accepting behaviour required of an exploited labour force.

An empirical application of Althusser's ideas to the US education system can be found in S.Bowles and H.Gintis, 'Schooling in Capitalist America' (1976), where they analyse the personality characteristics which they claim are fostered and developed by the US education system. Using primary research and results from other studies, Bowles and Gintis discovered that high grades equalled conformity and submission to authority, while low grades equated with anti-authoritarian attitudes and originality. They found that the teacher-pupil relationships in schools replicate the hierarchical division of labour in the workplace. Inequalities in the wider society are thus mirrored in schools, with the illusion of meritocracy promoted to ensure the myth of equal opportunity. Bowles and Gintis argue that rewards in education and in the job market are not based on merit, but on social class backgound. The class system is thus reproduced and legitimised by the education system.

The main problem with the Marxist perspective on education is that it assumes that teachers and pupils are acting out roles which are beyond their control. Not all teachers reward and punish pupils along class lines in order to promote capitalism. Prior to state education, capitalism still existed, which illustrates that indoctrination via the state education system is not required to uphold capitalism. Furthermore, there are many socialist societies which do not provide educational systems which offer equal opportunities and freedom.

Empirical evidence to contradict the work of Bowles and Gintis can be found in P.Willis, 'Learning to Labour: How Working Class Kids Get Working Class Jobs' (1977). He studied twelve working class boys ('lads') during their last eighteen months at secondary school and their first few months at work. He found no evidence to indicate that school and work were directly related, for the lads were not shaped by the school, but rejected it in order to create their own school counter culture. The attitudes and views of this counter culture were a better preparation for the low-skilled and low-status jobs which the lads were destined to enter. Thus, 'having a laugh', breaking the rules, and 'messing about' were all forms of behaviour developed by the lads themselves in their rejection of the school system. However, the lads' behaviour does recognise that capitalism does not bring them success, and therefore they need to develop collective action against capitalism. This was illustrated in the lads' opposition to the 'lobes' (or 'ear 'oles) who were hardworking pupils who demonstrated conformist behaviour. Although Willis's study is small-scale and unrepresentative it nevertheless indicates how pupils respond in an active way to school, and shows the importance of pupil sub-cultures within a capitalist system.

THE INTERPRETIVE THEORY

The interpretive view, as used by Willis, focuses on small-scale interaction in the classroom. Rather than seeing behaviour being shaped by the social system (as the functionalists and Marxists do), the interpretive perspective concentrates on describing the behaviour which is created and shaped by the individuals themselves. Examples of such studies include J.Benyon, 'Initial Encounters in a Comprehensive School' (1985), which describes the way in which children classify and evaluate each other in the first few months of secondary school, where they are labelled as teachers' pets, bullies, wierdos, etc. H.Becker has described the process of labelling by teachers in the classroom, showing that teachers tend to share a common picture of the 'ideal pupil' (well behaved, intelligent, highly motivated) which is used to judge all pupils. Middle-class children are more likely to fall into the 'ideal pupil' category, with working-class children largely featuring in the non-ideal role. Another example of the interpretive approach is provided by D. Hargreaves, 'Social Relations in a Secondary School' (1967) who describes how teachers and pupils are constantly 'bargaining' in the classroom, or negotiating order. For example, rewards and punishments are often negotiable, and pupils frequently play one teacher off against another to obtain what they want.

The interpretive perspective on education is, by its very nature, small-scale, in-depth and unrepresentative. Although it does not pay much attention to the social system, as the macro theories do, it does provide a valuable insight into the nature of classroom interaction and the power relations which exist between teachers and pupils.

THE LIBERAL THEORY

The liberal view of education is not recognised as a sociological perspective as such, but is important because of its influence on changes in the structure of education. This view upholds the democratic notion of equality of opportunity in education for all members of society. Self-development and social mobility in an open society are both seen as essential aims in an education system. The liberal view can best be seen as a reforming political perspective, concentrating on the achievment of educational reforms (for example abolition of the eleven-plus exam) as a means of increasing equality in education.

I. Illich, 'Deschooling Society' (1971) is highly critical of the role of education in advanced industrial societies. He argues for an education system where specific skills should be learnt alongside creative development. Illich believes that schools in industrial societies are repressive institutions which stifle individual creativity and contribute to many of society's problems. Illich proposes the 'deskilling' of society, with schools to be replaced by 'skill exchanges' and 'learning webs' where individuals can meet in groups to learn through 'creative and exploratory learning'. However, Illich fails to describe exactly how these arrangements would operate in practice on a large scale. Also, he has been criticised by Marxists for attacking the schools rather than society. The education system cannot provide equality of opportunity and achievement while the wider society is based on massive inequalities.

CHECK YOUR UNDERSTANDING

After reading this chapter you should now be able to define the following terms.

1 Tripartite system
2 Eleven-plus exam
3 Parity of esteem
4 Comprehensive schools
5 Public schools
6 Direct grant schools
7 Grant-maintained schools
8 National Curriculum
9 New Vocationalism
10 Elaborated and restricted linguistic codes
11 Long-term gratification
12 Short-term hedonism
13 Compensatory education
14 Streaming
15 Self-fulfilling prophecy
16 Delinquescent sub-culture
17 Positional theory
18 Cultural reproduction
19 Cultural relativism
20 Meritocratic principles
21 Role allocation
22 Ideological State Apparatuses

SELF-ASSESSMENT QUESTIONS

1 Briefly describe the main provisions of the 1944 Education Act.
2 How does the tripartite system fail to provide 'equality of educational opportunity'?
3 In what ways do comprehensive schools overcome the problems of the tripartite system?
4 Does the independent sector of education help to provide 'equality of educational opportunity'?
5 How can working-class under-achievement be explained?

6 How does 'cultural reproduction' benefit middle-class children?
7 In what ways do girls have a different educational experience to boys?
8 Give reasons why ethnic minorities under-achieve in the education system.
9 What do the functionalists regard as the essential purpose of the education system?
10 Summarise the Marxist view of the education system.

CHAPTER NINE

SOCIAL STRATIFICATION

LEARNING OBJECTIVES

ON COMPLETION OF THIS CHAPTER THE STUDENT SHOULD BE ABLE TO:

1 DEFINE THE NATURE OF STRATIFICATION, AND DESCRIBE THE MAIN SYSTEMS OF STRATIFICATION
2 DESCRIBE AND EVALUATE THE MAIN THEORIES OF SOCIAL STRATIFICATION
3 ASSESS THE INFLUENCE OF SOCIAL CLASS ON PEOPLE'S LIVES
4 DEFINE THE MAIN TYPES OF SOCIAL MOBILITY, AND DESCRIBE THE CAUSES AND PATTERNS OF MOBILITY
5 ANALYSE THE CLASS STRUCTURE OF MODERN BRITAIN, INCLUDING THE NATURE AND EXTENT OF CLASS CONSCIOUSNESS, EMBOURGEOISEMENT, AND PROLETARIANISATION

The nature of stratification

Strafication is a term used in geology to denote the layering of rocks into strata. It can also mean dividing up a population according to some particular characteristic such as age, sex, income, occupation. Although a person's age, sex, or personality may be accorded prestige in many societies, they do not provide the basis for social stratification. One of the most important characteristics of social stratification is that status is passed on from the head of the household to his or her spouse and children. Thus, age, sex, and personality are not forms of social stratification as they are not dependent on family background. A direct passing on of status would be an inherited title or position, or inherited wealth or power. An indirect passing on of status would be the advantages, (for example language, occupation, education), children were given because of their home background. This continuity of status through the family in social stratification has been emphasised by F. Parkin, 'Class, Inequality and Political Order' (1972). People are accorded high or low status in a society according to various criteria such as wealth, power, race, education, occupation, lifestyle. In Western societies, occupation is often used to identify a person's social status. Linked to occupation are a number of other characteristics, such as education, income, property, power. M. Weber

Class stratification at Royal Ascot

makes a distinction between **'social class'** and **'status group'**, with the former referring to a person's income or property, and the latter referring to lifestyle, honour and prestige in society. Although there are instances where income does not overlap with status, in most societies they are found together. Social stratification thus has the following key principles.

It is a characteristic of the society itself, and not just a result of individual differences. Almost all societies, pre-industrial and industrial, are stratified, with increasing technology leading to the production of more resources which in turn leads to more stratification.

Social stratification is universal throughout the world, but varies in nature. Thus, in pre-industrial societies stratification is minimal, and confined mainly to age and sex. In industrial societies there are more complex and rigid systems for distributing goods, based on education, occupation, wealth, prestige, etc.

Social stratification persists over time from one generation to the next. Children initially assume the ascribed social positions of their parents, but eventually achieve similar positions to their parents.

Social stratification is upheld by belief patterns, which may be based on religion, culture, or tradition. Generally, the people with the greatest social privileges in a society are the strongest supporters of such belief patterns.

Another important aspect of social stratification is its connection with social inequality. M.M. Tumin, 'Social Stratification' (1967) argues that the resources distributed in society lead to social inequality. The scarce resources which are available for distribution are: property (income and wealth), power (political and physical), and prestige (status and honour). The manner in which these resources are allocated determines the type of stratification system, for example slavery, caste, feudal, class, socialist. Tumin proposes four processes of stratification:

Differentiation occurs as a result of the division of labour, which allocates individuals to social positions according to their functions and responsibilities. The level of differentiation increases with the complexity of the society.

Ranking can be used in terms of occupation, race, sex, intelligence, technical expertise, etc. In industrial societies, ranking in education and occupation is more important than ascribed characteristics (sex, age) which often take precedence in pre-industrial systems.

Evaluation is based on the assessment of the relative value of a particular status. Some roles are more highly thought of than others because of their relative importance or contribution to society. The assessment is dependent on the dominant values of a society at a particular time, with the most powerful groups often defining their own roles as being more important than those of less powerful groups.

Rewarding occurs when social positions have been differentiated, ranked, and evaluated. The rewards which are given may be in terms of property, power, and prestige.

Systems of social stratification can be classified according to whether they are **closed systems**, which offer little or no social mobility, or **open systems** which provide the means to become socially mobile. Examples of both types are described below.

THE CASTE SYSTEM

The caste system is a system of stratification based on ascription, where social position is fixed at birth and determines people's destinies for life. Two good examples of the caste system are the traditional Hindu social system in rural India, and racial apartheid in South Africa. The Indian caste system comprises four main castes plus an outcast group known as the untouchables. Each caste is sub-divided into several thousand sub-groups or jatis. Individuals are born into a particular caste, which then dictates a person's lifetime occupation, with families in each caste performing one type of work. There are few occupations which are open to all (for example farming), which means that castes are socially identified with the work their members do. As it is the family's responsibility to transmit social standing from one generation to the next, a rigid system of social stratification insists that marriages are endogamous (between people of the same social standing). Couples thus marry within social categories rather than between them, with arranged marriages being the norm. There are occasional instances of social mobility within the caste system (a female might marry into a higher caste) but essentially it is a closed system of stratification. Powerful religious and cultural beliefs underpin the Indian caste system, with the higher castes regarded as 'pure' and the untouchables as 'unclean'. This leads to social distance between the castes, reducing social communication and economic co-operation. Movement from one caste to another is via the process of karma, where moral behaviour in one lifetime will lead to re-birth into the next higher caste in the cycle of reincarnation.

Until recently, racial apartheid in South Africa mirrored the Indian caste system, with racial groups allocated particular occupations, inter-marriage illegal, and extensive social segregation enforced between the groups. This system was enshrined in law, and also maintained by strong cultural and moral values.

THE CLASS SYSTEM

The class system is found predominantly in industrial societies, where the emphasis is on individual achievement, extensive education, and a high division of labour. These societies have greater legal and political freedoms than caste systems, with occupation based on achievement rather than on ascription. Classes are not as rigidly defined as the categories are in caste systems, and there is greater opportunity for social mobility via occupation or through marital choice. This open system of social stratification derives partly from the breakdown of social categories caused by migration from traditional villages to cities during industrialisation: S.M. Lipset and R. Bendix, 'Social Mobility in Industrial Society' (1967). The growth of democratic political systems in industrial societies also helps to promote a class system by providing education, legal rights, and greater job opportunities. Class systems tend to have low status-consistency, where an individual may have high status but little wealth, for example a vicar. In contrast, caste systems have high status-consistency, where there is consistent ranking of wealth, position and power.

CASTE AND CLASS COMBINED

Many societies have stratification systems which are a mixture of elements taken from the caste and class systems. This happens particularly in those societies where a long established agricultural economy becomes industrialised, for example the industrialisation which followed the English feudal system.

The estate or feudal system existed throughout Europe for much of the middle ages. The first estate was the hereditary nobility, the second estate was the clergy, and the commoners made up the third estate. Feudalism operated on the basis of legally defined rights and duties concerned with the ownership of land. The nobility controlled the system and had extensive wealth and power which was maintained by the law of primogeniture, whereby the eldest son inherited titles and land. The clergy also had large landholdings, with other members of the nobility employed in the military or the law. The serfs or commoners owned no land, and were dependent on their landlords for their livelihood. The industrial revolution, and the extension of legal rights and educational opportunities blurred the social rankings which were clearly defined under feudalism. However, not all the elements of the feudal system disappeared, and the class system in Britain today still retains remnants from that era. Thus, the nobility still have extensive wealth and landholdings. Inherited titles still confer power and prestige, with the monarch as the Head of State and the House of Lords containing a substantial number of inherited peerages. Even within the class system there is less social mobility than is found in other industrial societes such as the USA. Feudal culture may also continue to survive as D. Snowman, 'Britain and America: An Interpretation of their

Culture' 1945–1975' (1977) found that British people tend to be more resigned to their social position than Americans are.

Theories of social stratification

Social stratification in modern industrial societies can be viewed in terms of a single hierarchy of occupationally-based **status categories**. Most people are aware of this model, and often use it in their own interpretation of the class system: professionals are in social class 1 and unskilled labourers fall into social class 5. This classification is also used by governments, for example in the form of the Registrar-General's five-point scale of occupations or the seven categories of occupation used by Hall-Jones.

THE FUNCTIONALIST THEORY OF STRATIFICATION

The occupational approach to social stratification is the basis of the functionalist theory of stratification, which argues that stratification is a **functional necessity** in a society. Social inequality is necessary to motivate talented and trained personnel to fulfil the demands of social positions which are functionally more important than others. The functionalist view is most clearly expressed by K. Davis and W.E. Moore, 'Some Principles of Stratification' (1967) and is summarised below:

1. Certain positions in any society are functionally more important than others, and require extended education and special skills for their performance.
2. Only a limited number of individuals in any society have the talents which can be trained into the skills appropriate to these positions.
3. The conversion of talents into skills involves a training period during which financial and social sacrifices are made by those undergoing the training.
4. In order to induce the talented persons to undergo these sacrifices and acquire the training, their future positions must offer sufficient rewards to attract them from less important occupations. These rewards are in the form of income, prestige, and power.
5. Differential access to the scarce resources of income, prestige and power creates a system of social stratification, which in turn institutionalises and legitimises social inequality.
6. Social inequality in the amounts of scarce resources allocated to different groups within society is thus seen as both functional and inevitable.

Davis and Moore do not seek to justify social stratification, but only to explain why it exists. Some criticisms of their theory are outlined below:

M.M. Tumin, 'Some Principles of Stratification; A Critical Analysis' (1953) argues that Davis and Moore's concept of 'functional importance' is tautological: a society must by definition be functional in order to exist. Also, the functional importance of an occupation is difficult to define, and does not only depend on talent, but on access to education and training, for example entry into medicine is restricted by the profession itself. Tumin further observes that the rewards allocated to individuals are often unconnected to functional importance, for example sports personalities can earn huge sums of money but their functional importance is difficult to justify.

F. Parkin, 'Class Inequality and Political Order' (1972) argues that the dominant class in capitalist society has most of the scarce resources because it ensures that the system works in its favour, not because it is more 'functionally important'. Also, there is no societal consensus amongst different groups as to which positions are functionally more important than others.

The definition of talent and who defines it is unclear. What is defined as talent is frequently decided by those occupying the top positions in society, and thus the search for talent is restricted to their own children, and to members of their own group.

If the new talent derives from the children of those in the most privileged positions in society, then there are few, if any, sacrifices to be made by these children or their parents.

There is an assumption that without differentials in rewards individuals would not want to occupy the 'functionally important' positions. There are some individuals who have genuine vocational calling, irrespective of rewards.

Davis and Moore ignore the influence of privilege, inherited wealth, and ascribed characteristics such as sex and race, which all affect access to the top positions. Thus, there is much talent and ability which often lies 'undiscovered'.

Davis and Moore assume that social stratification benefits society as a whole, ignoring the dysfunctions of inequality and the conflict between groups of different strata.

The theory does not explain how any stratification system begins or changes. Stratification is seen as both inevitable and necessary, therefore it exists.

THE MARXIST OR CONFLICT PERSPECTIVE

The model of stratification based on the views of Karl Marx is essentially a conflict perspective. An outline of Marx's views on society has already been given in Chapter 1, so only his ideas concerning stratification in industrial societies will be summarised here.

Marx maintained that capitalist industrialisation led to the creation of a two-class society, arising from two basic relationships to the means of production. The **bourgeoisie** owned the means of production whereas the **proletariat** sold their labour in return for wages. Marx saw the start of the decline in the bourgeoisie as industrial companies sought monopolies and reduced the number of owners. The proletariat, however, were becoming poorer, as their exploitation increased with the advance of industrialisation. According to Marx, **polarisation** or increasing separation of the classes would occur. The proletariat would eventually realise their 'class position', become class conscious (aware of their exploitation), and unite together. Using trade unions as a means of uniting the workers, the proletariat would gain economic and political power, and take over the control of industry from the bourgeoisie. The proletariat would then change the values in society from those based on competition to ones based on co-operation, ultimately resulting in the creation of a classless socialist society.

J. Westergaard and H. Resler, 'Class in a Capitalist Society' (1976) is a contemporary Marxist view of the nature of class relations. They believe that the private ownership of capital explains class differences, and use empirical evidence on the distribution of income and wealth to support their argument. According to Westergaard and Resler, the dominant class represents between five and ten percent of the population, and includes top directors, senior civil servants, and company directors who are all large shareholders in private industry. Westergaard and Resler reject the view that the arrival of joint stock companies separated ownership and control, leading to an increase in the number of salaried managers with no property.

The Marxist or conflict perspective on social stratification also attracts a number of criticisms:

It is essentially based on Marx's observations of capitalism in the nineteenth century, when limited educational opportunies and primitive welfare provision were available. During this century greater educational opportunities have increased social mobility, thus diverting group conflict into individual competition. In addition, the massive expansion in welfare state provision this century has improved the condition of much of the working class since the last century, further reducing the level of class conflict.

The conflict view is founded on the social ideal that income will be given to each according to his need, from each according to his ability. It ignores the crucial fact than unequal rewards motivate people to perform various social roles within society.

According to R. Dahrendorf, 'Class and Conflict in Industrial Society' (1959) the capitalist class became fragmented this century due to the decomposition of capital (see J. Burnham, 'The Managerial Revolution' (1943)), the arrival of joint stock companies, and the increasing power of managers rather than owners. The decomposition of labour has also occurred, with the working class increasingly diversified because of technological change introducing new skills and knowledge. Managerial control has further expanded with the growth of the service class, involving more people in bureaucracies in positions of authority.

F. Parkin, 'Class Inequality and Political Order' (1972) criticises Westergaard and Resler for failing to explain the privileged position of propertyless professionals and higher civil servants. Doctors do not receive higher rewards than nurses because of their property-owning capacity, therefore other factors must be at work. Even in socialist societies with communal ownership of property, social inequalities persist.

Institutionalisation of conflict occurs through trade unions representing working-class interests. Rules and procedures developed to confine disputes to the work situation, although conflict may still be directed at the state as well as at the capitalists.

As a result of all the above changes, Dahrendorf argues that a '**structurisation**' of classes has occurred, and the two broad classes of Marx are structured or divided within themselves. A. Giddens, 'The Class Structure of the Advanced Societies' (1973) takes up this argument to show how different groups within the classes have differing educational opportunities, levels of militancy, etc.

WEBER AND THE MULTI-DIMENSIONSAL PERSPECTIVE

Max Weber considered Marx's two-class model of stratification to be too simplistic, and instead wanted to emphasise the variety of different criteria which can be used to classify people. He argued that instead of a single hierarchy there are several hierarchies or dimensions of social stratification, based on occupation, education, wealth, etc., with individuals holding different positions on each hierarchy. This multi-dimensional view was used by Weber to distinguish between class (based on income and wealth), status (based on social prestige), and party (based on the exercise of power by political parties, trade unions, pressure groups, etc.). Weber disagreed with Marx that social prestige and power are derived from economic position, because in class systems there are many examples of status inconsistency, for example government officials may have considerable power, but little wealth or prestige. Weber felt that classes were not clearly defined categories and preferred to rank people on a multi-dimensional hierarchy. This has led to the term '**socioeconomic status**' which refers to a composite social ranking based on various dimensions of social inequality.

The Weberian view of stratification is difficult to apply and measure compared to Marx's economic model. In practice individuals could be ranked on numerous hierarchies making it hard to group people for the purposes of comparison.

F. Parkin, 'Class Inequality and Political Order' (1972) argues that the multi-dimensional approach tends to cover up the fact that in industrial societies stratification is based on occupation, which is dependent on education, and which determines a person's income and status. Parkin is critical of Weber's belief that inequality is dispersed in society by ranking over a number of criteria. In practice, he argues, wealth, social status, power, a high level of education, etc. are invariably linked. Parkin thus maintains that in modern Western societies a two-class model is much more useful than a multi-dimensional approach. He argues that the differences between manual and non-manual workers are greater than the differences within the two groups. Manual workers have poorer working conditions, work longer hours for less money, and have fewer fringe benefits than non-manual workers.

A. Giddens, 'The Class Structure of the Advanced Societies' (1973) argues that two forms of stratification exist in modern capitalist societies: status categories, based on a hierarchy of occupations, and classes, based on people's relationship to the means of production. He goes on to develop the notion of a 'three class' model of stratification consisting of: the owners and controllers of industry, the rest of the non-manual stratum, and the manual sector. Three factors separate the three classes: the division of labour, the level of authority, and variations in consumption patterns.

The three approaches to social stratification outlined above (the occupational hierarchy approach, the multi-dimensional view, and the two/three class model) clearly indicate that to understand social life no one perspective is adequate. Each one has its usefulness depending on what is being studied.

THE CONVERGENCE THESIS

The convergence thesis is based on the ideas of C. Kerr et al, 'Industrialism and Industrial Man' (1960), which put forward the hypothesis that industrialisation tends to create similar social structures – that all industrial societies are converging or moving towards what they termed 'pluralistic industrialism'. Here, the state would regulate competition and conflict between a variety of different interest groups. The convergence thesis claims that all industrial societies (regardless of culture, history, or political structure) are converging towards pluralistic industrialism. Kerr et al predict that all industrial societies will undergo the same four changes:

1. Social mobility will increase, as technology will encourage selection based on merit, not on social background.
2. Differences in social strata will decline because of increased mobility, free education for all, and the provisions of a welfare state.
3. The middle strata groups will expand as a response to pressure from industry for more trained and skilled workers.
4. Status consistency will evolve as a result of the above factors. People with high qualifications will receive high incomes and high status occupations, and vice versa.

Criticisms of the four changes predicted by the proponents of the convergence thesis have been made as follows:

J. Goldthorpe, 'Social Stratification in Industrial Society' (1967) uses comparative data to show that social mobility has not increased in all advanced industrial societies. He also argues that rates of social mobility are not dependent on social mobility alone, but are influenced by cultural and political factors. Evidence from the Oxford Social Mobility Studies shows that in Britain high-status positions have only been opened up to other non-manual strata, not to manual groups.

J. Goldthorpe and D. Lockwood, 'The Affluent Worker' (1968) found that skilled manual workers were distinct from the rest of the manual workers in political attitudes and lifestyle. Research on poverty (R. Titmuss, D. Wedderburn, P. Townsend) shows that income inequalities have not diminished, and have probably increased since the war.

A. Giddens, 'The Class Structure of the Advanced Societies' (1973) argues that any expansion in the middle strata groups has arisen as a result of the increase in female workers in low-skill service occupations.

J. Goldthorpe and D. Lockwood (op. cit.) argue that there is evidence for status inconsistency, as the manual workers they studied who were well paid and owned their own houses did not have, or seek, non-manual status. The functionalist view that the educational system is based on merit, rather than social background, has been disproved in much research on differential educational achievement (see Chapter 8).

The convergence thesis is generally criticised for its deterministic approach, in that it claims that 'industrialisation' (which is not defined) will influence stratification irrespective of other factors. H. Davis and R. Scase, 'Western Capitalism and State Socialism' (1985) argue that there are major differences between capitalist and socialist societies which prevent convergence. For example, socialist states have relied more on political planning and control rather than free-market forces in their economies. Also, extensive public ownership in socialist societies has meant that differences in income and wealth have been smaller than in capitalist countries where personal property and inheritance are more widespread.

However, there may be increasing convergence between the East and the West as a result of the recent changes in Eastern Europe, such as the collapse of the Berlin Wall in 1989, and the subsequent dismantling of the old USSR. The new unified Germany and the new republic states emerging from Russia are embracing Western-style liberal democracy, and with it, associated Western social problems of unemployment, crime, poverty, and homelessness.

The influence of social class

In order to assess the influence of social class on people's lives, it is first of all essential to understand how social class is measured, and which groups of people are being compared. R. Crompton, 'Class and Stratification' (1993) describes two approaches to the measurement of social class. The **theoretical approaches** of Marx and Weber do not use categories which are practical to use in order to compare people's lives. 'Bourgeoisie' and 'proletariat' are very general terms which cannot easily be applied to groups of people. Similarly, Weber's dimensions of class, status and power are not feasible in practice. In contrast, **descriptive approaches** measure social class by using categories based on empirical data concerning occupations, educational achievement, health, attitudes, lifestyles, etc. Descriptive classifications may be subjective or objective.

Subjective definitions of social class involve asking people to rate themselves in terms of social class, or asking them to select which class they are in from a list. G. Marshall et al, 'Social Class in Modern Britain' (1988) argues that this method is fairly reliable as most people accept their class position and are usually honest in declaring it. I. Reid, 'Social Class Differences in Britain' (1989) found that there was a high level of agreement between people's self-ratings and other objective assessments used by social researchers.

One of the problems with subjective measurements of class is that people use the same word to mean different things: the term working class may be interpreted differently by various people. It may therefore be possible for a self-made millionaire from humble beginnings to claim working-class status, and a labourer winning the lottery declaring middle- or even upper-class allegiance!

Objective definitions of social class consist of groups of categories which are constructed by social researchers to determine the social classification of people. They are difficult to devise as there are many criteria which could be used to categorise people: education, occupation, income, housing, health, lifestyle, etc. Most social researchers use occupation as the major classifying factor as it is readily obtainable and directly linked to the other criteria. It is also used by the government in the most well-known classification, the **Registrar-General's Social Class Scheme**. This consists of thousands of occupations which are divided into groups and then placed into five social classes.

Social Class 1 (Professional) includes accountants, doctors, lawyers.
Social Class 2 (Intermediate) includes nurses, teachers, managers.
Social Class 3NM (Skilled Non-Manual) includes secretaries, shop assistants.
Social Class 3M (Skilled Manual) includes hairdressers, electricians, plumbers.
Social Class 4 (Semi-skilled) includes postmen/women, farm workers, packers.
Social Class 5 (Unskilled) includes labourers, cleaners, refuse collectors.

Obviously, as occupations become obsolete they are removed from the scheme, while others are re-classified, and new occupations are added. Variations of this scheme are used by social researchers and market research personnel. Classes A, B, C1, C2, D, E are based on consumption patterns, whereas the ACORN system is based on housing locality (A Clasification Of Residential Neighbourhoods).

Once people have been categorised into various classes it is possible to look for class differences. These class differences may be in terms of people's social lives (attitudes, leisure interests), lifestyles (possessions, housing), or more importantly lifechances (educational opportunities, health, life expectancy).

Research on educational achievement (see Chapter 8) and on health and life expectancy (see Chapter 17) show that non-manual or middle-class workers are more likely to gain more qualifications, to have higher standards of health, and to have a longer life expectancy. Further disparities in lifechances are found in the areas of poverty and crime, with manual workers more likely to be on welfare benefits (see Chapter 14), and also more likely to feature in criminal statistics (see Chapter 10). Differences in lifestyles, such as smoking and drinking habits, holiday preferences, and leisure interests are summarised in various editions of *Social Trends*.

Many of the advantages in lifechances which are enjoyed by the non-manual or middle-class group are related to differences in income between the middle class (social classes 1, 2, 3NM) and the working class (social classes 3M, 4, 5). 'Income' refers to a flow of resources over a period of time (weekly, monthly, etc.) and includes earned income (wage or salary), unearned income (share profits and investment interest), and social income (state benefits and allowances). Income statistics can be obtained from a number of sources, including the Inland Revenue, Family Expenditure Survey, and New Earnings Survey. Generally, figures from these sources indicate that weekly disposable income declines as you move down from social class 1 to social class 5. On average they show that the median gross weekly income of manual men is approximately 70% of that of non-manual men. In addition non-manual workers enjoy a number of fringe benefits such as company pension schemes and company cars, paid sick leave, and expense accounts. The Commission on Social Justice (1994) found that up to the late 1970s income inequalities had narrowed, but since the 1980s there has been a reversal of this trend, with greater increases in top salaries and cuts in income tax at the higher levels.

Similar class differences can be found in the figures concerning the ownership of wealth. Wealth is defined as the total stock of goods at a point in time, which can be used to generate income (sometimes called marketable wealth). Thus, houses, land, shares, possessions are all defined by the Inland Revenue as marketable wealth. I. Reid 'Social Class Differences in Britain' (1989) argues that wealth is undoubtably related to social class, but it is difficult to measure, as the effects of inheritance are almost impossible to separate from an individual's own accumulation of wealth. Although there has been an increase in share ownership in the past ten years, wealth still continues to be concentrated amongst the higher social classes. Thus *Social Trends* (1994) found that the wealthiest one percent owned 18% of the marketable wealth in 1991, with the most wealthy 50% owning 92% of the marketable wealth.

J. Westergaard, 'Who Gets What?' (1995) argues that class differences continue to persist largely in terms of people's lifechances. However, it does seem that lifestyles based on traditional class divisions are beginning to blur, with lifestyle 'identity' determined less by social class and more by consumer demands and personal choices.

Social mobility

Social mobility is concerned with the extent to which people move up or down the social class hierarchy. It can be vertical, with movement up or down the social ladder, or horizontal, with movement within the same social class. Social mobility has two major forms.

Inter-generational social mobility, which is considered to be the most significant, is where a person moves up or down the social ladder relative to parental class position (usually father/son). An example of upward inter-generational social mobility would be the son of a bus driver becoming a doctor.

Intra-generational social mobility is where a person moves up or down the social ladder within his/her own lifetime, for example a hairdresser becoming the owner of a chain of salons.

CAUSES OF SOCIAL MOBILITY

As already described at the beginning of this chapter, social mobility in closed systems of stratification such as the caste system or feudalism is either non-existent or very limited. However, in open systems of stratification, such as modern industrial societies, social mobility is an important feature. T. Bottomore, 'Classes in Modern Society' (1965) points out that social mobility has generally increased with the economic development of the industrial societies. This increase has been largely due to changes in the **occupational structure**, primarily the expansion of white-collar and professional jobs, combined with the contraction of the industrial base and manual jobs. The tertiary or service sector (sales, distribution, administration, the new 'sunrise' computer age) has increased its proportion of the total job market, and upward social mobility has filled the new positions in the middle ranges. The class structure has supposedly changed its form from a pyramid to a diamond shape.

However, according to J. Westergaard and H. Resler, 'Class in a Capitalist Society' (1976) the effects of changes in the occupational structure on social mobility have often been exaggerated. The shift to white-collar work has affected women far more than men. Thus, while the majority of women are in non-manual jobs, more than three in five men are still in blue-collar occupations, and it is still largely the men's position which sets living standards (women often work part-time). Westergaard and Resler suggest that much of the expansion of white-collar work has been into low paid and low grade work, particularly as it affects women. Thus, movement from skilled manual work into low level white-collar jobs does not always represent upward social mobility.

Another factor which affects social mobility is '**differential fertility**' or the difference in fertility rates between the middle class and the working class. D.V. Glass, 'Social Mobility in Britain' (1954) has pointed out that some upward movement from the manual working class had to occur in each generation to make up for the relatively low rate of natural replacement among non-manual families. However, as the fertility rates of both classes are now similar, differential fertility has virtually disappeared.

Education remains the most important cause of social mobility in modern industrial societies, with the private sector maintaining the educational and occupational advantages of the upper class, and the middle class taking advantage of the state system (T. Bottomore, 'Classes in Modern Society' (1965). The way in which social mobility is achieved via the educational system has been described by R. Turner, 'Modes of Ascent, Through Education' (1961), who argues that sponsored mobility or contest mobility can be found in the educational systems of all industrial societies.

SPONSORED MOBILITY

Turner argues that sponsored mobility is characterised by the following features:

1. It exists in all societies where there is a small elite.
2. This small elite (or upper class) is unable to recruit sufficient of its own people to fill all the top positions in society.
3. The inability to recruit from its own ranks means that the elite must look to other social classes for new recruits.
4. Selection of new recruits must occur early, to enable the elite to socialise the candidates into the norms and values of the elite.
5. Selection must ensure that no talent is left untapped, and sufficient time must be allowed for the removal of unsuitable candidates.
6. Once a possible candidate is selected, the elite then sponsor their progress through the education system, from primary level through to university level.

CONTEST MOBILITY

Turner argues that contest mobility is characterised by the following features:

1. It exists in societies where there are numerous elites and no one social class dominates.
2. The elites therefore have to compete with each other in the selection of recruits for the top positions in society.
3. Selection is left as late as possible to ensure that late developers will not be missed.
4. The candidate must compete for the final selection by tests or exams.

5. Through the process of competition the candidates eliminate themselves, leaving behind the talented few who will then go on to occupy the top positions in society.

From Turner's analysis, it would appear that Britain has a sponsorship system of education. The private and state systems of education both promote sponsorship. Thus, the relationship between private education and the top positions in society has been clearly shown by many pieces of research, indicating that the majority of politicians, directors, judges, and higher civil servants benefited from a public school education. Selection for sponsorship via the public schools is based partly on the ability to pay, and partly on family background. Under the tripartite system, sponsorship took place after the eleven-plus selection process, with grammar schools receiving more resources and attracting more highly qualified teachers. Although the comprehensive system was intended to reduce such sponsorship, much evidence (see Chapter 8) indicates that streaming and the differential treatment of the streams results in the sponsorship of the middle class.

THE EXTENT OF SOCIAL MOBILITY

The measurement of social mobility gives rise to a number of problems, including the following:

1. Information is often not available for the mass of the population, but only for professional groups and elites. Thus, the samples are often unrepresentative, and frequently ignore female social mobility.
2. As occupation is used to measure differences between groups, those who do not work (unemployed, housewives, retired, wealthy) cannot be identified and assessed.
3. Definitions of occupational categories between which individual movement is measured are often a rough guide to differences in socioeconomic position.
4. Occupations may be redefined over time in terms of status, so that a person may be defined as mobile because he has been re-graded by the Registrar-General.
5. Social mobility may be assessed differently in different countries, and occupations may be categorised in different ways. This makes crosscultural comparisons open to doubts about validity.

Except for D.V. Glass, 'Social Mobility in Britain' (1954) and the Nuffield Studies (1972 onwards) much of the research and evidence on patterns of social mobility in Britain is very fragmentary.

INTER-GENERATIONAL SOCIAL MOBILITY

The extent of inter-generational social mobility, based on the available studies and research on recruitment to elite occupations, indicates the following trends.

D.V. Glass (op.cit.), using the seven occupational levels of the Hall-Jones scale, found that more than two-thirds of his sample of men were at a different level to their fathers. Furthermore, four out of ten had moved more than one level up or down. However, chances of mobility were affected by social background, with the top groups marked by a high degree of self-recruitment. Glass found little social descent, and what there was usually stopped short of the white collar/blue collar divide. It appears that occupations which are clustered around the manual/non-manual divide act as a form of brake on social mobility. Most mobility is between levels which are close together, for example 3M to 3NM. This is supported by R. Miliband, 'The State in Capitalist Society' (1969) who suggested a generally high degree of social mobility, but little of it to positions of power. Most upward mobility stopped short of the white collar/blue collar divide.

Evidence to support the view that the service class is essentially self-recruiting comes from R.K. Kelsall, 'Higher Civil Servants in Britain' (1955), who found that in the higher civil service, 45% had attended public schools, while 30% came from families of property owners and professionals, who comprised only three percent of the whole population. Twenty years on, J. Goldthorpe and C. Llewellyn, 'Class Mobility in Modern Britain' (1977) suggest that there is still a strong relationship between parental background and mobility chances.

The Nuffield Studies or Oxford Social Mobility Studies started in 1972 with interviews of over 10,000 men aged between 20 and 64 in England and Wales. The resulting studies were entitled 'Social Mobility and Class Structure' (1980) by J.H. Goldthorpe and 'Origins and Destinations: Family, Class, and Education in Modern Britain' (1980) by A.H. Halsey. Rather than using a scale based on occupational prestige, as Glass had done, Goldthorpe and Halsey used a classification of occupations centred around market rewards (income, security of employment, promotion prospects, etc.) After dividing the men into occupational classes the researchers then grouped the men into three broad groups:

Service class, formed of people with well-paid jobs and career prospects in the professions, national and local government, senior management, and higher technical jobs.

Intermediate class, formed of people with routine, non-manual, mainly clerical jobs, also sales personnel, self-employed, supervisors, and lower grade technicians.

Working class, formed of skilled, semi-skilled, and unskilled manual workers.

Their work shows that considerable **absolute mobility** had taken place, that is the total mobility within a society measured by the numbers of individuals within each class who have been socially mobile. Thus, Goldthope and Halsey found that 750 men had moved up from the working class to the service class, while another 1,400 had moved up into the intermediate class. Goldthorpe and Halsey argue that these high rates of absolute mobility can be wholly explained by Britain's general postwar economic expansion, and that social reforms have contributed nothing to this process. Furthermore, they argue that measurements of relative mobility (calculated by comparing the mobility prospects of different social groups at the same point in time) show very little class movement. Although there may have been an expansion of jobs 'at the top' these continue to be filled by the higher social classes, leading to what Goldthorpe and Halsey call the '1:2:4 Rule of Relative Hope'. This rule states that whatever chance a working class boy has of making it to the top, that is to the service class, a boy from an intermediate class family has twice the chance, and a service class boy has four times the chance of getting into the service class. An important implication of Goldthorpe and Halsey's work is that if the absolute upward mobility which has occurred is due entirely to economic expansion then the economic contraction of the 1970s and '80s should result in less social mobility, with little significant reduction in class inequalities. Some evidence of this was found by Goldthorpe in his updated work based on the British General Election Survey of 1983, and G.Payne, 'Mobility and Change in Modern Society' (1987) in his Scottish mobility study found that relative mobility was limited. However, the importance of absolute mobility should not be under-emphasised, as it represents greater opportunities for both the working class and the middle class. P.Saunders 'Social Class and Stratification' (1990) goes further, and believes that talents are unevenly distribute across classes because of genetic inheritance and social factors, which will inevitably lead to better mobility prospects for the service class.

INTRA-GENERATIONAL SOCIAL MOBILITY

Intra-generational mobility refers to mobility in the course of a working life. J.Goldthorpe and C.Llewellyn, 'Class Mobility in Modern Britain' (1977) suggest that there is a greater degree of intra-generational mobility than had previously been thought to exist. They found only 29% of sons of social class one and 2 enter the same class in their first occupations, but by the age of thirty-five some 63% were in such occupations. It thus appears that downward mobility occurs early in a career, then upward mobility develops later on. Clearly, different pictures of mobility and the extent of self-recruitment are obtained depending on whether movement is measured inter- or intra-generationally.

S.M. Miller, 'Comparative Social Mobility' (1960) provides a comprehensive range of research into social mobility between various countries. He suggests that there is more inter-generational movement across the manual/non-manual divide in Britain than in other Western societies (including the USA), but in Britain recruitment to the small elite remains class based. Limited research in social mobility in Eastern European countries indicates that there is no more movement than in some Western societies, and that any movement can be explained by changes in the occupational structure associated with rapid industrialisation, rather than with ideological change.

The importance of social mobility within a society can be interpreted in different ways, depending on a person's perspective on society. Thus, a conservative viewpoint would hold that social mobility has created 'egalitarianism', and allowed society to maximise the talent available for the continuing benefit of society. From this perspective, society is seen as an 'open' hierarchy in which it is possible to move up or down according to personal ability. Failure thus becomes a personal matter.

An alternative viewpoint is that social mobility creates a pool of frustrated individuals who have either failed to rise up the occupational ladder, or who have descended through personal circumstances or economic conditions.

Research has indicated that most mobility has been upward and, furthermore, that it was mainly filling a 'vacuum' created by industrial expansion and associated changes in the occupational structure, as well as by differential fertility. A Marxist perspective would suggest that the end of differential fertility coupled with industrial decline will lead to an increase in downward mobility. This, taken with the tendency for the upper groups to self-recruit, will result in a less mobile working class.

The class structure of modern Britain

Critical to the ongoing debate on social stratification have been various attempts to analyse the nature of the class structure of British industrial society. This involves the interrelationships between the major classes, as well as the movements and changes both between and within the major classes. Although sociologists hold different interpretations over the number and type of classes which exist, most would agree with A.Giddens, 'An Anatomy of the British Ruling Class' (1979) that there are four recognisable classes in modern Britain: the upper class, the middle class, the working class, and the underclass.

THE UPPER CLASS

The upper class is a rather vague term which is used to describe the small group of people at the top of the social class hierarchy. It is also frequently referred to as the rich, the ruling class, the capitalist class, the establishment. Some sociologists consider the upper class to be too small to be considered a significant class in itself, but its extensive power and influence within society mean that its importance cannot be underestimated.

J.Westergaard and H.Resler, 'Class in Capitalist Society' (1976) present a Marxist view of the upper class which sees the group as a distinct ruling class who own the means of production. Westergaard and Resler maintain that the ruling or upper class, which represents between five and ten percent of the population, retains the greatest share of the wealth in Britain. They reject the view that the development of joint stock companies (with resultant increase in share ownership) has dissipated this power and wealth, which remains concentrated in the hands of the owners of capital and the top decision makers/directors of companies. This view has been challenged by J.Scott, 'The Upper Classes. Property and Privilege in Britain' (1982) who argues that the historical development of the upper class illustrates a more complex picture of the group than that portrayed by Westergaard and Resler. Scott describes the origins of the upper class in feudalism, with the largest landowners being the aristocracy/nobility. The arrival of the commercial or trading class in the fifteenth and sixteenth centuries created another upper group of financiers and merchants. The late eighteenth and early nineteenth centuries witnessed the Industrial Revolution, and the emergence of a third high-ranking group comprised of factory owners or industrialists. Thus, by the late nineteenth century there were effectively three upper classes derived from **landowning**, **commerce**, and **manufacturing**. According to Scott, the development of joint stock companies in the late nineteenth century resulted in 'managerial revolution' which increased the wealth and power of the business class, linking commerce and manufacturing industry. These groups are not distinct, but are interrelated by marriage and family ties, by overlapping business interests and investments, and by a common culture and lifestyle.

A.Giddens, 'The Rich', (1976) also believes, like Scott, that the upper class is not one distinct group, and he identifies three types of upper class: **the jet set** or 'pop' aristocracy who have accumulated their wealth via the pop industry, sport, or the media (for example, Paul McCartney); **the landowning aristocracy** who have passed their wealth down through the generations (for example, the Duke of Westminster); and **the entrepreneurial rich** who are essentially 'self-made millionaires' (for example Richard Branson). Giddens does, however, make the point that despite the diversification of the upper class into different groupings, there is much evidence to indicate that the upper class is still distinct in terms of its wealth and power from the rest of the population. In his article 'An Anatomy of the British Ruling Class' (1979) Giddens shows how industry is dominated by the same key individuals who often hold directorships in several large companies, creating a number of 'industrial elites'. These elites, and the upper class generally, are reproduced via the socialisation process, the education system, marriage, social networks, etc. which ensure that the wealth remains amongst a small group within the population.

THE MIDDLE CLASS

Prior to the industrial revolution the 'middle orders' were to be found between the nobility and the serfs. Following industrialisation in the late eighteenth and early twentieth centuries, the 'old' property–owning middle class was joined by a 'new' propertyless middle class comprising professionals, managers, and others employed in the service industries. From a Marxist perspective the middle class is working class as they do not own the means of production. However, sociologists who adopt a Weberian approach take into account not only the relationship to the means of production, but also class in terms of income, status, occupation, and power.

The generally accepted definition of the middle class is the one used by the Registrar-General, which classifies non-manual groups into three categories (social classes 1, 2, 3NM). This division of the middle class into three groups is reflected by a number of sociologists, including W.C Runciman, 'How Many Classes Are There in Contemporary British Society' (1990), who recognises three 'types' of middle class: **the upper middle class**, consisting of high level professionals and managers, small business owners; **the middle middle class**, consisting of lower grade professionals and managers, technicians; **the lower middle class**, consisting of routine non-manual workers, clerical, sales.

The distinction between different 'levels' of middle class is shared by K.Roberts et al, 'The Fragmentary Class Structure' (1977) who state that prior to the second world war there existed the 'old' middle class of land and property owners and the established professions, along with the commercial middle class of entrepreneurs, traders and shopkeepers. After the war there emerged the 'new' middle class or salariat of salaried public sector employees (teachers, health workers, social workers, etc.). Census data illustrates this growth in the middle classes, with 25% of the population belonging to social classes 1, 2, 3NM in 1901, with an increase to 51% in 1991.

The problem of defining the middle class has led to an attempt by boundary theorists such as E.O. Wright to show that the Marxist bourgeoisie/proletariat division is not applicable, and contradictory class locations are more appropriate. Thus, Wright argues that the middle class is split into a number of different groups based on structure, class position, etc., which might involve property ownership or might not. M. Savage et al, 'Property, Bureaucracy and Culture' (1992) has divided the upper middle class into three such groups: **professionals**, who rely on cultural assets, educational qualifications, moral values for their class position; **managers**, who rely on bureaucratic assets or organisational positions; **petty bourgeoisie** or entrepreneurs and traders, whose class position is based on property assets or economic capital.

The professionals are the most distinctive group within the upper middle class, and as such have been written about extensively. The functionalist view of the professions has its origins in Durkheim's account of organic solidarity in advanced industrial societies, where moral order will be maintained via the interdependence of individuals through the division of labour. The professions and their associations will lead the way, by providing a code of conduct, control of behaviour, and a sense of responsibility and duty towards the community at large. Durkheim legitimised the high rewards given to professionals by arguing that they were based on a consensus of the occupation's value to the community. More recent interpretations of the functionalist view of the professions include the following.

B. Barber in several articles in the 1960s, presented a functionalist interpretation of the role and rewards of higher professionals. According to Barber, **professionalisation** involves 'four essential attributes':

1. A basis of systematic theory comprising possession of knowledge or skill not widely or generally available.
2. Community sanction and approval of the authority of the professional group.
3. A code of ethics regulating professional/client/colleague relationships.

4. High rewards which symbolise their achievement and reflect their contribution to the well-being of society.

Barber also emphasises the 'public service' aspect of professionals, which serves to increase their 'functional importance'.

P. Halmos, 'The Personal Service Society' (1970) also envisages Durkheim's moral order being implemented in industrial societies with the aid of the professions. Halmos regards the 'personal service professions' (social work, teaching, nursing, etc.) as the vanguard of the movement in the creation of a new set of moral values in Western societies. He believes that the emphasis in these professions on concern for others will eventually spread to other areas of industrial life, leading to true organic solidarity. Halmos quotes examples from business and commerce, where the employment of personnel managers and industrial relations experts are interpreted as an indication that management are concerned with the well-being of the workforce and the community.

Criticisms of the functionalist view of the professions derive largely from sociologists holding a Marxist perspective. Critics of the supposed benefits to be gained from professionalisation put forward the following arguments:

Professionals do not make an important contribution to the well-being of society as a whole, but in many instances they actually have negative or harmful effects on individuals. P.Wilding, 'Professional Power and Social Welfare' (1982) argues that welfare professionals have too much power over policy-making decisions, client needs and problems, and resource allocation. Teachers can create negative self-fulfilling prophecies; architects and planners can design houses and neighbourhoods which are harmful to health. The most comprehensive study of this view of the professions is 'Medical Nemesis' by I. Illich (1975) where Illich shows how the medical profession has become a major threat to health by helping to encourage diseases and illnesses caused by modern industrial life. Far from eradicating ill-health, the enormous number of prescriptions given out to patients each year often cause further illness through various side effects. Modern 'ills' such as ulcers, heart attacks, and depression, are caused by alienation and 'commodity fetishism' (obsessional acquisition of material goods), and can only be cured by changing people's lifestyles and environment, that is by treating the cause, not the symptoms.

The professions do not serve the interests of society as a whole, but support the interests of the rich and powerful. In modern industrial societies, most professionals are employed by the state or industry, and therefore serve the interests of their employers rather than their clients. In 'The Power Elite' (1956) C.W. Mills showed how the legal profession in US increasingly acted as the servants of large corporations, rather than as guardians of the law for everyone. Mills rejects the functionalist argument that professionals receive high rewards because of their contribution to society, Instead, he reasons, their rewards are directly related to the demand for their services by the rich and powerful sector of society.

Professionalism is used as a means by which an occupational group can improve its market situation. A good account of how the medical profession does this can be found in N. Parry and J. Parry, 'The Rise of the Medical Profession' (1976), where they describe how doctors control the profession in the interests of their members, through restricted entry, control of training, code of ethics, etc. This particular view of the professions provides another explanation for the differing rewards of various occupations. Thus, those occupations (such as medicine, law, and accountancy) which control entry and training through their professional association enjoy greater rewards than occupations controlled by the state (such as teaching and social work).

A third perspective on the professions is provided by the interactionist view, expounded by T. Johnson, 'Professions and Power' (1974). Johnson criticises the functionalist and Marxist views for not taking account of the historical development of the professions, and the extent to which professionals are subjected to three types of control. These are: **client control** (royalty/aristocracy in pre-industrial society, organisations and individuals today); **third party control** (church in feudal times, the state today); **colleague control** (the increase in professional associations from the nineteenth century onwards). On the basis of these three types of control, some occupations may be more professional today, others less so.

H. Wilensky argues that since the 1960s there has been a move towards **de-professionalisation**. He observes that this counter-trend has been particularly apparent in the fields of social work and nursing. These occupational groups have taken the view that over-professionalisation will result in the loss of basic humanitarian values, and will draw its members away from social reform. These **semi-professions** believe that the emphasis on methods and techniques is often at the expense of participation and practice. As the semi-professions tend to be more bureaucratic than the established professions, this can create conflict in their relationships with clients. Wilensky proposes the development of '**mixed professionals**', people who combine technical competence with practical skills, such as pharmacists.

The other group within the middle class which has attracted as much, if not more, interest than the professions is the lower middle class, because of its tendency towards **proletarianisation**. This is the process whereby an increasing number of routine white collar workers and clerks are becoming working class. Marx noted the process occurring in periods of economic crisis, when the lower strata of the middle class sank into the proletariat, partly as a result of their specialised skills being overtaken by new methods of production (deskilling). H. Braverman, 'Labour and Monopoly Capitalism' (1974) has described how recent changes in automation and computerisation have led to the deskilling of many non-manual jobs, leading to large sections of the middle class effectively becoming working class.

However, the most detailed study on the process of proletarianisation has been provided by D. Lockwood, 'The Blackcoated Worker' (1958). Lockwood disagrees with Marx that clerks suffer from a false consciousness because of their class position (that is, they do not realise that they are part of the working class). From a Marxist viewpoint, clerks are in the same objective position as the working class, but on a subjective level their class consciousness is different. Lockwood adopts a Weberian perspective in order to analyse the class position of clerks, and examines them in terms of their market situation, work situation, and status situation.

Clerks and manual workers both have to sell their labour in return for wages, but they do not share the same **market situation**. In terms of income, job security, and occupational mobility clerks can not be considered proletarian. However, over the past thirty years, the clerks' advantages have been eroded as manual workers have improved their income and working conditions.

In the **work situation**, clerks are not on the shop-floor, but in offices alongside their employers. Most clerks originate from the lower middle class, and contact with middle class employers in the work situation encourages them to emulate their lifestyle. Thus the distinction between clerks and manual workers persists, with clerks regarded by the shop-floor workers as part of 'them'.

Differences in market and work situation are reflected in status consciousness (**status situation**). This is when people's objective social situation and their subjective perception of their situation coincide. Lockwood identified three features of class or status consciousness:

1. A sharp awareness of being in a similar situation to other workers and having interests in common.
2. The sharing of a definition of these interests as basically in conflict with the interests of another class.
3. The perceptions of class conflicts as pervading all social relationships and containing within them the seeds of a future social order.

Lockwood believed that the erosion of differentials between clerks and manual workers heightened the status consciousness of clerks, but status rivalry between the two groups means that status consciousness has not materialised.

As a result of all the above, Lockwood rejects the Marxist view that clerks suffer from false consciousness and as a result do not see themselves as part of the proletariat. Instead, Lockwood believes that there are significant differences between clerks and manual workers in terms of their market, work, and status situations. Although the differences have reduced over the years, indicating some proletarianisation, there has been no merging of the classes.

Recent evidence to support proletarianisation tends to focus on the extent of 'deskilling' in various occupations. Thus, G. Jones, 'White Collar Proletariat' (1984) found empirical evidence for the deskilling of female clerks, essentially due to the widespread use of computer technology. However, G. Marshall et al, 'Social Class in Modern Britain' (1988) reject the proletarianisation thesis for the majority of routine white collar workers, finding that a large number of their sample continued to have substantial job autonomy combined with middle-class attitudes and values. They did admit, though, that 'personal service workers' such as shop assistants and clerical staff appeared to be moving more towards the working class, with increasing attitudes of **instrumentalism** towards their work (seeing work primarily as a means to earning money, rather than for job satisfaction). The identification of clerks as a separate, distinct group between the working class and the service class has been made by a number of sociologists, including J.H. Goldthorpe, 'Social Mobility and Class Structure in Modern Britain' (1980) who has described them as the intermediate class.

THE WORKING CLASS

The Registrar-General's classification is also used to define the nature of the working class, with social classes 3M, 4, and 5 generally grouped together into the manual or working class. According to census data, these three classes made up 75% of the total population in 1951, but had decreased to just under 50% by 1991. K. Roberts et al, 'The Fragmentary Class Structure' (1977) argues that although the working class is now smaller it is more homogenous, or similar, in terms of pay and status. However, there are some sociologists such as W.G. Runciman who believe that there are still significant differences between skilled manual and unskilled manual workers. I. Crewe, in his analysis of working-class voting patterns, has also distinguished between different groups within the working class, in particular between the **'old' working class** (council tenants in manufacturing and public sector employment) and the **'new' working class** (home owners, employed primarily in the private sector). Other, more complex divisions within the working class based on ethnicity, region, housing, consumption styles, etc. have been made by E. Hobsbawm. Thus, in a similar way to the middle class, there is no such group as 'the working class', but rather several distinct groups which together are referred to as the working class.

Research into the nature of the working class has focussed on two areas or debates. One is the **embourgeoisement thesis**, or the extent to which the working class is becoming middle class. The other is concerned with how far the working class has developed **class consciousness**, becoming a class both in and for itself. These debates are examined in detail below.

THE EMBOURGEOISEMENT THESIS

The embourgeoisement thesis is a view of changes in the class structure which emerged after the second world war. Its two most prominent theorists, F. Zweig and J. Klein, argued that not only was there general agreement between the classes, but that the working class was gradually losing its identity and being absorbed into the middle class. This process of absorption was expected to continue until the working class disappeared completely. The theory was fairly powerful during the 1950s and 1960s, and was based on the following factors.

Economic factors. In the 1950s there was a gradual improvement in the incomes of the whole British population. It was estimated that average real earnings of industrial workers had risen by more than 20% between 1951–58. The increase in incomes was reflected in changing consumption patterns amongst the working class, who were buying cars, TVs, houses, etc.

Political factors. In 1945 the Labour Party gained power by an overwhelming majority, but then lost the next three general elections in a row. Labour, although regarded as a working-class party, appeared to be largely losing the support of working-class voters. The decline in the Labour vote was most marked in the prosperous and economically progressive areas.

Industrial changes. It was argued that more affluent workers were employed in the newer advanced industries (cars, chemical, engineering), and because of their skills were becoming equal in status to non-manual staff in those industries. It was also argued that wide differences in working conditions between clerical and blue collar occupations were disappearing.

Redevelopment and rehousing programmes. The break-up and destruction of old traditional working-class communities, with rehousing on new council estates, contributed to the weakening of working-class perspectives and class socialisation.

J.H. Goldthorpe and D. Lockwood were sceptical of the embourgeoisement thesis, and during the 1960s decided to test its validity by empirical research. They did not argue against the political and economic changes which had occurred after 1945, but questioned the interpretation of these changes. J.H. Goldthorpe and D. Lockwood, 'The Affluent Worker, Vols. 1, 11, 111' (1968–69) was based on the study of 250 married men, aged between 21–46, earning £17 a week or more, in three industries (Skefco Ball Bearing Co., Laporte Chemicals, and Vauxhalls) in Luton. The study revealed a great deal of information concerning industrial attitudes, family life, social class, and political views. The major findings in relation to the concept of embourgeoisement are as follows.

Economic. Although standards of income and consumption were converging between middle class and affluent workers, differences in the work situation remained. Thus, in terms of working conditions, amenities, fringe benefits, pensions, etc., white collar workers were better off than affluent workers.

Political. The affluent workers were found to be considerably more pro-Labour than the working class sample as a whole. This support is connected with the affluent workers' membership of trade unions, and the extent to which they see the unions as the major means for securing an improvement in wages and conditions. Working-class Conservatives were not therefore to be found within the affluent worker group.

Industrial. Wide differences in promotion opportunities and working conditions between white collar and blue collar workers were found. Goldthorpe and Lockwood also discovered that the working class did not seek satisfaction in their work like the middle class, but saw work as a means to an end to get money (an instrumental attitude).

Home environment. The affluent workers were found to be very family- and home-centred, and did not develop relationships between work and home. Goldthorpe and Lockwood thus argued that the affluent workers were privatised, unlike the middle class who often combined work and social life.

On all the above grounds Goldthorpe and Lockwood found no evidence that the working class was identifying, imitating, or wishing to join the middle class. They thus held the view that the theory of embourgeoisement was not proven, and replaced it with the concept of '**normative convergence**' between the affluent worker and the white collar worker. Normative convergence suggests that the affluent workers converge, or have areas in common, with the middle class, including the following.

1. 'Companionate' or joint conjugal roles in the home between husband and wife.
2. An emphasis on family or home-centredness.
3. Similar consumption patterns.
4. Educational and occupational aspirations for their children.
5. Instrumental collectivism, as practised by the affluent workers, being adopted by the middle class. Thus, the use of trade unions by middle-class groups to achieve economic security and advancement.

Despite these areas of convergence between the middle class and the affluent workers, Goldthorpe and Lockwood maintain that there are still differences between the affluent workers and both the traditional middle class and the rest of the working class. The affluent workers do not view society in terms of 'us' and 'them', but do not see status as based on prestige and power either. Instead, they see social status as being based on income, patterns of consumption, and standards of living. The traditional working-class collectivism has given way to the 'privatised worker', whose world is based on money, family, and home. As affluence extends to the rest of the traditional working class, Goldthorpe and Lockwood argue that a transformed 'new working class' will emerge, similar to the middle class, but different from both the traditional middle and working classes.

Goldthorpe and Lockwood assumed that the 'new working class' would remain affluent, and that this affluence would spread to the rest of the working class. Although this may have occurred in the 'boom' years of the 1960s, increasing inflation and rising unemployment in the 1970s may have halted, if not reversed, this development of a new working class.

However, evidence from the 1970s and 1980s appears to indicate that there is still sufficient embourgeoisement to maintain a class between the lower middle class and the skilled manual class. R.E. Pahl, 'Divisions of Labour' (1984) describes the emergence of a '**middle mass**' between the two groups.

The embourgeoisement thesis has not, however, been accepted by Marxists such as J. West, 'The Rediscovery of the Cash Nexus' (1970), who argues that affluent workers are not content with their lifestyles, but are alienated at work, and thus seek compensations outside the job, with rewards being purely monetary (the 'cash nexus'). West argues that if wages are sufficiently depressed then the affluent workers would turn militant, reverting to their 'true' working-class nature.

CLASS CONSCIOUSNESS

Marx's view of class consciousness and the working class must be seen in the context of his revolutionary theory concerning the overthrow of capitalism. Thus, the exploitation of the working class in the nineteenth century would create increasing class conflict with the bourgeoisie. However, essential to the increasing polarisation of the classes was the development of class consciousness amongst the working class. Marx argued that the need for class unity, shared class interests, and the need to build a revolutionary union and political organisation would lead the proletariat to develop both as a class in itself and for itself.

The Integrationist view of class relationships emerged in the late nineteenth and early twentieth centuries, led by sociologists such as Max Weber and Karl Kautsky, and the Fabian Movement in Britain. Their view of the class structure and the role of the working class within it is based on evolutionary change, rather than Marx's revolutionary change. The Integrationists did not see the working class becoming a class for itself, but argued that in place of a revolutionary role the proletariat was gradually becoming integrated into the institutional structures of capitalism. Through their trade union and political leaders the working class accepted the status quo and sought to reform capitalism through peaceful means (R. Miliband, 'The State in Capitalist Society' (1969)). The Integrationists thus believed that the working class constituted a class in itself, but by seeking to improve its position through negotiation rather than conflict it could not be considered as a class for itself. The Integrationist argument against Marx is based on the following factors:

1. General and substantial improvements in wages and living standards have occurred as a result of economic developments in capitalist societies.
2. These improvements produced an 'intermediate' strata of non-manual workers, which has minimised the process of polarisation.
3. Social welfare policies and reforms have reduced class conflict arising from exploitation of the proletariat.
4. Industrial and trade union legislation has established procedures for negotiation between employers and employees.

D. Lockwood, 'Sources of Variation in Working-Class Images of Society' (1975) argues that much research into class consciousness has concentrated on variations between the classes rather than differences within the strata. Lockwood suggests that it is possible to identify at least three models within the working class, each group generating different forms of class consciousness. These variations can be outlined as follows:

The proletarian traditional workers (power conscious model). Strong working class collectivism characterises this group, with workers viewing society in terms of 'us' and 'them'. This type of worker is found in manual industries in traditional working-class communities, such as mining, docks, ship-building.

The deferential traditional workers (status conscious model). These workers view society in terms of a hierarchy whereby they defer to their 'superiors' both socially and politically. This group is found in a variety of occupations, such as craft jobs, small family businesses and agricultural work, in which they are exposed to paternalistic forms of industrial authority.

The privatised worker (pecuniary or consumer conscious model). Workers in this group see class divisions in terms of differences in income and material possessions. Attitudes to work are instrumental, and family is regarded as more important than fellow workers and community. In contrast to proletarian traditional workers, the privatised workers join trade unions for instrumental rather than class solidarity reasons.

It would appear from the above that working-class consciousness in the sense of being a class for itself is unfounded. Lockwood has, however, been criticised by J. Westergaard, 'Radical Class Consciousness – A Comment' (1975). Westergaard is critical of Lockwood's three categories of workers, claiming that he does not allow for **'universalistic class consciousness'**. This involves identification with workers in other occupations outside the immediate locality. This form of consciousness is developed by the labour movement, socialist and Communist parties within Western capitalist society. Westergaard quotes Chartism, the establishment of the Labour and Communist Parties, and the 1926 General Strike as periods in history when there was universalistic class consciousness.

Other explanations for the lack of class consciousness amongst the working class tend to consist of variations of Lockwood's analysis. Thus, G. Marshall et al, 'Social Class in Modern Britain' (1988) argues that **instrumentalism** and **ambivalence** account for the limited desire for class action. Instrumentalism means that workers gain financially from the capitalist system, and have their living standards raised. Industrial action is not, therefore, a class action, but simply an attempt to secure more money from their employers. Ambivalence refers to the reluctance of the working class to wholeheartedly condemn the capitalist system. S. Hill, 'The Dockers (1976) found that the manual workers he studied held conflicting radical and conservative views. To some extent Marshall et al believe that the working class has a form of **'informed fatalism'**, or a sense of resignation to the status quo, based on a lengthy period of Conservative government. A lack of working-class leadership from the 'top' from the Labour Party has therefore held back the development of class consciousness.

THE UNDERCLASS

The term 'underclass' can be used to refer to any disadvantaged and marginalised group at the bottom of the social strata. Marx used the expression **'lumpenproletariat'** to describe the poor and destitute of nineteenth century capitalist society. During the 1970s the word underclass came to be used to describe the disadvantaged position of racial and ethnic minorities. J. Rex and S. Tomlinson, 'Colonial Immigrants in a British City' (1979) found in their study of Handsworth that there was a distinct difference between the white working class and the black working class in areas such as education, employment, and housing. Although many sociologists thus view the underclass as a separate class in its own right, a Marxist perspective would argue that it is an integral part of the working class, and separating it out from the rest of the working class diverts attention from the problems experienced by the whole working class.

The underclass can be defined according to economic, social, and cultural features. Poverty and unemployment are economic features which can result in increased numbers of single parent families as well as extreme deprivation and hardship. F. Field, 'Losing Out' (1989) has described the social features of the underclass, identifying three main groups: the **long-term unemployed** (including a large number of women and ethnic minorities), **single parent families**, and **elderly pensioners**. Finally, the cultural feature of the underclass implies that this group of people have certain defining characteristics, attitudes and values. This argument is similar to the one underlying the culture of poverty theory (see Chapter 14), and assumes that the poor have 'pathological values' (laziness, fatalism, etc.) which prevent them from moving up the social ladder. C. Murray, 'Losing Ground' (1984) blames 'welfare governments' for creating these attitudes, with too many benefits and support creating a 'dependency culture'.

The underclass concept is often criticised because of its reliance on cultural explanations, which result in the lower groups within society being stigmatised and blamed for their social situation. These critics, such as F. Field and R. Dahrendorf, argue that the existence of an underclass is due to the structural inequalities of society. Educational and employment opportunities for this group are highly restricted, resulting in high levels of unemployment and poverty. However, once established, the underclass develops its own cultural values which serve to reinforce people's dependency and powerlessness. The motivation and incentive to move up from the underclass is diminished, leaving a permanent group of people at the bottom of the social stratification system.

WOMEN AND SOCIAL STRATIFICATION

Theories of social stratification, social mobility studies, and accounts of class consciousness, make little reference to, or completely ignore, gender differences. This has implications for women in terms of their position within the class structure, and in relation to an assessment of their opportunities for social mobility.

Women's occupational classification. In the Registrar-General's classification men and women have different social class profiles, with women over-represented in class 3NM and under-represented in class 3M. The Registrar-General's scale also tends to differentiate more between 'men's jobs' than 'women's jobs', for example all nurses are placed in social class 2 even though ward sisters obviously carry more responsibility and status than staff nurses. Furthermore, sex discrimination in the workplace can mean that although men and women may officially be in the same social class they may not share the same market and work situations.

Whilst women can be classified on the basis of their occupation, for women who are not employed outside the home there are difficulties in placing them in the social hierarchy. 'Work' roles involving housework and childcare are not included in the Registrar-General's classification, which means that women without paid employment are judged either by their previous occupation or by their husband's occupation. The conventional view is that the family is the basic unit of stratification, determined by the head of the household (usually male), therefore women should derive their class position from men. As women often have 'career breaks' for childbirth and child-rearing their occupational status may not be an accurate reflection of their class potential, for example male clerks are usually promoted to management posts, whereas female clerks frequently remain in the same social position (A. Stewart et al, 'Social Stratification and Occupations' (1980)). In cases where the head of the household is a female, or if a woman's occupation is more 'salient' than the male's (longer hours, higher educational level, status and pay) then the social class would depend on the female. However, J.H. Goldthorpe, 'Women and Class Analysis' (1983) remarks that a man's occupation will invariably influence a woman's employment opportunities, for example families are more likely to move location because of a man's promotion prospects. Goldthorpe also believes that the the number of cross-class families where men and women have differently classified occupations is small, and usually consists of a lower middle class woman married to a skilled manual worker, where status and skill levels are similar.

An alternative to the conventional approach to classification is the view which is described as **revisionist**. From this perspective J. Acker, 'Women and Social Stratification' (1973) argues that social classifications must take account of gender and use either individual or joint measures rather than ignoring women. Revisionists argue that the increasing feminisation of the workforce means that women's social class positions cannot be ignored, and their potential for social mobility is not necessarily determined by their partners' occupations. M. Stanworth, 'Women and Class Analysis' (1984) suggests that households can no longer be taken as the basic unit of stratification, and individual or dual assessments need to be made. Another approach would be to use a joint classification (Britten and Heath) which combined couples' occupations into a composite measure.

Social mobility. Women have generally been omitted from social mobility studies, with a few recent exceptions, for example G. Payne, 'Scottish Mobility Study' (1987). Some of the reasons for this apparent neglect have been summarised by J. Gold and C. Payne, 'On the Class Mobility of Women' (1986):

1. The inclusion of women would require extremely large samples.
2. It is more expensive and time consuming to include women in mobility studies.
3. Comparisons with earlier generations are easier to make with males.
4. It is difficult to know whether to compare women to their mothers' or to their fathers' occupations when measuring inter-generational mobility.
5. Mobility studies cannot take account of career breaks which affect women's mobility.

J.H. Goldthorpe, 'Women and Class Analysis' (1983) would maintain that, as women normally take their class from men, separate studies of women's mobility patterns are unnecessary. However, G. Payne and P. Abbott, 'The Social Mobility of Women' (1990) argue that generalisations based on male samples do not apply to women, as females have a different occupational distribution and different patterns of movement between occupations. Thus, men and women have different absolute mobility rates (the actual number who move up or down an occupation) which are often a reflection of social inequality. Unequal opportunities in education and employment mean that less women are likely to enter the service class, leaving more positions for men to occupy.

Women's mobility patterns have been described in several studies. G. Payne, 'Scottish Mobility Study' (1987) and P. Abbott and R. Sapsford, 'Women and Social Class' (1987) indicate that women have less chance of upward social mobility than men. The importance of career breaks for women means that many females do not always stay in the same class; Payne found that 77% of women experienced downward intra-generational mobility due to spending time away from the workplace. The greatest amount of female mobility occurs within the 'buffer zone' of class 3M and class 3NM, with women moving up from skilled manual to routine non-manual occupations, where they tend to remain.

Class awareness. It is frequently assumed that women are less class conscious than men, and that for working-class adolescents class is less significant in their lives than gender. However, class awareness seems to be more apparent amongst upper-middle-class and upper-class girls, who see the relevance of class for self-identity and lifestyle. S. Lees, 'Losing Out' (1986) found that middle-class girls were more career oriented than working-class girls, who were often expected to place domestic chores above school work. Differences in class awareness are therefore due to the interaction of gender and class. M. Stanworth, 'Women and Class Analysis' (1984) argues that the operation of the class system creates gender inequalities, which in turn affects women's levels of class consciousness.

CHECK YOUR UNDERSTANDING

After reading this chapter you should now be able to define the following terms.

1   Stratification
2   Social class
3   Status group
4   Closed stratification systems
5   Open stratification systems
6   Caste system
7   Estate system
8   Registrar-General's social classification
9   Functional necessity
10 Bourgeoisie
11 Proletariat
12 Polarisation of classes
13 Structurisation of classes
14 Multi-dimensional view of class
15 Status inconsistency
16 Socioeconomic status
17 Convergence thesis
18 Subjective social class
19 Objective social class
20 Lifechances
21 Income
22 Wealth
23 Social mobility
24 Inter-generational social mobility
25 Intra-generational social mobility
26 Absolute mobility
27 Relative mobility
28 Upper class
29 Middle class
30 Working class
31 Professionalisation
32 Instrumentalism
33 Embourgeoisement
34 Normative convergence

35   Instrumental collectivism
36   Privatised worker
37   New working class
38   Class consciousness
39   Underclass
40   Dependency culture

SELF-ASSESSMENT QUESTIONS

1   What is the difference between 'social class' and 'status group'?
2   Describe a closed system of stratification.
3   Why do Davis and Moore regard stratification as a 'functional necessity'?
4   Give four criticisms of the functionalist theory of stratification.
5   How applicable is Marx's theory of social stratification in modern industrial societies?
6   What problems are there with Weber's multi-dimensional view of social class?
7   How do class differences affect people's lifechances?
8   What is the difference between inter-generational and intra-generational social mobility?
9   What are the main causes of social mobility?
10   To what extent has proletarianisation affected the lower middle class?
11   How does Goldthorpe and Lockwood's theory of normative convergence differ from the embourgeoisement thesis?
12   What explanations can be given for the lack of class consciousness amongst the working class?
13   How useful is the concept of an underclass?
14   What problems are there in attempting to classify women's occupational status?

CHAPTER TEN

CRIME AND DEVIANCE

LEARNING OBJECTIVES

ON COMPLETION OF THIS CHAPTER THE STUDENT SHOULD BE ABLE
TO:

1 UNDERSTAND THE DIFFERENCE BETWEEN CRIME AND DEVIANCE
2 SUMMARISE THE EVIDENCE ON THE EXTENT OF CRIME
3 DESCRIBE THE USES AND LIMITATIONS OF OFFICIAL STATISTICS
   ON CRIME AND SUICIDE
4 REVIEW FUNCTIONALIST EXPLANATIONS OF CRIME AND
   DEVIANCE, INCLUDING ANOMIE AND SUB-CULTURAL THEORIES
5 EVALUATE THE USE OF THE INTERACTIONIST PERSPECTIVE AND
   LABELLING THEORY IN EXPLAINING CRIME AND DEVIANCE
6 ASSESS THE CONTRIBUTION OF MARXISM TO AN UNDERSTANDING
   OF CRIME AND DEVIANCE
7 DESCRIBE THE EMERGENCE OF NEW THEORIES TO EXPLAIN
   CRIME AND DEVIANCE, SUCH AS REALIST CRIMINOLOGIES

Crime and deviance

Crime is defined as any activity which is against the laws of a society, and which incurs
some form of punishment for breaking that law. Thus, in Britain crime covers a range
of incidents from minor infringements of the law such as parking on double yellow lines,
to more serious offences such as murder, rape, burglary. Distinctions can also be made
between utilitarian or profit-making crimes such as theft, and non-money-making
offences such as vandalism, and between violent and non-violent crimes.

Individuals who are prosecuted for committing crimes are tried in a court of law,
which in Britain will be in a Magistrates Court for non-indictable or less serious
offences, and a Crown Court for indictable or serious offences. An individual found
guilty of an offence will be sentenced by magistrates in a Magistrates Court, and by a
judge in a Crown Court. Punishments can vary from fines, to community service,
probation, and ultimately custodial sentences in young offenders institutions or in
prisons.

Deviance has been described by D. Downes and P. Rock, 'Understanding Deviance'

(1988) as any form of socially unacceptable behaviour which attracts punishment and/or disapproval. This includes criminal acts such as murder and theft as well as unsocial acts, such as promiscuity, shouting in libraries. Thus, all crime is deviant, but not all deviance is criminal. A person who ignores or breaks the rules of a social group or of society is acting against accepted norms or mores, and is called a **deviant**. If the social rules which are broken are not considered to be very important, for example unusual fashion statements, then the people who break the rules are merely regarded as eccentrics. If the rule is a more significant one, or it is a law, then the people who persistently transgress these forms of behaviour may be seen as a social problem by others in society.

Characteristics of deviancy and deviants

There is nothing about an action in itself that makes it a deviant one. Deviancy is a result of the ideas and values that prevail in society about what actions and behaviour are right and appropriate. Deviance may occur in public or private, by individuals acting alone, or as group behaviour.

Behaviour which is regarded as being deviant in one society may not be seen as such in another: drinking alcohol is a sociable activity in Britain, but is strictly forbidden in Moslem countries.

Deviance varies over time as the norms and values of society change. The idea of women having careers was not acceptable in the early part of the twentieth century, but is considered appropriate today.

The mass media tends to present stereotypes of deviants by portraying fixed images of certain groups, such as alcoholics, homosexuals, drug takers. These images tend to reinforce our own stereotypes of these people, and may lead to a labelling process whereby the ex-prisoner, the single parent, or the homosexual are refused a job or somewhere to live.

Not all forms of deviancy are equally condemned. It is usually considered wrong to steal money from a friend. However, where a person steals from his workplace, or avoids paying income tax, this deviant behaviour may be tolerated or even encouraged.

To try and remedy deviant behaviour society looks for explanations as to why a person has wandered from the norms of acceptable behaviour.

The extent of crime

The extent of crime is measured by official statistics collected by the police, courts, and government agencies. M. Maguire et al, 'The Oxford Handbook of Criminology' (1994) summarises many of these figures, and comments that between 1876 and the 1930s there was little change in the crime rate. From the 1930s there was a gradual rise up to the mid-1950s, followed by a sharp continuous rise up to the present day. Thus, in 1951 there was one offence per 100 of the population, and in 1992 ten offences per 100 of the population (*Social Trends*, 1994). Official statistics compiled by the police show that there were 5.1 million crimes in the year to June, 1996, including more than 330,000 crimes of violence (a rise of 10% on the previous year). Other trends indicate that during the last ten years crimes of violence have increased, whilst burglary and vehicle theft have decreased.

Official statistics are published annually, enabling comparisons to be made from one year to the next. The figures show only those crimes which are 'known to the police', which means that a proportion of crimes go 'unrecorded'. This unrecorded crime is called the '**dark figure**' of crime, and can be estimated in several ways.

VICTIMISATION STUDIES

These studies consist of surveying a representative sample of the population, and asking them whether they have been a victim of crime in the previous year. Usually, drug offences, fraud, and crimes against business are not included as it can be difficult to ascertain if someone has been a victim of these crimes.

In Britain, the Home Office Research and Planning Unit has conducted biennial victim surveys since 1982, published as the British Crime Surveys. They have found that only one-third of crimes are reported to the police, with nearly 50% of people not reporting crimes because they thought the offence was too trivial. The surveys suggest that the overall increase in crime is less steep than the police figures indicate, with more vandalism and violence recorded by the police. The 1996 British Crime Survey has shown that the overall number of crimes in 1995 increased compared to the previous two years, but at a slower rate than before. The survey estimated that 19 million crimes occurred during 1995, which is four times more than the police recorded. Although most people thought that crime was getting worse, they felt less anxious about being a victim of crime.

Increases in crime, either from police figures or from victimisation surveys, may not be caused by an increase in the number of criminals, but by other factors. The 50% rise in the number of police officers in the last fifteen years, coupled with better technological and forensic methods of detection, have led to more criminals being apprehended.

There are several problems with victimisation surveys, such as the refusal of people to co-operate, the difficulty of obtaining a representative sample, and the concealment of sexual and violent crimes.

SELF-REPORT STUDIES

These are studies where a sample of the population is asked whether they have ever committed one or more of a series of offences. These self-admission surveys are intended to ascertain the size of the 'dark figure', and also to discover the characteristics of offenders. The responses from self-report studies can be checked by asking friends to confirm or dispute the answers, or even by using lie detectors, which indicate that approximately 80% of people give truthful answers. M. Maguire et al, 'The Oxford Handbook of Criminology' (1994) found that convicted offenders admit to more serious crimes and more frequent offending than people who have not been previously convicted. However, although these studies confirm that street crimes are more likely to be committed by young, working-class males, this group are not responsible for crime as a whole. This is supported by S. Box, 'Deviancy, Reality and Society' (1981), who reviewed 40 self-report studies in different countries, and found that the offender profile of 'young, working-class male' could be rejected.

Characteristics of offenders

Official statistics on crime and deviance indicate that there are certain social characteristics associated with those people who are arrested and processed by the criminal justice system. Although self-report studies dispute this offender profile (young, male, working-class, black, poor, low educational achievement), the appearance of these categories of people in the official figures can be explained in a number of ways.

Juvenile delinquency refers to criminal offences committed by 14–17 year olds. The highest rates of crime for both sexes occurs between the ages of 14 and 21. This adolescent peak seems to indicate that crime is a transitory activity for most teenagers. As D. Matza, 'Delinquency and Drift' (1964) argues, young people 'drift' into crime, often influenced by their peer group, and on assuming adult roles and responsibilities their criminal career ceases. However, a small hard core of persistent offenders remains to continue their criminality into adulthood. This group were studied as part of a twenty-year investigation by D.J. West, director of the Cambridge Institute of Criminology, into mostly white, all working-class boys growing up in London in the 1960s and 1970s. West found that poverty, a large family, parents with criminal records, and low intelligence in the child were key factors leading to delinquency. The link between the persistent offenders and home background indicated that the worse the family background, the greater the child's tendency to continue in crime.

Sex differences in crime according to official statistics indicate that male offenders outnumber female ones by a ratio of 6:1. Women commit less crimes than men at all ages and at all periods in history. However, since the 1950s, the rise in female crime has been far greater than that for male crime, particularly in the 14–17 age group. Some explanations for the sex-ratio of criminality include the following.

Sex-role socialisation means that males develop attitudes and skills which aid their criminality, for example aggression, technical knowledge, and confidence to walk city streets late at night. In contrast, girls are socialised into more passive behaviour, and are expected (by parents and teachers) to conform to norms and morals more strictly than boys. Most offences committed by females are non-violent, with theft, including shoplifting, remaining as women's biggest category of serious crime. However, over the last two decades the proportion of women convicted of violent crime has risen, especially in the 14–21 age group. This could be accounted for in terms of the greater emancipation of women, leading to increased self-confidence and assertiveness.

Opportunities for many women to commit crimes are much reduced because of their domestic responsibilities. For non-working women shoplifting is often the commonest offence. Crimes such as burglary, stealing cars, and theft from employers require mobility, freedom, and employment, all of which are unavailable to many women. Again, with emancipation, these crimes have increased among females.

Finally, there exists a 'dark figure' of unreported female crime. Thus, self-report studies on females suggest that the real ratio of male offenders to female offenders is possibly as low as 2:1. It does not appear that women are intrinsically less criminal than men, but that they are more likely to be treated leniently by the police, courts, teachers, etc. Some evidence to support this view is outlined in an article in *New Society* by A. Campbell, 'What makes a girl turn to crime?' (27/1/77). The increase in the number of female offenders picked up by the police may in part be explained by the 145% increase in women police officers from 1970–79 (compared to 13% for male police officers).

Class differences are apparent in the official statistics on criminal offences, with more crimes recorded for the working class than for the middle class. Even accounting for the proportionately larger number of working class in the population, the figures still present a national picture of working-class crime. Several explanations for this discrepancy follow.

Middle-class crime is under-reported by the police because middle-class people are

Police activity can affect the 'dark figure' of crime

treated differently than working-class people when a crime is committed. The elaborated language code, education, and status of a middle-class person are often regarded favourably by the police, who may not regard such people as immediate suspects. This differential treatment by the police is developed in the account of labelling theory in the section on the interactionist perspective on crime later in the chapter.

Middle-class crimes are not as visible as working-class crimes, and are therefore less likely to be reported. Such crimes include embezzlement, fraud, and tax offences. This type of crime is referred to as '**white-collar crime**', and its under-representation in official statistics was first described extensively by E. Sutherland in the 1940s. He found that pilfering from work, as well as serious crimes of bribery and corruption, often passed unnoticed or were dealt with internally.

Middle-class crimes concerned with law-breaking in businesses and corporations reflect the power and wealth of this group of people, who can use their positions of influence to control the law enforcement and judicial systems. W. Chambliss, 'On the Take' (1978) showed how organised crime networks in Seattle, USA were controlled by influential personalities in business, the legal profession, local government, and even the police force. This view of 'crimes of the powerful' will be developed in the section on the Marxist approach to crime later in the chapter.

Members of **ethnic minorities** according to official statistics are more prone to crime. P. Gilroy, 'The Myth of Black Criminality' (1983) argues that the intensely capitalist nature of Britain in the 1970s and 1980s crated a political revolt of blacks and Asians against the racist policies of the police. Thus, Gilroy claims that ethnic minority crimes are often conscious, deliberate political acts in the fight against racism, and that many beliefs about blacks and crime, for example that blacks are poorly socialised, pathological, etc. are 'myths'. As a result, the police hold negative stereotypes of West Indians and Asians as 'wild', 'lawless', and 'muggers'. This view has been criticised by J. Lea and J. Young, 'What is to be done about Law and Order?' (1984), who argue that the majority of crimes (90% plus) are brought to the attention of the police by the public, and are therefore due to general discrimination rather than to police discrimination. Lea and Young point out that some crime rates are actually lower for ethnic minorities than for whites, for example West Indians have lower figures for burglary than whites. Lea and Young do, however, accept that there has been a real rise in certain crimes committed by blacks, particularly street crimes arising out of unemployment and discrimination. Thus, relative deprivation and marginalisation of ethnic minorities may be as significant in explaining ethnic minority crime as the effects of police policies and practices.

It has also been found that more offences are committed in urban areas than in rural localities. This may be because there is greater opportunity to commit crimes in cities, as there are more cars, larger shops, banks, etc. Also, informal methods of social control operate more strongly in rural areas, as people tend to know each other better, and are reluctant to commit offences against their neighbours. This may mean that much rural crime is committed by people from outside the locality. Policing in rural and urban areas may be different too. A study by M. Cain, 'Society and the Policeman's Role' (1969) involved a detailed comparison of the different methods of operation of rural and urban policemen, and how community, family, and colleagues all affect the level of crime recorded by the police.

Official statistics

In Western societies there exists a general belief that it is only possible to know something when it has been counted and measured. Thus, it is only a case of collecting the figures, and they will speak for themselves. The great influence of this conventional belief is shown by the importance and reliance given to statistical evidence in sociology. One of the biggest areas of statistical material is what is termed '**official statistics**', which are collected mainly be government organisations. Sociologists have relied very heavily on such sources, and therefore it is important that they are critically examined to uncover and understand the **social processes** and **social definitions** involved in the construction of such figures. Official statistics on suicide and crime are used here to illustrate some of these problems.

DURKHEIM'S STUDY OF SUICIDE

Emile Durkheim (1858–1917), who occupied a chair of sociology at the Sorbonne, Paris for twenty years, was the first sociologist to apply the use of official statistics to a social problem – suicide. Durkheim's own theoretical position was presented in his 'Rules of Sociological Method' (1895).

1. Sociology is the study of **social facts** and the explanation of these in a sociological manner. Social facts must be regarded as **'things'**.
2. Social facts can be recognised by the constraints which they exercise on members of society.
3. Sociology must be an objective science conforming to the model of the natural sciences.

Suicide and crime are examples of social facts that can be objectively studied. These social facts are '. . . any way of behaving which is universal throughout a given society and has an existence of its own independent of its own individual manifestations'. (from R. Aron, 'Main Currents in Sociological Thought' (1968), p.73). Sociologists must look for causal explanations for these facts. A given effect always proceeds from the same cause: thus, if there are several causes of suicide, there will be several types of suicide.

Durkheim saw society as an autonomous reality, existing outside the individual. Society is formed by a **collective conscience** – a combination of all the consciousnesses of individuals in society. The **organic analogy** is implicit in Durkheim's work, and helps to provide his explanations for the different types of suicide.

In his study of 'Suicide' (1897), Durkheim sets out to investigate the phenomenon sociologically by demonstrating that suicide is caused by the social factors belonging to society, rather than alternative explanations such as climate, race, heredity, etc., which were prevalent theories at the time of his writing. He believed that success in explaining suicide by social causes would add weight to his goal of establishing sociology as an academically respectable discipline with its own subject matter – the social world.

Durkheim starts by defining suicide as being '. . . every case of death resulting directly or indirectly from a positive or negative act, performed by the victim himself, and which strives to produce this result'. (E. Durkheim, 'Suicide' (1970), p.42). This includes suicide by hanging or shooting, as well as those caused by hunger strikes and death before dishonour.

With the use of some 26,000 suicide cases collected from official statistics, Durkheim challenges arguments which attribute suicide to **'psychopathic states'** such as insanity, race, heredity, temperature/climate, imitation. He states that there is a particularly high rate of insanity in his sample of Jews, but their frequency of suicide is low. After discarding these alternative theories, Durkheim sets out his own sociological theory of suicide. He argues that the rate of suicide within a society is directly related to the degree of social integration which binds individuals into common beliefs (i.e. the collective consciousness). Durkheim suggests that there are three main types of suicide.

Egoistic suicide is caused by the lack of integration of the individual into society. This emerges from correlations between suicide rates and integrating social contexts such as religion and family life. Thus,

– suicide increases with age;
– it is higher in men than women;
– it is more frequent in unmarried and widowed people;
– it is more frequent amongst Protestants than Catholics.

Durkheim argues that Catholic countries and regions consistently have lower rates of suicide than Protestant ones. He explains this by social integration, in that the Catholic community has more shared beliefs and rituals which integrate the individual into the Church. In contrast, the Protestant religion leaves the individual to find his/her own way to God, and is not as collective as the Catholic religion. In a similar way, people who are not part of an immediate family (and particularly men) suffer from a lack of 'belonging', and are thus more likely to commit suicide.

Altruistic suicide is caused by an excess of social integration into society. In these cases, an individual kills himself/herself because of their duty towards the community. Collective life is so integrated that the individual counts for very little, and is prepared to take his/her life for the good of the whole. In some non-Western societies, such as the Eskimos, individuals are expected to commit suicide under certain prescribed circumstances, including old age and infirmity. Religious beliefs may also encourage altruistic suicide: in India, the practice of Suttee requires that the wife of a dead man is expected to die on his funeral pyre. Although most commonly associated with primitive tribes, Durkheim argues that altruistic suicide still exists within the armed services. The soldier is socialised into the impersonality of existence which makes him prepared to sacrifice himself for others. The longer the service in the army means an increased risk of suicide. Also, officers have a higher rate of suicide than privates possibly caused by their greater commitment to the force. A more recent example of altruistic suicide is the Japanese Kamikaze pilots of World War Two, who purposely killed themselves in the act of bombing for the benefit of their country.

Anomic suicide is caused by the society failing to control and regulate the aspirations of the individual. **Anomie** is a condition peculiar to modern industrial society, where previously held norms, values and beliefs are crumbling, and none are developing to take their place. It is a state of **normlessness**, or a breakdown of social control. This type of suicide, argues Durkheim, is characteristic of modern society, and is directly related to the changes brought about by industrialisation. Industrial relations, the role of the state, and the aspirations of the workers, are all affected by increasing industrialisation. Such suicides occur within times of political and economic crises when the value system cannot explain or legitimate the new changing roles, attitudes, and power relations. In times of prosperity the suicide rate decreases, and in times of recession the suicide rate increases. Anomie can also occur when an individual is without the social control provided by a sense of moral obligation. Hence, divorce leads to an increased risk of suicide because the individual is no longer regulated by family commitments.

Durkheim concluded that there were social forces running through society, the origin of which is the collective consciousness, and these forces are the determining causes of suicide. Consequently, the suicide rate for a particular society is compounded of the values and hence social integration within the society. The values in a society must therefore be in equilibrium. As soon as society fails to balance altruism(collective) /

egoism(individual) and anomie(freedom) / fatalism(constraint), suicide rates will rise. In his concluding chapter Durkheim studies ways in which the suicide rates could be made to decrease, by integrating the individual more into social groups, families, trade unions, etc.

GENERAL CRITICISMS OF DURKHEIM'S WORK

Suicide definitions vary widely from one society to another, which means that it is both impossible and invalid to compare the suicide rates of one country against those of another. Approval or condemnation of suicide in a society will affect the way in which it is defined. In Japan the act of Hari-Kari is seen as honourable and acceptable, and openly defined as suicide. However, in Catholic countries suicide is regarded as a very serious sin, with the result that there are strong social pressures to have the incident defined as a 'normal' death.

Definitions of suicide may change over time, both within and between societies. Thus, in France, up to 1910, two sets of suicide statistics were kept by separate government departments: the Ministry of Interior and the Ministry of Criminal Justice. On analysis, it was discovered that the Ministry of Criminal Justice's figures were on average 16% higher than those of the Ministry of Interior. In these cases it is difficult to know which figures should be used.

The death of the individual makes interviewing impossible, and obesvation is rarely possible due to the (usually) secretive and solitary nature of the act.

The most comprehensive critique of Durkheim's use of statistics and his analysis of suicide is to be found in J. Douglas, 'The Social Meanings of Suicide' (1967). Douglas argues that Durkheim's **positivistic** approach to the subject (necessary to establish sociology as a science of society), combined with his **functionalist** theory about society having a common value system, encouraged Durkheim to look for 'social facts' to fit his already formulated theoretical perspective. Douglas directs the following particular criticisms at Durkheim's work:

Durkheim fails to clarify the meaning of his three types of suicide, and does not challenge the value system which produces the equilibrium between altruism/egoism and anomie/fatalism.

As a consequence of his functionalist approach, Durkheim assumes that there is only one central belief or value system, and therefore the suicide rate reflects the amount of social integration into that value system. Durkheim does not account for the existence of different value systems within a society leading to other reasons for suicide.

Douglas also examines the contribution of later, mostly US, sociologists on the subject. All of them are criticised in much the same way as Durkheim for their reliance on official data. The J. Gibbs and W. Martin study 'Status Integration and Suicide' (1964) attempts to measure Durkheim's concept of integration, with ecological studies pointing to the social disorganisation which exists within the centres of towns (for example bedsits, anonymity). Other theorists, including Gibbs and Porterfield, develop Durkheim's concept of anomie to show how society fails to regulate individuals in times of crises. Consequently, they argue that a change of status (up or down) leads to tensions which may be resolved by suicide. An alternative view by Henry and Short postulates that both homicide and suicide are based on aggression causing anomie.

Douglas concludes that all of these studies on suicide are based on official statistics, and do not therefore question the definitions of suicide implicit in such figures. Instead, it is assumed that definitions of suicide are obvious to both participants and observers who are analysing the official data. Douglas argues that all sociologists since Durkheim have failed to ask the crucial question: 'What are the official definitions of suicide?'. Sociologists operate with different definitions from officials who classify and compile the suicide statistics. Douglas argues that the data used is, in fact, a human product produced within organisations. This raises problems concerning the objective criteria used to categorise a death, and the procedures used by coroners and courts to determine how these criteria are met.

In an article in S. Cohen, 'Images of Deviance' (1971), Maxwell Atkinson takes up Douglas's approach to suicide and proceeds to study the meanings that coroners attribute to suicide deaths. The actual 'intention to commit suicide' is deduced by the coroner from the available evidence plus that of the post mortem. Atkinson lists the main areas of suicide intent indicators thus.

Suicide notes: it is essential that these are not faked to conceal a murder. From research of police in Essex, only 30% leave suicide notes; police feel that many are destroyed by the family of the deceased. Notes provide crucial evidence as to the meaning of suicide.

Modes of death: hanging is defined by coroners as intentional. Difficulties emerge in labelling certain deaths as suicides, for example car accidents, drowning, falling from heights, drug overdoses. These rules of thumb or stereotypes of suicide cases decide which people and which deaths find their way into official statistics: one coroner regards less than ten sleeping pills as an accident; therefore ten pills is recorded as a suicide.

Location and circumstances of death: the implicit belief is that if individuals really want to kill themselves, they will make a successful job of it. Thus, suicides are usually embarked upon in situations where they are unlikely to be discovered.

Life history and mental condition: coroners operate with an implicit model of suicide. Certain conditions have to be present if a death is to be labelled as a suicide rather than as an open verdict of death by misadventure. Common stories to explain suicides involve separation from parents in childhood, mental illness, fits of depression, etc. Open verdicts are usually recorded when evidence does not fit in with the accepted model.

Atkinson concludes that the coroners' definitions serve to re-affirm the common sense definitions of suicide held by members within the community. It is only by understanding the processes involved in the compilation of official statistics that the sociologist can evaluate the validity of the statistics he uses. Atkinson goes on to criticise Douglas for using case studies and reports to draw up his own classification of suicidal types. It is perhaps best to regard Douglas's contribution to the study of suicide as an attempt to examine the social processes involved in labelling certain deaths as suicides, rather than being a complete and definitive alternative to the work of Durkheim.

The study of crime

Many of the major problems of definition and compilation of suicide statistics equally apply to official statistics on crime. Theories about the origin and nature of crime have often erroneously been based on these figures, with the social processes involved in the construction of the statistics largely ignored. The major types of official statistics on crime are those collected by the police, and those collected by the courts (judicial statistics).

The 'dark figure' in all official criminal statistics is the unreported percentage of events which the sociologist is trying to measure. Reasons for the non-reporting of crimes include the following:

1. The witnesses or victims involved simply fail to realise that an offence is being committed, for example, motoring offences, assaults.
2. Those involved may know that an offence has been committed, but are willing parties to it, for example illegal abortions, under age sexual relations, drinking alcohol under age.
3. The offender may know that he/she has committed a crime, but the victim may not, for example shop lifting, sexual assaults on children.
4. The failure of victims to report crimes for a number of reasons: fear of retaliation by the offender; a belief that the crime is unimportant; the view that the police will be unable to find the offender; embarrassment, for example rape cases.
5. As the public are involved in the construction of official crime statistics through defining the existence of crimes, the police as individuals and as an organisation are also involved in selecting what offences will be recorded. The police may fail to record crimes because of: lack of physical and human resources; a desire not to antagonise the public by pursuing every incident; problems of administration of the data.

Attempts have been made, particularly in the US, to calculate the size of the dark figure of unreported and undetected offences. One such early American study was conducted in 1967, when the National Opinion Research Centre selected 10,000 households throughout the country, and interviewed each adult to discover if anyone in the household had been the victim of a crime during the previous twelve months. These victims were then given a half hour interview and a questionnaire to complete concerning the unreported crimes. The results indicated that the figures for virtually all categories of crime were substantially increased when the victims' crimes were added to the national figures. As described in the previous section, similar '**victimisation surveys**' have been carried out in Britain since 1981 by the Home Office Research and Planning Unit. These biennial British Crime Surveys have found that on average only one-third of crimes are reported to the police, with non-reporting largely due to the belief that the offence was too trivial to report, or that the police would not be interested. In addition to these victim surveys, it is possible to conduct '**self-report studies**', which are based on self-admissions of criminal behaviour, to ascertain the size of the dark figure. The problem with both of these attempts to measure unrecorded crime is that the samples are often unrepresentative of the whole population. Also, people may be reluctant to participate, or may conceal crimes connected with sex and/or violence.

The collection and recording of criminal statistics by the police is complicated by the division into 'offences known to the police' and 'offences cleared-up by the police'.

Although the Home Office publish a set of instructions for the preparation of crime statistics in order to try to establish uniformity in the counting of crimes, there is no guarantee that all police forces interpret these in the same way. Thus, if a man commits what at first appears to the police to be malicious wounding, but is later found guilty of a lesser crime of assault, which offence should the police record? How many offences are recorded when several crimes are committed on the same occasion? Fluctuations in the crime rate from year to year are also due to increased reportability by the public of crimes, and increased police activity in particular areas such as drugs or pornography.

An offence is regarded as 'cleared-up' by the police if they can trace it to a suspect who is then prosecuted and convicted. But, there are circumstances where the police are allowed, indeed instructed, to classify an offence as 'cleared-up'. Thus, an offender who asks the court to take other offences into consideration when being tried for another offence, cannot be tried in the future for these other offences, which are regarded as 'cleared-up'. An offender who is prosecuted and found innocent or acquitted by the court has his offence recorded as 'cleared-up', although it has not been solved.

These major problems regarding the labelling and counting of offences makes it impossible to use the official crime statistics as an index or measure of police efficiency. It is also impossible to compare one year's figures with those of another (locally or nationally), one police force's figures with those of another, and one country's crime statistics with other countries'.

J. Douglas, 'American Social Order' (1970) provides a comprehensive summary of the major problems and dangers in using official statistics. His arguments rest heavily on ethnomethodological and interactionaist critiques on the meanings behind the figures, and include the following points.

1. The early social scientists conducting statistical studies of deviance and other social problems were themselves officials, or were directly or indirectly involved in official work. Thus statistical sociology, especially statistical studies of 'social problems' such as deviance, was created by officials for the purposes of better understanding and solving the officially defined social problems.
2. Official statistics are created and controlled by officials. The officials then become the legally defined 'gatekeepers' of information on social problems.
3. The reliance on official statistics and the officials' definitions has meant that sociological theories are often predetermined by the nature of the official information.
4. Official statistics do not explain what is really going on in society, but give a false idea of the nature of deviant behaviour.

In spite of these difficulties Douglas does, however, point out the usefulness of official statistics in generating a **'critical sociology'**, which has questioned the nature of social processes, and attempted to develop new and alternative methods of social research, such as participant observation into the study of suicide, crime, and deviance in general.

Explanations of crime and deviance

Sociologists have attempted to explain criminal and deviant behaviour from a number of different perspectives. These sociological explanations are a response to biological and psychological theories which locate the roots of criminality in the individual genetic makeup or in the psyche.

Thus, in the 1870s Cesare Lombroso, an Italian army doctor, came to believe that criminality was inborn when he examined the skull of a notorious bandit, and found characteristics which he believed to be a 'throw back' to an earlier evolutionary type. In his book 'L'Uomo Delinquente' Lombroso claimed to have identified a number of genetically determined characteristics which were often found in criminals, including large ears, insensibility to pain, extremely acute eyesight, high cheekbones. Other biological or physiological theories of criminality include the work of Sheldon and Eleanor Glueck in the 1940s who claimed to have found a causal relationship between physical build and delinquent activity. They defined three body types (**'endomorphs'**,

'ectomorphs', 'mesomorphs'), and then related body type to personality, and hence criminality. Although this theory is largely discredited, it is possible that body type might lead to role expectations, for example round, jolly ectomorphs and strong, aggressive mesomorphs. During the 1960s chromosomal theories of criminality became popular, and in particular the high proportion of male prisoners with the **'XYY Syndrome'** led many criminologists to support a genetic theory of crime. However, the 'extra chromosome theory' was discredited when it was discovered that these particular males had a tendency to be much taller and less intelligent than XY males, and therefore more likely to be caught and imprisoned. In the last twenty years biochemical theories of crime have gained some support. H.E. Kelly believes that chemical imbalances in the body can cause crime, and vitamin deficiencies may also contribute to criminality. Recent theories concerning genetic predispositions towards criminal behaviour have also gained credence but, as in all biological theories of crime, are difficult to prove.

Psychological theories of crime also view criminality as an individual aberration, with a mental abnormality predisposing the individual towards deviant behaviour. Thus, J. Bowlby, 'Forty-Four Juvenile Thieves' (1946) puts forward the belief that if a child is deprived of maternal love, particularly during its formative years, a psychopathic personality can develop. Similarly, R.G. Andry claimed that boys who had hostile and unsatisfactory relationships with their fathers projected this hostility, and acted it out in their relationships with others. Other psychological theories include H. Eysenck, 'Crime and Personality' (1964), which maintained that there is a connection between personality traits such as extraversion and criminal behaviour, with extraverts craving excitement and exhibiting impulsive behaviour which could lead to criminality.

Sociologists have criticised both biological and psychological explanations of criminal behaviour because of their emphasis on individuality, and their neglect of the social and cultural factors which affect criminality. In spite of this, these views are still widespread, and lead to the labelling of deviants as 'sick', with treatment provided in the form of 'cures', such as electric shock treatment and psychotherapy.

Functionalist explanations of crime and deviance

Functionalist theories of crime and deviance start with society rather than the individual, and emphasise the positive functions of crime for society. E. Durkheim, 'The Rules of Sociological Method' (1984) presents the functionalist view of crime and deviance, which sees crime as a normal phenomenon which is functional for societies. Durkheim stresses the importance of shared norms or social solidarity in societies. This shared consensus can only exist if people can break the shared values, leading to a reaction against the law breakers, which reinforces the social norms. Thus, crime is necessary for the maintenance and reinforcement of acceptable behaviour in society. Furthermore, **social control mechanisms** such as the police and the courts, are essential to keep deviance in check and to preserve the social order.

Durkheim also argues that crime and deviance are necessary in order for social change to occur. Hence, people with deviant views are often expressing individual originality rather than deviant behaviour, which in time is recognised and becomes acceptable, for example Darwin's theory of evolution.

Functionalists do not ignore the dysfunctions of crime and deviance, expressed in the work of people such as Samuel Smith, who sees such behaviour as pathological and therefore undesirable. According to functionalists, once crime reaches a certain level in society, steps must be taken to ensure that it is removed or reduced, in order to maintain the predominance of shared norms and values.

R.K. Merton writing in the 1930s, starts with the functionalist view that society can only exist with a shared set of norms. He then develops an explanation of crime in terms of the structure and culture of society, that is a **structural theory of crime**. Using the example of American society, Merton suggests that the goals of success are measured in terms of material possessions such as houses, cars, expensive clothes, etc. Although these goals are emphasised as being available to everyone, in reality the means for obtaining them are not available to many people. As legitimate methods of acquiring the goals are not successful in many cases, some people decide to abandon the accepted 'rules of the game' and attempt to achieve the goals via different routes. The abandonment of the accepted rules creates a state of anomie or normlessness. Merton outlines five responses to the situation where society emphasises certain goals but does not provide the means whereby everyone can achieve them:

Conformity: people accept the goals of success and the legitimate methods of achieving them.

Innovation: people accept the goals of success, but reject the legitimate methods of achieving them. This is the group most likely to turn to crime, although Merton does not explain why some people 'innovate', nor does this category account for non-materialistic crimes such as vandalism.

Ritualism: people reject the goals of success, but are strongly socialised to conform to accepted norms. They often lack ambition, and pride themselves on their strict adherence to rules and conventional values.

Retreatism people reject the goals of success and the legitimate methods of achieving them. This group is resigned to failure, and include people who 'drop out' of society, for example drug addicts, vagrants, etc.

Rebellion: people reject the goals of success and the legitimate means of achieving them, and replace them with different goals and means. This group often wishes to create an alternative society, based on their own norms, for example political groups using terrorism as a means of achieving a new political order.

Merton has been criticised for not taking account of the power relationships within society which determine the nature of the goals of success. However, his structural theory of crime, based on functionalist principles, did prepare the way for a number of theories based on the notion of **sub-culture**: that certain groups develop their own particular norms and values which are distinctive from the general culture of society.

A.K. Cohen, 'Delinquent Boys' (1955) takes issue with Merton on two counts. Firstly, Cohen sees delinquency as a collective rather than as an individual response to the class structure. Secondly, Cohen questions whether delinquent behaviour is a direct social consequence of the desire for material goods, for Merton's theory is an inadequate explanation for **'non-utilitarian'** crime such as vandalism or violence. Taking Merton's basic point that individuals hold the 'success goals' of the mainstream (general) culture, Cohen makes the following observations:

1. The education system emphasises the middle-class goals of success, ostensibly based on merit.
2. Lower-working-class boys are likely to fail in school because of cultural deprivation.
3. The lack of opportunity afforded to the working-class boys creates 'status frustration', for they want the goals but cannot achieve them.

Rather than turning to crime for material gain, as Merton suggests, the boys reject the success goals and replace them with their own, completely opposite, goals from which they can derive status and success. The **delinquent sub-culture** is thus a collective solution to the problem, with activities such as vandalism, joy-riding, and truancy, carried out for peer group prestige, not for material gain.

However, Cohen, like Merton, can be criticised for assuming that delinquents desire middle-class goals, such as educational success. According to D. Downes, 'The Delinquent Solution' (1966), there is also little evidence to suggest that status frustration leads to a complete reversal of the mainstream norms. The emphasis on the collective response does not explain individual acts of violence or vandalism. Finally, Cohen's account cannot explain non-utilitarian acts by middle-class boys who do not suffer from status frustration.

R.A. Cloward and L.E. Ohlin, 'Delinquency and Opportunity' (1961) combine the views of Merton and Cohen to present the argument that there is more pressure on the working class to become criminal because they have less opportunity to succeed legitimately. They support Cohen's notion of delinquent sub-cultures, but argue that he does not take account of different sub-cultures which give rise to different types of crime. Cloward and Ohlin suggest that as there are many ways to succeed via the legitimate opportunity structure, so there are a number of ways to succeed in the illegitimate opportunity structure.. They propose three methods by which individuals can succeed in the illegitimate opportunity structure, which correspond to three types of sub-culture.

A criminal sub-culture, which exists in areas with a high level of organised adult crime. Adolescents are socialised into criminality, and have the opportunity to rise in the criminal hierarchy. Most of the crimes are financially rewarding, or utilitarian.

A conflict sub-culture, which exists in areas where adolescents have little opportunity to enter the criminal hierarchy, as there is little organised adult crime. **Status frustration** results from the lack of access to either the legitimate or illegitimate opportunity structures, often resulting in gang violence and non-utlitarian crime.

A retreatist sub-culture, which exists when individuals fail to achieve success in either the legitimate or illegitimate opportunity structures. These sub-cultures are often organised around illegal drug use, and may form an explanation for middle-class as well as working-class criminal behaviour.

An alternative response to the work of Merton and Cohen is provided by W.B. Miller. Writing in the 1960s, Miller rejects both Merton's and Cohen's views that working-class delinquency is a response to, or reaction to, mainstream success goals. Instead, he places gang delinquency in the distinctive culture of the working-class, where a number of **'focal concerns'** such as toughness, smartness, excitement, and freedom from authority are emphasised. Conformity to this working-class culture, achieved through socialisation and the need to gain satisfaction which is not available via education or work, is the main cause of delinquency.

However, Miller has been criticised for ignoring the structural factors which sustain this working-class culture. A Marxist approach, as expounded by the Centre for Contemporary Cultural Studies, argues that changes in the structure of society have led to the emergence of distinctive working-class sub-cultures. Hence, S.Hall and T.Jefferson (eds.), 'Resistance Through Rituals' (1976), D. Hebbdige, 'Subculture: The Meaning of Style' (1979), and S.Frith, 'The Sociology of Youth' (1984) have demonstrated how the post-war economic changes have led to the emergence of the '**teenage market**' and the concept of 'teenage consumers'. However, working-class adolescents who suffer from economic disadvantage cannot participate in this consumer society, and consequently feel marginalised. One solution to this is the creation of distinctive working-class sub-cultures, such as 1950s Teddy boys, 1960s Mods, 1970s Skinheads, etc. By creating their 'own' teenage sub-cultures, with particular 'styles' (clothes, hair, music), they are also indicating a working-class resistance to capitalist society and domination. Although their sub-cultures do not solve their problems of alienation and unemployment, they do represent a symbolic refusal to accept capitalist society and the changes which have occurred since the war. The above views are sometimes called '**new subcultural theory**', but as D.Downes and P.Rock, 'Understanding Deviance' (1988) have commented, it is difficult to know whether these young people are actually reacting to changes in their communities and unemployment, or whether they are simply expressing their existing attitudes and beliefs via these sub-cultures.

Structural and sub-cultural theories both regard the origins of crime and deviance as 'outside' the individual's control. D.Matza criticises this deterministic view of the individual, who is seen as a passive victim of his circumstances. In 'Juvenile Delinquency and Subterranean Values' (1961) D.Matza and G.Sykes argue that delinquent values are not substantially different from the values reflected in the leisure activities of the middle-class. Thus, excitement, toughness, the search for thrills, etc. can all be experienced in legitimate leisure pursuits such as gambilng, night-clubbing, flying, etc. Matza and Sykes argue that all social classes hold these '**subterranean values**', and in most situations they can be expressed in a legitimate fashion. However, the greater amount of leisure time available to adolescents means that they have more opportunity to pursue subterranean values, which might develop into forms of delinquent activity. This explanation of juvenile delinquency would apply equally to middle-and working-class adolescents.

Another strand in the functionalist approach to crime and deviance is provided by the **ecological theory** which developed from the work of a group of sociologists based in Chicago in the 1920s, who demonstrated that the relationship between organisms and their environment could equally apply to humans and their environment. In particular, the sociologists of the 'Chicago school' applied the ecological concept to the growth of cities, arguing that behaviour could be explained in terms of the urban environment. Using Burgess's '**concentric zone model**' of city growth they showed how cities could be divided into a number of zones, each radiating outwards from the central business district in the centre. C.Shaw and H.McKay, 'Juvenile Delinquency and Urban Areas' (1942) used the concentric zone model to show how male juvenile delinquency rates steadily decreased from the first zone (surrounding the central business district) to the fifth zone (on the outskirts of Chicago). The high number of delinquents in the first zone, known as the '**zone of transition**' or **twilight zone**, is explained by the high level of '**social disorganisation**' in the area as a result of a shifting population. The social disorganisation (crime, prostitution, vilence, drug use, violence, etc.) arises out of the breakdown of norms which occurs in an area where people remain for only a short time.

The ecological theory does not explain how social disorganisation originates, and does not account for organised criminal activities. Also, the theory is very deterministic, in that it assumes people respond to their environment in a passive way, and play no active role in determining their own behaviour.

The functionalist perspective on crime and deviance is based on the assumption that there is general consensus in society about what forms of behaviour are defined as criminal or deviant. The functionalist view, as described in terms of structural and sub-cultural theories, concentrates on the criminal or deviant responding to social situations. Thus, criminals and deviants are seen as being distinct from the general population. There is also no explanation from this perspective of how agencies of social control respond to different individuals committing the same crimes. As a result of these criticisms, alternative explanations of crime and deviance have developed to take account of these problems and provide further insight into the nature of crime and deviance.

Interactionist explanations of crime and deviance

The interactionist perspective offers an alternative view of crime and deviance, based on the theory of social action. Interactionists are concerned with explaining how and why certain individuals and groups are defined as deviant, and the effects of this **labelling** on their future behaviour.

Labelling theory is the process whereby individuals and groups define certain behaviour as acceptable or undesirable, that is as non-criminal and normal, or criminal and deviant. H.S.Becker, 'Outsiders' (1963) is one of the first exponents of this theory, in which he claims that 'The deviant is the one to whom that label has been successfully applied; deviant behaviour is behaviour that people so label'. Becker argues that many people break laws and norms in society, but the ones who are discovered and labelled as criminal or deviant are a minority. The labelling of a person is often carried out by **agents of social control**, such as the police, teachers, social workers. The effects on an individual of being labelled as deviant are described by Becker as follows.

1. The label attached to a person creates negative responses from others, who assume that the individual has the characteristics of the label.
2. Rejection from family and friends may encourage the deviant to see himself in terms of the negative label, thus creating a **self-fulfilling prophecy**.
3. The labelled individual may join an organised deviant group which provides reinforcement of his deviant status

The intensification of deviance as a result of the labelling process is not inevitable, or no drug addicts or ex-convicts or homosexuals would ever be accepted in mainstream society. However, the **'social reaction'** which follows the labelling process strongly encourages entry into a deviant sub-culture.

In the late 1960s E.M.Lemert, like Becker, described the importance of societal reaction to deviance. He distinguishes between two types of deviation.

Primary deviation consists of deviant acts before they are publicly labelled as deviant, and thus includes the numerous deviant acts which are committed, but not discovered and labelled as such. Lemert does not regard primary deviation as important, because the individual's self-concept and standing in the community is not affected.

Secondary deviation is concerned with the response of the individual or group to the societal reaction of their deviance. Lemert regards societal reaction as the major factor in the creation of further deviance, with implications for the individual's self-concept and status in society.

In his paper 'Stuttering among the North Pacific Coastal Indians' Lemert examines the relationship between societal reaction and deviance. The presence of stuttering amongst this tribe, and not amongst neighbouring tribes, is attributed by Lemert to their strict insistence on word-perfect performances in ceremonial rituals. Children are pressured to speak without fault, or risk shame and ridicule of themselves and their families. The stuttering occurs as a societal reaction to the concern about speech defects, which actually results in the acceleration of speech irregularities.

Societal reaction is thus the major factor in the **amplification of deviance**, which describes the 'snowballing effect' which creates further deviant behaviour. A detailed example of its operation is given in J.Young, 'The Drugtakers' (1971), whose account of hippies in Notting Hill in London in the late 1960s illustrates how police reaction encouraged the hippies to form an organised drug sub-culture, which in turn increased police activity and an amplification of the deviance.

Amplification of deviance has also been described by S.Cohen, 'Folk Devils and Moral Panics' (1987). Cohen used labelling theory to explain how various activities are identified as 'problems' and subsequently result in censorious action. The media have an important role to play in developing and reinforcing the deviant labels, creating what Cohen calls **'folk devils'**. Cohen used the example of 'mods and rockers' in the 1960s', and in particular the social reaction to disturbances over the Easter bank holiday weekend at Clacton in 1964, to show how the media used a selective choice of material to present the teenagers as folk devils. Cohen recognised three main methods by which the amplification of deviance occurred in the media. These were **exaggeration** of actual events, accompanied by emotive language; the **prediction** that similar incidents would occur in the future; and the **symbolisation** of words, clothing and hairstyles with delinquent behaviour. These three processes combine to produce a **'moral panic'**, where people perceive the folk devils as a threat to the major values and institutions of society. These moral panics occur most frequently in times of social, economic, or political crisis, creating scapegoats for social problems, and serving to legitimate the status quo. Later moral panics over mugging in the 1970s and football hooligans in the 1980s are described in chapter 18.

The actual process of defining deviance, and the interaction between individuals and the agents of social control has been described by A.V.Cicourel, 'The Social Organisation of Juvenile Justice' (1976). His research centred on the differential treatment of juveniles in two Californian cities. The characteristics of the populations were similar, and should logically have revealed a similar number of delinquents arrested by the police. However, Cicourel found significant differences in the delinquency rates in the two cities, and explained this discrepancy in terms of societal reaction. Thus, the size and organisation of the police, as well as their policies and those of the juvenile courts, were all involved in the negotiation of justice.

Cicourel describes how the stereotyping of individuals can help to explain the relationship between social class and delinquency. The police and courts interpret language, appearance, race, neighbourhood, and manner as indicators of deviant or non-deviant behaviour. Hence, white, middle-class juveniles from good neighbourhoods are rarely perceived as deviant, and even if they are caught they have less chance of being charged because their parents are able to negotiate justice on their behalf. The interactionist perspective on crime and deviance can be criticised in a number of ways:

1. The perspective does not actually explain the origins of crime and deviance; it is only concerned with the consequences of labelling such behaviour as criminal or deviant.
2. The interactionists do not explain why certain people commit criminal or deviant acts, and other people do not.
3. The interactionist view assumes that criminals and deviants are passive individuals subject to labelling. Little blame is placed on the individual for his actions, whereas the agents of social control are condemned for labelling such people.
4. Not all criminals and deviants respond to labelling in the same way, so that the amplification process is not inevitable.
5. The interactionists do not examine the reasons why societal reaction to crime and deviance occurs. They do not explain who constructs the laws and who defines the norms which prohibit certain behaviour. No account is given of the power which underlies the police and judicial system.

H.Becker, 'Labelling Theory Reconsidered' (1974) defends the interactionist approach and outlines its main contributions to the study of crime and deviance. In particular, he states that the perspective explains the importance of agents of social control and the consequences for individuals of the labelling process, and demonstrates the negotiation of rules based on relationships of power.

Marxist explanations of crime and deviance

Theories of crime based on the Marxist perspective are similar to functionalist views in that they emphasise the influence of the structures and institutions of society on individuals. However, whereas functionalist explanations of crime and deviance stress consensus and integration, the Marxist view sees the conflict and class struggle arising out of the capitalist system as more significant in causing crime. Hence, because capitalism encourages greed and the acquisition of material goods it emphasises individual gain rather than collective well-being. There is pressure on people to break the law to achieve this material success, thus explaining crimes with a financial motive. Non-financial crimes represent the hostility and frustration felt by people who cannot achieve significant financial success.

Theories of crime based on the Marxist perspective are often referred to as **radical** or **critical criminology**. These ideas emerged in the 1970s, criticising the Marxist view that people are forced by economic circumstances into committing crime. In radical criminology people choose to break the law, but the way in which the state defines certain activities as criminal and criminalises certain groups is seen to be of greater significance than pure economic considerations. Crime is thus related to the power structure, and seen as a direct product of the capitalist system. In a capitalist society the dominant economic group is the middle class, who control the superstructure (legal, political, cultural, religious aspects of society), and therefore ensure that the legal system and agents of social control operate in their own interests. Thus, laws reflect the interests of the dominant capitalist class, for example the protection of private property. Certain laws, aimed at helping the working class, such as health and safety legislation, are seen as concessions by the middle class to gain loyalty and to ensure the health of the working class. W.G. Carson, 'White-Collar Crime and the Enforcement of Factory

Legislation' (1970) illustrates how law enforcement operates in favour of the middle class. Out of 3,800 recorded factory violations, 663 specific enforcement decisions were made, but only 10 resulted in prosecution. Selective enforcement of the law results in bias in favour of the dominant group: corporation crime (tax evasion, breaking trade laws, etc.) results in few criminal prosecutions. W.J. Chambliss and M. Mankoff, 'Whose Law?' What Order?' (1976) contains an historical review of laws created to aid the powerful. Medieval vagrancy laws in England ensured a constant supply of cheap labour by making any support for vagrants illegal. Chambliss's ten-year study of crime in Seattle, Washington DC, USA revealed many connections between organised crime (gambling, prostitution, drugs, etc.) and ruling groups in society.

A significant contribution to radical criminology is the work by I. Taylor, P. Walton and J. Young, 'The New Criminology' (1973). This contains the critique of what they describe as the 'old criminologies', and calls for a 'fully social theory of deviance'. This model comprises seven dimensions, which examine how the deviant act must be seen within the context of the capitalist system, and at the same time takes account of who has the power to define and label certain acts as deviant. Radical criminology is an attempt to integrate a Marxist perspective and an interactionist approach to crime and deviance. An example of its application to a specific crime can be found in S. Hall et al, 'Policing the Crisis' (1978), where the moral panic over 'mugging' in the early 1970s is largely attributed to the class divisions of British capitalism and the process by which labelling leads to the creation of moral panics.

Some criticisms which can be made of the Marxist view of crime and deviance include the following:

1. In theory, if crime is caused by private ownership and the capitalist system, then a socialist society, with communal ownership, ought to have a lower crime rate. There is little conclusive evidence though to indicate that crime rates in socialist societies are lower than those in capitalist countries. M. Mankoff, however, argues that the lower crime rate in Western Europe compared to the USA can be explained by the greater provision of welfare benefits and more efficient organisation of working-class interests in Western Europe.
2. Marxist theory fails to explain the existence of crime and deviance in socialist societies, assuming that it will be a transitory problem which will disappear with the full communal ownership of the forces of production.
3. Not all criminals commit offences because they oppose the capitalist system; there are other motives for crime.
4. There is an over emphasis on the link between capitalism and crime, as many crimes, such as traffic violations, are not expressions of class interests. These laws and others are necessary even in socialist societies.
5. D. Downes and P. Rock, 'Understanding Deviance' (1988) argue that Hall et al do not prove the link between moral panics and a crisis in British capitalism, and there is no historical correlation between economic crises and moral panics.

Recent developments in theories of crime and deviance

The 1980s and 1990s have seen the emergence of several new approaches to the study of crime and deviance. Increasing concern for the victims of crime, especially for vulnerable groups within society, led to theories based on a **realist approach** to crime. Thus, right realism and left realism emerged as alternatives to, and a reaction against, labelling theory and radical criminology. In both labelling theory and radical criminology attention is focused away from the victim and concern expressed for the labelled criminal or the unfair structure of society. Realist theories attempt to redress the balance and treat crime as a real and serious problem. The increased concern in the UK and the USA over crime in the 1980s (expressed via the media as well as in political circles), coupled with a rise in recorded crime, led to the 'law and order' debates of both the Thatcher and Reagan Governments which were critical to their re-election.

RIGHT REALISM

In the USA J.Q. Wilson, 'Thinking About Crime' (1975) lay the foundations of this approach, with the assertion that criminals are wicked, immoral individuals who must be severely punished for their criminality. In Britain right realism has been expounded by N. Dennis and J. Erdos, 'Families Without Fathers' (1992) and P. Waddington, 'Strong Arm of the Law' (1991). Right realists dispute the Marxist view that poverty and inequality cause crime by arguing that despite increased affluence in the post-war era crime has continued to rise at an unprecedented rate. After dispensing with these economic explanations of crime they focus on the possibility that cultural factors may be a more likely source of criminality. In particular, N. Dennis and J. Erdos suggest that as high unemployment in the 1930s did not lead to increased crime levels, changes in family life, such as the increase in lone parent families, may be more significant. A decline in family values, and the meteoric rise in 'fatherless families' is seen by Dennis and Erdos as critical factors in rising crime rates. C. Murray, 'The Emerging British Underclass' (1990) criticises the welfare state for creating dependency and reducing the will to work, thus encouraging the potential for criminal behaviour. Another aspect of right realism features 'control theory' espoused by R. Clarke and P. Mayhew, 'Designing Out Crime' (1980), who emphasise that people can choose whether to commit crime or not, and therefore by making it more difficult to do so crime can be controlled. Crime prevention measures such as surveillance techniques and redesigning buildings can help to achieve this, and increasing punishments as well as custodial sentences, can also lead to the 'control' of crime.

LEFT REALISM

This view is outlined in several key texts, such as J. Lea and J. Young, 'What is to be done about Law and Order?' (1984), J. Young, Ten Points of Realism' in J. Young and R. Matthews (eds.), 'Confronting Crime' (1992). The main proponent of left realism is J. Young, who, despite his contribution to the new criminology, is critical of certain left-wing theories of crime. Left realism developed as a reaction to the right-wing law and order debates in the 1980s. In particular, left realists wanted to develop an alternative left-wing view that did not see crime as merely as product of the capitalist state. Rather, they were concerned that crime, especially street crime, should be taken seriously, since much of it consists of crime committed by working-class people against other working-class people. In a similar approach to the right realists, left realists such as Lea and Young reject the view that poverty and unemployment are directly responsible for the surge in crime in recent years. The increase in white-collar/corporate crime is obviously unaffected by poverty and unemployment, and low-income groups such as pensioners have low crime rates. They therefore attempt to explain crime using three key concepts.

Relative deprivation is more important than deprivation itself, for it is how deprivation is perceived by individuals which leads to crime. The media and advertising stress middle-class lifestyles and patterns of consumption which create more 'felt' deprivation. The groups most at risk from being criminalised in the 1980s and 1990s are ethnic minorities, and young Afro-Caribbean males in particular. Their expectations are far removed from reality, and the opportunities available for this section of the population are severely curtailed.

Sub-cultural values develop when a group of people share a sense of relative deprivation, and create lifestyles which aid their adaptation to their deprived situation. Crime thus represents one aspect of the process of cultural adaptation to oppression and capitalist dehumanisation.

Marginalisation occurs when deprived or marginal groups in society find that the use of violence and rebellious behaviour represents forms of political action. Marginal groups are not generally represented by political groups and therefore find participation in society's goals difficult. Lack of trade union membership and little involvement in pressure groups means that many ethnic minorities have a lack of representation which leads to resentment and to street crime.

Left realism is similar in many respects to subcultural and structural theories, but goes further by suggesting solutions to the problem of street crime, such as more democratic control of the police, the involvement of marginal groups in political decision making, and a smaller prison population. The criticisms made of structural and sub-cultural theories also apply to left realism, for example the extent to which police policies influence criminal statistics. A further criticism of left realism has been made by P. Scraton et al (eds.), 'Law, Order and the Authoritarian State' (1987), who argues that the approach is anti-working class, and even racist, and uncritically accepts the ways in which the criminal justice system reinforces these tendencies.

Other developments in the sociology of crime and deviance have concentrated on social categories which are largely ignored by mainstream theories of crime. Hence, research in the areas of gender and crime and ethnicity and crime has become more commonplace in the last twenty years.

GENDER AND CRIME

Although biological explanations are still common in explaining female criminality, there is an increasing trend towards theories based on socialisation. F. Heidensohn, 'Gender and Crime' in M. Maguire et al (eds.), 'The Oxford Handbook of Criminology' (1984) argues that the low levels of female crimes compared to males may be caused by women's socialisation patterns, which lead to greater conformity amongst females. Research by N. Campbell, 'Delinquent Girls' (1981) and P. Carlen, 'Criminal Women' (1985) on female gangs has shown that women continued to be controlled by men, so that their 'criminal careers' are limited. Women who are prosecuted and subsequently imprisoned are labelled by the prison officers and by society as a whole as both criminal and 'unatural' or 'unfeminine': A Worrall, 'Offending Women' (1990). Similar reflections of the perception of women are apparent throughout the criminal justice system, which may treat women more harshly for failing to conform to the mother/ homemaker stereotype: M. Eaton, 'Justice for Women' (1986).

Gender differences in crime rates are frequently due to different opportunity levels between the sexes. F. Heidensohn, 'Crime and Society' (1989) suggests that the higher levels of male crime are due to greater freedom of movement, as most women are still restricted in some way to the domestic sphere. Hence, the highest rates of female crime are to be found in areas such as shoplifting, handling stolen goods, and prostitution.

ETHNICITY AND CRIME

The 1970s and 1980s witnessed a deterioration in relations between the police and ethnic minorities. A series of racial attacks across the country led to an investigation of the possible causes, resulting in the Scarman Report (HMSO 1981). Scarman argued that many of the riots were the result of anger and resentment of Afro-Caribbeans about police treatment. This concern over the increasing appearance of ethnic minorities in the criminal justice system led to a number of research studies which attempted to find reasons for this high level of representation. D. Smith, 'Race, Crime and Criminal Justice' in M. Maguire et al (eds.), 'The Oxford Handbook of Criminology' (1994) found that Afro-Caribbeans were disproportionately represented in the prison population, comprising more than 10% of the male prison population and about 25% of the female prison population. Smith argues that the criminal justice system is racist, with stop-and-search powers, juvenile arrests, and sentencing affecting Afro-Caribbeans more than any other group in the population. He believes that this treatment of Afro-Caribbeans is extended to other minorities, and ultimately leads to the criminalisation of all black people.

Racism within society is also suggested by S. Hall et al, 'Policing the Crisis' (1978) as the most likely reason for the disproportionate number of ethnic minorities within the prison population. They argue that high unemployment amongst ethnic minorities, coupled with extensive racism, leads to the development of crime as a survival strategy for these groups within society. Thus, explanations for criminal behaviour amongst ethnic minorities may include theories which are different to those which are applied to the white population.

CHECK YOUR UNDERSTANDING

After reading this chapter you should now be able to define the following terms.

1 Crime
2 Deviance
3 Dark figure
4 Victimisation surveys
5 Self-report studies
6 Juvenile delinquency
7 White-collar crime
8 Social facts
9 Collective conscience
10 Organic analogy
11 Egoistic suicide
12 Altruistic suicide
13 Anomic suicide
14 Normlessness

15 Gatekeepers of information
16 Social control mechanisms
17 Structural theory of crime
18 Status frustration
19 Delinquent sub-culture
20 Focal concerns
21 Ecological theory
22 Labelling theory
23 Agents of social control
24 Primary deviation
25 Secondary deviation
26 Amplification of deviance
27 Folk devils
28 Moral panics
29 Radical criminology
30 Social theory of deviance
31 Right realism
32 Control theory
33 Left realism
34 Marginalisation

SELF-ASSESSMENT QUESTIONS

1 How does deviance differ from crime?
2 Briefly explain why crime occurs most frequently amongst young, working-class males.
3 How did Durkheim's theoretical position affect his examination of suicide statistics?
4 What reasons are there for the existence of a 'dark figure' of crime?
5 Describe **one** biological explanation of criminal behaviour.
6 List Merton's **five** responses to anomie.
7 How does A. Cohen explain the existence of 'non-utilitarian' crime?
8 Name Cloward and Ohlin's **three** types of sub-culture.
9 What part does the self-fulfilling prophecy play in labelling theory?
10 What is the difference between Lemert's 'primary deviation' and 'secondary deviation'?
11 According to Cicourel, how do the agents of social control affect the relationship between social class and delinquency?
12 How is Marxism applied to the study of crime to create a 'critical criminology'?

13 What do right realists see as the main causes of crime?
14 How do left realists attempt to explain rising street crime?
15 How do explanations of crime amongst ethnic minorities differ from
     mainstream theories?

'A' LEVEL SOCIOLOGY ESSAY QUESTIONS

1 Evaluate the claim put forward by some sociologists that both the nature and
    the extent of deviance are socially constructed (AEB, summer, 1992).
2 Critically discuss the Marxist argument that deviance ought to be explained in
    terms of a person's social class position (AEB, summer, 1995).
3 'Many sociological approaches to deviance have ignored the extent to which
    females are involved in crime.'
    Discuss the evidence and arguments for and against this view (AEB, summer,
    1995).
4 'The usefulness of crime statistics in sociological research depends on the
    theoretical approach adopted by the sociologist.'
    Critically explain this view (AEB, summer, 1996).

CHAPTER ELEVEN

RACE AND ETHNICITY

LEARNING OBJECTIVES

ON COMPLETION OF THIS CHAPTER THE STUDENT SHOULD BE ABLE TO:

1 DISTINGUISH BETWEEN THE TERMS RACE AND ETHNICITY
2 DESCRIBE THE RANGE OF ETHNIC GROUPS IN BRITAIN
3 EXPLAIN THE NATURE OF RACISM, PREJUDICE, AND DISCRIMINATION
4 ANALYSE THE RELATIONSHIP BETWEEN RACE AND SOCIAL CLASS
5 REVIEW THE POSITION OF ETHNIC MINORITIES IN THE WORKPLACE

Race and ethnicity

The terms 'race' and 'ethnicity' are often used interchangeably, even though the former is based on physical or biological differences, and the latter is a form of social or cultural categorisation. There are several other overlapping classifications which are used in relation to race and ethnicity, such as black/white and minorities. These distinctions are described in some detail below.

RACE

Race is a biological concept whereby human beings can be classified by a number of physical criteria, such as hair type, eye colour, skin colour, nasal shape, lip form, etc. During the nineteenth century attempts were made to classify people into racial types, resulting in the familiar three categories:

Negroid: characterised by dark brown or black skin, brown eyes, black curly hair, broad nose, and wide lips. This group of people are found mainly in Sub-Saharan Africa.

Mongoloid: characterised by yellow or brown skin, brown slanted eyes, black straight hair, small nose, and high cheekbones. This category of people derive from North and South America, the Pacific Islands, South and East Asia.

Race and ethnicity in modern Britain

Caucasoid: characterised by white to dark brown skin, light blue to dark brown eyes, straight or wavy light or dark hair, narrow nose, and thin lips. This group originate from Europe, the Middle East, Africa, and India.

It is often assumed that the three categories are mutually exclusive, yet modern genetics has shown that the majority of people are genetically mixed, with a combination of genes from all categories. Race is not, therefore, a straightforward 'black and white' issue.

Although there is no scientific evidence that racial differences have a direct effect on behaviour and cultural attitudes, biological traits have been used to rank people in systems of social inequality. The importance of racial categories thus lies in how they affect social relations. M. Banton and R. Miles, 'Racism and Migrant Labour' (1982) use the term **'racialisation'** to describe the way in which people 'frame' the social world in racial terms. Hence, people construct racial categories which use physical appearance to create social barriers between groups, and then conclude that intellectual and behavioural characteristics of the groups are due to physical factors. The term race is thus used most frequently in the context of its social effects, rather than in its strict biological sense.

BLACK/WHITE

The term black/white, used in reference to race and/or ethnicity, is very confusing as it does not allow for the placing of 'intermediate' groups such as Arabs, Chinese, Native Americans. Also, individuals of mixed race parentage cannot be satisfactorily placed in either a black or white category. A further problem with the black/white terminology is that the word black is often used, inaccurately, to refer to all minorities, and at other times it is used specifically to denote black people of Afro-Caribbean origin. At an individual level, a person may not define him/herself as black: Indians do not classify themselves as black.

ETHNICITY

Ethnicity is a term which refers to the cultural heritage shared by a category of people which gives rise to a distinctive social identity. Thus, while race is a biological classification, ethnicity is a cultural differentiation between groups. Ethnicity is usually thought to be a more useful concept than race because it describes the significant social and cultural features which are often behind racial conflicts. It is quite difficult to classify people into ethnic groups because of inconsistencies in shared culture and religion. Ethnic groups are frequently classified by 'territory', for example people connected through birthplace or descent with the New Commonwealth countries are assumed to belong to the same ethnic group. However, these countries (for example India, Pakistan, Kenya, Jamaica, etc.) contain people with different histories, language and traditions, which means that they cannot all be described as belonging to the New Commonwealth ethnic group. It is more feasible to view ethnicity as a cultural or religious concept which is not specifically tied to territory.

The legal requirements for defining a group as an ethnic category were spelled out in a House of Lords ruling in 1983. Two fundamental criteria were laid down: a long, shared history, and a specific cultural tradition. Other features were also included, such as common geographical origin, shared language, common literature and religion, and 'an oppressed status'.

MINORITIES

Minorities may be based on race or ethnicity, but essentially they are catergories of people, defined by physical or cultural traits, who are socialy disadvantaged within a society. Thus, the term 'minority group' can also be used to refer to women, people with disabilites, and even political radicals. However, race and ethnicity are the most common bases of minority groups, which have two major characteristics:

A distinctive identity, whereby minorities view society in terms of 'we' and 'us' versus 'they' and 'them'. This identity is more apparent in racial minorities as ethnicity tends to be more variable and open to change. This identity is frequently maintained via **endogamy**, or marriage within one's racial or ethnic grouping.

Subordination, which is an aspect of social stratification. Minorities suffer social disadvantage and discrimination, and are more likely to have lower incomes, less occupational prestige, and less educational qualifications than the majority population. Although subordination is common in minority groups, there may be individual exceptions where some people have achieved wealth and prestige. However, these individuals may still continue to experience abuse and racism, as their master status based on race or ethnicity overrides their personal characteristics and achievements.

Minorities usually form a small proportion of a society's population, with exceptions such as blacks in South Africa and women in industrialised countries. The struggle for rights that are formally guaranteed by law is the source of many social conflicts for minority groups, for example in South Africa, Northern Ireland, and the former Soviet Union. An unusual reversal of this situation is found in Malaysia, where ethnic inequality is mandated by law as a means of increasing the social equality of Malays by giving them preferential treatment in education and employment.

Relationships between the majority group and the minority groups can take a variety of forms, **assimilation** (trying to incorporate the minority into the majority so that it loses its distinctiveness); **pluralism** (peaceful co-existence between the groups); and in extreme cases **genocide** (the systematic killing of one group of people by another). Although minority groups may often accept assimilation or segregation, they may also try various means (violent and non-violent) in order to gain power for themselves.

Ethnic groups in Britain

It is very difficult to categorise ethnic groups in Britain as the 'English' have always had immigrant ancestors such as the Irish, Scottish, Welsh and French. In fact, although the term 'immigrant' is often used to denote black minorities, the largest category of migrants into Britain has been whites. J. Walvin, 'Passage to Britain' (1984) estimates that between 1945 and 1950 approximately 457,000 European refugees entered Britain. The 1981 census indicated that out of 3.4 million people 'born overseas', 1.89 million were white. More recent information, such as the International Passenger Survey 1989, estimates that over 70% of immigrants are white. It is thus important that the term immigrant is not applied solely to black migrants, or indeed to second and third generation black Britons.

The migration of people into Britain from other cultures is affected by '**pull factors**' and '**push factors**' The former refers to the features which attract immigrants to a country, such as economic prospects, education, joining relatives. In contrast, push factors are those which drive people out of their country, such as poverty, unemployment, religious or political persecution. Very often a combination of push and pull factors are responsible for making people decide to emigrate.

PATTERNS OF MIGRATION INTO BRITAIN

Between 1825 and 1905 there were high levels of Irish immigrants, and also a large number of Central European Jews entering Britain. The 1905 Aliens Act restricted the numbers of (largely European) immigrants into Britain, and it was not until the 1948 British Nationality Act that levels of immigration once again increased to high levels. Post-war immigration was essentially from the New Commonwealth countries of the

West Indies, India, and Pakistan. The 1950s and 1960s saw large numbers of New Commonwealth immigrants, pushed by poverty and unemployment, and pulled by the large proportion of unfilled jobs in the new National Health Service and in the transport industry. These figures peaked in the early 1960s as legislation was introduced in order to restrict entry to those with certain skills and qualifications. Thus, the 1970s and 1980s witnessed a continuing decline in the numbers entering from the New Commonwealth, with several 'emergency' influxes, such as Ugandan Asians, Greek Cypriots, and Vietnamese boat people. The vast majority of immigrants today are dependants of first and second generation immigrants from the New Commonwealth.

STATISTICS ON ETHNIC MINORITIES

Although general trends in immigration can be ascertained, it is difficult to obtain accurate figures on the total number of people belonging to various ethnic groups. The 1981 census was the first attempt to officially 'count' ethnic minorities, by including a question on 'birthplace of the head of household' (a rather unreliable method as an increasing number of Britain's black population are British born). Thus, out of 3.4 million people born outside the UK only 1.5 million originated from black ethnic minorities. The 1985 Swann Report on 'Education for All' estimated that six percent of the British population were non-white, and of these, 40% were born in the UK. In addition to ethnic minorities from the New Commonwealth, Swann emphasised the distinctive nature of many other white ethnic groups, such as Italians, Cypriots, Ukranians, Vietnamese, and Travellers. Diversity within ethnic minorities makes it difficult to obtain precise figures on all minority groups: Asians are often 'counted' as one ethnic group, yet there are clear differences between Hindus, Sikhs, and Muslims. The 1991 census incorporated a direct question on ethnicity for the first time, and found that ethnic minorities represent five and a half percent of the total population, with the highest three categories being whites, Indians, and, jointly, black Caribbean and Pakistani.

Other sources of data concerning country of birth, nationality, and ethnic group include the Labour Force Survey and the International Passenger Survey. Although these surveys are based on small, often unrepresentative, samples they nevertheless provide valuable information on the nature of ethnic minorities and the movement of people from one country to another.

Racism, prejudice, and discrimination

Prejudice is a rigid and irrational generalisation about an entire category of people. It is a form of prejudgement, based on strong, inflexible attitudes. Prejudice can be positive or negative, and range from mild to severe. As it is shaped by culture, it is found to some degree in everyone. G. Allport, 'The Nature of Prejudice' (1958) describes how prejudices are based on stereotypes, which are a series of often factually incorrect or exaggerated beliefs about a group of people. Allport suggests that there are two components of racial prejudice: unfavourable attitudes (which are evaluative statements such as 'I don't like Indians'), and mistaken beliefs (which are supposedly factual statements such as 'All Pakistanis have large families'). Races and ethnic groups are frequently depicted in stereotypical form in the media as well as amongst individuals, for example 'mean Jews', 'lazy Africans', 'autocratic Germans'. Prejudices are thus not just located in individual attitudes and beliefs, but are developed and sustained by cultural factors.

Racism is an extreme form of prejudice, based on the belief that one racial group is innately superior or inferior to another. Racism has existed throughout world history, from the Ancient Greeks, through European colonialism, to the Nazi regime in Germany, up to the present day racist views held about immigrants. The racial classifications developed in the nineteenth century are an example of **'scientific racism'**, whereby different racial 'stocks' were ranked in a hierarchy in order of superiority/inferiority. M. Banton, 'What Do We Mean By Racism?' (1969) describes how this view was politically convenient as it helped to justify the colonisation of inferior 'savages'. It also illustrates how racism, like prejudice, is not just an individual concern, but is often embedded in the culture of society to the extent that racist attitudes become an acceptable part of the dominant group's ideology.

Some of the reasons which have been put forward to explain prejudice and racism are summarised below.

AUTHORITARIAN PERSONALITY THEORY

This theory has been expounded by T. Adorno et al, 'The Authoritarian Personality' (1950), who argue that extreme prejudice may develop as a personality trait. They found that people who displayed strong prejudice toward any minority were usually prejudiced against all minorities. These individuals can be identified as having an authoritarian personality, which is characterised by rigid conformity to conventional cultural values, a clear notion of right and wrong, and extreme ethnocentricity. Adorno et al discovered that people with such personalities generally had little education, and strict and demanding parents. It is therefore possible that under such circumstances authoritarian personalities develop aggressive and hostile traits which may be directed at scapegoats in society.

SCAPEGOAT THEORY

J. Dollard, 'Frustration and Aggression' (1939) links prejudice to frustration, with prejudice likely to be more pronounced among people who are themselves disadvantaged. This prejudice is then directed at scapegoats, who are individuals or groups of people who are unfairly blamed for the problems of others, for example Jews under the Nazi regime, Pakistanis and West Indians in Britain today. It appears that, whenever a society is experiencing social and/or economic problems, those who are suffering from widespread frustration or disadvantage may direct their anger at racial or ethnic minority groups. Therefore, housing problems, unemployment, and rising crime may all be blamed on the black population. E. Cashmore, 'The Logic of Racism' (1987) found that many whites in his Birmingham sample blamed blacks for the confusion and distress caused by rapid social change. Another example, from S. Hall et al, 'Policing the Crisis' (1978), illustrates how the state can also scapegoat, such as the attempt to direct attention from the government's failure to stem industrial decline in the 1970s by emphasising the rising tide of black 'muggers'. By cracking down on the perceived problem, the government gained support and diverted attention from the economic issues. Scapegoating may therefore exist on an individual or personal level, or may be part of the state's attempt to protect itself from criticism and win public support at the same time.

CULTURAL THEORY

This theory is based on the premise that certain forms of prejudice are linked to widespread cultural values. E. Bogardus used the concept of 'social distance' to assess prejudice, by measuring how closely people are willing to interact with members of various racial and ethnic categories. He found that measurements of social distance were similar to a society's evaluations of racial and ethnic groups. It appears that cultural perceptions of prejudice become widespread in society, even among non-prejudiced people. The fact that such attitudes are widely shared suggests that there is a 'culture of prejudice' which affects everyone. J. Rex, 'Race and Ethnicity' (1986) argues that racist ideologies are developed and circulated by the dominant group within society in order to maintain the status quo and to discourage movement between racial and ethnic groups. Another view of 'cultural racism' is described by M. Barker, 'The New Racism' (1982), who argues that **'new racism'** is the major form of cultural racism in Britain today. He claims that this ideology has been developed by a group of 'New Right' politicians, intellectuals, and activists, who hope to introduce extreme right-wing policies. By emphasising cultural differences, and focussing on distinctly 'British' symbols such as flags, anthems and traditions, they have established a view that black people are a threat to the 'British way of life'. Fears about jobs and housing are also used to illustrate the threat posed by 'aliens'. P. Gilroy, 'There Ain't No Black in the Union Jack' (1987) suggests that new racism is based on the false assumptions generated by 'ethnic absolutism,' that cultural boundaries are fixed and permanent. Whereas, in reality, cultures are not clearly differentiated, but overlap and interact in a variety of ways.

Ultimately, the cultural theory poses problems of measurement, for it is not possible to accurately assess how much the cultural values of prejudice affect individual perceptions of different racial and ethnic categories.

CONFLICT THEORY

The conflict theory argues that prejudice results from social conflict among various categories of people. From a Marxist perspective, prejudice can be used as an ideology to justify the oppression of minorities, and it can also serve the interests of the elite by dividing the working class and thus reducing class opposition. This view is developed more fully in the section on race and stratification later in this chapter.

Race discrimination or racialism is where people of different races and ethnic minorities are treated unequally in society. Whereas prejudice refers to attitudes and beliefs, discrimination is a matter of behaviour. Like prejudice, however, discrimination can be either positive (conferring special advantages) or negative (causing disadvantage), and it can be overt (open and obvious) or covert (hidden and indirect).

Prejudice and discrimination often occur together although, as R. Merton has described, it is possible for a prejudiced person not to discriminate (possibly fearing legal action), and become a 'timid bigot'. In reverse, Merton labels as 'fair-weather liberals' people who discriminate without being prejudiced (for example a worker discriminating when a superior demands it). Merton completes his typology with the 'active bigot' (someone who is prejudiced and discriminatory), and the 'all-weather liberal', who is free of both prejudice and discrimination.

Prejudice and discrimination are inextricably linked and mutually reinforcing. They can be seen in terms of a vicious circle or cycle, which perpetuates itself over time, and from one generation to the next, as illustrated on the next page.

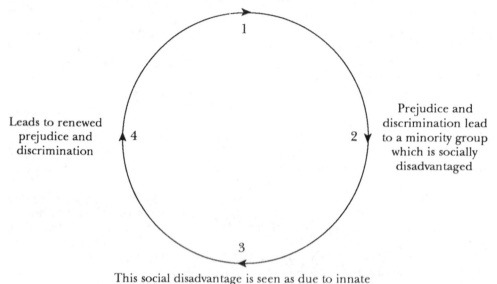

Prejudice and discrimination emerge as an attempt to justify economic exploitation or as a result of ethnocentrism

1

Leads to renewed prejudice and discrimination

4

Prejudice and discrimination lead to a minority group which is socially disadvantaged

2

3

This social disadvantage is seen as due to innate inferiority, not prejudice and discrimination

Substantial evidence exists to show that racial discrimination pervades all areas of life in Britain. In particular, a major series of studies by the Political and Economic Planning Group (PEP), later renamed the Policy Studies Institute (PSI), found that although racial discrimination had lessened a little since the passing of the anti-discrimination laws in the 1960s, it was still evident, particularly in housing and employment. One of the most recent studies by C. Brown, 'Black and White Britain' (1984) conducted under the PEP series, used a wider sample than the studies of the 1960s and 1970s, including a greater variety of classes and localities. However, Brown still found similar results to the previous studies, indicating that blacks continue to suffer greater disadvantages than whites.

Institutional discrimination refers to patterns of discrimination that are incorporated into the fabric of society and embedded in social institutions such as education, the law, employment, housing, etc. Prejudice and discrimination against racial and ethnic groups can thus lead to institutional racism, whereby racism becomes acceptable in society, and is built into its rules and routines. Although enforced racial discrimination has existed in South Africa with the apartheid system, it is questionable whether institutional racism exists in Britain today. R. Jeffcoate, 'Ethnic Minorities and Education' (1984) argues that with anti-discrimination legislation in Britain there is no systematic racism, but social institutions vary in the extent of their racism, with some adopting specific anti-racist policies such as multicultural education, and others simply abiding to the minimum requirements of the legislation. Even with legal equality, however, social institutions can still discriminate in a covert way, as laws do not affect people's behaviour and attitudes.

It may also be queried whether, in fact, racism always leads to racial disadvantage, as the latter may be due to other factors such as unemployment and language difficulties. Finally, it should be noted that not all black people are disadvantaged, and as T. Jones, 'Britain's Ethnic Minorities' (1993) has noted, some ethnic groups (such as the Chinese and Jews) are more successful than others (such as Pakistanis and Bangladeshis).

Race and social class

Racial stratification is concerned with the relationship of immigrants to the class structure of the society in which they have chosen to live. The functionalist view, implicit in most of the legislation regarding immigrants, views all problems to do with immigration as problems of integration. The post-war influx of migrants from the New Commonwealth (mainly India, West Indies, and Pakistan) resulted in the emergence of the **'immigrant-host' model** to explain the consequences of migration. The main assumptions of this model are as follows:

1. The host community is the country into which the migrants are moving, with groups of immigrants holding different norms and values to the host community. This 'strangeness' of the immigrants is a major barrier to their social acceptability and success, as described by S. Patterson, 'Dark Strangers' (1965).
2. The model assumes a homogeneous host community, with a single and distinguishable value system. The immigrants simply have to be integrated into this unitary culture.
3. The host population will be apprehensive about the immigrants' ways and habits, reacting in either a hostile or tolerant manner.
4. Disorganisation in the value system of the host country will occur until the immigrant population has been assimilated into the country's value system, thus restoring the equilibrium.
5. The process of assimilation is thought to follow a particular sequence, from 'contact' to 'competition' to 'accommodation' to 'assimilation', as described by R. Park, 'Race and Culture' (1950).

Criticisms of the functionalist model have been made by many sociologists, notably M. Banton, 'Race Relations' (1967):

1. The immigrant-host model fails to take into account the class nature and divisions which exist within the host community.
2. It fails to recognise the specific role which an immigrant population plays within the existing class structure.
3. The existence of prejudice and discrimination is underestimated, and no explanation is offered for the differential treatment of black immigrants and white migrants.
4. Assimilation into the host culture is automatically seen as 'natural' and 'desirable'. No allowance is made for the wishes of migrants, who might desire to retain their particular culture.

5. The sequence of events leading to assimilation is regarded as non-problematic, with the host population presumably willing to assist in the process.

A Marxist view of the relationship between race and stratification tends to concentrate on the class position of racial and ethnic minorities, and in particular their position in relation to the working class. There are three main models which reflect the Marxist perspective:

THE 'UNITARY' VIEW

This view, as supported by J. Westergaard and H. Resler, 'Class in a Capitalist Society' (1976), takes the strict Marxist line that the relationship to the means of production is the only significant factor regarding stratification. Thus, racial and ethnic minorities are not classified according to their race, but like the indigeneous population, according to their occupation. As the majority of racial and ethnic minorities hold manual jobs they are therefore assigned to the working class. Westergaard Resler believe that class is the key position which people hold in society, and that race acts as a distraction from the major issue, which is the unequal nature of capitalism.

The main criticism of this approach is that it neglects the racial conflicts which exist within the working class itself, and it pays little attention to the existence of racial and ethnic minorities who are in the middle class.

THE 'DIVIDED WORKING CLASS' VIEW

The idea that the working class is 'split' by the existence of racial and ethnic minorities has been proposed by S. Castles and G. Kosack, 'Immigrant Workers and Class Structure in Western Europe' (1973). The central point of the book is that all Western European industrial societies have a migrant population, representing between five percent and 25% of the labour force. The nature of the migrant population depends on particular historical ties between countries, for example in Britain many migrants come from former British colonies. One crucial distinction between migrants in Britain and other parts of Western Europe is that, in the latter, migrants are usually a transitory labour force with no citizenship rights (often called 'guestworkers'). In Britain, migrant labour competes openly and freely with no legal constraints. Castles and Kosack argue that, irrespective of their legal position, the actual functions of migrant populations in different parts of Europe are the same. They make the following general propositions about immigrants in Western Europe as a whole:

1. The presence of migrant workers is structurally essential for the national economies of Western European societies.
2. In all Western European societies immigrants have a specific socio-economic position, in that they take on the most low-paid and least desirable jobs.
3. This low socioeconomic status is reflected in a generally inferior social position in terms of housing, education, etc.
4. There is a tendency for the indigenous working class to perceive immigrants as a competing and alien group, rather than as members of the same class. As a result, racial and prejudicial attitudes develop in the host group.
5. The presence of a stratum of immigrant workers allows for social advancement on the part of the indigenous population. The migrants thus 'split' the working class both objectively (in terms of the jobs they do) and subjectively (migrants have a lower

social status and suffer from racial prejudice). This division in the working class reduces the possibility of achieving class consciousness.
6. Finally, Castles and Kosack argue that labour migration can only be understood as part of the historical development of international capitalism. Thus, there is a relationship between industrial development in Western Europe and underdevelopment in the Third World.

THE 'RACIALISED CLASS FRACTION' VIEW

This variation, expressed by R. Miles, 'Racism and Migrant Labour' (1982), accepts the strict Marxist view of a single working class (the unitary view), but recognises that the class position of racial and ethnic minorities is complicated by the process of '**racialisation**'. R. Miles, 'Racism' (1989) describes racialisation as the way in which racial categories are imposed on people, and lead to social, cultural and moral inferiority. Miles suggests that within social classes there are 'racialised class fractions', for example some blacks may be members of the working class, but within the working class they are singled out as a racialised 'fraction'. These fractions may seek out their own forms of political action, separate from the indigenous working class.

Miles extends his argument to show how black groups do appear in the middle class, but in a 'marginalised' position, where they are seen as a distinct 'fraction', and often treated as racially inferior. This view is often considered as an alternative 'divided working class' theory, but without the use of the term 'migrant labour', which is now considered inappropriate as the majority of the black population have been born in Britain.

The Weberian view of racial stratification reflects Weber's belief that social class should be defined in terms of people's positions in the economic market place, rather than just the relationship to the means of production (as in the Marxist view). Thus, people's property, prestige, and power are all significant indicators of social class. One of the most notable studies which has adopted a Weberian approach to immigrants is J. Rex and R. Moore, 'Race, Community and Conflict' (1967), based on research in Sparkbrook, Birmingham. Rex and Moore attempt to analyse the class position of immigrants and the nature of racial conflict by examining access to housing in the community. Following Weber, Rex and Moore regard ownership of domestic property and ownership of the means of production as equally important in determining social class. Thus, each person participates in two different class systems: one determined by position in the labour market, and one by position in the housing market. Rex and Moore distinguish between five different housing 'classes', with three filled by the indigenous population (owner-occupiers, council house tenants, and tenants of private houses), and two filled by immigrants (lodging house proprietors and tenants of lodging houses). Rex and Moore argue that the 'housing class theory' helps to explain the origins of racial conflict and prejudice, with the immigrants blamed for generating housing problems, and creating the deterioration of property in the inner-city twilight area by multi-occupation and sub-letting. The 'housing classes' identified by Rex and Moore are no longer applicable as many ethnic minorites now occupy their own homes and council houses. However, J. Rex and S. Tomlison, 'Colonial Immigrants in a British City' (1979), found in their study of Handsworth that there still existed a distinct difference between the white working class and the black working class, in areas such as housing, education, and employment. They use the term 'underclass' to describe the diadvantaged position of the black population. Although Rex and Tomlinson reserve the word underclass for racial or ethnic minorities, D. Glasgow, 'The Black Underclass' (1981) uses the term to describe any group of people who are more or less permanently trapped at the bottom of the social ladder. According to P. Saunders, 'Social Class and Stratification' (1990) the underclass has the following features.

Multiple deprivation, where the underclass is disadvantaged in terms of a number of criteria, such as education, employment, housing.

Social marginality, whereby the underclass do not have the power to ensure that their views are heard. Even within political parties and trade unions, the underclass do not find that their interests are promoted.

Culture of fatalism and depair, which arises from marginalisation, and may include feelings of alienation or disaffection, or may even erupt into violent behaviour.

Welfare state dependency, which is often caused by a combination of the above factors which lead ethnic minorities to claim benefits. Thus, rather than having a 'welfare mentality', the underclass may be dependent on the state because of their unemployment and poverty, and because of race discrimination.

The use of the term underclass is not without criticism, mainly because it is not clear whether it applies solely to ethnic minorities or includes white people as well. Another criticism levelled at the use of this term is the extent to which it encourages the labelling and 'victim blaming' of a certain category of people. Links are often made between deviant behaviour and the underclass, thus generating further marginalisation and discrimination against this group of people. Finally, there is a danger that the differences between ethnic minorities and the white population are emphasised at the expense of the overlap between the two. J. Rex, 'Race and Ethnicity', (1986) argues that although immigrant minorities continue to have a much higher statistical risk of disadvantage, there does exist a convergence between what he calls the 'native economy' and the 'minority economy'. This view accepts that the two groups interact, and also that within ethnic groups there is considerable scope for social mobility.

Ethnic minorities in the workplace

The extent of participation in the workplace is generally measured by 'economic activity' rates, which count the number of people in various categories who are in work, or, if unemployed, looking for work. *Social Trends*, 1994 shows that participation rates for white males and Afro-Caribbean males are similar (86% and 80% respectively), but rates for other ethnic minorities are much lower, for example Pakistani/Bangladeshi rate is 72%. For women the differentials are greater, with 72% of white females and 66% of Afro-Caribbean females economically active compared to only 25% of Pakistani/Bangladeshi women.

Although these figures give a generally positive picture of the position of ethnic minorities in the workplace, the areas in which they work are often those with low pay and low status. In 1982 the Policy Studies Institute found that, compared to whites, a significantly higher proportion of Asians and Afro-Caribbeans are manual workers or unemployed. The disadvantaged position of minorities in the labour market is further illustrated by their lower earnings compared to those of whites in similar occupations: C. Oppenheim, 'Poverty: The Facts' (1993). Ethnic minorities still tend to be concentrated in the areas of the economy where they were originally employed as new immigrants in the 1950s and 1960s, that is distribution, hotels and catering, transport and communications, health services. K. Amin, 'Poverty in Black and White' (1992) found that in addition to low status and pay, ethnic minorities also work longer hours, and have less access to training and benefits. It appears that many employers operate a 'dual market' jobs policy, with a primary market of high pay, secure employment, good training and promotion prospects, and a secondary market of low pay, insecurity of employment, and few opportunities for training and promotion. Access to the primary market is often more difficult for ethnic minorities, where skills and qualifications may be suitable, but appearance and attitude may be unacceptable. Thus, R. Jenkins, 'Racism and Recruitment' (1986), found in interviews with managers and personnel officers in the West Midlands, that black candidates often 'failed' at the acceptability fence, when racial stereotypes and ethnocentric attitudes dominated assessments made by potential employers.

Further evidence of the disadvantaged position of ethnic minorities in the workplace can be found in unemployment rates, which are higher than those of the indigenous population. Although unemployment rates for all groups rose in the 1970s and 1980s, to fall back in the 1990s, they have remained higher for ethnic minorities than those for whites at all age groups and at all qualification levels (Labour Force Survey, 1989–91). The sustained increase in unemployment amongst ethnic minorities is partly due to the decline of old manufacturing town based industries, and the rise of new industries in areas away from cities where a large proportion of ethnic minorities live.

In contrast to the disadvantages outlined above, there is, however, evidence to indicate that there is significant upward social mobility amongst certain ethnic minorities, for example Asians and Chinese. Thus, P. Bachu, 'Twice Migrants' (1985) found that an increasing number of ethnic minorities were moving into the middle class, whilst T. Jones, 'Britain's Ethnic Minorities' (1993) describes the growth of Asian businesses and entrepreneurs in the retailing, manufacturing, and restaurant trades.

CHECK YOUR UNDERSTANDING

After reading this chapter you should now be able to define the following terms.

1 Race
2 Ethnicity
3 Racialisation
4 Minority group
5 Assimiliation
6 Pluralism
7 Segregation
8 Prejudice
9 Stereotypes
10 Racism
11 Authoritarian personality theory
12 Scapegoat theory
13 Cultural theory
14 Conflict theory
15 Racialism

16 Institutional discrimination
17 'Immigrant-host' model
18 'Racialised class fractions'

SELF-ASSESSMENT QUESTIONS

1 What is the difference between race and ethnicity?
2 Summarise the patterns of migration into Britain.
3 What are the main explanations for racist behaviour?
4 Why is the 'immigrant-host' model an unsatisfactory explanation of the role of immigrants?
5 According to Castles and Kosack, how do migrant workers 'split' the working class?
6 How does the Weberian perspective on immigration differ from the Marxist view?
7 Explain why ethnic minorities tend to be concentrated in low status and low paid occupations.

CHAPTER TWELVE

RELIGION

LEARNING OBJECTIVES

ON COMPLETION OF THIS CHAPTER THE STUDENT SHOULD BE ABLE TO:

1 DEFINE THE NATURE OF RELIGIOUS BELIEFS
2 SUMMARISE THE FUNCTIONALIST VIEW OF RELIGION
3 EVALUATE THE MARXIST PERSPECTIVE ON RELIGION
4 REVIEW MAX WEBER'S CONTRIBUTION TO THE STUDY OF RELIGION
5 DEFINE THE MAIN TYPES OF RELIGIOUS ORGANISATIONS
6 DESCRIBE THE SECULARISATION DEBATE

The nature of religious beliefs

Belief systems are ideas about the meaning of life that are shared among members of a group or society. If people are agreed that some divine force is guiding their destiny, then this belief system is called a **religion**. Belief systems which are centred on this world and emphasise a human rather than a divine agency, are called **secular ideologies**.

E. Durkheim, 'The Elementary Forms of Religious Life' (1912) produced one of the most famous definitions of religion, arguing that all religious beliefs classify all things into two groups: the **sacred** and the **profane**, or the **religious** and the **secular**. Any physical or supernatural object considered superior in force, invested with holy or mystical power, and accompanied by a set of rituals, can be sacred, for example gods, bones of ancestors, animals, etc. Sacredness is not built into any object, but is a characteristic which is imposed by a group of people. Religions in all societies allocate specific roles to people who are assigned the task of maintaining the sacred items and conducting the ceremonies associated with them, for example priests, ministers, witch doctors, etc. In contrast, profane objects such as possessions and money are wordly and understandable. There are a number of universal aspects of all belief systems, whether they are religious or secular:

1. Beliefs and rituals fulfil both individual and group needs.

2. Belief systems provide ways of understanding and explaining strange or unusual phenomena.
3. Beliefs can help to reduce the anger and injustice which people may feel, for example loss of a loved one, or living in poverty.
4. Ceremonies such as holy communion, bar/bat mitzahs, rain dances, witch hunts, animal/human sacrifices are all designed to bring people together, and to help people deal with the unknown and sometimes threatening aspects of life, such as disasters and personal tragedies.
5. Rituals help to reinforce group norms and mores, and encourage the persistence of customs and traditions.
6. Belief systems have rules of conduct which consist of proscriptions (forms of behaviour which are prohibited) and prescriptions (approved ways of behaving).
7. All belief systems have a vision of the future, which may be resurrection, reincarnation, or a mission to spread the faith to other people.

The functionalist view of religion

E. Durkheim, 'The Elementary Forms of the Religious Life' (1912) described the significance of sacred objects as symbols which represent the **collective conscience** (shared norms, values, etc. within a society). The rituals surrounding the worshipping of such symbols helps to bind society together into a collective unit. Durkheim describes how in technologically simple societies the power of society is represented by a **totem**, a symbol derived from an animal or plant. He uses studies of Australian aborigines to show how the totem of each clan represents both the aborigines' gods and the clan itself, and thereby becomes a focus for collective unity. Durkheim believed that, as the division of labour in modern societies becomes more complex, the collective conscience is weakened. Individuals then make more of their own decisions, with less reliance on and recourse to the collective conscience. Rather than society being seen as sacred, the individual is bound to society by a commitment to an inner spiritual belief which Durkheim called the '**cult of man**'.

In addition to the importance of symbols for the maintenance of the collective conscience Durkheim identified several other key functions of religion for the operation of society:

Social cohesion or the binding together of society's members is achieved through shared lifestage rituals, such as baptism, marriage, funerals. Traditions and customs, such as Easter, Christmas, Passover and Divali, also help to encourage a sense of membership or social solidarity.

Social control is maintained via the rules, mores and lifestyles which are advocated by the particular religion. The Ten Commandments in Christianity provide a moral framework for individuals' lives.

Meaning and purpose refers to the ways in which religion can help to explain uncertainties and disasters, and give comfort to people in times of personal crisis.

B. Malinowski, 'Magic, Science and Religion and Other Essays' (1954) studied Trobriand Islanders and described the importance of rituals in times of emotional stress when the social solidarity was threatened. Thus, life crises such as birth, puberty, marriage and death are surrounded by religious ritual, and give comfort and meaning to people's lives.

Malinowski also described how religious ritual was important as a response to the uncertainties and fears which individuals hold. Thus, the Trobriand Islanders were content to fish in the safety of the lagoon, but when they ventured outside the reef the danger and uncertainty led them to conduct specific rituals which relieved their anxiety and increased their sense of control over the unknown.

T. Parsons reinforces the views of Durkheim and Malinowski by arguing that religion provides and legitimises the **'core values'** of a culture, thereby promoting social solidarity. Thus, religion influences the development of laws and norms in a society as well as promoting values of democracy, self-discipline, etc. Parsons also emphasises the importance of religion for meeting individual needs, by helping to explain experiences of a contradictory or meaningless nature.

R. Bellah, 'The Broken Covenant' (1975) suggests that Durkheim's views on religion and the collective conscience may be suitable for small-scale pre-industrial societies, but in modern societies they cannot be sustained. He argues that present day societies are characterised by a rise in **civil religion** or semi-religion, where individuals are unified by the values and attitudes derived from mainstream religion (Protestantism in the case of Britain and the USA). Hence, individualism, self-discipline, moral worth, etc. create a loyalty towards the society which in turn binds individuals into a coherent group. Bellah uses the USA as an example, where faith in 'Americanism' is maintained via oaths and anthems which include references to God, and national holidays and cultural rituals which emphasise and embrace the 'goodness' of American society (Thanksgiving, Memorial Day).

The major criticism of the functionalist view of religion is that it ignores the dysfunctions or negative aspects of religion. Religious differences can often create divisions within a community, for example Catholics and Protestants in Northern Ireland. C. Glock and R. Stark, 'Religion and Society in Tension' (1965) argue that rather than contributing to social solidarity religion can often pose a threat to social order.

The Marxist view of religion

Marx and Engels did not write extensively on the role of religion in society. There are, however, a number of points they made concerning the relationship between religion and society.

They argued that religion is 'man-made': it is a system of beliefs and practices created by individuals to help people cope with their oppression in a capitalist society. If alienation and exploitation were removed from people's lives (for example in a socialist society) then Marx believed that religion would disappear. However, religion does not always legitimate or justify capitalism, for in communities such as the Israeli kibbutz religion and socialism are successfully combined.

Religion can offer consolation to people in poverty by promising them a brighter future in the afterlife (as in Christianity) or an improved lifestyle following reincarnation (Indian caste system). The notion that people can receive their rewards in another life helps them to come to terms with their situation on earth.

According to Marx religion also acts as an effective instrument of social control, which serves to justify the status quo. However, many neo-Marxists have described the way in which religion can be used by the working class as a means of resistance against oppression and exploitation. They dispute Marx's claim that as part of the superstructure religion is solely determined by the economic base or infrastructure of capitalism. A. Gramsci holds the view that religion can be used by the working class to express and support their ideas and beliefs, leading to **hegemony** – intellectual and moral leadership and control. Examples of this include the US black civil rights movement in the 1960s and the black South African church leaders fighting apartheid. More recent cases can be found in O. Maduro, 'Religion and Social Conflicts' (1982) which illustrates how religion as a conservative force in many Latin American countries (for example Catholicism in El Salvador) can transform itself into a dynamic, political force campaigning for the interests of the poor and downtrodden. This link between religion and politics is called '**liberation theology**'.

Marx applied his view of religion as an ideology to the role of Protestantism in justifying capitalism. Marx argued that the transition from feudalism to capitalism was marked by a decline in Catholicism and a rise in Protestantism. The rising merchant class of the sixteenth century used the individualistic values of Protestantism to further their exploitive interests. Thus, Protestantism satisfied commercial requirements more readily than Catholicism, for it encouraged money lending, and saw the accumulation of wealth as a sign of God's grace and favour. The Protestant ethic of hard work reaping high rewards enabled the early industrialists to justify their exploitation of the working class. M. Weber criticised Marx's analysis of religion as ideology, for whereas Marx viewed Protestantism as the product of capitalism, Weber argued that Protestantism helped to produce capitalism.

Max Weber and religion

The functionalist and Marxist views on religion both take a structuralist approach, whereas Weber takes an interpretive perspective as well as a macro view on the significance of religion. Weber conducted a number of detailed studies of some of the world's major religions, and agreed with Marx that religion did sometimes act as a form of social control. Weber was also concerned to emphasise the role which religion played in providing 'meaning' for people's lives and helping to define their identities.

Weber used his theory of social action to examine the nature of religion and social change. He criticised Marx's analysis of religion as ideology, and whereas Marx viewed Protestantism as the *product of capitalism*, Weber argued that Protestantism helped to *produce capitalism*. Weber's analysis of the relationship between Protestantism and capitalism is contained in 'The Protestant Ethic and the Spirit of Capitalism' (1958), originally published in 1904–05. Weber intended to demonstrate how the ideas and beliefs formed within the socioeconomic structure can change the material conditions of life. In particular, in western societies, the development of capitalism, or '**rational action**', required a particular set of values and economic conditions. The Protestant religion, and in particular Calvinism, which influenced many early Protestant movements such as Puritans, Baptists, Quakers, played a major role in creating the cultural atmosphere within which capitalism could develop. Calvinism refers to the strict form of Protestantism derived from the ideas and teachings of John Calvin (1509–64), the French reformer and theologian. His name is associated in particular with the concept of **predestination** – the doctrine that all human action is determined by God from birth, and that certain souls are predestined or selected for salvation, and others are assigned to damnation or to perish. Followers of Calvin aimed for salvation by adopting values such as hard work, disdain for idleness, and self-discipline. These ideas, values and ethics embodied what Weber called the **'spirit of capitalism'**, for the Calvinist values restraining spending led to the greater accumulation of wealth, thereby providing favourable conditions for the development of capitalism. The Calvinist theory of predestination led many people to assume that they were the chosen ones, and by 'intense worldly activity' proved their favoured position. Thus, hard work, frugality, and the re-investment of profits became signs of God's grace and evidence of their guaranteed salvation.

According to Weber, Protestantism thus had significant but unintended consequences for the economic system of capitalism by encouraging a rational, calculating, efficient approach to business. This represents a challenge to Marx's position of economic determinism which argues that religion merely reflects the economic base of society. However, although Weber argued that Calvinism played a major role in creating the climate in which the capitalist spirit could thrive, he was aware that Calvinism alone did not cause capitalism. Other factors, such as the development of technology, were also important in creating the 'right' conditions for the transition to capitalism.

CRITICISMS OF WEBER

Doubt has been cast on Weber's theory that Calvinism preceded capitalism. Eisenstadt and Tawney argue that the first great upsurges in capitalism occurred in Catholic Europe before the Protestant Reformation. K. Kautsky, 'Foundations of Christianity' (1953) defends Marx's view that early capitalism preceded and therefore led to the establishment of Protestantism, as a means of legitimating the position of the capitalist class. K. Samuelson, 'Religion and Economic Action' (1961), describes the existence of Calvininst communities in Scotland which were not based on capitalist principles, which would appear contrary to Weber's view.

Weber failed to realise that there are other religions such as Hinduism, Islam, and Judaism in particular, which contain elements which support rational capitalism.

There is doubt concerning Weber's interpretation of the attitudes of Calvinists. Many followers saw wealth as evil and the acqusition of it as a form of temptation. If followers truly desired salvation, why did Calvinists re-invest their profits rather than help the poor?

Weber's interpretive approach has been used by other sociologists. P. Berger et al, 'The Homeless Mind' (1974) argue that the rationalising nature of Protestantism has helped to 'demystify' the modern world and taken away the mystery and magic of the unknown. The spread of rationalisation has led to an increase in impersonal relationships, and left people cut off from social support and comfort – 'homeless' in Berger's terms.

Types of religious organisations

The earliest attempts to classify religious organisations were made by Max Weber and Ernst Troeltsch, who both focused on the range of religious groups within Christianity. Weber and Troeltsch both distinguished between a church and a sect, but Troeltsch emphasised the degree of tension between a religious group and the wider society to differentiate between the two. From Troeltsch's perspective churches and sects are almost opposites in the ways in which they relate to the larger society.

CHURCHES

A church is a formal religious organisation which is well integrated into the larger society. It is a long-established religious group, which has a complex, formal hierarchy with a bureaucratic structure. The aim of a church is to be 'inclusive' in its membership, by being open to all people in society. There is a professional clergy, organised hierarchically, and traditional rituals and services. Churches accept society's norms and are often formally integrated into the values and institutions of society. British schools continue to have a legal obligation to teach predominantly Christian values.

A church can take one of two forms. It may be an ecclesia, which refers to a church that is formally allied with the state, for example the Catholic Church and the Roman Empire, the Anglican Church and England, Islam and Iran. A church may also be a denomination, which is separate from the state, but accepts the norms of society and is recognised by most people as being very similar to the established churches. Denominations have less formal organisations, and in addition to a hierarchy of paid officials, also have a substantial number of lay preachers (non-clergy). Rituals are usually formal, although some denominations welcome spontaneity from the congregation during services. Examples of denominations include Baptists, Methodists, United Reformed Church.

SECTS

A sect is an informal religious organisation that is not well integrated into the larger society. Sects are 'exclusive', in that they they set clear barriers between themselves and the outside world, clearly distinguishing between members and non-members. They lack the rigid hierarchy of churches and professional clergy, and have leaders who display charismatic qualities. Sects have strict discipline codes, with rules concerning conduct and missionary activity, with active recruitment and proselytising expected of members. Entry into the sect is ususally by conversion or personal transformation, or sponsorship by an existing member. Sects regard themselves as select, chosen groups of people who are superior to other members of society. There is little ritual in services, with personal experience and emotion highly valued. The repression of individuality is a common feature of sects, with members participating in group 'devotions', or even group marriages (for example the Unification Church or Moonies). Historically, sects have arisen out of conflict with the established churches and are a result of religious schisms: Methodism emerged as a branch of Protestantism. Other examples include Jehovah's Witnesses and Seventh Day Adventists. Today, sects are more likely to be created outside the established churches, for example Hare Krishnas, Moonies.

M. Weber argued that sects are more likely to emerge amongst the under-privileged, or those at the bottom of the social hierarchy. These people form a 'theodicy of disprivilege' which is a religious explanation for their lowly position in society, arguing that they have been exclusively chosen ('enlightened') for salvation. C. Glock and R. Stark, 'Religion and Society in Tension' (1965) argue that membership of sects is not confined to the economically disadvantaged, but attracts any individual who feels a sense of relative deprivation. This includes economic, social, ethical, psychic, and organismic (physical ill-health) deprivations. In order for the sect to develop, the feeling of deprivation must be shared with other individuals; no existing outlet is available for the resolution of the deprivation, and a leader must emerge. Thus, in America in the 1960s many ethnic minority members turned to religious sects (such as the Black Muslim movement) in the hope of alleviating their social and economic deprivation.

Mass Moonie wedding in Korea

B. Wilson, 'Contemporary Transformations of Religion' (1976) uses the case of the rise of Methodism in England to show how sects develop in conditions of social change and disruptive social processes, or anomie.

C. Glock and R. Bellah (eds.), 'The New Religious Consciousness' (1976) explain the growth of sects from the 1960s onwards in terms of a 'crisis of meaning'. Traditionally, American culture has been based on the notion of **utilitarian individualism** which says that in an open society individual talent will be rewarded with economic success. In the 1960s the reality of the 'American Dream' was being questioned, and events such as the Vietnam War and the Black Civil Rights Movement led to the rejection of utilitarian individualism by many young people. The development of a counter culture could be seen in the growth of sects which emphasised integration, inner harmony and sensitivity, such as Krishna Consciousness, the Unification Church (Moonies), Happy-Healthy-Holy Organisation.

H.R. Niebuhr, 'The Social Sources of Denominationalism' (1922) argues that sects are necessarily transient groups, which either develop into denominations (such as Methodism) or disappear. The sect can change or disintegrate for a number of reasons:

1. Second generation members might not be committed to the values of the sect.
2. Existing members might come into contact with the outside world, and alter their views concerning the sect.
3. The death of a charismatic leader leads to the 'routinisation' of a sect (from Weber), and bureaucratic structures develop to continue the day-to-day work.
4. Social mobility by sect members brings greater wealth and security, and the desire to re-integrate within society.

B. Wilson, 'Religious Sects' (1970) argues that the question of whether sects develop into denominations depends on how the sects respond to the problem of 'What shall we do to be saved?'. Wilson describes seven responses to this issue: conversionist, revolutionist, introversionist, manipulationist, thaumaturgical, reformist, and utopian. Using this categorisation, Wilson argues that conversionist sects are most likely to become denominations, because their 'born again' message must be spread through a highly bureaucratic organisation, for example Jehovah's Witnesses. In contrast, introversionist sects are least likely to develop into denominations, as their sole aim is to achieve salvation by withdrawing into their own community. Although there is much debate concerning the transition from sect to denomination, little research has been carried out on the process by which a denomination changes into a sect, for example Salvation Army.

CULTS

The terms cult and sect are often used interchangeably, and although they are similar in some respects there are important differences. Roy Wallis suggests that cults, like sects, are highly unconventional in terms of the surrounding society and often have charismatic leaders, but unlike sects, they permit members' involvement with other groups in society. There is minimal organisational structure in cults, with an emphasis on 'inner divinity' and personal spiritual experiences. Cults therefore demand little formal commitment from their members. Cults can form and disperse very quickly, or may become incorporated into an established church, for example the Church of Jesus Christ of Latter-Day Saints (Mormons). Many cults arise from the diffusion of religious ideas from one society to another: Transcendental Meditation (TM) originates from India, but spread to Europe and the United States in the 1950s, reaching its peak of popularity in the 1970s.

NEW RELIGIOUS MOVEMENTS (NRMS)

The 1960s and 1970s witnessed a tremendous growth in the number of non-conventional religious movements, with many groups difficult to categorise as either cults or sects. Previous typologies (Broom, Selznick, Wilson, Yinger) proved inadequate in describing movements which often had characteristics previously identified exclusively with either sects or cults, for example the Siddha Yoga movement (a cult) is highly organised. The use of the term New Religious Movements (NRMs) came to be applied to any religious movement outside the established churches and denominations. R. Wallis, 'The Sociology of the New Religions' (1985) has attempted to classify NRMs into ones which draw on the Christian tradition (such as the Jesus People); those that are derived from non-western religions (such as Hinduism, Buddhism); and groups which have adapted ideas and beliefs from psychology and psychotherapy (Scientology). In addition, Wallis has divided all NRMs into three types:

World-affirming NRMs. These groups lack many of the characteristics of the established religions, and do not directly refer to God. They are not overtly 'religious', and accept the outside world, emphasising the positive aspects of society, stressing the potential of mankind to improve and transform his/her environment, for example Transcendental Meditation.

World-accommodating NRMs. These movements are also unlike the established religions, but nevertheless encourage their members to remain within society whilst remaining critical of it. Followers are taught to develop their 'inner power' in order to be able to come into contact with their spiritual self, for example Siddha Yoga.

World-rejecting NRMs. Whilst world-affirming and world-accommodating NRMs are more 'cult-like' in their organisation and attitude towards the outside world, the world-rejecting NRMs have more 'sect-like' characteristics. Thus, they share some of the features of the established religions, including a clear concept of God, an organisational structure, and a charismatic founder. However, they are openly critical of, and even hostile towards, the secular (outside) world, holding the belief that true salvation lies with their movement alone. They clearly differentiate between members and non-members, expect a high level of commitment to the group, and disprove of many secular activities such as joining a trade union or political party. Jehovah's Witnesses are a good example of a world-rejecting NRM which co-exists with the outside world, whereas some NRMs withdraw totally from mainstream society into a communal lifestyle: the Moonies created their own town in Oregon, USA.

Although there is evidence to support all three types of NRMs, individual members of NRMs may have a different relationship to the same movement. It is possible that some individuals seek self-fulfilment and escape from the 'real world' rather than rejection of society in a world-rejecting NRM. Also, the operation of a NRM at local, regional, national, and even international level may differ widely, and not always 'fit' a particular type. Finally, the use of the term *New* Religious Movement may imply that these groups have all emerged in the past thirty years, whereas many of them are long-established either in Britain or abroad.

MILLENARIAN MOVEMENTS

There is a tendency to concentrate on the development of religious organisations in industrial societies, at the expense of other areas of the world. New Religious Movements can be found throughout the world in many diferent cultures. Some of these NRMs are called 'millenarian movements' and are similar to Seventh Day Adventists and Jehovah's Witnesses in that they promise that the world will be suddenly transformed in a supernatural manner to a new social order. The movement is organised around the preparation required for this radical change in the social world. Millenarian movements thus predict a merger of the world of the supernatural and the world of people into a pain-free world of human perfection. These movements often develop in societies which are undergoing colonisation or have been colonised, or are being settled by outsiders. R.M. Itley, 'The Last Days of the Sioux Nation' (1963) has described how, in the 1890s, the Teton Sioux developed a millenarian movement in response to the American government's attempts to force them to live on reservations. The loss of their buffalo herds and the imposition of a farming economy, coupled with the erosion of their traditions, led the Teton to develop the 'Ghost Dance' religion. This was based on the belief that the world would one day be renewed, with the white people buried under the earth, the buffalo herds restored, and the traditions re-instated. The Teton danced the Ghost Dance, wearing 'ghost shirts' which were supposed to protect them from the white men's bullets. This growing movement made the American government uneasy, and they sent in troops to engage in a battle at Wounded Knee. The Teton were massacred, and the Ghost Dance religion consequently ended.

Millenarian movements are frequently found amongst deprived groups in the population, as a response to poverty or natural disasters such as plague or famine. N. Cohn, 'The Pursuit of the Millenium' (1957) argues that they also develop during periods of rapid social change when norms are displaced, for example during colonisation. Occasionally they can develop into political movements, as was the case in South Africa, where Marxists would argue that they represent a 'proletarian self-consciousness'.

The secularisation debate

The word secular refers to something which is not sacred or spiritual, but earthly or worldly. B. Wilson, 'Religion in Secular Society' (1966) defines secularisation as 'the process whereby religious thinking, practices and institutions lose social significance'. Supporters of the secularisation thesis argue the following:

1. The power and prestige of religious institutions has declined.
2. The influence of religion on people's attitudes and values has reduced.
3. Religious practices such as church marriages and collective worship are not as frequently followed as in the past.

There are particular problems with measuring secularisation, since statistical evidence may not always be reliable or valid. Definitional problems are also an issue, for example church membership is defined in various ways, such as according to baptism and/or confirmation, or attendance on significant days such as Easter Sunday. Finally, there are methodological questions concerning the representativeness of samples and the interpretation of people's answers. The evidence and arguments in favour of secularisation are summarised below:

There has been a steady decline in participation in formal religious activities, such as church attendance and rites of passage (marriage, baptism, etc.) The statistical evidence for secularisation raises the general problems of the use of official statistics (see Chapter 10). D. Martin, 'A Sociology of English Religion' (1967) argues that the figures must be judged for their validity, as many people attend church or participate in ceremonies for non-religious reasons. Also, the criteria used by the church organisations for defining church membership (attendance, electoral roll, baptism, etc.) must be taken into account when using such figures. With an awareness of these methodological problems, the statistics reveal the following trends:

(i) In 1851, just under 40% of the adult population attended church once a week, but by 1900 this figure was 35%, in 1950 it was 20%, and in 1970 only 12% were going to church once a week. Since the 1970s the figure has remained constant at between 10% and 12%.

(ii) In 1929, 56% of marriages in England and Wales were conducted in the Church of England, compared to 37% in 1973, and only 29% in 1976 and in subsequent years. There has been a corresponding increase in Register Office marriages, with civil marriages accounting for only 26% of all marriages in 1929, compared to 50% in 1976 and subsequent years.

(iii) In 1950, 65% of all babies born alive in England were baptised in the Church of England, compared to just under 50% in 1973.

The decline in the power of the church or religious disengagement provides further evidence for secularisation. From the Middle Ages up to Victorian times the church has been a central force in society, making a major contribution to political life, the professions (medicine, law, education), and the economy (one in every 30 males was in the service of the church during the Middle Ages). In Britain today the Church of England has less influence over government, education, law, welfare, and morals than it has had in the past.

There is an assumption that religious beliefs and influence were more significant in the past, and that **desacralisation** (or the rationalisation of the world), with an increased emphasis on rational or scientific thought, has occurred. M. Weber saw secularisation as an aspect of the wider process of rationalisation, with religious explanations of the world gradually being replaced with secular or material explanations. He argued that the physical separation of the urban industrial workers from their church led to the search for fulfilment in material consumption. However, there is evidence to indicate that clergy in the Middle Ages were concerned about the lack of religiosity, and the presence of superstitious and magical beliefs: D. Martin, 'General Theory of Secularisation' (1978). Despite the existence of these heretical beliefs and practices, B. Wilson argues that nevertheless people were still 'believers', and thus the amount of secularisation is difficult to measure.

The emergence of New Religious Movements is often cited as evidence that secularisation is taking place. Yet the fact that these groups have beliefs contradicts the notion that they are not 'religious'. B. Wilson claims that NRMs are 'superficially religious', but he accepts heretical beliefs of the Middle Ages as evidence of religiosity. There is thus a diversity of opinion over what does and does not constitute secularisation.

A number of criticisms of the secularisation debate have been advanced, most of which are contained in P. Glasner, 'The Sociology of Secularisation' (1977). Some specific arguments against secularisation include the following:

Statistical evidence of a decline in church attendance and participation in ceremonies and rituals cannot be accepted at face value, for individuals hold different reasons and meanings for their actions. N.J. Demerath and P.E. Hammond, 'Religion in Social Context' (1969) argue that there are methodological problems when attendance and belief are equated. Glasner criticises the over-concentration on measuring church-oriented religion, as many people worship in private. R. Jowell et al(ed.), 'British Social Attitudes' (1992) found that 69% of people in Britain believe in God, 55% believe in life after death, 54% accept the existence of heaven, etc. Further evidence for the prevalence of non-organised religion is to be found in descriptions of personal spiritual events which people have claimed to have experienced.

Religious disengagement has not meant a withdrawal of the church from wider society, but has led to specialisation in the issues with which it is involved. Thus, many churches have spawned a range of voluntary organisations, such as the Salvation Army, and are concerned with specific social issues such as divorce, nuclear weapons, poverty, euthanasia, etc.

Desacralisation has not necessarily occurred, as many people in Britain still claim to have experienced some sort of religious experience (D. Hay, D. Martin). Although secularisation has occurred in terms of religious institutions, P. Berger argues that religious pluralism, with the emphasis on private worshop, has emerged. The growth of sects also provides evidence of a religious revival or **'resacralisation'**, indicating religious transformation rather than decline. The argument concerning the replacement of religion by science depends on the definitions given to them, for if they are both interpreted as 'belief systems' then it is difficult to argue that 'spiritual' religion has been superceded by 'rational' science. As all ideas and beliefs are formed within a social context, both religion and science can be viewed as 'universes of meaning'.

Secularisation appears to be self-limiting. D. Martin, 'General Theory of Secularisation' (1978) and R. Stark and W.S. Bainbridge, 'The Future of Religion: Secularisation, Revival, and Cult Formation' (1985) argue that secularisation in Britain and Western Europe has reached a peak, and is reversing, resulting in religious revival. Thus, sectarian groups branch off as established religions become too worldly, new faiths are imported or developed to fill the gap left by the conventional religious organisations, and a process of re-birth in religiosity occurs. The growth of sects and cults, the popularity of the 'house-church' movement and bible groups, the increasing appeal of non-Christian religions, and the emergence of 'New Age' groups (pagan, UFO supporters, etc.) in Western societies has strengthened the case against secularisation.

Whilst the secularisation of religious institutions has occurred by a withdrawal from churches in Britain, it has happened within churches in America. Church attendance figures in America average 54%, compared to 20% in Britain (British Social Attitudes Special International Report, 1989), which seems to suggest that Americans are more religious. However, W. Herberg, 'Protestant, Catholic, Jew' (1955) argues that one aspect of 'being American' requires a public commitment to religious beliefs within a religious organisation. It does not matter which religion is adhered to, so long as people claim allegiance to a set of beliefs. Herberg states that religion is thus part of the American way of life, and it became secular as a means of binding society together. The greater heterogeneity of American communities and the absence of an established church provided the conditions under which religious institutions have accommodated religious differences and promoted a sense of community rather than specific religious beliefs.

The rise in **religious fundamentalism**, particularly in the United States, indicates that there is religious revival rather than decline. Religious fundamentalism is when conservative religious organisations seek to restore what are viewed as fundamental elements of religion, such as restoration of traditional values, literal interpretation of the Bible, etc. The process is most evident among Protestants, and to a lesser extent among Catholics and Jews. It came to significance in the US during the 1980s presidential campaign of Ronald Reagan, who was supported by a number of conservative Christian organisations, and illustrated how powerful many of these evangelical groups had become. The fundamentalist movement is most apparent amongst Pentecostals, Southern Baptists, Seventh-Day Adventists and other 'born again' religions, with their influence extending to the establishment of schools, Bible colleges, periodicals, and the increasing use of television (the 'electronic church') to promote their views.

The rise of **'televangelism'** or the **'electronic church'** has shown that religion is capable of attracting a large audience. J.K. Hadden and C.E. Swain, 'Prime Time Preachers: The Rising Power of Televangelism.' (1981) describe the increasing use of television as a vehicle for religion from the 1960s, when satellite and cable TV became popular. Televangelism peaked in the 1980s, declining due to a series of sex and money scandals featuring several nationally known presenters (for example Jim and Tammy Bakker). It is difficult to know whether viewers are already pre-disposed to religious beliefs, or whether the programmes actively encourage an upsurge in religious beliefs. As approximately 25% of the American population are already fundamentals or evangelicals it is likely that the programmes are preaching to the converted, rather than recruiting large numbers of new members.

Views concerning the nature and extent of secularisation can be seen in the theoretical approaches which were outlined at the beginning of this chapter.

K. Marx argued that secularisation would continue to increase as capitalism advanced and socialism gradually replaced capitalist relations of production. He argued that in a socialist society religion would no longer be necessary to give people 'false consciousness' as there would no longer be any need or reason to justify differentials in wealth and income. It was thus inevitable that religion would decline and eventually disappear.

E. Durkheim viewed secularisation as representing a decline in the collective conscience and social solidarity of society. Increasing **industrialisation** and **urban-isation** fragmented society, leading to excessive individualism and anomie, which would undermine religious beliefs and practices. Greater social and geographical mobility would further reduce social cohesion, leading to secularisation. Durkheim did not see secularisation as an inevitable or irreversible process, but that if people wanted religion to survive then they would have to promote its practices and rituals.

M. Weber was concerned with the increased rationality of the social world which came with industrialisation. He believed that many religions actually contributed to this rationality, for example Calvinism and Protestant denominations such as Methodists and Quakers promoted a more practical and less 'spiritual' approach to the world. As a result of the decline in ritual and tradition fostered by these religions, people have lost ways in which religion can give meaning to their lives. The emphasis on norms, values, and a sense of spirituality offered by sects and cults has led to a resurgence of religious belief and meaning which is at odds with the rationality of the more established religious organisations.

P. Berger argues that twentieth century modern industrial societies have witnessed the enormous growth of a wide range of religious beliefs and practices – a **plurality** of belief systems. Greater geographical and social mobility, combined with media influence, ensure that people are exposed to so many belief systems that they undermine each other, leaving no overall religion or single belief system. As a result people follow their own personal or **'privatised' belief system**, which is often comprised of various elements taken from a range of available religions.

CHECK YOUR UNDERSTANDING

After reading this chapter you should now be able to define the following terms

1 Belief systems
2 The sacred
3 The profane
4 A totem
5 Core values
6 Civil religion
7 Hegemony
8 Liberation theology

 9 Calvinism
10 Predestination
11 Spirit of capitalism
12 A church
13 An ecclesia
14 A denomination
15 A sect
16 Religious schisms
17 Theodicy of disprivilege
18 Utilitarian individualism
19 New Religious Movements
20 Millenarian movements
21 Secularisation
22 New Age groups
23 Religious fundamentalism
24 Televangelism

SELF-ASSESSMENT QUESTIONS

1 What are the main characteristics of belief systems?
2 How did Durkheim view religion?
3 How do neo-Marxists differ from Marx in their perception of the link between religion and social control?
4 According to Weber, how did Calvinism aid the development of capitalism?
5 What is the difference between a church and a sect?
6 What are New Religious Movements?
7 Summarise the evidence in favour of secularisation.
8 What examples of religious revival exist to contradict secularisation?

'A' LEVEL SOCIOLOGY ESSAY QUESTIONS

1 Compare and contrast functionalist and Marxist explanations of the role of religion in society (AEB, summer, 1992).
2 Evaluate the usefulness of the distinction between church and sect in explanations of the changing nature of religious beliefs and religious participation in modern society (AEB, summer, 1995).
3 'Sociologists do not agree on the meaning of secularisation but they do agree that it is taking place.'

Critically discuss this statement with reference to relevant sociological evidence (AEB, summer, 1996).

CHAPTER THIRTEEN

POLITICS

LEARNING OBJECTIVES

ON COMPLETION OF THIS CHAPTER THE STUDENT SHOULD BE ABLE TO:

1 DESCRIBE HOW POWER CAN BE DEFINED AND MEASURED
2 DISTINGUISH BETWEEN DIFFERENT FORMS OF POLITICAL SYSTEMS
3 EXPLAIN AND EVALUATE ELITE THEORIES OF POWER
4 EXPLAIN AND EVALUATE PLURALIST THEORIES OF POWER
5 EXPLAIN AND EVALUATE MARXIST THEORIES OF POWER
6 DESCRIBE AND EXPLAIN PATTERNS OF VOTING BEHAVIOUR IN THE U.K.

The nature of power

Politics refers to any set of social relationships which involve power, rule, or **authority**. This broad definition includes parental authority over children, the rules of a social club, authority of management over workers, and the power of government to legislate. These examples refer to particular political relationships found in all societies. This chapter, however, is concerned with the overall nature and distribution of power in Western industrialised nations.

Power is defined by M. Weber, 'Economy and Society' (1978) as the ability to achieve desired ends despite resistance from others. Weber identified two forms of power **coercion** is based on physical or psychological force, whereas **authority** involves the exercise of power which is socially sanctioned. Weber believes that authority is more effective than coercion because it involves consensus about cultural values and the means of attaining them. He identified three types of authority, based on **tradition**, **charisma**, and **rationality** (see Chapter 6), with rational legal authority the dominant form in industrial societies.

Another view of power is presented by S. Lukes, 'Power: A Radical View' (1974), which argues that there are 'three faces of power' which must be appreciated in order to understand the full nature of power. The first face of power he calls 'success in decision making', which is a pluralist view insisting that power can be seen from the outcome of a decision-making process. The distribution of power can be ascertained via the 'issue method', or the study of specific issues to examine who gets their own way in the decision-making process. Those most frequently successful in getting the results they want will have the most power. From this first face of power, it would appear that western industrial democracies are based on a number of groups exercising various degrees of power. The second face of power Lukes calls 'managing the agenda', which is supported by critics of the pluralist view, such as P. Bachrach and M. Baratz, who argue that power depends on control of the agenda for debate. Power involves the promotion of some issues for discussion, and the exclusion of other issues from the agenda. The third face of power described by Lukes is called 'manipulating the wishes of others', in which power is seen as the ability to shape the wishes and desires of others. The general public are persuaded that their interests are the same as those who are in power: from a Marxist view, the ruling class exploits a subject class through an imposed consensus.

The nature of power can also be examined from the viewpoint of the three main sociological perspectives.

The functionalist view of power reflects the emphasis on **value consensus** in this perspective. The government thus implements the collective goals in a power relationship which promotes the whole of the social system. According to T. Parsons, 'Sociological Theory and Modern Society' (1967) the amount of power in society varies with the rate at which the collective goals are achieved. This is known as a '**variable-sum**' concept of power, as power is not fixed or constant, but may increase or decrease according to how effectively the social goals are achieved. However, it has been argued (by A. Giddens and M. Mann) that in modern industrial societies institutions such as armies and economic organisations have much greater power than in the past, because of their organisational effectiveness. In other words, these organisations can intervene more extensively in people's lives because of bureaucracy, tax, official records, etc., and therefore have greater power than in pre-industrial societies.

M. Weber's view on the nature of power is in direct contrast to Parsons' analysis. For Weber, **power differentials** reflect the extent to which some individuals hold power over others. He rejects the notion of collective goals, arguing that governments and organisations have **sectional interests** which are designed to further their own ends, rather than those of society as a whole. Weber's concept of power can be referred to as a '**constant-sum**' view or '**zero-sum**' approach: the amount of power in a society is fixed, and fluctuates between competing groups and individuals.

K. Marx saw power relationships as a reflection of economic relationships, with the infrastructure or economic base determining the superstructure or social institutions. In a capitalist society the bourgeoisie holds power over the rest of the population. According to Marx, the state is not impartial, as Parsons argues, but it represents sectional interests, favouring the bourgeoisie at the expense of the proletariat. In order to legitimise their class power the bourgeoisie use social institutions (schools, mass media, etc.) to wield **ideological power**. The dominant economic class is therefore the **ruling class**.

Political systems

Political activity is usually associated with government, and in particular the methods by which governments implement their power and rule the population. There are a number of political systems which can be used to govern people.

MONARCHY

This is a type of political system in which power is passed on from generation to generation within a single family. Its history can be traced back to Biblical days, with the power legitimated by traditional authority. In medieval Europe absolute monarchs enjoyed power based on the **divine right of kings**. Today, many European countries (UK, Spain, Netherlands, Sweden, Denmark) have **constitutional monarchies**, in which the monarchs are merely symbolic heads of state, and government is conducted by elected officials, legitimated by rational authority.

DEMOCRACY

Democracy literally means 'government by the people', from the Greek words demos (people) and kratos (power). A **direct or participatory democracy**, such as the one which operated in Ancient Athens, is not feasible in a modern nation state. Instead, large complex societies in which people cannot participate directly in decision making have evolved a system of **representative democracy**, where authority is placed in the hands of elected leaders who are accountable to the people. Democracy is based on **rational-legal authority**, with an extensive bureaucracy underpinning the elected representatives. In addition, there are a wide range of competing organisations (businesses, trade unions, pressure groups) which are also a part of a modern democracy. Both capitalist and socialist economic systems have claimed to be democratic, and since 1989 the break-up of communist Eastern Europe and the Soviet Union has led to more countries moving towards a democratic state. Modern liberal democracies, which are generally found in affluent industrial societies, have the following characteristics:

1. The people have some form of control over the representatives in power. This is usually achieved by means of regular and fair elections. In Britain a general election must be held at least every five years.
2. People have the right to vote and to engage in political activity.
3. All voters are equal under the law, and each voter has only one vote.
4. People have the freedom of speech and opinion.
5. When people have exercised their democratic rights, a decision will be taken according to the wishes of the majority.

In theory, in a democracy the people have power, but in practice, this may not be so. In democracies there exist 'undemocratic' elements, such as censorship of the press and television, the existence of an unelected monarch, the presence of unelected Lords, and an Official Secrets Act which controls people's access to government information.

It has been suggested that **regional devolution** of power (Wales and Scotland having their own parliaments or even counties having greater autonomy) would increase the level of democracy and participation in the decision-making process.

TOTALITARIANISM

Totalitarianism refers to a political system which denies the majority participation in the government of the country, and at the same time extensively regulates people's lives. The fascist states of Germany and Italy in the 1930s under Hitler and Mussolini are examples of totalitarian systems, as well as the former Soviet Union and present day China. Totalitarianism can therefore span the political spectrum from the far right of

Nazism to the extreme left of the People's Republic of China. It is also found in countries with capitalist economies as well as socialist ones.

Totalitarian governments exert total control over the population, and attempt to persuade people to support the government by a range of methods. No organised political opposition is permitted, with no legal right to assemble for political purposes. Any pro-democracy actions, such as Beijing's Tiananmen Square show of force in 1989, are swiftly quashed, with family and friends encouraged by the government to inform on the dissidents. Access to information is severely restricted, and only recently in the Soviet Union has the mass media been able to act independently from the government. Totalitarian governments also aim to control people's lives by encouraging inward commitment to the system: posters of leaders and political banners and flags are widely displayed, and political messages are continuously broadcast to socialise citizens into supporting the government and the system.

AUTHORITARIANISM

A political system based on authoritarian government or dictatorship also denies the majority of the population participation in government, but has no interest in controlling areas of people's lives. Examples from the recent past include Haiti, Panama, and Chile. Under this system there is no legal means of removing and replacing the leaders, who may be absolute monarchs or military juntas. Any political opposition under this system is suppressed by force, with people's civil rights ignored.

Elite theories of power

Elite theories emerged in response to Marx's view that true democracy can only be achieved under a socialist system. However, the 'classical' elite theories of V. Pareto and G. Mosca are based on the belief that in all societies, even socialist ones, the population can be divided into two main groups: a **ruling minority** and the **ruled**. They reject Marx's theory of a proletarian revolution leading to communism and equality, but argue that a new ruling elite will simply replace the one which existed under capitalism. The elite in any society directs the nation, usually in a manner which aids the interests of the elite. The ruled, however, are seen by Pareto and Mosca as largely uninterested in the main issues concerning the nation, accepting the propaganda issued by the elite to justify its position.

V. Pareto (1848–1923) proposed that the concentration of power in the hands of a minority was inevitable, because such people are 'better fitted' for such a role. The innate abilities and talents of these people make them 'natural leaders', in contrast to the ruled masses, who are inherently unfit to hold power. Pareto's view is based on the leaders holding personality characteristics. **'Lions'** (such as military dictators) achieve power because of their directiveness and force, whereas **'foxes'** (such as political leaders in western democracies) cunningly manipulate the masses. Social change encourages the development of new elites, so that there is a never-ending **'circulation of elites'** in all societies throughout all periods of history. These cyclical patterns in elite rule often mean that new recruits have to be assimilated from the non-elite, and trained accordingly. Although the internal composition of the elite may change, the fact or omnipresence of elite rule continues.

Pareto's views have been criticised for being too simplistic, particularly for not making any distinction between different types of political systems. He assumes that all societies are characterised by the same process of elite circulation, when in fact many elites remain unchanged throughout history, for example the ruling Brahmin caste in India. T. Bottomore, 'Elites and Society' (1993) concludes that there is a lack of sound evidence to support Pareto's ideas.

G. Mosca (1858–1941) shares Pareto's distinction between the masses and the elite: 'In all societies . . . two classes of people appear – a class that rules and a class that is ruled' ('The Ruling Class' (1939)). Mosca, however, disputed Pareto's claim that all societies, even modern democracies, were dominated by self-interested elite rule. Instead, Mosca distinguished between different forms of elite rule, with democracies having more open forms of elite power than the caste or feudal systems. Mosca believed that elites could exercise power in a representative way, for as they draw new recruits from a wider range of social backgrounds a greater variety of interests will be represented. This concession to the masses was tempered by Mosca's view that the vast majority of people will never be capable of decision making, and thus elite rule is always inevitable. For these reasons, Mosca was contemptuous of the masses, and opposed the extension of the vote to the working class.

The inevitability of elite rule has been questioned by C.W. Mills, 'The Power Elite' (1956), who argues that elites have only recently emerged in the USA in the mid to late nineteenth century. He uses classical elite theory in his critical examination of post Second World War American society. Mills argues, from a radical perspective, that there are three unrepresentative elites in American society: political, military, and industrial, which together make up the '**power elite**'. The relative power of the elites varies according to the country's political and economic situation. Mills includes within the 'masses' the middle class, working class, and the poor. In post-war America, the middle class were concerned with their own sectional interests, the working class lacked trade union organisation (compared to Europe), and the poor consisted of the unemployed, the elderly and the black minorities. Mills did not accept the power elite as inevitable (as Pareto and Mosca did), but argued that they were a result of the **centralisation of power**, which allowed a disproportionate amount of power to be held by certain individuals, holding '**command posts**' or '**pivotal positions**' in key institutions.

Mills has been criticised for the circumstantial nature of his argument, and lack of documented evidence to support his claims. R.A. Dahl, 'A Critique of the Ruling Elite Model' in J. Urry and J. Wakeford (eds), 'Power in Britain' (1973) argues that Mills has only demonstrated the 'potential' for control, not 'actual' control. In order to prove the latter, a number of case studies where key decisions are made must be examined. If it is found that a minority group in such situations decides the policies and overrules any opposition, then the existence of a power elite is proven. Dahl himself, however, can be criticised for ignoring the process by which certain issues are raised for decision making, such as who decides the issues to be decided?

There is, however, substantial empirical evidence for the existence of elites in British society:

Inheritance. P. Stanworth and A. Giddens (eds.), 'Elites and Power in Britain' ((1974) studied British company chairmen, and found that 26% of those in industry and 47% of those in merchant banks, had entered the family firm. In addition, at least 66% of all company chairmen came from upper-class backgrounds, with just one percent from the working class.

Kinship links. The importance of kinship ties between elite members has been described by T. Lupton and S. Wilson, 'The Social Background of Top Decision-Makers' (1959), indicating that many government ministers, top civil servants, and financial leaders are related by kinship and marriage. R. Whitley, in P. Stanworth and A. Giddens has shown how the people controlling economic institutions are mostly descended from the commercialised aristocracy and gentry. Also, many large firms are linked by overlapping directorships, which creates cohesion and unity between elites.

Educational privilege. Access to the senior civil service, management, banking, and positions of power in industry and politics, are determined to a significant extent by the type of education which individuals receive. In particular, products of the public school system are overrepresented in elite positions. In a 1971 study of 460 British company chairmen, P. Stanworth and A. Giddens found that 65% of chairmen had attended public schools, a further 17% had also experienced private education, 11% were uneducated in other forms of secondary schooling, and 17% were of unknown educational background.

Integration of elites. W. Guttsman, 'The British Political Elite' (1963) found that in the British Conservative Government of 1951–55 ministers had an average of 18 links with other elite groups, nearly half of which were with banks or firms. In Guttsman's 1974 study, in P. Stanworth and A. Giddens he found that in 1970 32% of Conservative MPs and 12% of Labour MPs had occupations connected with industry or commerce.

FRAGMENTED ELITE MODEL

The fragmented elite model is a modified version of classical elite theory, which suggests that although connections exist between elites, it is difficult to prove that they are united in a self-interested power elite. The fragmented elite model, as proposed by I. Budge et al 'The New British Political System' (1983) argues that there are a number of elites in Britain who, despite their common social origins, compete for power, rather than work together. Thus, instead of a unified, cohesive power elite (as Mills described), Budge et al see conflict between different groups seeking to influence government, as well as competition between government departments for funds or control.

Pluralist theories of power

Pluralism is an alternative view of the nature and distribution of power in societies, and is the dominant model for portraying the organisation of power in the West. Pluralism has its origins in the work of Max Weber, who questioned the possibility of direct democracy in Western industrial nations, and accepted that a representative democracy, with a large number of elected officials from all parties, was the best form of government. Pluralism thus rejects classical democratic theory and direct participatory democracy as unrealistic in modern industrial societies, and proposes the existence of **'pluralist democracies'** in Western power structures, in which a diffusion of power exists. The main features of the pluralist model are outlined below:

Modern industrial societies are characterised by increased **social differentiation**, leading to a heterogeneous network of social and occupational roles. Interests have therefore become progressively diversified, with large numbers of groups holding different viewpoints.

R. Dahl, 'Who Governs?' (1961) argues that **classical pluralism** has replaced **classical democracy** in modern Western power structures, where different groups pursue different political interests. Groups may form political organisations to promote their aims, for example political parties, trade unions, pressure groups. In this way, although elites exist in a pluralist democracy, they form a political system of 'open' power groups, where no one elite holds a monopoly of power. Thus Dahl states that 'there are multiple centres of power, none of which is or can be wholly sovereign'.

The role of the state in pluralism is to mediate between the various interest groups to ensure the operation of democracy.

The wider distribution of political resources means that no single elite group predominates in Western societies, but instead a variety of elite groups compete for power. S. Keller, 'Beyond the Ruling Class' (1963) argues that in modern societies a system of '**strategic elites**' operates, whereby business, government, labour, education, and culture influence decision-making, but retain their own values and interests.

According to D. Riesman, 'The Lonely Crowd' (1950) the various elites act as '**veto groups**', and exercise countervailing power against each other as and when necessary.

In modern industrial societies the development of public ownership, the increased separation between ownership and control (and the rise of the managerial class), and the growth of joint stock companies have all reduced the emphasis which economic power gives to elites.

In a pluralist democracy **political parties and pressure** (or interest) **groups** are crucial in ensuring that democracy is representative of the majority of the population. Political parties are accountable to the electorate if they wish to retain power, and must reflect the wishes and interests of the population in their policies. Interest or pressure groups aim to influence political parties by representing a particular interest or cause. They will be discussed in more detail later in the chapter.

Empirical support for the pluralist model can be found in a number of studies on the decision-making process in the USA and Britain. Some particular examples include the following:

R. Dahl, 'Who Governs?' (1961) conducted an investigation of local community politics in New Haven, Connecticut, USA, concentrating on decision making in three main issue areas (educational policy, political nominations, and urban renewal). Dahl found no evidence of a ruling elite, but '**dispersed inequalities**' where power was shared among various interest groups whose involvement in the issue depended on their relevant interest. The only people involved in all three areas were the mayor and others in official positions, and they had to make their final decisions with reference to the demands of the relevant groups.

A.M. Rose, 'The Power Structure' (1967), in a study of power on a national level in the USA, proposes a '**multi-influence hypothesis**', with a number of competing elites (economic, political, military, etc.) influencing decisions. Rose shows that legislation in the 1960s on social welfare programmes emerged as a response to the demands of various interest groups, rather than as a direct policy intended to benefit economic interests.

C.J. Hewitt, 'Elites and the Distribution of Power in British Society' in P. Stanworth and A. Giddens (eds.), 'Elites and Power in Britain' (1974) studied the passage of legislation in the British Parliament from 1944–1964. The 24 policy issues reviewed fell into four main areas: foreign policy, economic policy, welfare policy, and social policy. Hewitt compared the decisions of Parliament with the views of interest groups and public opinion at the time, and concluded that no one interest group prevailed.

W. Grant and D. Marsh, 'The Confederation of British Industry' (1977) examined four pieces of legislation between 1967 and 1972, to see how influential the CBI (representing three-quarters of the top 200 manufacturing companies) was on the government. The Labour Government rejected the CBI's opposition to the 1967 Iron and Steel Act, and after pressure from conservationist groups the CBI compromised over the 1972 Deposit of Poisonous Wastes Act (introduced by the Conservatives). The Clean Air Act of 1968, also opposed by the CBI, conceded more to the demands of the National Society for Clean Air than to the demands of the manufacturing industry. The 1972 Industry Act, introduced by the Conservatives to give the government the right to buy shares in private industry, was unsupported by the CBI. The TUC, however, supported the Act as a means of investing in industries at a time of growing unemployment. These examples illustrate that the CBI has little direct influence over the government, but that the demands of the electorate and interest groups are more significant in determining government policies.

The pluralist view of the nature of power has been criticised on a number of grounds. The pluralist model assumes that all the major interests in society are equally represented, yet the economically more powerful groups in society are more successful in gaining representation than others. In reality, therefore, many individuals and groups (such as ethnic minorities, the elderly and people with learning difficulties) do not have an effective mouthpiece for their demands.

Pluralism ignores what P. Bachrach and M. Baratz call '**non-decision-making**', which refers to the process by which certain groups have the power to decide which issues are discussed and which are excluded from consideration. Thus, issues which are particularly contentious, for example poverty, unemployment, are not permitted to be 'opened' to individuals and groups who are not directly involved. In the absence of such participation '**safe decisions**' are taken, which reflect existing power relationships, and do not fundamentally alter the status quo. Extreme or violent interest groups are marginalised or 'organised out' so that their demands are unlikely to succeed, and other more 'subversive' or 'eccentric' groups (such as women's groups, peace campaigners, Irish Republicans) are branded as 'outsiders' and excluded from the decision-making process. The illusion of a representative government is maintained through the mass media, the education system, and public participation in elections. A. Gramsci uses the term '**ideological hegemony**' to describe the capacity of the dominant class to rule not only by controlling the means of production, but by controlling ideas as well.

The pluralist concentration on the decision-making process ignores the more important results and consequences of such decisions. According to J. Westergaard and H. Resler, 'Class in a Capitalist Society' (1976) 'power is visible only through its consequences'. The effects of decisions invariably reveal benefits for the ruling class, with occasional concessions made to the masses to avoid radical opposition to the status quo.

Pluralism emphasises the importance of governments consulting with a wide range of interest groups and responding to them accordingly. However, many New Right theorists such as S. Brittan, 'The Role and Limits of Government' (1983) suggest that this creates an '**overloaded government**', whereby issues and concerns have to be dealt with, usually by financial concessions, in order to buy electoral support. This in turn creates economic inefficiency and a government which is swayed by interest groups, distracting it from its main policies.

ELITE PLURALISM

Elite pluralism emerged as a result of the criticisms of classical pluralism, and is a modification of the pluralist position. R. Dahl, 'Dilemmas of Pluralist Democracy' (1982) accepts that the unequal distribution of income and wealth in the USA makes equal political influence impossible. This has been described by D. Marsh as 'elite pluralism', and results in many groups being under-represented (such as unemployed, blacks), whilst other groups have greater access to government departments. The government will consult with interest groups in order to minimise conflict, but will concentrate on 'insider groups' (those with regular access to government departments), with few 'outsider groups' included in the process.

Elite pluralism can also be criticised, for it undermines the pluralist view that power is widely dispersed in society. It further assumes that the leaders of interest groups are acting on behalf of the well-being of their members, when in reality corruption and self-interest may motivate some of these leaders.

PRESSURE GROUPS

Pressure groups are considered by many pluralists as playing a crucial role in the decision-making process. Pressure groups are organisations which try to influence government – usually national government, but often local government too. They are different from political parties, which seek to become the government: pressure groups very seldom put up candidates in elections, preferring to focus on a small range of issues and trying to persuade the government to take their views into account in policy making.

There are a vast number of interest groups in our society, with variations in size, structure, and objectives. The group may come together to fight for one specific issue, and remain in existence until this aim is realised. The Abortion Law Reform Organisation was founded in 1936, and it was not until 1967 that the Abortion Act was passed. The pressure or interest group may exist only briefly in order to prevent some specific action that they feel threatens their locality, such as the building of a motorway, or the holding of a pop festival. Other distinctions may be made between local and national pressure groups, those with short-term aims and those which are permanent groups (for example the RSPCA), 'open' groups which anyone can belong to (for example the Ramblers' Association) and those with a 'closed' membership (such as the BMA). There are organisations which exist solely as pressure groups, for example ASH (Action on Smoking and Health), and those which pursue a range of activities (such as the National Trust).

Pressure groups can also be divided into two main types.

Protective groups, which seek to protect the interests of some section of society. They are sometimes described as economic interest or sectional groups, and serve to protect the interests of trade unions, professional associations, and employers' organisations.

Promotional groups, or non-economic interest groups, which seek to promote a cause or idea, for example, Friends of the Earth, NSPCC.

W. Grant argues that the distinction between protectional and promotional pressure groups is not always appropriate, and suggests an alternative classification based on **'insider groups'** and **'outsider groups'**, which depend on how they are treated by the government. Insider groups (usually protectional) are those which the government consults on major issues, and which make a significant contribution to the policy-making process, for example CBI, BMA. Grant uses the term outsider groups to refer to groups (usually promotional) which have less influence on and access to the government. It is possible for groups to move from one to the other. The trade unions under the

1974–79 Labour Government were insiders, but since 1979 have become outsider groups.

Grant's views are supported by M. Smith, 'Pressure, Power and Policy: State Autonomy and Policy Networks in Britain and the United States' (1993), who argues that many pressure groups (insider ones) are linked to government departments and other influential groups in society. Governments need pressure groups to support their policies and provide vital research information, so they develop **policy networks** with certain groups. In some circumstances these may develop into a **policy community**, which is a more closed network, with one or more government departments maintaining close contact with a limited number of insider pressure groups over a period of time. The existence of policy communities means that insider groups are more likely to be involved in decision making, and thus have more influence with the government, reducing pluralism in society.

Pressure groups operate via a number of methods, including petitions, marches, demonstrations, strikes, disruptive action, and advertising. It is also possible to lobby MPs, to persuade one or more to represent the group's interests in Parliament, and even to introduce a Private Member's Bill. Some Labour MPs are sponsored by trade unions, while many Conservative MPs act as representatives of business organisations. Ultimately, the success of a pressure goup will depend on whether it can persuade Parliament to introduce or withdraw legislation, or whether it can persuade a local authority to adopt a particular course of action. Pressure groups do have a number of advantages in a pluralist society:

An example of a promotional pressure group

1. They increase the level of democracy by bridging the gap between elections, and giving people a means of showing their support or disfavour for the government's policies.
2. Pressure groups increase democracy as they allow more people the opportunity to participate in decision making at local and national levels.
3. They provide an enormous amount of specialised information (for example Shelter, Friends of the Earth, NSPCC) which is often used to promote the group's cause, or used by the government in formulating policies.
4. Protectional groups such as trade unions or professional associations are important in watching over the interests of their members, ensuring wages and working conditions are fair.

Pressure groups have also been subject to a number of criticisms:

1. They lead to an oligarchic society where a number of important groups compete (political parties, trade unions, CBI) for power and influence, but shut out the general public, thus reducing democracy.
2. Pressure groups form a kind of self-government in which some associations carry more weight than other with groups representing minorities (such as the elderly, or handicapped) having little support or power.
3. Pressure groups which can afford to pay an MP to act for them obviously carry greater power than those who cannot.
4. They can weaken government as it tries to gain popularity with all groups, but cannot satisfy all the demands, diverting it away from the policy issues planned.

Marxist theories of power

Marxist theories of power are based on Marx's view of the structure of society, and his emphasis on how the economic mode of production determines the social relations. Thus, a capitalist economic system based on private ownership and control leads to social relations based on class dominance and subordination of the masses. Marxist theories of the role of the state in capitalist society are in direct contrast to the 'liberal-democratic' view of the nineteenth century which envisaged a 'democratic revolution' following the transition from feudalism to capitalism. The enfranchisement of the working class, the growth of political parties, and the development of trade unionism were all seen as elements in the democratic process. The Marxist view of these developments is that they are merely palliatives designed to diffuse working-class protest and discontent. Whereas the liberal-democratic model sees the state as an independent body in the democratic system, Marxists regard the state as a democratically elected elite. Marx argued that only in a socialist society, with the abolition of private property, would true democracy be achieved, with the working class taking on the governing of the country. Marx's views on power and the relationship between the state and the ruling class have been modified by a number of Marxist writers as follows:

A. Gramsci, 'Selections from the Prison Notebooks of Antonio Gramsci' (1973), writing in the early years of the twentieth century, argued that under certain conditions the superstructure (ideas and beliefs) may change the infrastructure (economic system), via the actions of particular individuals. Gramsci also saw the state as divided into two parts: the political society or the institutions which rule by force (for example police, army), and the civil society or institutions which rule by consent (for example political parties, mass media, trade unions).

Gramsci uses the term '**hegemony**' (intellectual and moral leadership) to describe the way in which the bourgeoisie impose their ideas and values on other groups in society, thus influencing the views of the masses. Revolution is therefore only possible if working-class movements can develop their own hegemony to sway the interests of the working class. Gramsci challenged Marx's two class model, and stressed the divisions within the ruling class and within the subject class. In order to maintain hegemony, the ruling class must create alliances or power blocs between different groups, and the subject class must also develop alliances if they are to challenge the ruling hegemony.

R. Miliband, 'The State in Capitalist Society' (1969) includes within the term 'state' the government, civil service, parliamentary assemblies, and the judiciary. Miliband takes an **instrumentalist view**, with the state acting as the instrument of those with the economic power, the ruling class. The power of the state also extends to the ideological power which it holds in order to maintain its position. The '**process of legitimation**' involves massive indoctrination of the masses into the acceptance of inequalities as normal and desirable. Miliband describes how the ruling class or elite is selected on the basis of social and educational background, with the vast majority drawn from the professional middle classes.

N. Poulantzas, 'Classes in Contemporary Capitalism' (1975) criticises Miliband for concentrating on the social background of occupational elites and the ruling class. Poulantzas presents a **structuralist** version of the Marxist approach, where he argues that it is the structure of the capitalist system itself which is the main factor in the concentration of power in the hands of the few. Attempts by socialist parties to implement their policies are doomed to failure, because the structure of capitalism cannot accommodate socialist principles. Hence, even socialist governments have to conform to capitalist economic systems. The relationship of the state to the rest of the capitalist system limits the extent to which a socialist party can effect change. In the 1970s the Marxist President Allende of Chile was overthrown by a conspiracy between several elites (military and political) in order to protect their interests. In contrast to Marx, Poulantzas does not believe that the replacement of capitalism by socialism is economically inevitable, but that the transition can only come about through political struggle.

In a similar way to Gramsci, Poulantzas sees divisions within the capitalist class, with the state acting as a partially independent representative of the capitalist class. He claims that the state must have **relative autonomy** from the ruling class. In other words, the state must retain a level of independence from sectional interests so that it can promote the long-term interests of capital. It can do this by mediating between the demands of different capitalist groups, by acceding to some working-class demands and thus minimising conflict, and by directly intervening in the economy to improve long-term capital interests. Miliband and others have criticised Poulatzas for overemphasising the way in which the structure of capitalism affects state action. The concept of relative autonomy is difficult to prove, and it is not easy to decide when the state is autonomous, and when it is controlled by capital.

The existence of a ruling class which controls the means of production as well as having political control, is increasingly open to doubt. The spread of wealth from a small capitalist class to the wider society has occurred through share ownership and share possession. Over 50% of all shares in private companies are held by insurance companies, pension funds, and other institutions. Another key factor which casts doubt on the Marxist theory of power is the increasing separation of ownership and control in modern industrial sociéties. As ownership passes from owners to salaried managers it is difficult to sustain a theory which envisages a ruling class which both owns and controls the means of production. In response, some neo-Marxists have attempted to explain how a Marxist theory of power can be applied to advanced industrial societies.

D. Coates, 'The Context of British Politics' (1984) has tried to demonstrate how, in Britain, a divided ruling class will result in the emergence of Gramsci's 'power blocs' or alliances at different periods of historical development. Different groups will become part of the power bloc under varying circumstances, although financial capital remains the dominant group throughout all periods. According to Coates and other neo-Marxists, the ruling class controls the means of production by developing power blocs and alliances to suit the prevailing economic conditions, with financial capital retaining overall control over the process.

Patterns of voting behaviour in the UK

National and local elections in which people can exercise their vote are an essential part of the democratic process. Although voting takes place in secret, sociologists have attempted to find out how people vote, and the extent to which social factors influence voting intentions. The scientific study of voting behaviour is called **psephology**. The main factors which influence voting behaviour in Britain are as follows:

POLITICAL SOCIALISATION

This is the view that political ideas and attitudes are transmitted from one generation to the next. D.E. Butler and D. Stokes, 'Political Change in Britain' (1974) found that political attitudes such as respect for leaders in authority, and loyalty to the monarch, tend to be related to early family experiences. Large national surveys consistently bear out the importance of the long-term influence of parents, and show a fairly high degree of consistency in inter-generational voting behaviour, especially in the first few years of voting experience.

SCHOOL

Certain political ideas and attitudes may be informally acquired from teachers in the day-to-day teaching and learning process, for example in history or social studies. In addition, through mixing with children who come from politically conscious homes, other children may acquire particular political attitudes.

GENDER

J. Blondel, 'Voters, Parties and Leaders' (1969) suggests that women tend to vote Conservative more than men, in a ratio of about 6:4. The main reason given for this Consevative bias of women, particularly those who do not go out to work, is that they are thought to be less influenced by industrial conditions and trade union activity. It has also been suggested that women are more passive than men, and therefore more consevative in temperament.

This female bias towards Conservatism has been apparent in most elections up to

1974, but studies of elections since 1979 indicates that this gender difference has almost disappeared, most probably as women have entered the labour force, and become more involved in industrial relations. B. Campbell, 'The Iron Ladies: Why Do Women Vote Tory' (1987) provides evidence to show that there are variations among women of different ages, classes, and domestic circumstances. There also exists a **'gender gap'** in particular issues: in the nuclear agenda of the 1980s more women than men were against the use of nuclear defence systems.

AGE

Young people tend to be more radical in outlook, while older people are more conservative in their attitudes. Young people are more likely to have problems establishing themselves economically, and thus tend to seek immediate political solutions for their problems, hence their radical views. Although middle-aged people often vote Conservative, wishing to preserve their hard-won financial and social status, many elderly people vote Labour as their standard of living in retirement declines.

OCCUPATION

It has been claimed that traditionally the work situation has been significant for political communication, especially on the shop floor. However, contrary evidence can be found in J. Goldthorpe and D. Lockwood, 'The Affluent Worker' (1968) where affluent workers (or **'instrumental collectivists'**) were committed to the unions and the Labour Party for what they could get out of them, and would readily change their voting behaviour if it was in their interests to do so. In contrast, they found that the traditional working class (or **'proleterian traditionalists'**) were staunchly Labour, and resisted the influence of Conservative values even when these appeared to be in their own interests.

ETHNICITY

According to several opinion polls in the 1980s Afro-Caribbean and Asian ethnic minorities tend to be strong Labour supporters (with between 70% and 90% voting Labour). This tendency can be explained in class terms, as these groups contain a large proportion of working-class voters. However, it appears that many non-manual black voters also support Labour, as it is seen as the party which is most sympathetic to the needs of ethnic minorities.

Recently, there has been evidence to indicate that this ethnic minority support for the Labour Party may be fragmenting. A 1987 poll by the Harris Research Centre found that only 72% voted Labour in the general election, compared to 18% for the Conservatives and 10% for the Alliance. Surveys by the Commission for Racial Equality have shown that the strong support for Labour in the 1979 general election declined by the 1983 election, and again in the 1987 election. The strongest supporters of Labour were the West Indian community, perhaps because they are more likely to be unemployed, or in low-paid and low-status jobs. It appears that during the 1980s the affluent Asian voters who were experiencing upward social mobility were more likely to vote Conservative or Liberal-Democrat. Examples of this switch in allegiance as ethnic minorites increase their prosperity include Jewish immigrants in the 1930s, who initially voted Labour, but as their standard of living and wealth increased, were more likely to vote Conservative.

The 1987 election of four black Labour MPs to Parliament may help to present a party image which is more favourable to ethnic minorities, and may also reinforce the belief that Labour is more likely than other parties to champion the rights of minorities in society.

REGION

Within Britain, Scotland and Wales are more Labour inclined than Conservative, and in England, the south-east and south-west have more Conservative voters than Labour ones. Explanations for regional differences in Britain centre on the influence of industry, business, and standards of living in the areas concerned.

In recent years the north/south divide has become more apparent. In the 1987 general election Labour held only three seats south of a line drawn from the Wash to the Bristol Channel. In the same election, in Wales and Scotland Labour held more seats than all the other parties put together. I. Crewe suggests that Labour has become a '**regional class party**'. However, R.J. Johnston, C.J. Pattie, and Allsopp, 'A Nation Dividing' (1988) suggests that there are important regional variations in the level of support for different parties from each social class. Thus, the Labour Party gains more votes from middle-class voters in industrial areas of Scotland, Wales, and northern England, while the Conservatives are more successful in gaining working-class votes in the south. Local influences and conditions, rather than social class, may therefore have a greater effect on voting tendencies.

MASS MEDIA

It has been suggested that the effect of television on political attitudes is strongest amongst the least politically minded viewers (J.G.Blumler and D.McQuail, 'Television in Politics' (1968)). **Floating voters** are people who change their party allegiance from one election to the next. They tend to be the least politically minded voters, and are easily swayed by election propaganda. Political parties therefore direct their broadcasts, newspaper articles, and interviews at the floating voters to try and gain their support. Newspapers have been found to be a relatively unimportant influence on voting behaviour during election campaigns, and party meetings seem fairly ineffectual as a means of spreading political propaganda. The increasing use of the media during election campaigns may lead people to believe that it plays a significant role in deciding voting behaviour, yet most research seems to indicate that media influence is small.

OPINION POLLS

Opinion polls aim to measure public opinion, by measuring a sample of the total electorate's intentions at the time of the interview, and using this information to predict the result of the election. Opinion polls are important as a means of informing the electorate about the progress of the election, and the issues which people feel are relevant. It has been claimed that at least 50% of the total electorate take notice of polls during pre-election periods, and, they are more popular than party political broadcasts. Political party images are built up through opinion polls, and can indicate to a government the popularity of various policies.

There is, however, little evidence that media coverage of opinion polls influences the way in which people vote. Although, in the 1992 general election, it is possible that some Liberal-Democrat voters may have switched to the Conservatives at the last moment, fearing opinion poll predictions of a Labour victory.

Some of the reasons why opinion polls may wrongly predict the result of an election include: The '**Late Swing Argument**' where the polls are unrepresentaive of the electorate, or they missed a late swing to another party; the '**Differential Turnout Argument**' where less people turn out to vote than was expected from the poll; the '**Boomerang Effect**' where the polls predict a victory, and so a large proportion of people believe that 'their' party will win and do not bother to vote.

SOCIAL CLASS

Social class is usually regarded as the greatest determining factor of voting behaviour. D.E. Butler and D.Stokes, 'Political Change in Britain' (1974) conducted a series of surveys between 1963 and 1970, and found that social class was a significant influence on voing behaviour, with most people voting in the same way as those with similar occupations. The majority of people therefore consistently voted for the party which represented their class (a process called '**partisan alignment**') with most manual workers voting Labour, and a majority of middle-class non-manual workers voting Conservative. The main problem with the partisan alignment theory was that it could not explain the existence of '**deviant voters**', or people who vote against class lines, such as middle-class people who vote Labour, and working-class people who vote Conservative.

J.Raynor, 'The Middle Class' (1969) argues that there are two types of middle-class deviant voter. Firstly, there are the '**intellectual left**', or those with considerable higher education, working in vocational or 'helping' professions, such as social work, teaching, etc. They vote for the Labour Party because they have first-hand knowledge of the disadvantaged, and believe that Labour will give the greatest help to these people. Secondly, there are the middle-class people with low status, who vote Labour because of their resentment towards the establishment for failing to utilise their educational qualifications.

J.Goldthorpe, 'Social Mobility and Class Structure in Modern Britain' (1980) argues that the second generation of affluent workers, who have become white-collar workers, will vote Labour because of loyalty to their background. It may also be the case that as the traditional working class declines, the Labour Party is broadening its policies to appeal to the new generation of affluent workers.

Working-class deviant voters or '**working-class Tories**' are of much greater significance than middle-class Labour voters because they effectively determined the results of post-war elections, when manual workers formed a majority of the population, but because a third of the working class consistently voted Conservative they prevented a perpetual Labour government. Deviant working-class voters are also significant because they contradicted the claim that class was a major influence on voting behaviour. Much research in the 1960s concentrated on these voters and their behaviour, resulting in a number of explanations for their voting inclinations:

The embourgeoisement, or affluence argument emerged during the late 1950s, and proposed that the working class were gradually losing their identity to become absorbed into the middle class. The political evidence for this merging of the classes was based on the fact that the Labour Party, after having achieved a huge majority in 1945, then lost three general elections in a row (1951, 1955, 1959). During this period the

Labour Party's share of the total vote fell from 49% in 1951 to 44% in 1959. It was argued that increasing affluence among the skilled working class led to a change in voting behaviour.

In their critique of the embourgeoisement thesis, J.Goldthorpe and D.Lockwood provided evidence to show that affluent workers were not voting Conservative, but in fact were more pro-Labour than the traditional working class. The major reason for this was due to the fact that they were members of strong and militant trade unions who had been able to improve their wages and conditions. Goldthorpe and Lockwood argued that affluence, or the lack of it, is only one element in the formation of a worker's political attitudes and voting behaviour. Other factors, apart from money, may prove to be significant.

The sunken middle class argument suggests that working-class Conservative voters are ex-members of the middle class who have, for various reasons, such as marriage, bankruptcy, occuptional change, suffered downward social mobility: in other words, they have 'sunk' into the working class. Although this group are objectively members of the working class in terms of income, occupation, etc., they have retained their middle-class attitudes and values. These attitudes include support for individualism, enterprise, privatisation: a Conservative political viewpoint.

The major criticism against the sunken middle class argument is that this group of people represent only a small proportion of the working class, certainly not sufficient to account for one-third deviant working-class voters. Although the argument explains the behaviour of some working-class Conservative voters, it is inadequate as a complete explanation.

The subjective social class argument is based on the view that the way in which a person thinks of his/her position in the class structure (subjective social class) is a greater influence on voting behaviour than objective social class. M.Benny, A.P.Gray, and R.H.Pear, 'How People Vote' (1956) concluded that subjective class seems to be more related to party choice than objective class. This argument has a limited value in that it can only explain some of the working-class Conservatives, but not all.

The deference argument was proposed as long ago as the nineteenth century by Walter Bagehot, who believed that British people of all classes deferred decision making to people who were 'born to rule'. Members of the Conservative Party in the nineteenth century were predominantly wealthy, privileged, and well educated, which led many working-class people to think they were the 'best' individuals to vote for. This **'deferential authority'** view of working-class voting behaviour has been developed in recent years.

R.McKenzie and A.Silver, 'Angels in Marble' (1968) found that deference accounted for the behaviour of abour half the working-class Conservatives in their sample. These deferential Conservative voters were more likely to be female, on low incomes, and tended to be older. McKenzie and Silver described the non-deferential working-class Tories as **'secular voters'**, because they voted Conservative on the basis of specific policies rather than on party image.

E.Nordlinger, 'Working Class Tories' (1967) suggests that working-class Tories can be sub-divided into three groups, each of which votes Conservative for different reasons. Thus, the **'solid Conservative voters'** have always voted Tory and would continue to do so if there was a general election tomorrow; the **'deferential voters'** select Conservative candidates on the basis of their ascribed status 'born to rule' but they will vote Labour if the candidate is from a high ascribed social position; the **pragmatist voters**' choose candidates on the basis of achieved status, that is, their 'proven ability', and are just as likely to vote Labour as they are to vote Conservative.

Although the majority (two-thirds) of working-class people vote Labour, that is they are **'conformist'** working-class voters, their reasons for doing so may differ. D.E. Butler and D.Stokes, 'Political Change in Britain' (1971) suggested that manual workers may be motivated by varying perceptions of the class-based nature of politics. Thus, a minority of people view politics purely in terms of class conflict, while others see the Labour Party as the sole representative of working-class interests, yet others view the act of voting Labour as part of their class sub-culture.

F.Parkin, 'Class Inequality and Political Order' (1971) and R.Jessop, 'Traditionalism, Conservatism and British Political Culture' (1974) argue that in spite of voting Labour, many working-class people embody conservative values and beliefs which are critical of Labour Party policy. Parkin and Jessop argue that the dominant institutions in society (the monarchy, church, media, etc.) are essentially conservative, and unless the working class are 'shielded' from their influence they will absorb these conservative values. Working-class sub-cultures can act as barriers to these influences (traditional working-class communities tend to be more radical and class conscious than affluent workers). J.Goldthorpe and D.Lockwood, 'The Affluent Worker' (1968) found that the affluent workers (or **'instrumental collectivists'**) were committed to the unions and the Labour Party for what they could get out of them, and would readily change their voting behaviour if it was in their interests to do so. In contrast, the traditional working class (or **'proletarian traditionalists'**) were staunchly Labour, and resisted the influence of conservative values, even when these appeared to be in their own interests.

SOCIAL CLASS AND VOTING BEHAVIOUR IN THE 1970S AND 1980S

During the 1970s it appeared that traditional class patterns of voting behaviour were weakening, leading to what B.Sarvlik and Crewe, 'A Decade of Dealignment' (1983) call a process of **'partisan dealignment'**. Partisan dealignment is where fewer voters are associated or aligned with one or other of the two main parties. This was shown by the trend away from the two main parties towards the centre parties of the Liberals, the Social Democratic Party, the Welsh Nationalists, and the Scottish Nationalist Party between 1974 and 1983. Thus, in 1951 the third or centre parties only gained three percent of the vote, but managed to win ten percent in 1970, with an increase to 25% in 1974, and with the Liberal-SDP Alliance boosting the centre parties share of the vote to 26% in 1983. A second factor in partisan dealignment is the decline in political partisanships, or the way in which people switch allegiance from one election to the next, particularly as the media has intensified its coverage of political issues and the image of the party leaders.

Crewe further argues that the process of partisan dealignment has been accompanied by **'class dealignment'** or the decline in the influence of social class on voting behaviour. In the 1960s approximately two-thirds of voters regularly supported their 'natural' class party, but the 1970s saw a decade of dealignment as class and voting were no longer synonymous, and by the 1980s this figure fell to less than half of voters.

Explanations for class dealignment focus on changes in the class structure caused by the decline of heavy industries and the fall in union membership. Crewe suggests this has led to a divided working class, with an expanding **'new working class'** of manual workers in the south, who are owner-occupiers, private sector employees, and non-unionised, voting Conservative, and an old or **'traditional working class'** with the opposite characteristics. According to Crewe, the 1983 general election results indicated that an increasing number of 'new working class' were voting Conservative. Furthermore, he argues that the 1987 election revealed a similar 'split' in the middle class, with university educated and public sector non-manual workers rejecting the Conservatives, and middle-class non-university educated and private sector workers continuing to vote Conservative.

There are a number of critics of the view that the relationship between social class and voting behaviour has declined. A.Heath, R.Jowell and J.Curtice, 'How Britain Votes' (1985) use research and analysis of elections from 1963 to 1983 to question the process of class dealignment. Heath et al argue that the boundary between the middle class and the working class is not as clearly defined as it was in the past. They use an alternative classification to the one usually preferred by psephologists (A, B, C1, C2, D, E), and instead use a class analysis based on economic interests, as follows:

The salariat: professionals and semi-professionals, managers, supervisors of non-manual workers.

Routine non-manual: clerks, secretaries, salesworkers.

The petty bourgeoisie: farmers, self-employed manual workers.

Foremen and technicians

The working class: skilled and semi-skilled workers.

In their classification, manual workers of different types fall into classes 3, 4, and 5, and they further classify women by their own occupation if they are in paid employment. Heath et al argue that in terms of **'absolute class voting'** (the percentage of the electorate supporting their 'natural' class party) measurements are misleading, because the Labour Party's share of votes from all classes has declined. Dealignment would only occur if the working class were rejecting the Labour Party in relatively larger numbers than other classes. To measure the relative strength of the relationship between class and voting behaviour they use the 'odds ratio', that is the odds of a member of the salariat voting Conservative divided by the odds of a working-class person voting Labour. Using this measurement Heath et al found no evidence of class dealignment from 1964 to 1983, but instead they describe **'trendless fluctuation'** in the strength of class alignments. They propose that a change in the class structure has affected dealignment, for example the working class decreased from 47% to 34% of the electorate between 1964 and 1983, whilst the salariat and non-manual groups increased from 18% to 27%. The combination of a decline in natural class support and the rise of the third parties explains changes in voting patterns. A number of criticisms have been made of the research and analysis of Heath et al:

1. Their definition of the 'working class' excludes manual workers who are most likely to vote Conservative.

2. An absolute decline in class voting is evidence of a weakening of class alignment.

3. The use of the odds ratio exaggerates the changes in class voting behaviour by

focusing on the two main parties and ignoring the centre ones. The odds ratio only includes the working class and the salariat, ignoring the other groups which might be more likely to dealign.

4. The changes in voting patterns within the classes are more significant than changes in the relative size of classes.

In response to these criticisms Heath et al conducted follow-up studies on the 1987 and 1992 elections ('Labour's Last Chance? The 1992 Election and Beyond' (1994)). This time they developed a log-linear analysis to study the relationship between class and voting behaviour. This measurement allowed for changes in the relative size of classes, as well as fluctuations in support for different parties. Heath et al continued to maintain their original conclusions: in absolute terms fewer people vote for their 'natural' party, with changes in the class structure remaining more significant. According to Heath et al, there is evidence that Labour has lost support relatively evenly across all classes, and therefore no dealignment has taken place. A disillusionment with Labour leaders and policies in the 1987 and 1992 elections, coupled with an increase in support for third parties, were seen as the main reasons for Labour Party defection.

Ultimately, acceptance of the theory of class dealignment depends on the definition of the term itself. If, as in the case of I.Crewe, it is seen as a decline in absolute numbers of a class voting for a particular party, then dealignment has occurred. On the other hand, if the relative definition of Heath et al and measurement is used, then there has been no class dealignment.

ISSUES AND VOTING BEHAVIOUR

H.T.Himmelweit et al, 'How Voters Decide' (1985) argue that class loyalty is not as significant today as a voter's position on specific issues. However, the relationship between issues and voting behaviour is not straightforward. I.Crewe shows how, in 1987, the main issues were education, unemployment, defence, and the NHS, and although the majority of the electorate favoured Labour's policies on all these issues except defence, the Conservatives still won the election. Crewe suggests that people are more concerned with issues which directly affect their personal prosperity, rather than with general issues. As most people thought the Conservatives were more likely to improve prosperity compared to Labour, the Tories attracted more votes, and won.

In summary, R.Rose and I.McAllister, 'The Loyalties of Voters: A Lifetime Learning Model' (1990) suggest that voting behaviour is a combination of short-term and long-term factors. Rose and McAllister propose a **'lifetime learning model'**, whereby voters are influenced throughout life by a range of factors including family, school, work, region, etc. These long-term factors may be reinforced or overtaken by short-term circumstances such as policy issues, performance of parties, and media campaigns.

TRENDS IN GENERAL ELECTIONS 1979 TO 1997

During the 1950s the Labour Party suffered three consecutive defeats by the Conservatives, largely explained by the **embourgeoisement thesis**. M.Abrams and R.Rose, 'Must Labour Lose?' (1960) questioned whether Labour would ever be able to win another general election. Labour did, however, win in 1964, and intermittently in the 15 years after that. Subsequently, from 1979 to 1992 the Conservatives won four elections in a row, and the same question was asked again – whether Labour could ever regain power. Some general explanation of why Labour was so unsuccessful during the 1980s include the following:

1. The declining influence of class on voting behaviour, and an increasing number of floating voters changing their allegiance from one election to the next.
2. A rapid increase in the number of 'deviant voters;' with a minority of manual workers voting Labour in the 1983 and 1987 elections, and a correspondingly increasing number of Conservative voting manual workers.
3. The change from a two party to a three party system. In 1981 four members of the Labour Party broke away to form the Social Democratic Party, which joined with the Liberal Party as the Alliance to fight the 1983 and 1987 elections.
4. The general decline in support for the Labour Party during the 1980s, with success remaining only in the traditional 'heartlands' of England, Wales, and Scotland.
5. The replacement of the embourgeoisement thesis with an explanation based on the policy preferences of individual voters.

B.Sarlvik and I.Crewe, 'Decade of Dealignment' (1983) argue that from the 1979 election the importance of voters' opinions on issues (such as privatisation and the reduction of trade union power) became more significant in determining voting behaviour. This view has been backed up by H.T.Himmelweit et al, 'How Voters Decide' (1985), who propose a 'consumer model of voting', where an elector's choice of party is similar to a consumer making a purchase. However, Health et al, 'How Britain Votes' (1985) reject the consumer theory, for they claim that in 1983, if the six most important issues are taken into account, then Labour and the Conservatives would have received the same share of the votes. They also argue that party image was significant, rather than just policies, with Labour regarded as too left-wing in 1983.

THE 1987 GENERAL ELECTION

I.Crewe argues that the Conservatives continuing success in the 1987 election confirms his analysis of trends in voting behaviour that divisions are continuing to grow within both the middle class and the working class. The split is most apparent between the university-educated, public sector non-manual workers, and the non-university-educated, private sector non-manual workers. Crewe also found divisions between the 'new working class' (owner-occupiers, non-unionised, private sector workers in the south) and the 'traditional working class' (council housing, unionised, public sector workers in the north).

Crewe further commented on the influence of policy preferences on voting behaviour, with people feeling more prosperous under the Conservatives, and therefore trusting them to continue providing this for the people. Crewe attributes the 1987 defeat for Labour as a consequence of social trends, as follows:

1. The decline of manual work and therefore a decrease in 'natural' class support.
2. An increase in home ownership, and a corresponding decrease in council house owners, with owner-occupiers more likely to vote Conservative.
3. A decrease in trade unionism (between 1979 and 1985 membership decreased from 51% of the workforce to 38%), and thus a decline in traditional Labour supporters.
4. Changes in electoral geography, with people moving away from Labour strongholds and industrial areas in the north to rural areas and the south.
5. Changes in electoral demography (increased life expectancy and a declining birth rate), leading to a larger elderly (and Conservative) population.

Crewe also mentions several social trends operating in Labour's favour, such as the increasing turnout amongst black voters, and the increasing number of female white-collar workers joining unions.

A.Heath and S.K.McDonald argue that Crewe has exaggerated the degree of harm to Labour caused by social changes. They suggest that there are a number of factors which would limit the damage of the social changes.

1. The upwardly mobile working-class people with manual origins are not as likely to vote Conservative as non-manual workers with non-manual parents.
2. Much of the post-war expansion in housing had seen an increase in both owner-occupation and council housing. Many of the manual workers who bought council houses in the 1980s had always been Conservative voters.
3. The expansion of non-manual work was largely the result of increasing employment amongst the wives of non-manual workers, who were always likely to have voted Conservative.
4. The core working class of manual workers, who rent council houses and belong to unions, has always been small. Furthermore, Crewe's 'new working class' is not new at all; the working class has always been divided.

THE 1992 GENERAL ELECTION

Following the three Conservative victories, J.Benyon claimed that there were four main factors which must cease to act if Labour was to win in the 1992 general election:

1. The split between Labour and the Alliance of non-Conservative votes which benefited the Conservatives.
2. Many voters believing that the economy was stronger under a Conservative government.
3. The Labour Party's defence policy of unilateral nuclear disarmament damaged its support.
4. The image of Labour as an extreme left-wing party.

By 1992, though, conditions appeared perfect for a Labour victory. An effective election campaign, a new public image, and the dropping of unilateral nuclear disarmament in favour of multilateral disarmament all helped swell Labour's support. In contrast, the Conservatives were facing high inflation and rising interest rates, coupled with the unpopularity of many key Conservative policies, such as the community charge (poll tax), the privatisation of water, and reforms of the NHS. Even the opinion polls predicted a Labour victory, but this was not to be, for the following reasons.

Issues: although Labour had changed their defence policy, there was a fear of Labour tax increases and possible mismanagement of the economy.

Party leaders: the Conservative change of leadership from Margaret Thatcher to John Major resulted in a fresh image, whereas Neil Kinnock, the Labour leader, was facing his second election contest in opposition.

Mass media: there was extensive tabloid support for the Conservatives, with *The Sun* especially denigrating Kinnock as a potential Prime Minister.

Liberal-Democrat defection: following the 1987 election the Liberal Party/SDP Alliance ended, as the two parties moved apart, with some remaining with the SDP and others joining the new Liberal-Democrat Party. This weakened support for the centre parties, and reduced the extent to which the non-Conservative vote was split. In addition, the fear of a Labour-Liberal Democrat coalition government persuaded many Liberal Democrat supporters to defect to the Conservatives.

Late swing argument voters changed their minds at the last moment, making a late decision to vote Conservative.

On the positive side, an increase in ethnic minority voting increased Labour support, and an increasing number of people in higher education also helped the Labour vote. However, the biggest barrier to success remained the declining proportion of the electorate who were manual workers and 'natural' Labour supporters.

THE 1997 GENERAL ELECTION

After four consecutive defeats by the Consevatives, Labour won the 1997 election with a landslide majority of 179 seats, the greatest swing of votes since 1945. There was a substantial increase in Labour's vote, from 35% in 1992 to 45% in 1997, with a virtual collapse in Conservative support from 43% in 1992 to 31% in 1997. In Scotland and Wales the Conservatives were left without a single seat. The Liberal Democrats gained 46 seats (twice as many as they had won in 1992), although their share of the vote actually fell from 18.3% in 1992 to 16.7% in 1997. Reasons for the predicted Labour victory include the following:

Issues: in 1992 the Conservatives led on six issues (inflation, defence, industrial relations, law and order, Europe, and taxation), but by 1997 they led on only three of these – defence, inflation, and 'the unity of the United Kingdom'. In the 1997 election Labour led the Conservatives on Europe, taxation, and law and order, which were more significant in the electorate's minds.

Europe: the Conservatives were increasingly split over the issue of Europe, with the party committed to 'negotiate and decide' about the abolition of the pound, and the creation of a single European currency. The most damage was inflicted by 200 Tory MPs (the 'Eurosceptics') who broke rank before polling day and came down against the single currency in their election addresses.

The 'sleaze' factor: this was concerned not so much with sexual improprieties, but with financial ones. The publication of the Nolan Committee in 1994 on MPs finances, followed by the suppressed Downey Report on the 'cash for questions' issues reduced the confidence of the electorate in the Conservatives. One Tory MP implicated in the affair, Neil Hamilton, gained public notoriety as he refused to resign as candidate for Tatton in Cheshire. Martin Bell, the journalist, decided to oppose him as an 'anti-corruption' candidate (later changed to Independent), and was overwhelmingly successful, particularly as the Labour and Liberal Democrat candidates stood down.

Labour U-turns: the Labour Party adjusted or abandoned their commitments on a huge range of issues, from Europe and the economy to the trade unions and Sinn Fein talks. Also, Labour's rejection of privatisation was reversed, and they promised to delay the abolition of the pound until into the next century.

The Labour Left: in all previous elections since 1979 the Labour Left had attacked the Party leadership, and split the party on defence, nationalisation, and union power. In 1997 the Labour Left kept its silence and all but disappeared for the duration of the campaign. Even Clause 4 (the commitment to socialist principles) was revised without the left objecting too strenuously. Perhaps, after four election defeats in a row, even the Labour Left had had enough of opposition and wanted a chance at government.

Tactical voting: it has been suggested that many voters were keen to see the Conservatives ousted at all costs, and for those who would not vote Labour, the Liberal Democrats were an attractive alternative, doing particularly well in target seats where they were a close second to the Conservatives in 1992. Also, in 17 seats where the Conservatives came second, the Referendum Party polled more votes than the margin between the Tories and the winners. Based on the assumption that most of those who voted for the Referendum Party would otherwise have voted Conservative, there was a definite vote against Conservatism.

Election campaign: Labour's campaign organiser Peter Mandelson aimed to construct an image of the Party which would attract the anti-Conservative vote, and appear united under a strong and popular leader. The concept of 'New Labour' was born, to herald a Party competent to govern into the next century. The ideas of 'New Labour' and the phrases 'Blairism' and 'Young Country' were picked up by the media to project the image of an electorable Labour Party. Even *The Sun* newspaper abandoned the Conservatives and supported Labour's vision.

Party leadership: following the death of the Labour leader John Smith in 1994 the Labour Party 'skipped a generation' and elected Tony Blair as Party Leader (who at 43 was to become the youngest Prime Minister since 1812.) From 1994 until the election Blair transformed the Labour Party, leaving its left-wing, union influenced image behind, and remodelling the Party for the 1990s and beyond. Blair's young, classless image with no union ties represented a radical change for Labour, but a necessary one if it was to be an electorable Party.

Mass media: the defection of *The Sun* newspaper to backing Labour enhanced the mass support for the Party. Also, the media images of Major and Blair were very different, with Blair thought to be more 'caring' than Major, better 'able to unite the nation' 'more likely to stick to principles', and above all, more 'effective'.

Boredom: after 18 years of Conservative Government the country may simply have wished for a change.

It is too early to assess the consequences of Labour's victory, but there is certainly evidence of a shift from a blue-collar to a white-collar party. Out of 419 newly elected Labour MPs, 55 are lecturers/academics, 49 are teachers, and 111 are other white-collar workers. The party is also predominantly a young one, with three-quarters of Labour MPs aged 40 to 60, with 64 under the age of 40, and only 41 over 60. The number of female MPs has doubled from the 1992 election (to 120), with 101 of them Labour. The impact of these changes in composition in Party membership may filter down to policy, with an emphasis on issues concerned with the young, with women, and with white-collar workers. The imminent signing of the European Social Chapter will have an effect on working conditions and health and social benefits for the population.

CHECK YOUR UNDERSTANDING

After reading this chapter you should now be able to define the following terms.

1 Politics
2 Power
3 Value consensus
4 'Variable-sum' concept of power
5 'Constant-sum' view of power
6 Monarchy
7 Democracy
8 Totalitarianism
9 Authoritarianism
10 'Circulation of elites'
11 Power elite
12 Fragmented elite model
13 Pluralism
14 Pluralist democracies
15 Ideological hegemony
16 Elite pluralism
17 Protectional pressure groups
18 Promotional pressure groups
19 Policy networks
20 Process of legitimation
21 Structuralist view of power
22 Psephology
23 Political socialisation
24 Instrumental collectivists
25 Proletarian traditionalists
26 Floating voters
27 Partisan alignment
28 'Deviant voters'
29 Embourgeoisement thesis
30 Deferential voters
31 Pragmatist voters
32 Partisan dealignment
33 Class dealignment
34 'New working class'
35 'Traditional working class'
36 Absolute class voting

37 Odds ratio

38 Lifetime learning model

SELF-ASSESSMENT QUESTIONS

1 What is meant by the 'variable-sum' concept of power?
2 How does the Marxist view of power differ from the liberal-democratic view?
3 Briefly summarise 'classical' elite theory.
4 How do studies of the decision-making process lend support to the pluralist view?
5 Describe several key influences on voting behaviour, apart from social class.
6 What reasons have been given for middle class 'deviant voters'?
7 Summarise the debate on class dealignment, in the light of recent election results.

'A' LEVEL SOCIOLOGY ESSAY QUESTIONS

1 Critically examine sociological contributions to an understanding of the nature and distribution of power in industrial societies (AEB, summer, 1992).
2 To what extent has the concept of the 'deviant voter' been relevant and useful in sociological accounts of voting behaviour? (AEB, summer, 1995).
3 Compare and contrast Marxist and New Right perspectives on the role of the state in society (AEB, summer, 1996).
4 Critically examine the view that voting behaviour in the United Kingdom during the last 30 years has been increasingly influenced by factors other than social class (AEB, summer, 1996).

CHAPTER FOURTEEN

POVERTY AND INEQUALITY

LEARNING OBJECTIVES

ON COMPLETION OF THIS CHAPTER THE STUDENT SHOULD BE ABLE TO:

1 EXPLAIN AND EVALUATE DIFFERENT MEASUREMENTS OF POVERTY
2 REVIEW WELFARE STATE LEGISLATION FROM 1906–1996
3 ANALYSE FUNCTIONALIST, SOCIAL DEMOCRATIC, MARXIST, NEW RIGHT, AND FEMINIST VIEWS OF POVERTY
4 SUMMARISE THE DISTRIBUTION OF POVERTY BY CLASS, ETHNICITY, SEX AND REGION
5 DESCRIBE THE REASONS FOR THE PERSISTENCE OF POVERTY
6 DESCRIBE THE EXTENT OF INEQUALITY IN INCOME AND WEALTH, AND GIVE REASONS FOR THE DIFFERENCES

Measurements of poverty

Before the late nineteenth century the prevailing view was that poverty was caused by individual laziness, and any attempt to alleviate poverty would only encourage idleness and discourage thrift (S. Smiles, 'Self Help' (1859)). Governments were reluctant to take any responsibility for the poor; it was mainly left up to individuals to support each other. If this mutual support system failed, then local parishes stepped in, but the workhouses provided for paupers were degrading and regarded by many as a dire fate to be avoided at all costs.

When increasing industrialisation brought people into the towns and cities from the early nineteenth century onwards, this primitive welfare system broke down. Disease, dirt, and overcrowding posed major threats to the health and well-being of the whole population. However, it was not until the end of the nineteenth century, following the publication of two influential studies on the poor, that attitudes began to change, and reforms were initiated.

C. Booth, 'The Life and Labour of People in London' (17 volumes appeared in stages between 1889–1903), was an attempt to examine the real extent of poverty, to discover the figure behind the often quoted 'starving millions', and to shed light on the validity of the distinction between the 'deserving' and the 'undeserving' poor.

In order to study the conditions of the poor in London in the 1880s Booth had to construct his own '**poverty line**', a measure used to define those in poverty. He pioneered methods of investigation, virtually inventing his own social classifications, such as 'the lowest class', 'the very poor', 'the regularly employed', etc.

Using his own estimates of subsistence levels for families of different sizes (his poverty line), Booth concluded that some 30% of London's population was living in poverty. He was also able to show that the great majority of the poor were unable to escape from their poverty, which was frequently caused by problems of ill-health, unemployment, widowhood, inadequate housing, and old age.

S. Rowntree, 'Poverty: A Study of Town Life' (1901, 1936, 1950), was inspired by Booth's study, and wanted to examine the extent to which a provincial city, York, compared to London in terms of its poor. Rowntree also used a poverty line based on subsistence levels, that is the minimum amount necessary to maintain physical efficiency. Rowntree calculated his estimates more scientifically than Booth, by consulting the British Medical Association and various nutritionists to draw up appropriate dietary needs for children, male adults, female adults, etc. He translated these nutritional needs into quantities of food, and thence their cash equivalents. To these amounts Rowntree added minimum sums for rent, clothing, fuel, and household sundries, according to the size of the family. Thus, the poverty line for a family of five (two adults, three children) was 17 shillings and 8 pence (approximately 90p) per week, not including rent. Such a family was regarded as being in poverty if its income, minus rent, fell below this amount.

Rowntree's finding of 28% in poverty in York was near enough to Booth's figure suggesting that approximately one-third of the urban population of Britain was in poverty.

Rowntree distinguished between '**primary poverty**', where a family's total earnings are insufficient to obtain the minimum necessary for physical efficiency, and '**secondary poverty**', where total earnings are sufficient, but expenditure is wasteful.

Rowntree added allowances for newspapers, stationery, and trade union subscriptions in his later studies, with the percentage of his sample population in poverty dropping to 18% in 1936, and 1.5% in 1950. Nearly all subsequent inter-war studies on poverty were influenced by the subsistence levels used by Rowntree. Some criticisms of Rowntree's methods are as follows:

1. His estimates of nutrients for different family sizes were broad averages, and did not vary in sufficient detail by age, family composition, or occupation.
2. The food allowances given required extremely skilled budgeting, and did not account for the non-availability of certain foods, or regional variations in diet.
3. Rowntree's estimates of the costs of necessities other than food were based either on his own and others' opinions, or, as in the case of clothing, on the actual expenditure of a small sample of poor families.

The surveys of Booth and Rowntree, and additional descriptive accounts concerning the plight of the poor, led to the origins of state welfare by the reformist Liberal Governments of 1906 and 1910. Old-age pensions and a limited scheme of national insurance were the major initiatives.

ABSOLUTE POVERTY

Absolute poverty refers to a poverty line based on the minimum basic needs for all people, in all societies. Thus, Booth and Rowntree used poverty lines based on subsistence levels, and were describing the number of people in absolute poverty.

Absolute poverty is thus a measure of **objective deprivation**, obtained by costing the basic necessities of life (food, clothing, shelter), drawing up a poverty line using these costs, and defining the poor as those whose income falls below the line.

Absolute poverty, or subsistence poverty, does not take into account general rises in the standard of living of the population, or different cultural requirements. Thus, the poor in Britain today are better off than their Victorian counterparts, and also compare favourably with poor people in many Third World countries. Nevertheless, in relation to the rest of the population in twentieth century Britain, they are poor.

The concept of absolute poverty as a poverty line was also used by W. Beveridge in his proposals for National Assistance in the 1940s. National Assistance Benefit (later changed to Supplementary Benefit, then to Income Support) was designed to provide a minimum income below which nobody should fall. In a similar way to Rowntree, Beveridge argued that national assistance should be sufficient to provide the essentials for physical survival.

Although this measurement is not an official 'poverty line', levels of Income Support are nevertheless used by researchers to measure absolute poverty. However, evidence from Child Poverty Action Group studies indicate that even Income Support rates exclude people who are unable to afford even the basic necessities.

The main drawback with absolute poverty as a poverty line is that it does not take into account general rises in the standard of living of the population as a whole.

RELATIVE POVERTY

Throughout the 1950s and early 1960s the concept of **relative poverty** (or normative poverty) as a true estimate of the number of people living below the average standard of living began to gain support. Using this measure of poverty, rather than an absolute poverty line, many social scientists estimated that rather than disappearing, the numbers in poverty were increasing. Hence, the **'rediscovery of poverty'** in the early 1960s.

Since Rowntree's 1950 study, which showed that only one and a half percent of the survey population were in poverty, very little post-war research had been undertaken until the early 1960s. The work of D. Wedderburn and R. Titmuss are of particular note, but the most significant piece of research was B. Abel-Smith and P. Townsend, 'The Poor and the Poorest' (1965). Abel-Smith and Townsend took as their (relative) poverty line the National Assistance (now Income Support) rates, and added 40% to these figures to provide a 'reasonable standard of living' which was comparable with lifestyles in the 1950s and 1960s. They calculated that in 1953 to 1954 7.8% of the survey population was in poverty, compared to 14.2% in 1960. Nationally, this represented four million people in 1953 to 1954, and nearly 7.5 million in 1960.

Although the data used by Abel-Smith and Townsend are not strictly comparable, the figures nevertheless indicated that poverty was hardly disappearing. Abel-Smith and Townsend were also able to show that 'inadequate wages and/or large families' represented the major cause of poverty for 40% of people, in contrast to Rowntree's 1950 study, where only 4.2% of the poor fitted into this category.

Relative poverty thus emerged as a measure of poverty in the 1960s, to take into account not only subsistence levels, but also the standard of living within a society. It therefore differs from time to time and place to place. P. Townsend, 'Poverty in the

UK' (1979) argues that poverty can only be understood in terms of **relative deprivation**.

> Individuals, families and groups in the population can be said to be in poverty when they lack the resources to obtain the types of diet, participate in the activities and have the living conditions and amenities which are customary, or at least widely encouraged or approved, in the societies to which they belong (Townsend, 1979, p.31).

Townsend extends the government's concept of relative poverty (people with incomes less than Supplementary Benefit rates) by drawing up an index of 60 deprivations, which he claims reflect the style of life which is customary in British society. These include the possession of material goods (for example radio, washing machine, TV) as well as social activities and working conditions. Using these deprivations to measure relative poverty in Britain in the late 1960s, Townsend argues that Supplementary Benefit rates are too low, and people whose incomes are 40% above these rates should also be regarded as being in poverty.

Townsend estimated that in the late 1960s, using Supplementary Benefit rates as the poverty line, 6.4% of the population were in poverty. However, using Supplementary Benefit rates plus 40%, to give what Townsend believes to be a realistic 'average standard of living', the number of people in poverty rises to 21.5%. Thus, using the concept of relative poverty to calculate the number of poor raises methodological problems, for there is no consensus over where the poverty line should be drawn. Some researchers suggest that Townsend's 140% Supplementary Benefit rate poverty line is too generous and arbitrary (why not 120% or 150%?) and today would involve 14 million people, many on average incomes.

Critics of Townsend's concept of relative deprivation argue that rather than measuring poverty, he is actually measuring inequality. Other critics have attacked his methodology. D. Piachaud argues that Townsend's deprivation index contains an arbitrary list of lifestyle activities, many of which depend on cultural behaviour, such as eating habits, social outings. Townsend did not consult the population to discover what a 'normal, reasonable lifestyle' might consist of.

SOCIAL CONSENSUS DEFINITION OF POVERTY

J. Mack and S. Lansley, 'Poor Britain' (1985) represents an attempt to address some of the problems raised by Townsend's study. They conducted a survey in 1983 for the LWT programme *Breadline Britain*, in which they also drew up a list of items in order to measure deprivation. However, the items they included were based on the views of the general public on what they considered to be essentials, and excluded items which people lacked through choice rather than lack of money. Mack and Lansley surveyed 1,174 people, asking them which of 35 items they regarded as essentials. 22 items were selected by at least 50% of the sample, and these comprised the deprivation index. People who lacked three or more of these necessities were defined as poor.

A follow-up survey, *Breadline Britain: 1990s*, used a sample of 1,319 people and included 32 essential items, to reflect the increase in living standards since the original survey. Using the index from the 1985 study, Mack and Lansley estimated that 7.5 million people were in poverty, and by the 1990 survey this had risen to 11 million.

Although Mack and Lansley can be applauded for asking the respondents to identify their own list of essentials, they can be criticised for subsequently imposing their own definition of poverty by counting the poor as those who lack three or more of the items.

There is no evidence that society would approve of this definition, although Mack and Lansley argue that people with less than three of the items are not deprived in other ways, whereas those who lack three or more have other deprivations as well. In spite of this criticism, Mack and Lansley have attempted to achieve a social consensus definition of poverty based on how people actually perceive poverty.

SUBJECTIVE POVERTY

This refers to an individual or group feeling that they are poor. W.G. Runciman, 'Relative Deprivation and Social Justice' (1966) was one of the first to elaborate the term relative deprivation to include 'feelings' of deprivation relative to others, and not conditions of deprivation relative to others. Some individuals may feel poor relative to former circumstances in their lifetime, or a group may feel subjectively poor, even though objectively they are not.

The definition of poverty thus determines the extent of poverty, for example an absolute definition results in few people in Britain being defined as poor. However, if relative definitions are used, a much larger number of people are classified as poor. There is no doubt that absolute poverty has declined this century (Rowntree, Abel-Smith and Townsend), but relative measurements (Abel-Smith and Townsend, Mack and Lansley) would indicate that the number of poor has increased. There are a number of factors responsible for the increase in poverty, such as increased life expectancy, a rise in divorce rates, more lone parent families, and higher levels of unemployment.

Welfare state legislation

The development of welfare legislation results from the notion that poverty is not a natural state, and that the government has a responsibility to provide for the welfare of all its citizens from cradle to grave, or 'womb to tomb'. Welfare provision in Britain dates back to the Elizabethan Poor Law of 1601, which provided **parish relief** for the destitute. Officials in each village had the power to collect a poor rate from every household and distribute the money to those in need. Help was classified as '**indoor relief**' (moving into an institution such as a workhouse) and '**outdoor relief**' (where help was given in the family's own home). The Poor Law Amendment Act 1834 extended this system by grouping parishes into unions and electing Boards of Guardians to oversee the workhouses.

The role of government in the provision of welfare was still essentially one of laissez-faire: the government should not interfere in the economy. However, as the poor law system started to break down in the mid-nineteenth century, the government began to take a more active role in welfare provision. Thus, during the 1870s advances were made under both Conservative and Liberal governments, leading to a number of initiatives such as a national system of elementary education, slum clearance programmes, the start of council housing, and a series of Public Health Acts appointing a Medical Officer of Health and a Sanitary Inspector for each area.

LIBERAL GOVERNMENT REFORMS 1906–1914

It was, however, the 1906–1914 Liberal Governments which laid the foundations of our present welfare state by targeting certain areas for welfare support, leading to the following reforms:

- free school meals and school medical inspections (1906, 1907);
- old age pensions for those over 70 years of age (1908);
- labour exchanges for the unemployed (1909);
- wage councils which set minimum wages for low-paid workers in certain industries (1909);
- a national insurance scheme, limited to certain workers, involving contributions from employers, employees, and government, to fund benefits for unemployment and sickness (1911).

This government involvement in welfare provision marked a change in direction from the laissez-faire attitudes of the eighteenth century, leading to the idea that government responsibility for welfare should be extended into other areas.

THE BEVERIDGE REPORT AND SUBSEQUENT LEGISLATION

The 1942 Beveridge Report laid the foundations for the development of the welfare state, in the post-war years. Beveridge believed that a comprehensive welfare state was essential if the '**five giants**' of want, disease, squalor, ignorance, and idleness were to be eradicated. His belief that poverty was caused mainly by unemployment, old age, and ill-health led him to devise a welfare system which would attack these areas. As a result of his report the Labour Government of 1945 introduced the following legislation:

Butler's Education Act, 1944 established a universal system of education at all levels (primary, secondary, further).

Family Allowances Act, 1945 introduced a non-contributory benefit for each child except the first, payable until the child finished full-time education.

National Insurance and National Insurance (Industrial Injuries) Acts, 1946 provided a system of flat-rate contributions and benefits to provide for unemployment, retirement, sickness, disability, widowhood, maternity, and funeral costs.

National Health Service Act, 1946: to implement in 1948 a comprehensive system of healthcare, free at the point of use.

National Assistance Act, 1948 introduced national assistance, which was intended to be a 'safety net' for those who were not included in the national insurance scheme.

The benefits provided were based on an assessment of needs, and took into account the means of each claimant. Thus, it became a **means-tested** benefit. It was envisaged that the number of people claiming national assistance would decrease, as increasing numbers of people paid into national insurance for their pensions, and the NHS would reduce the amount of sickness in society.

DEVELOPMENTS FROM THE 1950s–1979

The 1950s witnessed a consolidation of the above legislation, with the Conservative Governments of 1951 to 1964 continuing to develop Labour's policies during a period of economic growth and almost full employment. Changes which were introduced included the following.

National Insurance Act, 1959 introduced graduated pensions, increasing with the level of contributions paid in, to a maximum level.

1966 – the Ministry of Social Security was created to replace the role of the National Assistance Board. National Assistance was re-named Supplementary Benefit, and the Supplementary Benefits Commission was introduced.

Family Income Supplement, 1970: a new means-tested benefit which was introduced to supplement the income of low–paid workers.

Child Benefit Act, 1975 replaced Family Allowance and income tax relief for children. Child Benefit was payable for all children including the first.

State Earnings Related Pension Scheme (SERPS), 1975 was introduced to give higher levels of pensions in the future, with those on higher salaries paying in more than those on lower incomes, and subsequently receiving higher pensions.

The 1960s and 1970s also saw both Conservative and Labour governments increase the number of **selective benefits** and services, for example targeted at specific groups within the population. This served the dual role of saving money, as well as aiming welfare provision at those most in need. There was increasing concern too that the insurance scheme was becoming less important that the Supplementary Benefit 'safety net'.

WELFARE STATE LEGISLATION FROM 1979–1996

The election of Margaret Thatcher as Conservative Prime Minister in 1979 marked a replacement of the social democratic consensus on welfare (based on cross-party support for extensive state provision) by a **market liberal attitude**, characterised by an approach to welfare based on minimal state intervention. Ideas were suggested to reduce the bureaucracy of the social security system, and to encourage a self-help culture to replace the **'dependency culture'** which had resulted in increasing numbers of people on benefit. Changes introduced throughout the 1980s and 1990s included the following.

Social Security Acts, 1980 introduced a number of cut-backs in social security, and a 'tightening up' of the rules on discretionary benefits. The link between increases in earnings and increases in benefits was broken, and replaced by benefits linked to increases in prices. Most earnings-related supplements for benefits were abolished.

Social Security and Housing Act, 1982 moved the responsibility for payment of Housing Benefit to local authorities.

Social Security Act, 1986 this implemented the most radical changes since the introduction of social security in 1948. **Income Support** was introduced to replace **Supplementary Benefit**, and was intended as a way of restricting money and reducing the dependency culture by excluding young, single people from claiming. At the same time, extra payments were provided for those in greatest need, including lone parents and the disabled. **Family Credit** replaced Family Income Supplement and was extended and used to encourage people to take low – paid jobs which would effectively be 'topped up' to Income Support levels. It was heavily criticised for acting as a form of subsidy for employers, and creating a poverty trap whereby people on Family Credit who improve their income lose benefits (such as free prescriptions) and can become worse off than people who are not working. The **Social Fund** was introduced to curb the demands for payments for exceptional needs, such as furniture or clothing. These payments were abolished under the 1986 Act, to be replaced by the Social Fund, which retained a small budget for grants in cases of exceptional needs, but introduced a system of loans for the majority of applicants. Eligibility for grants and loans was tightened up at the same time. The 1986 Act also substantially reduced the earnings-related part of SERPS, encouraging people to contribute to occupational or private pension schemes.

Child Support Act, 1991 which became operational in 1993, required absent parents, usually fathers, to contribute to the maintenance of their children. The aim was to reduce the dependence of lone parents on welfare benefits.

Job Seekers Allowance, 1996 – which replaces Unemployment Benefit and Income Support for the unemployed. Under JSA regulations the unemployed will have to show that they are available for, and actively seeking, work. In addition, they are required to sign and keep the Jobseekers Agreement, with harsh penalties imposed if directions are not complied with. There are two forms of JSA. **Contributory JSA** replaces Unemployment Benefit, and is payable for a maximum of 26 weeks. **Means-tested JSA** replaces Income Support, and is payable up to pensionable age.

The period since 1979 has been characterised by a move away from a belief in **collective welfare provision** towards as **'residual model'**, in which help is selectively given to those in desperate need, rather than to all as a right. The greater use of discretionary payments and loans, cuts in benefits, privatisation of certain services, increasing community care, and the encouragement of **welfare pluralism** (private and volunatry sector expansion), are all essential elements of the recent changes in welfare state legislation.

Perspectives on welfare provision

There are a number of theoretical perspectives which can be applied to the study of the welfare state and to poverty. Each perspective differs on how it believes the welfare state should develop, and whose interests it should serve.

FUNCTIONALIST THEORIES

Functionalism is a theory based on the belief that everything which exists in society fulfils some kind of function. Thus, societies are made up of social institutions which perform identifiable functions, and together make up the social system. When functionalism is applied to the study of welfare and poverty, the following assertions can be made.

The welfare state, poverty, and inequality are functional or necessary for society's survival because they maintain social integration by limiting the amount of deprivation people suffer. However, it is important that the levels of poverty do not fall too low (leading to complacency) or rise too high, as the latter may lead to social unrest. The welfare state thus needs to continuously change in order to monitor and adapt to different circumstances so as to maintain balance or 'homeostasis'.

H.Gans, 'More Equality' (1973) argues that if poverty has dysfunctions for individuals, it follows that it must also serve certain functions, or positive effects, for particular groups in the population. Gans lists 15 functions of poverty, including the following:

- It ensures that menial, dirty, and dangerous jobs are performed.
- It creates employment for certain professional groups, such as social workers, the police, etc.
- The poor consume the inferior goods and services in society.
- The low status of the poor raises the social status of the non-poor.

Individuals are seen as relatively unimportant, rather it is the demands of the whole social system which determine the development of welfare institutions, which operate for the benefit of the whole society.

SOCIAL DEMOCRATIC THEORIES

These theories originate from the ideas of J.M. Keynes on economic theory, and W.Beveridge on social matters. Keynes argued that governments were able to manage demand for goods and employment levels by careful intervention in the economy through tax policies and control of spending. Beveridge's views were based on a belief in **collective welfare provision** to modify the hazards of a capitalist economy. Beveridge thus favoured a system of **compulsory insurance** for everyone, to protect them against the pitfalls of a market economy, such as unemployment. The view that everyone should be insured, and therefore eligible to receive state benefits is called an **'institutional model'** of welfare. This model is based on the premise that the majority should contribute to the welfare of the needy minority. Even though some people will pay in more than they receive, they will have the satisfaction of knowing that they can receive support in hard times. T.H. Marshall, 'Sociology at the Crossroads' (1963) suggested that the right to healthcare and state benefits leads to the development of **'citizenship rights'** and ensures loyalty to the state as a provider.

This collective approach to welfare favours the use of **collective benefits** (available to all as of right), rather than **selective benefits** (targeted at certain groups). The creation of the welfare state in the 1940s heavily reflected a social democratic approach, with extensive universal benefits and a limited number of selective benefits.

MARXIST THEORIES

Marxism is a theory which sees society as being divided into two social classes, with opposing interests. Thus, in Britain the capitalist class own the means of production, and want to maximise their profits by paying the lowest possible wages to the workers. This brings them directly into conflict with the workers who are trying to sell their labour for the highest prices.

The Marxist view sees the welfare state as serving the needs of the capitalist system and the interests of the capitalist class, with the main features of the Marxist approach to welfare including the following:

1. The welfare state developed as a concession by the ruling class to the working class, in order to modify their exploitation, and to encourage commitment to the state.

2. The welfare state was created to benefit the capitalist class by giving them a healthy, adequately housed, and well-educated workforce, with a reserve of labour (the unemployed, supported temporarily by social security).

3. The welfare state benefits the rich as well as the poor. Thus, the 'hidden welfare state' gives the capitalist class benefits through the tax system, such as tax relief on mortgages, expense accounts, etc. as well as direct benefits such as healthcare and free or subsidised schooling.

4. Marxists such as J.O'Connor, 'The Fiscal Crisis of the State' (1973) argue that the welfare state is functional for the capitalist economic and social system, but it has to balance two functions. Firstly, the capitalist state is concerned with the accumulation of profits, and secondly, the state must make the system appear fair to everyone (legitimation). Conflict arises when the state has to increase taxes to fund public services, thus threatening profitability, leading to a 'fiscal crisis'. Cuts in expenditure, however, create a 'legitimation crisis' where people question the state's interests. Capitalism needs the welfare state to maintain order, but finds it difficult to reconcile the idea of a welfare state with the capitalist ethos of the accumulation of profit.

5. The welfare state is an adjunct to capitalism, helping to fulfil its needs. Therefore there is no prospect that the welfare state could eradicate poverty and unemployment, or reduce class inequality: it is not intended as a means of doing so.

NEW RIGHT THEORIES

The New Right approach (also known as **market liberal, neo-conservative**, or **anti-collectivist**) has its origins in the nineteenth century political economists of the 'old right', such as Adam Smith and J.S.Mill. These thinkers argued that a free market in both goods and labour was necessary for a capitalist economy to operate effectively. State intervention is seen as unnecessary and harmful, as it interferes with the **free market economy**. The New Right philosophy is seen as a resurgence of these views, which took hold in the 1980s and became supported by the Conservative Governments of Thatcher and Major in the UK and by the US Republican Governments of Reagan and Bush. New Right ideas have been developed in recent times by monetarist economists such as M.Friedman and political writers such as F.A.Hayek. The main features of the New Right approach are as follows:

Capitalism can provide wealth and happiness for all, as competition between individuals and companies leads to higher standards of living overall. The free market operates in such a way that prices and wages find their correct level, leading to full employment and a balance between supply and demand.

V.George and P.Wilding, 'Ideology and Social Welfare' (1985) argue that the market liberals are highly critical of state welfare beyond the bare minimum for a number of reasons. Thus, the welfare state interferes with individual freedom by forcing people to contribute to benefits and services; it is impossible to provide a comprehensive welfare state; the welfare state damages the economy and undermines individual freedom and choice.

Welfare state services are too bureaucratic and inefficient, partly due to a lack of competition for services. M.Friedman and R.Friedman, 'Free to Choose' (1980) argue that a free market economy should be applied to welfare, with the encouragement of private and voluntary provision to compete with state services.

Collectivism is an outdated concept, belonging to the the pre- and postwar eras, when there were no alternative sources of provision.

Many welfare sevices are taken over by professionals, who use them in their own interests, rather than those of the clients. A market place approach would give consumers choice, and eliminate wasteful services and services for which there is no demand.

The welfare state is too expensive, and becomes a drain on the economy. Constantly rising expectations encourage people to believe that services and benefits are unlimited, rather than leading people to consider what provision they could make for themselves.

The government becomes overloaded, with too many systems and groups to deal with. An increase in provision by private and voluntary sector services would reduce this bureaucratic overload.

Government spending on welfare services often increases in response to competing pressures and interest groups, particularly near election time. The idea of 'buying votes' is wasteful, and often no thought of the eventual cost or consequences of such actions is considered.

State intervention takes power away from individuals, leading to a decline in the importance of the family, and reduced incentives to work hard. The New Right argues that people should become more responsible for themselves and their families. Mrs. Thatcher was keen to reduce the role of the **'nanny state'** and its associated **dependency culture**. R. Segalman and D. Marsland, 'Cradle to Grave: Comparative Perspectives on the State of Welfare' (1989) argue that in a democracy citizens have duties as well as rights, including responsibility for themselves and their families.

State provision should be based on a **'residual model'** of welfare, where help is given selectively to those who cannot help themselves. Means-testing is the most efficient way of identifying groups in need, as it is cheap and effective.

Welfare state legislation since 1979 has been heavily influenced by New Right theories. The Conservative Governments of both Thatcher and Major have aimed to reduce the quantity and value of universal benefits, whilst increasing the range of selective benefits and services. Increasing emphasis has been placed on the role of the individual in providing for their own welfare, for example people are being encouraged to take out private pensions to reduce state dependency (and state costs).

Although apparently opposed in views, the New Right and Marxist perspectives actually share a number of feature, for example they both want increased government expenditure, but not at the expense of higher taxes. They also believe that the government is overburdened and cannot cope with the demands on its services. However, their respective solutions to these problems are diametrically opposed.

FEMINIST THEORIES

Feminist theories, like Marxist ones, question in whose interests the welfare state operates. They argue that the welfare state not only maintains the interests of the capitalist class, but reflects the **patriarchal** (male dominated) ideology found throughout society. Ways in which the welfare state supports patriarchy include the following.

The conventional family structure has always been reflected in welfare state policies. The assumption that the male wage earner provided the family wage resulted in many benefits being restricted to males only, with females regarded as 'dependants' (for example the 1911 National Insurance Act incorporated an insurance scheme which largely excluded married women). This perception of **'female dependency'** was extended by the 1940's legislation, when married women were allowed to opt out of full national insurance cover and rely on their husbands' contributions instead. A more recent example of sex-segregated benefits is the Attendance Allowance which, prior to a European Court ruling in the mid-1980s, could not be claimed by a married woman looking after a disabled relative. However, single or married men were entitled to claim Attendance Allowance, the assumption being that men were losing an income by looking after their dependant relatives.

Families operate as miniature welfare systems, in which women are expected to undertake extensive **unpaid 'welfare work'**, such as caring for children, and looking after sick and elderly relatives. M. Barrett, 'Women's Oppression Today' (1980) argues that this welfare work helps to serve the interests of the capitalist class by supplying a free source of care.

Until recently, the tax system reinforced patriarchal attitudes, with the existence of the married man's tax allowance, and the legal obligation for wives to disclose their financial affairs to their husbands.

Women tend to be greater recipients of welfare as they are more likely to be in low-paid, part-time jobs, have a longer life expectancy, an increased likelihood of lone parenthood, and childcare responsibilities. For many childbearing women gaps in national insurance contributions inevitably lead to lower levels of benefits.

The ideologies/perspectives outlined above have been used by professionals, practitioners, and political groups to interpret the problems raised by health and welfare services, and to provide answers to them. Each of the approaches is equally valid, and helps in some way to explain how society and the state views the role of the welfare state.

The distribution of poverty

As described earlier on in this chapter, there are a number of methodological problems surrounding the measurement of poverty. However, using Mack and Lansley's 'index of deprivation', based on a consensus definition of poverty, approximately 12 million people can be considered to be poor in Britain today.

MINORITY GROUP THEORY

This is a method of identifying which particular groups within the population are more likely to be in poverty, because of their specific circumstances. These groups tend to be socially deprived in a number of ways, and can be described as follows:

The unemployed constitute the largest single group in poverty, comprising approximately 1.8 million people. Increased levels of automation, the decline of traditional industries, and foreign competition, have all led to significant changes in the economy, including high levels of unemployment. People who are most likely to be unemployed include the least skilled, people in the northern part of England, and ethnic minorities.

The low-paid are defined as workers who earn less than two-thirds of the male median hourly wage. The Low Pay Unit estimates that 45% of British workers are on low pay, including 78% of part-time workers and 29% of full-time workers. In addition, 71% of women workers are low paid.

The low paid with children are particularly at risk of poverty, especially since the early 1980s and the expansion of part-time employment, coupled with the freezing of Child Benefit from 1987–1990. The lowest paid families tend to also be the lone parent ones, the majority of which are headed by women, who are frequently in part-time, low-paid employment.

The elderly includes those over pensionable age, who curently comprise about 18% of the population, or 11 million people, with two-thirds being women. Increasing life expectancy is likely to swell the numbers of elderly people into the next century.

Elderly people who rely totally on state pensions for their income are most likely to be poor, as the state pension in 1990 was only about 16.5% of the average male weekly earnings. Poverty in old age does not affect all of the elderly, but those who were formerly in low-paid jobs are most at risk, as they have had the least opportunity to save money or to enter occupational or private pension schemes.

Lone-parent families have increased rapidly since the 1970s, with more than one in six families headed by a single mother. Childcare responsibilities, low-paid and part-time work contribute to poverty in this group of people.

The sick and disabled are estimated to number approximately six million adults (14% of all adults in the population), and 360,000 children (three percent of all children). This group of people are more likely than the general population to be in receipt of long-term or permanent benefits. Individuals within this group who do work are disproportionately found in the lower income occupations.

In addition to poverty being related to particular life situations, certain categories of people are more likely to be found in poverty than other. Thus, social class, gender, ethnicity, and regional locality all affect the distribution of poverty.

SOCIAL CLASS AND POVERTY

Most of the minority groups identified above derive from the working class (from unskilled or semi-skilled manual occupations). People employed in these areas are more likely than people from professional, middle-class backgrounds to experience low pay, job insecurity, and fewer opportunities to enter occupational pension schemes. J. Westergaard and H. Resler, 'Class in a Capitalist Society' (1975) argue that minority group theory ignores the class-based nature of poverty, and diverts attention away from the class inequalities present in society. They believe that it is not individual lifestyle situations which lead to poverty, but the extensive class inequalities generated by the capitalist system.

GENDER AND POVERTY

Women form the majority of the minority groups described above (except for the unemployed), with an estimated 4.5 million women in poverty, comprising 62% of adults who receive Income Support. The reasons why women form the majority of the poor include the following.

Childbearing: interruptions to the continuity of employment result in loss of earnings and lack of, or severly curtailed, promotion prospects.

Family responsibilities often restrict employment opportunities for both married and single women. Women are socialised into the primary care role, and are expected to look after their children first, and develop a career later. Also, the lack of childcare provision (and the expense when it is available), deters many women from obtaining employment.

Ineligibility for non-means-tested benefits. Due to their disrupted working life, many women fail to accumulate sufficient contributions for non-means-tested benefits. Therefore women tend to rely on Income Support. In 1990, 96% of lone parents on Income Support were women, and three times as many female pensioners were on Income Support compared to male pensioners.

Carers are predominantly female, looking after children, the elderly, and disabled relatives. It is estimated that there are almost four million female carers in the UK.

P. Townsend et al, 'Poverty and Labour in London' (1987) argue that there has been a **'feminisation of poverty'** since the 1980s, largely as a consequence of reductions in social security benefits, and less employment protection for part-time workers. Townsend identifies four main groups of female poor:

– lone women with children;
– women who look after children or other dependants;
– elderly women;
– low-paid women.

The feminist perspective on welfare described earlier in the chapter would argue that until the patriarchal nature of society changes, women will continue to experience poverty and inequality in relation to welfare services.

ETHNICITY AND POVERTY

High rates of poverty are found amongst certain ethnic minorities, in particular Asians and Afro-Caribbeans. As these two groups have unemployment rates approximately twice that of the white population, they are likely to experience greater poverty. Asians and Afro-Caribbeans are also more likely than whites to earn less and be employed in low-paid jobs. Discriminatory practices in employment as well as in the operation of the welfare services increases the chances of all ethnic minorities of being poor. R. Skellington and P. Morris, 'Race in Britain Today' (1992) describe how residency requirements and passports are necessary in order for many Asian and Afro-Caribbean people to forward a claim for benefits.

REGION AND POVERTY

Poverty appears to be distributed in Britain in an uneven fashion, with the persistence of the 'North-South divide' evident. There is a higher percentage of people on low incomes in the North of England compared to the South. The poorest region in the UK is Northern Ireland, and the most wealthy is South-East England.

The variations in poverty levels between the different regions is overwhelmingly due to differences in unemployment rates in the various areas. It can be seen that as unemployment started to affect the 'affluent' areas in the late 1980s and early 1990s poverty has increased in the South-East.

Poverty varies quite significantly within as well as between regions, with '**pockets of**

poverty' present in urban and rural areas. In London most of the inner city boroughs are likely to have high numbers of poor people. It also appears that many deprivations are linked, so that poor housing contributes to poor health, low educational achievement, and reduced employment prospects.

Reasons for the persistence of poverty

The nineteenth century view of poverty was that it was clearly the fault of the individual (**victim-blaming theories**) and the result of laziness and moral inadequacy. Writers such as S. Smiles, 'Self-Help' (1859) argued that people must help themselves to get out of poverty and accept responsibility for their situation. H. Spencer regarded any attempt by the state to alleviate poverty as a negative one, which would encourage dependency and moral decline. Hard work and moral virutes were considered to be the cures for poverty.

These individualistic or victim-blaming theories are not accepted today as sole explanations for the persistence of poverty, although the New Right approach includes elements of these views, arguing that there are groups within the population for whom poverty and unemployment are self-inflicted. However, the actual number of lazy people or 'social security scroungers' is estimated to be quite small, and certainly constitutes a much smaller percentage than the numbers who fail to claim benefits to which they are entitled to. Even the claimants (usually with large families) who receive more from social security than they would from work represent only about five percent of all people on benefit.

Current explanations for the persistence of poverty in modern industrial societies include the following:

DEPENDENCY THEORIES

These are derived from the views of the New Right, who argue that poverty is caused by excessive dependency on the welfare state, the '**dependency culture**', resulting from what Margaret Thatcher called the overprotectiveness of the 'nanny state'. She spearheaded policies which were intended to encourage an '**enterprise culture**', by reducing income tax and cutting benefit levels.

Another key feature of dependency theories is the concept (first developed in the USA by C. Murray) of an 'underclass' of people who exist below the working class and are dependent on state benefits. Murray distinguishes the underclass from the rest of the poor, claiming that the underclass make no effort to help themselves, squander their income, and often come from disorganised families with high levels of crime and low levels of educational achievement. This group of poor people are seen as irresponsible and immoral, with state benefits too easily available, helping to create a culture of dependency. Dependency theories can be criticised on a number of grounds:

1. This view blames the victim for the cirumstances in which they live, and makes scapegoats out of them by blaming social problems on the underclass. This diverts attention away from the government's ineffectiveness in dealing with social problems.

2. F. Field, 'Losing Out: The Emergence of Britain's Underclass' (1989) supports the views of many social democratic thinkers who argue that the welfare state itself

does not lead to dependency. Instead, as Field points out, it is the lack of resources which prevents poor people from improving their situation and becoming fully participating members of society.

3.   Other groups in society who receive benefits from the state are not regarded as 'spongers' or 'scroungers', for example people who claim tax relief on their mortgages.

4.   Removing state welfare support would not make the underclass disappear; it would simply shift the responsibility to family, friends, and voluntary agencies. Social democratic supporters argue that these groups could not provide adequate welfare support, and in any case the state has a duty to support its most vulnerable citizens.

THE CULTURE OF POVERTY

The underclass, as perceived by the New Right, is seen as having a distinctive way of life and attitudes which create dependency and prevent escape from poverty. The **'sub-culture of poverty'** refers to the view that poverty exists as a culture or sub-culture, with its own distinctive way of life, which is passed down from generation to generation through primary socialisation in the family group. The notion that the poor have a separate culture from mainstream society is one which was first proposed by O. Lewis, with his work among the urban poor in Mexico and Puerto Rico, 'Children of Sanchez' (1961) and 'La Vida' (1966). Lewis argues that the culture of poverty arises out of the marginal position of the poor, and results in a **'design for living'**. Some of the characteristics of the culture of poverty include attitudes of fatalism, feelings of helplessness and inferiority, and a lack of participation in the major institutions in society. Lewis does note that the culture of poverty is weakly developed in advanced capitalist societies, and is more commonly found in Third World countries. However, several American studies have argued that the culture of poverty does exist in advanced capitalist societies. M. Harrington, 'The Other America' (1963) claims that the poor in America have a distinctive sub-culture or 'world view', which is transmitted from generation to generation. The work of W.B. Miller on the American lower class provides evidence to show that the lowest stratum of the working class has a distinctive sub-culture, characterised by 'focal concerns', such as present time orientation, fatalism, and a search for thrills. Some criticisms of the culture of poverty theory include the following.

The actual existence of a culture or sub-culture of poverty has been challenged by research in slums in Peru by W. Mangin and in West Africa by K. Little. They have described the existence of a number of self-help groups and community organisations which do not indicate apathy and fatalism. Research in America by C.A. and B.L. Valentine found that although a sub-culture of poverty existed, it was not the dominant culture among the poor. M. Rutter and N. Madge, 'Cycles of Disadvantage: a Review of Research' (1976) found little evidence in the UK to support the culture of poverty described by Lewis. K. Coates and R. Silburn, 'Poverty: the Forgotten Englishmen' (1970) studied the slum area of St. Ann's in Nottingham, and although they found that there was some degree of resignation and hopelessness amongst the poor, this appeared to be a consequence, rather than a cause, of poverty.

It is argued that the behaviour which characterises the culture of poverty is due to **situational constraints** rather than to the transmission of a particular cultural lifestyle. Thus, the attitudes of the poor are determined by the facts of their situation, for example low income, inadequate housing, lack of facilities, etc. This argument suggests that the behaviour and attitudes, or '**focal concerns**', of the poor would change in response to a different set of circumstances. F. Liebow, 'Tally's Corner' (1967) supports the **situational constraints thesis**, with his participatory observation research on black 'streetcorner men' in a low income area of Washington DC. The behaviour of these men (unemployed or in unskilled jobs) in their family and social life can thus be understood in terms of their reactions to their circumstances, rather than as a distinct culture. U. Hannerz, 'Soulside' (1969) used his research in a black, low-income area of Washington DC to illustrate how the culture of poverty theory and the situational constraints view are compatible. He argues that situational constraints can lead to the development of sub-cultural values, which often remain or take some time to disappear, when the constraints are removed.

THE CYCLE OF DEPRIVATION (or poverty as a positive feedback system)

This approach to poverty is one favoured by the social democratic perspective, and argues that people become poor due to their situation, which may be caused by economic, social, or environmental factors. These situational constraints prevent the poor from escaping poverty, and participating in the norms of society. K. Coates and R. Silburn, 'Poverty: The Forgotten Englishmen' (1970) conducted a major study of poverty in St. Ann's, Nottingham, and found evidence that situational constraints did exist, with multiple deprivations trapping families into '**cycles of deprivation**'. Thus, parents in poor physical health, with inadequate housing, and low-paid employment, give birth to infants with a high risk of illness and death. Living in deprived conditions, these infants grow into sickly children, and education is frequently missed and given low priority. Lack of educational qualifications leads to low-paid and low-status jobs, resulting in inadequate housing and often poor diet and ill-health. Marriage or relationships develop between these deprived young adults, and with reproduction the cycle once again transmits its effects from one generation to the next, as illustrated in the diagram opposite.

Poverty is therefore seen as a **positive feedback system**, a system in which each part reinforces the others and so maintains the system as a whole, trapping people in a situation from which there is little escape. Further evidence to support the existence of a cycle of deprivation comes from D. Caplovitz in the USA and P. Harrison in Britain, who both show how the poor have to pay more for their goods and services because they are likely to live in inner-city areas with high insurance premiums and lack transport to supermarkets. Also, the poor cannot afford to buy food in bulk, or freeze it, so they pay more for it, and have to travel to shops more frequently if they have no transport. M. Rutter and N. Madge, 'Cycles of Disadvantage: a Review of Research' (1976) found significant evidence to suggest that cycles of disadvantage do exist, but they were reluctant to conclude that they were caused by poverty, for in many instances (for example labelling of children from low-income families) they may actually be the cause of poverty.

Critics of the cycle of deprivation argue that there is as much evidence against such a cycle as there is for it. M. Rutter strongly criticises the idea of a self-perpetuating cycle of deprivation, and even Rowntree had suggested that an individual can move in and out of poverty at particular stages in their lives. Furthermore, the theory is only a partial explanation of poverty, for it does not attempt to explain how poverty originates in a society, or describes ways in which the cycle can be broken, for example via the education system.

EXCLUSION THEORIES

These theories support a social democratic or Weberian perspective, which stresses the differences in power between various groups in society. Thus, the elderly, disabled, women, and ethnic minorities have less power in the marketplace and are either excluded from the labour market or are in a restricted position in it, which leads to low-paid work. The poor are therefore those who are excluded from mainstream society by the actions of others. This is also described as a **process of marginalisation**, with these groups of people on the periphery of society's economic and social activities. This view of poverty does not blame the individual, but suggests that certain people will inevitably become casualties of industrial and social change – a condition described as **'dyswelfare'**. Many social democrats believe that a welfare state can ameliorate some

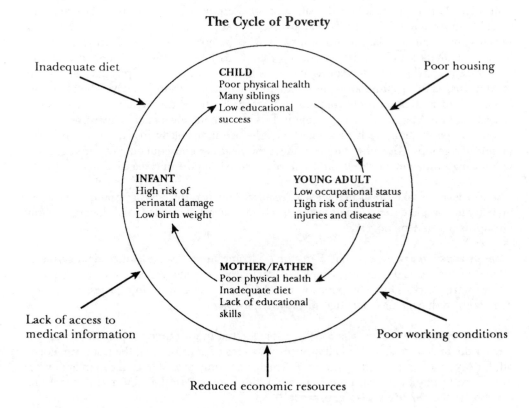

The Cycle of Poverty

of the problems caused by exclusion. Beveridge was a social democrat who hoped that state benefits and services could help to re-introduce the poor into mainstream society.

P. Townsend, 'Poverty in the UK' (1979) adopts the Weberian approach and argues that class, power, and poverty are interwined in such a way that the hierarchy of occuaptional classes, the different work conditions and life chances of these classes, and the institutions and professionals which control access to rewards, all comprise a significant part of any explanation of poverty. Townsend argues that the only solution to this situation is to introduce a series of radical social policies which would abolish excessive wealth and income, and introduce a more equitable income structure, restrict the power and rewards of professionals, increase public ownership, and encourage co-operation and responsibility for those less fortunate in society. Townsend sees the role of the state as instrumental in amending the system of social inequality.

The main criticism of this view is from a Marxist perspective, which argues that in a capitalist society the state will always represent the interests of those at the top, and will not therefore substantially reduce class inequalities.

MARXIST THEORIES

These theories are based on the Marxist premise that there is competition between the powerful groups in society and those with little power, with their power related to their economic position. Thus, the powerful hold the key positions in society, and are able to impose decisions on others in order to maintain their affluence. Hence, low pay and state benefits help to maintain the situation of the powerful. J. Kincaid, 'Poverty and Equality in Britain' (1973) argues that low pay is a key feature of a capitalist society as it benefits the capitalist class in a number of ways: it creates a 'reserve army of cheap labour'; it divides the working class; and maintains low benefits in order to increase work incentives. The structure of capitalism is therefore the cause of poverty, according to Marxists, as the accumulation of wealth automatically leads to poverty. The abolition of capitalism is thus the only solution to poverty for these theorists.

Critics of the Marxist view argue that it does not adequately explain why some groups within the population, such as women, elderly, are more likely to experience poverty than other groups. Also, the state can affect the negative consequences of capitalism by influencing employment levels, and enforcing equal opportunity legislation.

The low level of take-up of many social security benefits, through ignorance, pride, or inability to complete the relevant forms, has been suggested by the Child Poverty Action Group as a cause of poverty.

The poverty trap means that a person's income after tax and other deductions is often less than social security benefits, particularly as some benefits are lost when a person starts work. Thus, the poor are caught in the trap of working for less than they can claim, reducing the incentive to find employment.

The tax system operates against the poor, for the more money a person earns, the greater the tax concessions and allowances. In terms of housing, too, the poor are worse off, for tax relief on mortgage interest payments are only available to those people who can afford to buy their own homes. F. Field, the Labour MP, has referred to these tax benefits as the **'hidden welfare state'**.

Contrasting levels of wealth and lifestyles

Contrasting levels of wealth and lifestyles

The unequal distribution of income and wealth

The difference between income and wealth may be explained simply as being that the former represents a flow of resources over a period of time (weekly, monthly, etc.), whereas wealth is a stock of goods at a point in time, which can be used to generate income. Thus, houses, land, shares, and investments are classified as wealth. Sources of income can therefore be divided as follows:

Earned income, which people obtain by selling their labour in return for a wage or salary.

Unearned income, which is derived from an increase in the value of stocks, shares, land, etc., and interest from investment accounts.

Social income, which refers to state benefits and allowances.
The aims of social democrats such as Beveridge and R.H. Tawney, 'Equality' (1931) that a welfare state would redistribute benefits from the rich to the poor have not materialised. The rediscovery of poverty in the 1960s indicated that major redistribution had not occurred. In the 1982 edition of the government's Inland Revenue Statistics, little change in the distribution of wealth was discovered over the previous ten years. Thus, the richest one percent of the population owned 30% of the personal wealth in 1971, and 25% in 1981. The poorest 50% of the population owned only 9% of the personal wealth in 1971, which decreased to 5% in 1981. Income distribution shows a similar pattern, with the richest 20% increasing their income after tax from 37.5% in 1976 to 38.8% in 1980, and the poorest 20% reducing their tax income from 7.6% to 6.8% over the same period (*Economic Trends*, 1980).

More recent studies have shown that there has been a widening of income inequality throughout the 1980s and 1990s, with a reduction in real income after housing costs for those at the lowest income levels. The welfare state as a means of redistribution or **'strategy for equality'** appears to have failed. The re-organisation of state benefits, with increased selectivity, and tax reductions for high earners, contributed to this widening division between rich and poor. J. Le Grand, 'The Strategy of Equality' (1982) conducted an extensive review of the effects of taxation and welfare on social inequality. There are a number of areas in which the rich benefit more from the state than the poor: use of health services, education post-16, mortgage concessions for home buyers, and state subsidies on transport which benefit middle-class commuters.

In terms of gender and race inequalities a range of equal opportunities legislation has been passed, but it is difficult to measure or assess its effectiveness. Women are still found predominantly in low-paid, low-status jobs, and are still expected to bear the brunt of the 'unofficial welfare state', caring for children and elderly/disabled relatives. Many ethnic minorities are also found in lower occupational strata, and there is evidence to suggest that they suffer discrimination in education and housing.
Whether the welfare state should be aiming to reduce income and wealth inequalities depends on the perspective of welfare which is taken. Arguments against any substantial redistribution of income and wealth include the following:

1. It is human nature to accumulate wealth.
2. Heavy taxation will reduce the incentive to work hard.
3. Income and wealth is already distributed fairly: those who deserve the highest rewards and work hard for them receive high incomes and accumulate great wealth.

Those who are in favour of a much greater redistribution of income and wealth argue as follows:

1. The rich gain their wealth from inheritance, and as proprietors of business enterprises. Thus, two-thirds of people with more than £100,000 inherited more than £25,000 of it.
2. The rich do not work any harder than the sector of the population with little income and wealth.
3. The possession of wealth leads to power, so that an elite group in the population wields power over the less wealthy.
4. In an article in *New Society* in October, 1979, called 'An anatomy of the British ruling class', A. Giddens provides evidence to show how a particular type of social and educational background can lead to inequalities in income and wealth. Using the study of British elites carried out at Cambridge University in 1974, Giddens reports how three-quarters of the directors of industrial corporations had a public school background, as did 80% of the directors of financial firms. Giddens also uses a number of studies to demonstrate how direct kin relations exist between directors of a number of industrial and financial corporations.

A Marxist perspective of poverty, such as that provided by J. Westergaard and H. Resler and by J.C. Kincaid, argues that the private ownership of capital is the major cause of inequalities in income and wealth. Thus, in a capitalist society, low wages for the working class are essential if profit margins are to be maintained. Similarly, social security benefits are kept at a low level to ensure that the poor stay at the bottom of the class structure.

The problem with the Marxist analysis is that it fails to explain how non-property owners, such as top professionals, have high levels of income and wealth.

The functionalist view of stratification, outlined in Chapter 9, would explain inequalities in income and wealth in terms of the rewards which people deserve for their long training and talent. However, this fails to explain inherited wealth, or why some highly trained and talented people do not receive equivalent rewards.

A Weberian view of inequalities in income and wealth would examine the '**market situation**' of individuals, or the amount of power people have in society. Thus, minority groups such as the elderly and the handicapped often have little opportunity to compete in the market, but not all of them are poor. Those whose '**class situation**' is high often have a high level of income and wealth.

Examples where market situation and class situation coincide are found in E. Liebow's study of streetcorner men and in K. Coates and R. Silburn's study of poverty in Nottingham. In both pieces of research, the low class position of the poor corresponds to a low level of education and training, which makes their participation in the economy possible only at the lowest rungs, with the least pay. Some ways of redistributing income and wealth include the following.

1. Raising the level of social security benefits to a value commensurate with average standards of living.
2. Changing the tax system by raising thresholds, to enable the low paid to keep more of their income.
3. The introduction of a **national minimum wage** to eliminate low-paid workers from potential poverty.
4. A **tax credit**, or negative income tax scheme, which would pay benefits to those people below the tax threshold.

5. A '**War on Poverty**', which was the term given to the attempt in the mid-1960s in America to fight poverty. A series of measures designed to create employment, provide camps for unemployed youths, and provide massive pre-school education (Operation 'Head Start') were introduced. By concentrating on aspects of the culture and cycle of poverty, the 'War' failed to change the fundamental basis of poverty – the stratification system.

CHECK YOUR UNDERSTANDING

After reading this chapter you should now be able to define the following terms.

1   Poverty line
2   Primary poverty
3   Secondary poverty
4   Objective deprivation
5   Relative poverty
6   Subjective poverty
7   Laissez-faire
8   Beveridge's 'five giants'
9   Social democratic consensus
10 Market liberal attitude
11 Dependency culture
12 Residual model of welfare
13 Institutional model of welfare
14 Welfare pluralism
15 Collective benefits
16 Selective benefits
17 Legitimation crisis
18 Female dependency
19 Pockets of poverty
20 Victim-blaming theories
21 Underclass
22 Sub-culture of poverty
23 Cycle of deprivation
24 Marginalisation
25 Dyswelfare
26 Strategy for equality

SELF-ASSESSMENT QUESTIONS

1 Describe why relative poverty is a more useful concept than absolute poverty.
2 How has recent welfare state legislation changed the system which was introduced following the Beveridge Report?
3 What are the main differences between the social democratic and New Right perspectives on poverty?
4 Which groups of people in the population are most likely to be poor?
5 How valid is the culture of poverty thesis?
6 How do exclusion theories explain the existence of poverty?
7 Why do explanations for inequalities in income and wealth depend on the perspective which is taken?

'A' LEVEL QUESTIONS

1 Assess the argument that, rather than eliminating poverty, the Welfare State has created a form of 'dependency-culture' (AEB, summer, 1992).
2 Assess the argument that different definitions and explanations of poverty reflect different ideologies (AEB, summer, 1995).
3 'Some have argued that the major reasons for the continuation of poverty are the behaviour and attitudes of the poor'.
    Critically discuss the sociological arguments and evidence in support of this view (AEB, summer, 1996).

CHAPTER FIFTEEN

WORK AND NON-WORK

LEARNING OBJECTIVES

ON COMPLETION OF THIS CHAPTER THE STUDENT SHOULD BE ABLE TO:

1 DEFINE WORK, NON-WORK, AND LEISURE
2 DESCRIBE THE NATURE OF WORK IN INDUSTRIAL SOCIETIES
3 EVALUATE THE IMPACT OF TECHNOLOGICAL CHANGE ON WORKPLACE PRACTICES
4 ANALYSE THE NATURE OF INDUSTRIAL RELATIONS
5 DESCRIBE THE NATURE, CAUSES AND CONSEQUENCES OF UNEMPLOYMENT
6 SUMMARISE LEISURE PATTERNS IN MODERN INDUSTRIAL SOCIETIES

Work, non-work, and leisure

In sociological terms work is any form of activity which results in the production of either goods or services, in return for which financial and social rewards are given. Thus, people work for money, status, job satisfaction, self-respect, companionship, etc. P. Berger characterises three types of work:

1. Work which leads to self-fulfilment and satisfaction, such as medicine, music, art.
2. Work which reduces the individual to an appendage, such as mass production factory work.
3. Work which is 'grey and neutral', such as clerical work.

Definitions of work have concentrated on work as wage labour or paid employment, but the growth in the informal economy (work outside paid employment) has led to a number of other classifications. Thus, R. Pahl and J. Gershung, 'Britain in the Decade of Three Economies' (1980) have produced the following definitions of work:

Formal economy, which is work that is recognised by the state, recorded in some way, and subject to tax and national insurance contributions on the income received.

Informal economy, sometimes referred to as the 'black economy', is work which is not officially recorded, and is not subject to tax and national insurance contributions. The income received is often in the form of cash, but may also include pilfering from work and fiddling expenses. People working in the informal economy may at the same time be in receipt of social security benefits.

Household economy, which refers to domestic work carried out by members of the household to provide essential services for themselves, such as cooking, cleaning, washing, etc. Much of this work is carried out by females within the household, and may be described as housework or domestic labour. It is unpaid labour, and as such, in sociological terms, is not defined as 'work', but as 'non-work', for it involves duties and responsibilities but not the choice which is associated with leisure time.

R. Pahl, 'Divisions of Labour' (1984) added a fourth type of work which he called the '**communal economy**' which is used to describe unpaid work outside the household, such as voluntary work, church activities, involvement in a trade union or political party, etc.

'Non-work' is difficult to define, but is generally used to refer to activities outside paid employment, but which do not constitute leisure. Non-work can therefore be used to describe time spent in necessary but non-remunerative tasks such as shopping, cleaning, personal hygiene, etc. It is also possible to view unemployment as a form of non-work, for it does not offer a financial reward, and is a type of enforced leisure, with no choice. Thus, activities which comprise non-work are distinct from leisure, where there is free choice, enjoyment, and pleasure attached to the interests pursued.

The terms work, non-work, and leisure are difficult to define because they overlap, and in some situations may be interchangeable. Thus, work has different meanings for different people, so that gardening and decorating may constitute paid employment (work) for one person, be regarded as necessary domestic duties (non-work) by another, and may be non-remunerative activites chosen in someone's free time (leisure).

In summary, it can be assumed that work involves a financial reward, and is a necessity or a means to an end for most people. Leisure, however, is concerned with choice over activities which occupy someone's free time, and implies pleasure rather than obligation or monetary reward. Finally, non-work is time spent in activities which carry a duty or responsibility which make demands on people but offer no financial reward. It is a term which can also be applied to the unemployed, who generally do not choose their status, who receive no salary, and who are obliged to conform to certain duties and responsibilities, for example to look for employment.

The nature of work in industrial societies

Changes in the nature of work are a reflection of the social and economic changes resulting from the industrial revolution. The organisation of work varies in relation to the division of labour, that is the breakdown of work into a number of specialised jobs, carried out by different people. Thus, work can be categorised as follows:

Craft or domestic industries, such as weaving, carpentry, painting, etc. are labour intensive, but with little division of labour.

Mechanisation, which started to be used in craft industries from the early seventeenth century onwards, involved an increase in the division of labour accompanying the use of machines.

Mass production, using conveyor belts to move the product along as it was assembled, started in the car industry in the early twentieth century, and spread to a vast range of industries, such as food, household goods, etc. This type of work has a very high division of labour, but workers on the 'belt' rarely have any sense of satisfaction in the finished product.

Automation is where machinery increasingly takes over the jobs previously carried out by people. Since the 1970s micro-chip technology has enabled mass production factories to function at a highly efficient and productive level, without utilising a large workforce.

According to Durkheim, the division of labour is the most important characteristic of industrial societies. In pre-industrial societies there is a limited degree of division of labour, which means that social unity has to be maintained by '**mechanical solidarity**' where people are bound together by common social values and roles. In contrast in industrial societies a high degree of division of labour leads to much greater job specialisation, with social cohesion based on occupational interdependence i.e. **organic solidarity**.

Durkheim's work influenced later functionalists such as T. Parsons, 'The Social System' (1951), who argued that industrial societies were characterised by a high level of functional differentiation: there are a number of institutions which specialise in particular functions which were previously performed by the extended family, such as childcare, healthcare, catering, etc.

In contrast to the functionalists' emphasis on the division of labour, Marx stressed that the nature of work was determined by the mode of production. In pre-industrial societies work was organised around the system of feudalism, which resulted in an economic structure based on the ownership of land. The industrial revolution led to the replacement of feudalism by capitalism, where the production of goods and services is financed by the owners of private capital (land, property, industries). Work in a capitalist society is thus organised and controlled by a small number of wealthy owners aiming to create as much profit for themselves as possible. The labour of employees was seen by Marx as a commodity to be bought and sold. Hence, capitalism created 'wage slaves', who, while legally free to sell their services to any employer, were dependent on the capitalists for work. Unlike feudalism, where even the serfs had their own land, equipment and animals, the workers in capitalism do not own the means of production, and are therefore 'slaves' to the capitalist class. In order to extract maximum profit from their investment, capitalists will buy labour from the workers at minimum cost. By maximising their profits at the expense of their employees Marx argued that workers would suffer from alienation, or a lack of satisfaction in their work. This would ultimately lead to conflict between the two classes of capitalists and workers.

For M. Weber the most significant aspect of industrial society was the development of a rational approach to organising work and social life. Rational behaviour consists of actions which are designed to achieve a specific goal (rather than traditional or charismatic action). The origins of this rational approach could, according to Weber, be traced to the Protestant ethic and the 'spirit of capitalism'. Rational action is characterised by strict rules, bureaucratisation, and a clearly defined hierarchy of authority.

Recent views of industrialisation have focused on the belief that a new form of economic system is developing in advanced industrial societies, leading to post-industrial societies. According to D. Bell, 'The Coming of Post-Industrial Societies' (1973), in these societies unskilled work characteristic of many manufacturing industries is increasingly being taken over by machines. The workforce is thus becoming filled with highly skilled professionals working in the service sector.

Examination of the nature of industrial or post-industrial society has also included discussion on the forms of ownership and control in the economies of capitalist societies. Marx noted in the nineteenth century how there was a growing trend towards **monopolisation**, whereby the ownership of the means of production is increasingly concentrated in fewer numbers of companies. However, the form of monopoly capitalism has changed, as private industry is less likely to be owned by a family or individual, and more likely to involve professionals, salaried managers, and technical experts. By a series of takeovers, mergers, and interlocking directorships different companies are increasingly owned and controlled by the same groups of people. However, Marx did realise that the growth of joint stock companies, where ownership is in the hands of a number of shareholders, would transform ownership and control, with salaried managers being responsible for controlling the companies.

In recent times the rise of large corporations has encouraged and increased the number of **shareholding owners**, with control over decision making passing to professional managers. This pluralist view sees society in terms of competing interests, rather than domination by the capitalist class. The 1980s saw a series of privatisation issues of major British utilities, and combined with the conversion of a number of building societies to banks, this has resulted in a wider share ownership. However, despite the growth in private individual ownership, the majority of shares are still concentrated in the hands of companies, banks, building societies, pension funds, unit trusts, trade unions. Also, in most large firms, the major shareholders are often the senior management, with owners and controllers frequently represented by the same individuals. Furthermore, **mutual shareholdings**, where firms often have shares in other companies, and interlocking directorships (directors common to several companies), dispel the notion that ownership and control are increasingly separate in modern industrial societies.

Other changes in the nature of work which have occurred over the past thirty years include a number of **changes in working patterns**. Thus, the number of working women has increased, as the proportion of male workers has declined, since the 1950s, with women now comprising 45% of the full-time workforce. There has been a vast increase in the size of the part-time working population, who now make up 25% of the workforce. A part-time workforce offers greater flexibility for employers, as they are cheaper than fulltimers, less likely to be unionised, and easier to dismiss. Employers can use part-timers to fill the gaps during periods of peak production, and lay off part-timers in slack times. The majority of part-time workers are female (five million in 1994, compared to less than one million males), as women with dependent children are more inclined to welcome the flexible hours.

The growth of the service sector of employment has led to a huge expansion in part-time work, in the areas of health care, education, catering, shop work, hairdressing, and clerical work. The **expanding service sector** is a result of the process of deindustrialisation, or decline of the manufacturing sector, throughout the twentieth century, and in particular from the 1980s. As primary industries such as agriculture, farming, mining, forestry, and fishing have declined, and secondary industries represented by manufacturing have shrunk, the tertiary or service sector, comprised of education, health, leisure, personal services, transport, etc., have developed apace, with over 15 million employed in the sector in 1994 (compared to only four million in manufacturing industries). D. Bell, 'The Coming of Post-Industrial Society' (1973), argues that the expansion of the service sector of the economy is a key characteristic of post-industrial societies. Bell believes that once people's basic needs for material goods are satisfied (via the manufacturing sector) there is an increased demand for the satisfaction of social needs, such as education, health, and leisure. This leads to growth in the provision of service industries.

Bell also envisages that professional, scientific, and technical occupations will become more 'knowledge based', with the **information technology revolution** offering greater technical expertise and control over work. Bell's views have been criticised for their optimism, for while there has certainly been an increase in the service sector, many people are using goods from this sector to provide services for themselves, using washing machines instead of laundries, videos rather than going to the cinema, and purchasing and using DIY materials at the expense of decorators. J. Gershuny describes this as a trend towards a 'self-service economy', arguing that many service occupations involve selling the products from the manufacturing sector. However, the demand for these manufactured goods does not appear to have stimulated manufacturing industries in Britain; in many cases the goods are imported from abroad.

From a Marxist perspective neither Bell's nor Gershuny's arguments are valid, for in a capitalist society the accumulation of profit is the only goal, and the provision of services can just as easily generate profits as the manufacturing sector. E. Mandel, 'Late Capitalism' (1975) provides evidence to show that large transnational companies will often diversify from manufacturing into services when their profits are slipping. It certainly does not appear that the growth of the service sector has fundamentally changed the nature of capitalism.

Attitudes to work

The attitudes which people have towards work are influenced by a number of factors, both inside and outside the workplace. Some of the theories concerning people and their attitudes to work include the following.

MARX AND ALIENATION

Alienation is a term used to describe a situation where a worker feels a sense of powerlessness over his job, to the extent that the worker is alienated or separated from the product of his labour. K. Marx, 'Economic and Philosophical Manuscript of 1844', was one of the first to discuss the concept of alienation. Marx considered that workers in capitalist society are alienated from work because they own neither the products they produce nor the means of production. Marx derives a number of conclusions from his examination of the relationship between the worker and the production of labour.

1. Man is alienated from nature: the product becomes an alien object independent of the producer.
2. Man is alienated from his own activity: there is no creative act involved in the labour; it is seen purely as a means to subsistence.
3. Man is alienated from his species: estrangement from the products of his labour

distorts man's individual freedom and consciousness, the very things which separate the human species from other animals.

4. Man is alienated from man: if man is alienated from himself, then he will also be alienated from his fellow man.

Crucial to Marx's analysis of alienation is the origin of the estrangement not merely as part of a modern industrial society, but because the means of production are under private ownership. Thus, under private ownership of the means of production the worker not only loses control over the product of his labour, but also over the process. Work no longer becomes a means of self-expression, but merely a means of providing subsistence. The lack of self-expression in labour leads to the loss of the sense of identity and self.

M. Weber rarely used the term alienation, but in his work on bureaucracy and organisations, he illustrated how working particularly at the lower levels of bureaucracy can produce boredom and lack of control over the working environment. In contrast to Marx, Weber appreciated that alienation can equally affect clerks and typists, whether in state bureaucracies or in privately-owned organisations. Although Marx and Weber both agree on the definition of alienation, they differ over its attributed cause. For Marx, capitalism is the root cause of the problem, whereas Weber envisaged any bureaucracy under any economic system as capable of creating alienation.

BLAUNER AND ALIENATION

During the early 1960s a number of studies were published examining the relationship between technology and work satisfaction. These studies categorised work into different types, and attempted to 'measure' the amount of satisfaction workers derived from each particular type. One of these studies, by A. Touraine, took an historical stance to produce the following typology:

- Flexible machines – craft workers
- Standard machines – unskilled workers
- Automation – superintendents

He associated flexible machines/craft workers and automation/superintendents with relatively high levels of satisfaction, and standard machines/unskilled workers with a high degree of alienation.

J. Woodward used the terms unit, batch, mass, and process production in her research, and showed a relationship between increased mechanisation and increased alienation. She also commented on the overlapping roles of workers, technical and supervisory staff in unit and process production, which probably contributes to the low level of alienation found in these industries.

R. Blauner, 'Alienation and Freedom' (1964) is the most comprehensive study examining the relationship between work technology and alienation. Blauner uses empirical evidence from four different American industries based on different technologies.

- Printing as an example of craft technology
- Textiles as an example of machine tending technology
- Cars as an example of assembly line production
- Chemicals as an example of process technology

To measure the degree of alienation in each of the industries above, Blauner presents four dimensions of alienation, which are contrasted with four non-alienative states.

Powerlessness .... control
Meaninglessness .... purpose
Isolation .... social integration
Self-Estrangement .... self-involvement

With regard to the four industries, the printer is presented as the non-alienated worker, as craft technology features freedom from close supervision, control over the work situation, and an intrinsic interest in the work itself. The chemical worker is also presented as having a low degree of alienation, as a result of the responsibility and variety of work in process production. Textile and car workers are both seen as having a high degree of alienation, although Blauner does concede that textile workers achieve social integration in and through the local community, where kinship and religion are dominant institutions.

Using the work of Touraine, Woodward, and Blauner, it is possible to illustrate their findings by what Blauner terms 'The Inverted U-Curve of Alienation'. Blauner expresses the view that alienation has travelled a course that can be charted on a graph as shown opposite.

Blauner interprets the graph as follows. In craft technology the workers' freedom is at a maximum. This freedom is diminished by the introduction of machines, and is further reduced by mass assembly production lines. With the onset of automated industry, however, there is a counter trend, as the continuous process industries increase workers' control and their freedom. Blauner's work can be criticised on a number of points.

Blauner's major source of inter-industry comparison was derived from a re-working of a survey conducted in 1947 for *Fortune* magazine, supplemented by his own case study material from the early 1960s. The information is thus dated and limited in its scope.

The predominant character of an industry's technology may change over a period of time. Thus, in the case of printing, Blauner's example was useful some 25 years ago, but it would not apply to the dominant technology of the present day printing industry, which is largely automated.

There is no clear relationship between industry and technology. Not all the workers in an industry are involved in the same type of technology. In fact, in Blauner's study, only 18% of manual workers were actually classified as working 'on the belt' in the car industry.

Blauner does not explain how he measures alienation, or what he actually means by alienation being 'high' or 'low'.

The emphasis on Blauner's work is on expressed attitudes, rather than on observed behaviour. People do not always exhibit attitudes and behaviour which concur.

Whereas Marx saw alienation as inseparable from the capitalist mode of production, Blauner takes capitalism for granted, and sees alienation as a product of technology – 'technological determinism'. Marxists would argue that changes in technology cannot reduce alienation, for the latter is a fundamental aspect of the capitalist economy. They would go further, and suggest that technology is not 'neutral', but is actively used by both workers and employers to achieve certain gains. A good example is provided by H. Beynon, 'Working for Ford' (1973), who conducted interviews and used participant observation at the Ford car plant in Halewood on Merseyside. By studying both workers and management, Beynon found that technology was used by both groups in different

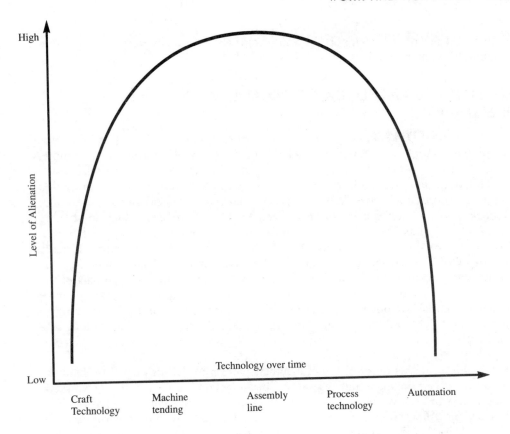

High

Low

Level of Alienation

Technology over time

Craft
Technology

Machine
tending

Assembly
line

Process
technology

Automation

ways. Thus, the management used the production technology to increase the speed of the belt to increase work output, and improve profits (essentially exploiting the workers). In response to their exploitive situation the workers would resist by pulling out the safety wire to stop the assembly line. Technology can therefore be seen as creating constant struggles between management and workers, leading to what Beynon described as a secondary source of alienation (the primary source being the capitalist economy).

Blauner implies a time scale, with one kind of technology supplanting another, with the result that industry is eventually automated, and all work becomes satisfying. Again, this is contrary to Marx, who suggested that no matter how work is organised, under capitalism workers will always be alienated because of their subordinate position.

Many sociologists accuse Blauner's work of being 'technologically deterministic': technology is the one independent variable affecting all other variables, such as the organisation of work, job satisfaction, leisure activities. J. Goldthorpe and D. Lockwood have challenged this view of the relationship between technology and work satisfaction, and their evidence does not support the argument that the former determines the latter. An outline of their research is given below.

GOLDTHORPE AND LOCKWOOD AND WORK ORIENTATIONS

J. Goldthorpe and D. Lockwood, 'The Affluent Worker Vols, 1, 11, 11 (1968–69) was based on the study of 250 married men, aged between 21 and 46, earning £17 or more, in three industries (Skefco Ball Bearing Co., Laporte Chemicals, and Vauxhalls) in the town of Luton. This study of affluent workers revealed a great deal of information concerning industrial attitudes, family life, social class, and political views. Goldthorpe and Lockwood question the importance given by Blauner to technology in shaping workers' attitudes and behaviour. They reject Blauner's positivistic approach which tends to see workers' behaviour as an automatic response to technology. Instead, Goldthorpe and Lockwood take a social action perspective, which emphasises the workers' own definitions of the work situation. They maintain that a large part of the behaviour of the Luton workers cannot be explained in terms of a rejection of mass production technology, but in the way in which workers define and give meaning to their work situation. Goldthorpe and Lockwood make the following observations as a result of their study:

In terms of job satisfaction, they found a similar pattern to that described by Blauner, with skilled workers having a higher level of job satisfaction than assembly line workers.

Goldthorpe and Lockwood found little relationship between technology and attitudes and behaviour. All workers saw work primarily as a means to an end, to earn money to raise their living standards, in other words they had an instrumental attitude to their work. This attitude did not develop in response to the work situation, but was brought to the work situation by the men.

Goldthorpe and Lockwood conclude that the attitudes and behaviour of the affluent workers are little influenced by technology. Instead, they derive from the instrumental attitude which the workers bring to the work situation. The authors argue that what happens outside the factory is more important in shaping attitudes and behaviour than what happens inside. The affluent workers' family life was home-centred and consumption-minded, which explained their instrumentalism more effectively than the influence of technology.

Most of the criticisms of Goldthorpe and Lockwood's study centre on the fact that the majority of the sample were married men with dependent children, who were obviously more likely to have an instrumental orientation to their work. It is not entirely clear in the study where these instrumental views originate – from the work situation or from domestic life. Although the authors imply that the affluent workers and their employers enjoyed a mutually beneficial relationship, shortly after the study there was an acrimonious strike at Vauxhalls, indicating that perhaps employer-employee relationships were not entirely compatible.

Another problem with the affluent worker study was that it neglected the work orientations of women workers. A. Pollert, 'Girls, Wives, Factory Lives' (1981) argues that girls from manual working-class backgrounds are socialised into marriage and childbirth, and develop an instrumental attitude to work because work is merely a temporary phase before the fulfilment of their major ambition. Once married with children, work is still viewed in an instrumental way by most manual women workers, as money becomes even more important.

Evidence to support Goldthorpe and Lockwood's conclusions can be found in international studies which take account of cultural differences in workers' attitudes. In four detailed studies of workers in automated oil refineries in France and Britain in 1978, D. Gallie found substantial differences between workers' attitudes according to their country of origin, with autocratic French management styles encouraging conflict and provoking strike action. Gallie also found that, contrary to Blauner, workers in process production felt 'indifference' towards their work, rather than satisfaction, indicating that non-technological factors may influence work orientations.

WEDDERBURN AND CROMPTON AND WORKERS' ATTITUDES

D. Wedderburn and R. Crompton, 'Workers' Attitudes and Technology' (1972), used the research of Blauner and Goldthorpe and Lockwood to conduct their study in terms of both viewpoints. They studied a large chemical complex in England which they called 'Seagrass', and concentrated on two works on the same site. One was a continuous process plant, and the other used machines to produce chemically-based yarn. The sample of workers were mostly born and raised in the area, with 30% over the age of 46, 10% unmarried, and nearly half of the men earned wages which were below the national average. Wedderburn and Crompton found that their sample, like the Luton workers, had an instrumental attitude to work. 'Job interest' was mentioned as important by fewer Seagrass workers than Luton ones.

The authors found that different attitudes and behaviour within the work situation could emerge in response to differences in technology. Thus, the process workers found their work more interesting, with more freedom and control over their work situation. In contrast, the machine shop workers found work boring, with little freedom and control over their work situation. Workers in the machine shop had a higher rate of absenteeism and a higher strike level than workers in the process plant. Finally, workers who found their jobs interesting tended to regard supervisory staff favourably, whereas the machine shop workers saw their supervisors as enforcers of authority, concerned with quality control.

Wedderburn and Crompton conclude that the general attitudes and behaviour of Seagrass workers cannot be accounted for by technology. They do, however, maintain that certain aspects of behaviour are influenced by production technology.

Technological change and workplace practice

Marx viewed technology in capitalist society as a means by which employers could increase their profits. In particular, if skilled workers could be replaced by machines then labour costs would be significantly reduced. Gradually, this would lead to a process of deskilling, whereby skilled workers would be downgraded to machine minders at an unskilled level. In practice, however, the twentieth century has witnessed an expansion in the diversity of occupations, particularly in the service sector, with automation seen as increasing the range of skilled jobs. Many Marxists though would argue that the level of skill required in work has been progressively reduced in the twentieth century as

Technological change and workplace practice

employers use deskilling to control the workforce. One exponent of this view of the labour process is H. Braverman, 'Labour and Monopoly Capitalism, The Degradation of Work in the Twentieth Century' (1974).

Braverman argues that deskilling, or the progressive degradation of work, has been achieved by management decisions rather than by technology. These management strategies are based on the 'scientific management' theories of F.W. Taylor (outlined in Chapter 5) which were implemented by Henry Ford in his car assembly line. By breaking down the labour process into a number of stages, unskilled workers can be increasingly used in the production line, with decision making removed from the workers' control. If workers are allowed to develop their skills, this may require them to organise their own work practices, thus threatening the ability of management to control the labour process. Braverman describes three stages by which managers take control of the labour process via the deskilling of workers:

Using F.W. Taylor's scientific management principles, management should study the skills required in particular industries, and use the knowledge to control the production process by redesigning jobs accordingly.

This is where management takes control of the planning and procedures ('brain work'), leaving the workers to execute or carry out the defined tasks. Braverman calls this stage the 'separation of conception from execution'.

Management specifies the tasks which are to be given to unskilled workers, thus reducing their bargaining power.

Braverman argues that management will make concessions to workers, such as improved working conditions and increased pay, in order to remove any potential conflict. In other words, the human relations school of management (see Chapter 5) may be used to make the strict scientific management approach more tolerable.

Case studies have been conducted by a number of Marxist researchers which support Braverman's views: A. Zimbalist (ed.), 'Case Studies on the Labour Process' (1979) reviews deskilling in coal mining, car assembly, carpentry, clerical work, and includes Zimbalist's own research on the printing and typesetting industries. Despite this evidence for deskilling, a number of criticisms can be levelled at the thesis:

R. Edwards, 'Contested Terrain, The Transformation of the Workplace in the Twentieth Century' (1979) argues that Braverman overestimates the importance of scientific management as a management strategy, and suggests that there are three forms of control which can be identified. Firstly, nineteenth century capitalism operated a form of 'simple control' of the labour process, with two levels of management, the owners and the foremen/managers. As the early twentieth century increased the range of skilled jobs available, employers had to resort to 'structural control' methods, such as production lines. During the post-war era the expansion in non-manual jobs required 'bureaucratic control', which was achieved by creating hierarchical authority structures and written rules.

Whereas Braverman saw scientific management (or Taylorism) as the only form of labour control, Edwards identified different forms of control which emerged at different stages in the capitalist process.

Edwards' views have been supported by S. Wood and A. Friedman, the latter describing a management strategy called 'responsible autonomy', where workers have limited freedom to control the labour process by working in teams rather than on production lines, for example Volvo and Volkswagen car plants.

There is evidence that workers do not passively accept management control of the labour process, but that worker resistance can affect, or even change, the type of control. Trade unions may be influential in negotiating these changes in working conditions, but there may be limits to this resistance because ultimately the employers own the organisation and materials, and can impose their will on the workers.

Feminist critics have argued that women have largely been excluded from the discussion on deskilling. V. Beechey and S. Walby argue that women's skills (for example cleaning, cooking, childminding) are often not recognised as such, and also that deskilling may be directed more at women as they have less trade union protection. Women may, in addition, be subject to male management strategies which deliberately exclude women from skilled work, reserving it for male employees.

The evidence for deskilling provided by Braverman is limited. Unlike Braverman's 'golden age' of skilled workers, only a small number of nineteenth century craftsmen were skilled artisans, with the majority either semi-skilled or unskilled, particularly in mining, transport, and food processing. Braverman's claim that many non-manual jobs have been deskilled (for example nurses, teachers, engineers, secretaries) is open to question. Although some non-manual and manual jobs have been deskilled by new technology, there is evidence to indicate that many occupations have undergone reskilling, with typists becoming wordprocessors, nurses becoming technicians, and new jobs have been created, for example computer operators, IT specialists.

FLEXIBILITY AND POST-FORDISM

Braverman's view of the labour process was one which was implemented by Henry Ford in his car assembly line, using scientific management principles. However, throughout the 1970s and 1980s a number of theorists have argued that the labour process typical of 'Fordism' has been replaced by more flexible methods of production, known as 'Post-Fordism'. The trend away from Fordism towards a post-Fordist era has resulted in what M.J. Piore calls 'flexible specialization', characterised by flexibility in the production process and the re-emergence of skilled crafts. This flexibility involves the use of technology, especially computer aided design and manufacture (CAD, CAM), to produce specialised products (small batch production) according to demand. Goods can thus be produced to order, often for a more discriminating and affluent consumer. An increase in skill levels and a more flexible workforce would result from the implementation of small batch production.

Another supporter of the concept of the 'flexible firm' is J. Atkinson, who argues that such flexibility has emerged as a result of technological changes, the reduction in the working week, and reduced trade union power. Atkinson recognises two main forms of flexibility:

'Functional flexibility' involves the redeployment of multi-skilled employees between different tasks. For this form of flexibility a core workforce is required, consisting of permanent, full-time and well rewarded managers, designers, technicians, and craftsmen.

'Numerical flexibility' involves the ability to increase or decrease the labour force as necessary and at short notice. For this form of flexibility a peripheral workforce is required, consisting of temporary, part-time, and often hourly paid staff, who are generally clerical or assembly line workers.

Piore and Atkinson do not accept that work has been deskilled. However, they have slightly different views on the future implications of flexibility. Thus, Piore believes that most workers will increase or broaden their skills in flexible companies (by operating computers or designing products), leading to increased control in the workplace. Atkinson, though, is more pessimistic, acknowledging that core workers will be rewarded with enhanced skills, promotion opportunities, and good levels of pay and conditions, whereas peripheral workers will experience less job security, poor promotion prospects, and lower financial rewards. Post-Fordism and flexibility can be criticised on a number of counts:

The move towards small-scale batch production is not new. As A. Pollert indicates, many specialist products have always been manufactured in this way, for example furniture. Conversely, mass production is still a crucial form of manufacturing in food processing, drinks, DIY, toiletries, etc., especially as many companies cannot afford the technology required for CAD and CAM.

It has been questioned whether flexible working will lead to increased skill levels and greater worker control. Flexibility may create conflict between employers and workers, as each group want different things from the process. This could result in either 'Taylorist' control or 'worker-centred' control, or a combination of both.

The idea of a peripheral workforce is not a new concept. Temporary, part-time, and contract workers have always played a significant role in manufacturing industry, and have not substantially increased in the last twenty years.

Both the arguments of Braverman and those of the post-Fordists are based on their respective fundamental views and perspectives of society and the nature of work. They claim that work is developing in a direction which is linked to their particular economic and political theories. Perhaps there is no single course of movement in which work is developing, and it may be more realistic to accept that different industries and workforces are affected to varying degrees and in diverse ways by technology, skills, flexibility, and control.

The nature of industrial relations

The field of industrial relations is concerned with the interaction between employers and employees, with the workplace frequently seen as an arena of disagreement between the two sides. This conflict is often presented in the media and by politicians as a social problem which disrupts services and reduces economic efficiency. Conflict is thus seen as an unavoidable but temporary feature of the industrial relations process. However, it is also feasible to view conflict as a normal part of the industrial system in a capitalist society, with the employers seeking to maximise their profits, and the workers simultaneously pursuing better working conditions and higher pay.

Industrial conflict involves many forms of industrial action, varying in severity and popularity. These include the following:

Official strikes: which have the recognition and backing of the trade union involved.

Unofficial strikes: (or 'wildcat strikes') which are not officially supported by the relevant trade union.

Industrial sabotage: where workers deliberately damage the product or tamper with the process of production. Many good examples can be found in the work of L. Taylor and P. Walton, 'Industrial Sabotage: Motives and Meanings' (1971) in S. Cohen (ed.), 'Images of Deviance' (1971).

Go-slows or work-to-rules, which are designed to disrupt the production of goods and services without the workers losing their income.

Overtime ban: which affects the production process.

Individual acts: which include absenteeism, resignation, or even theft from the company.

Strikes are the most visible and most reported forms of industrial action, and have therefore received the greatest interest from sociologists. One area which concerns sociologists is the problem of actually measuring what a strike is, and then collecting data on how frequently they occur. R. Hyman, 'Strikes' (1972) lists five elements in the definition of a strike.

1. An actual stoppage of work, as distinct from a go-slow.

2. A temporary stoppage of work, where workers intend to return to work within a short period of time.
3. A collective act, involving a group of employees.
4. The action taken is by employees, as distinct from students, etc.
5. It is nearly always a 'calculative act', designed to seek a solution to problems, express grievances, or put pressure on employers to enforce demands.

Data on the frequency of strike action is not always reliable, with official statistics on strikes suffering from the general problems of the collection of official data (see Chapter 10). In industrial relations, the government collects figures on the number of official and unofficial stoppages, the number of employees involved, and the number of working days lost. The collection of this data is dependent on reports by the employers, and therefore is not always reliable or valid. Hyman provides statistics for the three measures from 1900 to 1971, which indicate that the actual number of strikes has increased, but that the number of working days lost has decreased. Since 1971 the number of disputes (defined by the Department of Employment as strikes which last one full day, involve at least ten workers, or the loss of 100 days or more) has remained almost constant, but the number of days lost has increased. This may, however, appear misleading, as one strike may involve large numbers of workers, for example prolonged disputes by the miners in 1973/74 and 1984/85. Overall, the trend is towards local rather than national strikes, and a greater number (80–90%) of unofficial strikes. In general, the picture in Britain compares favourably with other countries (about half-way down the international strike table), with about 95% of manufacturing industries free of stoppages in any one year. Some of the major causes of both official and unofficial disputes include the following:

Economic: this is the most commonly stated motive, although research frequently demonstrates the existence of an underlying non-economic cause. Between 1966–74, problems relating to pay accounted for 57% of stoppages according to the Department of Employment. Most strikes in the 'winter of discontent' of 1978–79 were mainly about pay, and although the 1980 steelworkers' strike was superficially about pay, an underlying cause was the British Steel Corporation's decision to reduce its workforce by approximately one-third over a period of years. The economic motive tends to become more important when inflation is high, but is also related to an increase in consumerism and a rise in white-collar union militancy.

Non-economic or underlying factors. Two important case studies illustrate the relevance of these factors. A. Gouldner, 'Wildcat Strike; A Study of Worker-Management Relationship' (1957), described how the strike he observed was preceded by tension and conflict between workers and management over the introduction of new machinery and new management. The change from an informal structure to one more rigidly structured was the major source of conflict, with the workers eventually accepting a wage rise as compensation for the new authority structure. T. Lane and K. Roberts, 'Strike at Pilkingtons' (1971), pointed out that the strike was preceded by a good period of industrial relations, with no apparent or observable 'cause'. They concluded that it is possible for strikes to arise under 'normal conditions': they are a fact of working life, an accepted weapon in the bargaining process.

Strike-prone industries: this implies that some industries have higher strike 'risks' than others. An international comparison of strikes in eleven countries by C. Kerr and A. Siegal in 1954 found that miners, dockers, ship-builders and textile workers were involved in strike action more frequently than any other groups of workers. Their theory of explanation was that strike-prone industries are found in areas with close-knit communities, where worker solidarity is high, and the work is hard and dangerous. Their work has been criticised by R. Hyman, who argues that they do not explain variations in strike rates for those who live in loose-knit communities, or why workers in the same industry but from different countries have different strike rates. Recent studies, such as S. Hill, 'The Dockers' (1936), find the picture of 'strike-prone industries' rather dated now, as many traditional working class communities have disappeared, and workers have become privatised, with family and home taking precedence over work relationships.

Role of technology. Blauner's work on alienation would seem to indicate that all car assembly-line workers are alienated and thus likely to strike. This does not, however, account for variations within the same industry between different countries.

Workplace characteristics. W.W. Daniel and N. Millward 'Workplace Industrial Relations in Britain' (1983) suggest that particular workplace characteristics are associated with strike action. Thus, higher strike rates are found in workplaces with a higher proportion of male workers, with more full-time workers, local bargaining procedures, and agreed negotiating procedures between management and unions.

Multiple motivations for strike action have been put forward by R. Hyman as an interactionist view of industrial conflict. It is the strikers' definition of the work situation which determines the propensity to take action. The studies of H. Beynon, A. Gouldner, T. Lane and K. Roberts support the notion that strikes have underlying and complex causes, which can only be understood in terms of the workers' definitions and meanings attached to the working environment.

The belief that strikes are an inevitable feature of modern industrial societies is one largely held by Marxists. In a capitalist society where employees and employers have irreconcilable differences, industrial conflict provides a means of expressing grievances against the ruling class. Strikes are seen as inevitable in a situation where employers want to maximise profits, and workers seek to improve their pay and conditions. According to the Marxist perspective, no legislation can reduce the level of conflict, for the solution lies in the restructuring of capitalist society along socialist lines.

The functionalist view of strikes is not of inevitability. Their belief in a society based on consensus extends to employers and employees, who ultimately share the same goals, but play diferent roles in the production of goods and services. Strikes are seen as a problem which can be solved, providing adequate bargaining machinery is established to settle disputes. R. Dahrendorf, 'Class and Class Conflict in an Industrial Society' (1959) argues that conflict has not disappeared, but has been 'institutionalised'. Attempts to institutionalise conflict through the process of collective bargaining have been described by A. Fox and A. Flanders, 'Collective Bargaining: From Durkheim to Donovan' (1969). Trade unions are therefore viewed as interest groups, rather than conflict generators, able to influence industrial and political decision making, ensuring integration into capitalist society. More recent initiatives aimed at eliminating conflict include the encouragement of workers' participation in management via the ownership of shares in the industry. For Marxists, however, participation still does nothing to remove the fundamental inequalities within the system, which can only be removed by workers' control of the industry. The limited attempts at co-operative industries in Britain, such as Triumph Motorcycles at Meriden in the 1970s, have failed due to a lack of development capital and poor management. It has also been argued that historically the culture of the British working class is anti-industrial democracy, as workers are socialised to either conform or conflict, not to participate.

RECENT CHANGES IN INDUSTRIAL RELATIONS

The 1980s and 1990s have seen widespread changes in the nature of industrial relations, with a reduction in the power of the trade unions, and an increase in the importance of **collective bargaining**. These changes have arisen largely as a result of government legislation, initially with the 1974–79 Labour Government's 'Social Contract'. This initiative attempted to persuade the trade unions to accept pay restraint in return for the repeal of the 1971 Industrial Relations Act, and greater consultation between the government and the TUC. A number of organisations were created which were designed to bring together representatives of government, trade unions, and employers. The National Enterprise Board was set up in 1975 to develop policies for firms receiving state aid. During this period trade union growth peaked, with almost two-thirds of the workforce unionised in 1979. However, this successful era for the unions turned sour as pay restraint proved unpopular, particularly with low-paid workers. This resulted in an increase in strike action in the late 1970s, culminating in the 'winter of discontent' in 1978–79, when a number of public service unions went on strike.

The 1979 election of a Conservative Government under Margaret Thatcher marked a change of direction, with a commitment to reduce the power of the trade unions. A series of industrial relations legislation was introduced to restrict the ability of trade unions to take effective industrial action.

1. Laws were introduced affecting voting within the union, and the balloting of members for strike action.
2. Regulations concerning the election of union officials were implemented.
3. Trade union action against dissenting members within the union was prohibited.
4. Secondary action was outlawed, that is a union cannot support a dispute which is not at their own place of work.
5. Trade unions which infringe industrial relations legislation are liable to have their funds removed (sequestered).

The above changes affecting the operation of trade unions weakened trade union solidarity, and reduced the power of individual unions. In addition to the introduction of government policies, a number of economic changes in the 1980s have resulted in the weakening of trade union power. These can be summarised as follows:

Economic recession and the restructuring of the workforce. High levels of unemployment and redundancies in manufacturing industries have hit traditionally strong areas of union activity, such as coal mining, ship-building, and engineering. The provision of new jobs in the service sector has resulted in a large proportion of the workforce being female and part-time, (traditionally low areas of unionised activity). In addition, workers' bargaining power has been reduced by an increasing number of unemployed (a 'reserve army of labour') who are able and willing to take on jobs under poor conditions and with low pay.

Changing attitudes of employers. Many employers are now moving towards internal and local bargaining procedures, which make it difficult for a union to organise unified action. In some cases there is even individual bargaining over pay and conditions, with people accepting flexible working conditions and variable pay awards. These changes are a reflection of post-Fordism, indicating a more flexible workforce, and move away from collectivism towards individuality.

Union influence. The economic and political power of trade unions has decreased as they have increasingly been excluded from the membership of government organisations. Membership of large unions such as the TGWU and the GMWU have decreased due to the decline of semi-skilled and unskilled jobs. In order to improve their bargaining power smaller unions have combined or merged. The public sector unions of NUPE, NALGO, and COHSE joined together to form UNISON. In order to improve their power and increase their influence trade unions need to recruit more members, especially more women and part-time workers. As the distinction between manual and non-manual occupations decreases, unions seem more likely to have joint interests. It certainly seems the case that an increasing number of white-collar unions are prepared to take strike action in support of their working conditions and pay.

The nature, causes, and consequences of unemployment

THE NATURE OF UNEMPLOYMENT

Unemployment is a feature of all economies, and is an accepted part of capitalist society. However, prolonged periods of high unemployment in the 1970s and 1980s caused it to become a high-profile political issue. Although the measurement of unemployment suffers from all the problems of official statistics (see Chapter 10), it appeared to rise from less than two percent of the workforce between 1948–66 to over six percent in the late 1970s. Following a slight decrease, it rose rapidly to 9.5% in 1982, and reached a peak in the mid-1980s with 11.8% of the workforce unemployed (representing just over three million people). This figure declined in the late 1980s to reach just less than two million people in the mid-1990s.

Official statistics on unemployment can be criticised for representing an overestimation of the figure or an underestimation of the figure. Thus, it could be argued that there are people claiming to be unemployed who are not seriously looking for work, or who are working unofficially. However, R.E. Pahl, 'Divisions of Labour' (1984) found evidence to suggest that the unemployed were no more likely to take on unrecorded or 'informal work' than people in paid employment. It is equally valid to argue that the official figures underestimate the numbers of unemployed. Thus, the Conservative Governments between 1979 and 87 changed the method of calculating unemployment statistics 19 times, mostly involving the removal of people from the register, or making qualification for inclusion on the register more difficult, for example men over 60 years and young people under 18 years are now excluded from the register, and youth and adult training schemes have removed people from unemployment. The current official unemployment figure is based on the number of people who actually claim unemployment-related benefits, that is 'claimant unemployment', unlike the International Labour Organisation definition, which includes all people actively seeking work, whether they are eligible for benefits or not.

THE SOCIAL DISTRIBUTION OF UNEMPLOYMENT

Despite the above problems with the official measurement of unemployment, it is possible to see a number of patterns in the distribution of unemployment amongst different groups in the population:

Social class. According to D.N.Ashton's research in 'Unemployment under Capitalism' (1986) people who are in semi-skilled and unskilled work are more likely to be unemployed than skilled workers and managers/professionals. He also found that personal service workers and women suffered high rates of unemployment, with professionals, managers and employers having only one-third of the average rate of unemployment. Ashton's work is supported by evidence from the General Household Surveys and the *Employment Gazette* which add that manual occupations are more likely to experience periods of temporary unemployment as well as long-term unemployment.

Age. Unemployment rates are found to be disproportionately higher for people in younger age groups, especially for males under 24 years. Youth unemployment amongst 16–17 year olds has virtually disappeared, as teenagers can no longer claim benefit, but must take up youth training programmes. D.N.Ashton argues that, during economic recessions, first time entrants to the labour market will be most affected, with more opportunities available for this group during boom periods. He also adds that it is difficult to measure whether unemployment is a long-term problem for the young, or a temporary phase until they are qualified, more experienced, and established in the workplace.

Gender. Figures consistently indicate that women have lower rates of unemployment than men, but this is probably an underestimate as many married women are ineligible for benefits which entitle them to be officially registered. The existence of many female homeworkers, seasonal staff, and casual workers means that women are often omitted from the official unemployment statistics. Another reason for women's higher levels of employment is that they are more likely than men to accept low-paid work, temporary work, and part-time work, all of which have increased as a result of the growth of the service sector.

Ethnicity. Labour Force Surveys of the 1980s have shown that ethnic minorities consistently experience higher rates of unemployment than the white population. The group with the highest figures is Pakistani/Bangladeshi, who have approximately one-third unemployed, compared to 10% of the white population. Young ethnic minorities are particularly affected, and during economic recessions it appears that black groups find it especially difficult to obtain employment.

Region. Variations in unemployment between different parts of the country have been described by the Department of Employment. Using standard regions in Britain, the ranking of areas has remained relatively constant since the 1950s, with Northern Ireland, Scotland, Wales, North, and North-West regions suffering the highest rates of unemployment, and the South and South-East enjoying the lowest rates. Areas with the highest figures are those in locations which have been most affected by the decline in traditional industries, and those with the lowest figures have experienced the most growth in service sector industries. It also appears that there are variations within regions: inner-cities have higher rates than suburban areas within the same region.

THE CAUSES OF UNEMPLOYMENT

Market liberal theories arose in the 1970s as a response to the post-war Keynesian consensus that governments could and should maintain low levels of unemployment. Whereas the Keynesian view was supported by both Labour and Conservative governments in the years after 1945 with state intervention in the economy, market liberalism grew in the 1970s as an alternative view of the labour market. Market liberals such as Milton Friedman argued that state interference in the market over goods and services can actually create unemployment. Thus, union demands for higher wages increased inflation, higher taxation would reduce incentives for investment, while welfare benefits discourage people from working for low pay. Friedman advocated 'monetarist' policies to counter these effects and control inflation. Consequently, the Conservative Governments from 1979 to 1987 adopted these policies by reducing the role of the state in economic affairs via a reduction in union power, cutting public expenditure, and lowering benefits for the unemployed.

Critics of these policies have, however, questioned whether they have been successful in reducing unemployment, or in fact, may have led to an increase in unemployment rates. J MacInnes 'Thatcherism at Work' (1987) argues that unemployment was rising in the late 1970s and early 1980s as a result of the world economic recession, despite the government's monetarist policies. The decline in unemployment from the mid-1980s cannot be proved to be linked to free market policies, but may have been the result of other factors, such as the changing definition of unemployment, and the introduction of job and youth training schemes.

Marxist theories are based on Marx's belief that unemployment is a direct result of the capitalist system. Economic booms and troughs are seen as inevitable features of a capitalist economy, resulting in periods of full employment which will lead to a decline in profits, stimulating periods of high unemployment with low wages to increase profits. These periods of crisis when wages fall and unemployment rises would progressively increase according to Marx. Monetarism and government policies to weaken trade unions merely represent attempts by the capitalist class to keep the working class suppressed, and increase the profitability of the employers.

Structural unemployment is a situation which occurs when there are workers seeking employment, but they do not match the jobs which are available. One form of structural unemployment is 'regional unemployment', where the unemployed lack the relevant skills and appropriate qualifications to fill the vacancies; for example workers in traditional industries may find their skills obsolete, and unless they retrain may find it difficult to obtain employment.

Frictional unemployment occurs when workers change jobs, but do not move to their new employment straight away. Thus, they may be unemployed for a short time as they seek work, or wait to take up a new post.

Cyclical unemployment occurs when the supply of labour exceeds the demand for workers by employers. This results in the number of unemployed far outstripping the number of vacancies. Cyclical unemployment is a result of economic cycles of depression and boom, usually short-term, but occasionally long-term. Although the cycles may be affected by government policies, it is assumed that low levels of unemployment will occur naturally after a period of about five to seven years. However, this seems doubtful in the light of new technology and reduced demands for certain types of labour.

Technological change has resulted in a dramatic decline in manufacturing industries, with three million jobs lost between 1971 and 88. Other areas which have suffered decline through automation in the past twenty years include construction, energy and water supply industries. New technology, in particular information technology, may also threaten people in a range of occupations, such as printing, engineering, teaching, banking and insurance.

Competition from abroad has resulted in the loss of manufacturing jobs to countries with cheaper labour and production costs, in particular to Third World nations in the Far East. Overseas competition has also come from industrialised nations in the European Community and from Japan.

THE CONSEQUENCES OF UNEMPLOYMENT

Although it is difficult to measure, there is considerable evidence to suggest that unemployment has a number of negative consequences, not just for the individual, but for society as a whole. Often links are made between unemployment and 'social problems' such as crime, suicide, divorce, alcoholism, discrimination, and violence, although these are difficult to prove. A. Sinfield, 'What Unemployment Means' (1981) argues that unemployment devalues the standard or quality of life in society. It does this by threatening the security of those in work, reducing job mobility as people fear that other jobs are unavailable, creating wider divisions between the unemployed and the workers, and reducing equal opportunities as employers have no reason to employ minority groups. The unemployed may thus feel marginalised by society, leading to alienation, apathy, and discontent.

In individual terms it is difficult to separate the effects of unemployment from other variables in people's lives, and different people experience, and react to, unemployment in different ways. Nevertheless, there appear to be a number of consequences of unemployment for the individual, which can be summarised as follows:

Psychological effects. Studies from the 1930s onwards have claimed that unemployment causes negative psychological effects which vary between the newly unemployed and the long-term unemployed. Work deprivation is thought to result in apathy, depression, and alienation from society. L. Fagin and M. Little, 'The Forsaken Families' (1984) identified four stages which the unemployed pass through, based on their study of unemployed men in Liverpool. These were: shock; denial and optimism; anxiety and distress; resignation and adjustment. It is difficult to generalise from this sample to the whole unemployed population, as young unemployed people who have never worked will feel differently to middle-aged people who have been made redundant.

Financial effects. There is evidence to indicate that unemployment leads to poverty. A DHSS survey in 1978 found that the income of 30% of unemployed men fell to less than half what it had been in employment. More recently, the Joseph Rowntree Foundation, 'Inquiry into Income and Wealth vol. 1' (1995) found that during the 1980s and early 1990s the income gap between those on benefit and those who were employed significantly widened. One reason for this was that during the 1980s benefits changed from being linked to average earnings to being linked to prices.

WORK AND NON-WORK **261**

Social effects. These are difficult to quantify, but there is some evidence to indicate that people may suffer social disorganisation as a result of unemployment. B. Thornes and J. Collard, 'Who Divorces?' (1979) found that unemployment was twice as common in divorcing couples than in stable marriages. One reason may be that some women are resentful if their husbands are around the house all day, especially if they do not contribute to the housework or childcare. L. Fagin and M. Little, 'Forsaken Families' (1984) decribed how their sample of unemployed Liverpool men suffered from a loss of identity and role, in particular missing the ritual and routine associated with the 'obligatory activity' of work. Social contacts are reduced, time is difficult to structure, and leisure pursuits may have to be forsaken due to a lack of income. Although the social effects of unemployment focus on men, it appears that women also suffer a sense of loss of purpose during unemployment, and it is false to believe that domestic life offers an equivalent identity and role. For many divorced, widowed, or lone unemployed women the social effects may have greater consequences than for men.

Leisure patterns in modern industrial societies

As already described at the beginning of this chapter, work is defined as an activity for which a person receives some form of remuneration. Thus, any other activity that does not involve payment is defined as 'non-work' or leisure. In pre-industrial societies, people would often work with members of their family in cottage industries or farming, where there was no sharp division between work and leisure. In industrial societies, however, because people go out to work and return home at the end of the day, there is a much clearer division between work time and leisure time. According to Marx, writing in the mid-nineteenth century, factory workers barely had time for 'animal functions' (sleeping, eating, procreating), let alone leisure interests. Subsistence wages ensured that any time that was left over from work had to be spent very frugally. Marx regarded non-work time as simply a means by which the workforce could recover and recuperate from its labour in order to reproduce a new generation of workers for the capitalist system. Since the nineteenth century, a significant reduction of working hours, coupled with a general rise in living standards, has greatly increased the opportunity for self-fulfilment in leisure. However, many Marxists argue that this opportunity has not been realised.

A. Gorz, 'Work and Consumption' (1965) argues that alienation at work can also lead to alienation in leisure. Thus, rather than finding self-fulfilment in leisure, capitalism creates an entertainment industry which provides a means of escaping from alienation at work, but does little for self-fulfilment.

H. Marcuse, 'One Dimensional Man' (1972) extends Gorz's view to argue that in its leisure industries capitalism creates 'false needs' via the mass media, which is controlled by the ruling class. He argues that these 'false needs' prevent self-fulfilment in leisure, as people become obsessed with obtaining consumer goods as a form of leisure, a condition which I. Illich calls 'commodity fetishism'.

The Marxist perspective on leisure outlined above fails, however, to take account of the meanings which individual members of society have concerning their leisure. By condemning all workers to a lifetime of unfulfilled leisure, Marxists are not prepared to accept that some people may actually gain self-fulfilment in their leisure hours. If individuals do proclaim such fulfilment, the Marxist perspective would argue that they are suffering from 'false consciousness', that the mass media only makes them think that they are gaining satisfaction.

THE RELATIONSHIP BETWEEN WORK AND LEISURE

A number of relationships between work and non-work activities in industrial societies have been observed. These include the following.

The effect of time spent at work on non-work activities. Most people have a five day working week, with free weekends, annual holidays, and public holidays. As a consequence, organised leisure activities are arranged to fit in with this pattern. Sporting events, clubs, cinemas and theatres, design their functions around weekends, evenings, and public holidays. People who do not fit in with this general pattern of having available leisure time at weekends and evenings have particular problems filling their non-work time. Thus, shift-workers and weekend workers may have to look for alternatives, such as watching TV, walking, gardening, etc.

The effect of income received at work on non-work activities. People with high disposable incomes can obviously afford to pursue more expensive activities (such as sailing, skiing, flying) than those with lower incomes.

The effect of social contacts at work on non-work activities. The influence of other workers in the work situation on an individual's leisure time friendships depends on a number of factors. The nature of the work situation determines the amount of 'social mingling' which occurs: office workers are more likely to mix socially than assembly line workers. The age of fellow workers can encourage or discourage leisure friendships (people of the same age tend to mix socially outside working hours). People in professional occupations often mix their business and leisure interests, for example business lunches, golf course meetings, etc. Finally, the distance between work and home can limit a person's opportunity to share leisure activities with work colleagues, or in the case of close-knit communities with one industry, can encourage social mixing.

The effect of a person's social status at work on their non-work activities. The type of work a person does can affect his own and his family's social status, and can influence his leisure activities in two ways. Firstly, leisure can reflect the status of his job situation, so that certain clubs are joined (sports or social) which reinforce a person's status, and people with high occupational status generally hold positions of office in these organisations. Secondly, leisure can be used as a means of achieving social status, for example by holding offices in trade unions or political parties, or using sport or entertainment to provide status which is denied to a person in a job.

Several studies have attempted to examine the relationship which exists between the work a person does and the way in which they spend their leisure time. S. Parker, 'Work and Non-Work in Three Occupations' (1965) was based on a study of 200 men and women who worked in 10 different occupations, half in the business sector and half in service industries. Parker's main hypothesis was that people in different occupations would not only vary in their degree of commitment to their jobs, but also in the part that work plays in their lives as measured by the encroachment of work on leisure time. In turn, this would affect the extent of colleague friendships and the function of leisure in people's lives compared to their family and work. Of the 10 occupations studied, Parker found that bank employees were one of the least work-involved groups of people,

Parker's conclusions can be summarised as shown below.

Occupation	Leisure pattern	Relationship to work	Demarcation	Attitude to work	Function of leisure
Childcare Officer	Extension	Similar	Little	Involved	Development of personality
Bank employee	Neutrality	Some difference	Some	Indifferent	Relaxation
Coal miner	Opposition	Very much	Much	Hostile	Recuperation

whereas childcare officers were highly work-oriented. These two categories of occupations, together with a third group of youth employment officers, were chosen by Parker for more intensive study. Using his own research material, and also the studies on traditional extended working-class families by J. Tunstall and N. Dennis et al, Parker proposed three patterns to illustrate the relationship between work and leisure:

Extension pattern is where leisure activities are an 'extension'of working life, and help to develop the individual's personality. Parker found that childcare officers and youth employment officers frequently used their leisure time for work-related activities. The same could be said for teachers or musicians, whose work and leisure overlap.

Complementarity or neutrality pattern is where people neither enjoy their job enough to wish to carry it over into their leisure time, nor do they dislike it to the extent that they become hostile towards it. They feel indifferent towards their leisure activities, which might be spent in sport, hobbies, or just relaxation. Parker found that bank employees were most likely to have this particular pattern of a work/leisure relationship.

Opposition pattern is where there is a sharp division between work and non-work, with leisure time spent in activities which serve to compensate for work which is regarded with hostility. Parker argued that this pattern could be seen in fishermen and miners, who regarded their leisure-time drinking as a means of escape from the dangerous and hostile world of work.

Research on the leisure activities of managers casts doubt on Parker's extension pattern. American research indicates that managers fit into the extension pattern, with a working week of over 60 hours, and leisure often seen as a refresher to enable work to be performed better. This subordination of leisure to work is not found in Britain. J. Child and B. Macmillan, 'Managers and Their Leisure' (1973), studied 964 British managers, and found that only 2.3% mentioned the use of leisure as a means to improve their careers. In fact, almost a quarter admitted to using leisure as a means to escape from work, and appeared to fit into the neutrality pattern in terms of their leisure pursuits.

These cultural differences may be due to different attitudes to the work ethic, self-improvement, and individual achievement.

Research on the relationship between work and leisure has also concentrated on social class differences. J. Goldthorpe and D. Lockwood, 'The Affluent Worker' (1968) included a summary of the extent to which workers in the three factories they studied participated in work based clubs and societies. Their results are summarised below.

From this table it can be seen that workers with a high degree of alienation are least likely to participate in clubs and societies. Overall, all workers preferred to join a general works club, rather than specific sports or hobbies clubs or societies.

S. Parker, 'Professional Life and Leisure' (1974), was a small survey in the central London borough of Islington. Parker interviewed 96 men : 57 in full-time paid employment, 21 self employed, and 18 either retired or students. Parker found that although the self-employed had less leisure time, they were more likely than the employed to spend it in activities related to work. Only a small minority of all workers felt hostility towards their work, with the most popular leisure activities being walking, sports, cinemas, pubs, visiting relatives or friends, and going to the library.

M. Young and P. Willmott, 'The Symmetrical Family' (1975) included a survey of social class variations in leisure in two major areas home-based activities and sports activities. For home-based activities, they found that all classes listed 'watching TV' as their overwhelmingly favourite leisure activity. For social classes 1 and 2, over two-thirds participated regularly in gardening, reading, and listening to music. In contrast, only 28% of social classes 4 and 5 read regularly. Swimming was the most popular sports-based activity in all classes, with the more expensive sports (motor racing, sailing, water skiing) confined to social classes and 1 and 2. Young and Willmott also found that visiting the pub was enjoyed by between 45% and 50% of people in all social classes, but that men in social classes 1 and 2 were more likely to go out drinking with their wives than men in social classes 4 and 5.

Although it appears from the above evidence that work does have an impact on

	Skefco (Craftsmen)	Laporte (Process workers)	Vauxhalls (Assembly line workers)	All married men
% belonging to work clubs (general)	80%	52%	29%	53%
% belonging to particular clubs and societies	32%	22%	14%	23%
% regular attender	26%	4%	5%	13%

people's leisure time and interests, there are other social constraints which affect leisure. R. and R. Rapoport, 'Leisure and the Family Life Cycle' (1975) argue that choice of leisure activities is shaped by an individual's age or position in the family life cycle. Thus, the leisure interests of children, adolescents, young adults, married couples, and retired people are to a large extent determined by their income, social contacts, and family commitments. However, it could be argued that it is not necessarily the biological base which constrains leisure activities, but the ways in which society 'constructs' leisure around images and expectations of certain age groups, for example nightclubs for teenagers, gardening for the middle aged. Another key constraint on leisure is gender, which is largely ignored in studies on work and leisure. For women, their dual role of worker and wife/mother often restricts their leisure interests in particular ways. R. Deem, 'All Work and No Play: The Sociology of Women and Leisure' (1986) describes how women frequently combine their leisure with domestic activities: ironing while watching TV, reading and childminding. Family-oriented leisure seems to be of greater significance in women's non-work time than the pursuit of individual leisure activities.

PLURALIST VIEW OF LEISURE

Parker's conclusions on leisure, and many studies after it, tend to adopt a deterministic view of leisure, which assumes that work, age, gender, and family life all directly affect people's leisure activities. The pluralist approach stresses the individuality and choice which people have in their non-work time, whilst accepting that social factors may play some role as well. K. Roberts, 'Contemporary Society and the Growth of Leisure' (1978) claims that leisure must be viewed in terms of choice, so that leisure must mean that people have the freedom to choose how to spend their non-work time. This would exclude non-work obligations such as DIY, gardening, and visiting family, unless these were freely chosen as leisure interests. Roberts disputes Marxist theories which argue that people are manipulated by commercial leisure interests and controlled by state provided facilities. He argues that the provision of services does not necessarily guarantee that people will use them. There is certainly plenty of evidence to indicate that theatres, cinemas, libraries, etc. will close down if the public demand declines. There are also examples of ways in which state and commercially provided leisure interests have to respond to public demand, for example skateboarding parks, recreation centres, cheap package holidays abroad.

Finally, Roberts claims that the ultimate in choosing one's own leisure activities has to be the creation of leisure interests by individuals, such as hobby clubs, darts teams, sports groups. Although Roberts accepts that social factors such as family life, class, etc. may influence leisure choices, he disagrees with Parker that work determines leisure, for excluding the unemployed, approximately half the population do not have paid work.

MARXIST VIEW OF LEISURE

The Marxist perspective on leisure is essentially one of exploitation and control, with capitalism shaping leisure as well as work. J. Clarke and C. Critcher, 'The Devil Makes Work: Leisure in Capitalist Britain' (1985) describes how the state controls licensing laws (in pubs, clubs, and in gambling), censors films and videos, and passes health and safety legislation which restricts certain leisure pursuits (for example an adult cannot supervise more than two children under eight years in a swimming pool). Clarke and Critcher argue that consumers are exploited by large leisure industries which provide mass-produced leisure where people have little choice, such as theme parks, concerts, package holidays. Mass advertising is used to lure people towards these activities in order to make as much profit as possible for the leisure entrepreneurs.

Another Marxist approach is offered by H. Wilensky, who argues that in modern industrial societies, elites will increasingly plan and organise the work activities of the labour force. In response to this 'takeover' of the work situation, leisure will replace work as a central life interest. Wilensky envisages the worker withdrawing into a form of 'contented apathy' where family and friends will provide the satisfaction and security unobtainable from work and the community.

In a similar way, C.W. Mills sees the replacement of the work ethic by the leisure ethic. The leisure, however, will not provide the fulfilment denied at work, because the ruling elite will use the leisure industry to manipulate the mass society. Hence, the techniques of mass production used in industry are applied to leisure (organised sport, cinema, TV, etc.) to provide mass entertainment offering escape rather than fulfilment.

POSTMODERNIST VIEW OF LEISURE

Postmodernism is a more recent development of pluralism, stressing the new cultural mood of the post-war era, and emphasising the importance of personal identity, style, diversity, and choice. Many postmodernists, such as A.J. Veal, believe that individuals create a lifestyle around their own personal identity. This might include choice of clothes, furniture, food, hairstyles, and leisure pursuits. It is an idea which T. Burns also subscribes to, where leisure provides the freedom for individuals to choose activities to promote their own interests in order to find meaning and self-fulfilment. Burns uses Goffman's idea of '**styling of activities**' to describe the meaning and significance given to life by these leisure interests. 'Styling' will also influence work, rather than the other way, as people choose jobs which fit in with their leisure in terms of hours, location and social contacts. Although the postmodernist view suggests that people can escape their traditional roles to pursue leisure as they wish, there are still certain constraints which are still relevant in leisure choices. Thus, income, gender, race, and class will continue to affect the leisure activities available to, and chosen by, individuals in society.

CHECK YOUR UNDERSTANDING

After reading this chapter you should now be able to define the following terms.

1 Formal economy
2 Informal economy
3 Household economy
4 Non-work
5 Division of labour
6 Functional differentiation
7 Monopoly capitalism
8 Service sector
9 Deindustrialisation
10 Self-service economy
11 Alienation

12 Blauner's Inverted U-Curve of Alienation
13 Technological determinism
14 Instrumental attitude
15 Deskilling
16 Post-Fordism
17 Flexible specialisation
18 Functional flexibility
19 Numerical flexibility
20 Claimant unemployment
21 Market liberalism
22 Monetarist policies
23 Structural unemployment
24 Frictional unemployment
25 Cyclical unemployment
26 Leisure
27 Extension pattern of leisure
28 Complementarity pattern of leisure
29 Opposition pattern of leisure
30 Styling of activities

SELF-ASSESSMENT QUESTIONS

1 Describe some of the problems involved in defining work, non-work, and leisure.
2 How has the division of labour affected the organisation of work?
3 Describe the impact of alienation on workers in different occupations.
4 How has 'flexible specialisation' affected the nature of work?
5 Give evidence to support the view that although many strikes have an obvious economic motive, there are often more important underlying causes for disputes.
6 Which groups in the population are most likely to experience unemployment?
7 To what extent does work influence leisure activities?
8 How do the Marxist and postmodernist views of leisure differ?

CHAPTER SIXTEEN

COMMUNITY, URBANISATION AND DEVELOPMENT

LEARNING OBJECTIVES

ON COMPLETION OF THIS CHAPTER THE STUDENT SHOULD BE ABLE TO:

1 DISCUSS THE MEANING OF THE TERM COMMUNITY
2 DESCRIBE SIGNIFICANT EXAMPLES OF COMMUNITY STUDIES
3 DESCRIBE THE RELATIONSHIP BETWEEN COMMUNITY AND GENDER, AGE AND RACE
4 SUMMARISE THE KEY FEATURES OF URBAN SOCIOLOGY
5 DESCRIBE KEY SOCIOLOGICAL THEORIES OF DEVELOPMENT
6 REVIEW THE RELATIONSHIP BETWEEN DEVELOPED AND LESS DEVELOPED SOCIETIES
7 SUMMARISE THE MAIN FEATURES OF FIRST AND THIRD WORLD COUNTRIES

The meaning of community

The word community conjures up many different aspects of social life. It can be used to describe a village, a social group (for example a church community), the European Community, 'community' care, and racial and ethnic minorities (for example the Jewish community). The term can describe close, intimate relationships, or more distant social relationships. It certainly implies that people are bonded together in some way, or have some connection. The confusion over a clear definition of the term has been noted by G.Hillery, who found that the word had been used in 94 different ways by sociologists. However, according to H.Newby, 'Country Life' (1987), it is possible to group the definitions into three broad categories:

Community as a fixed locality, or a geographical area, in which there is a high level of social organisation.

Community as a social system, or a set of relationships which are found in a given locality.

Community as a type of relationship, in which there is a strong sense of shared identity and experiences. These relationships are not dependent on geographical locality or on close knowledge of one another. Members of the Jewish religion may be described as a community, even though they live in different parts of the world. Newby calls the quality of this relationship a **'communion'**.

'LOSS OF COMMUNITY'

An examination of the nature of community can be achieved by contrasting it with what a community is not. Several of the most influential theories on the 'loss of community' include the following.

F.Tonnies, 'Gemeinschaft und Gesellschaft' (1887), which can be roughly translated as 'Community and Society'. Tonnies described how **gemeinschaft** relationships are close-knit, involve primary groups, ascribed statuses, and diffuse roles (people are not just seen in terms of their occupational role, but as a whole person). In contrast, **gesellschaft** relationships are associational, involve secondary groups, achieved statuses, and specific roles. Tonnies applied gemeinschaft and gesellschaft to organisations as well as to roles and relationships. Thus, a church is typically gemeinscaft, but a business enterprise reflects gesellschaft characteristics. Tonnies was rather pessimistic about city life and gesellschaft lifestyles, believing that they led to the death of the community and gemeinschaft living.

E.Durkheim, 'The Division of Labour' (1893) described how **social solidarity** is achieved in pre-industrial or rural societies and in industrial or urban societies. He used the terms 'mechanical' and 'organic solidarity' to refer, respectively, to the way in which the division of labour in rural and urban societies contributed to social solidarity. Durkheim feared that a condition of **anomie** or normlessness would arise during the transition from mechanical to organic solidarity, with a consequent breakdown in community life.

G.Simmel, 'The Metropolis and Mental Life' (1903) used many of the ideas of Tonnies and Durkheim to explain how the growth of cities affected personal relationships. Simmel's approach is really that of a social psychologist, as he examines the emergence of 'market-place' values in human relationships, a sense of rationality, self-interest, and people viewed as commodities. Simmel also mentions the positive aspects of city life for those who are successful – wealth, freedom from restraint, and status.

R.Redfield, 'The Folk Society' (1947) was keen to illustrate the differences between **'folk societies'** and more industrialised **urban societies**, envisaging a continuum stretching from 'rural' at one end to 'urban' at the other. In a similar way to Tonnies, he found (based on research in Mexico) that folk societies were small, intimate, homogenous, traditional, and focused on ascribed statuses. In contrast, urban societies are large, impersonal, hetergenous, rational, and focused on achieved statuses. However, O.Lewis, 'Life in a Mexican Village: Tepotzian Restudied' (1957) found that, contrary to Redfield's 1930 study of the same area, the community was divided and distrustful of one another. Although this may have indicated a change in the nature of the community over a period of time, the differing perspectives of the area may also reflect the influence of personal values in this type of research.

CRITICISMS OF THE TERM COMMUNITY

The word community has been criticised for its inappropriateness in defining groups of people. M.Stacey argues that studies of large communities are impossible because of the size of the population, and small communities are not necessarily self-contained, but are influenced by outside agencies. She suggests using the term **'locality social system'** instead of community, because it more clearly describes the closeness of the institutions (family, school, work) within a particular locality. Another example of an alternative term for community is **'social network'**, used by F.Bott, 'Family and Social Network' (1957) to illustrate the pattern and density of relationships between people. The size, duration, and frequency of contacts are important in determining the extent of people's social networks.

The idea of a **'community spirit'** is derided by some sociologists, who argue that it is a myth to believe in a homely, small town neighbourliness. A.Vidich and J.Bensman, 'Small Town in Mass Society' (1958) studied Springdale, a small town in New York State, and although it appeared to be neighbourly, friendly, and democratic, there were underlying divisions based on class and racial differences, with a small group having political control. In contrast to this, A.Etzioni, 'The Spirit of Community' (1944) argues that the materialism, selfishness, and social problems of modern society require a move towards the creation of a more moral and democratic society – what Etzioni calls **'communitarianism'**.

Despite the above criticisms, some sociologists believe that the notion of community remains a relevant and useful concept. The alternative definitions of Stacey and Bott are difficult to apply, and are often used interchangeably. H.Newby, 'Community' (1980) argues that community is still useful for measuring social change and the impact on people's lives. The term **'spirit of community'** is increasingly used by politicians and journalists as a means of resurrecting the moral values and social relationships of a previous era, Finally, there is substantial evidence to indicate that communities have not disappeared from society, but are still significant in many people's lives.

Community studies

Community studies are based on particular localities, and attempt to describe the values, relationships, and lifestyles of the people who live there. They try to capture the essence of the community, whether it is a 1950s working-class district, an ethnic community in the 1990s, or a youth sub-culture such as Teddy Boys. Many community studies offer an opportunity to undertake field studies on a range of subjects, such as family, work, social class, age, race. However, there are a number of problems which are associated with community studies, including the following.

TIME DIFFERENTIAL

The fact that communities change over time means that studies may become outdated very quickly. On the positive side, however, it is possible to assess the social change which has occurred over a particular time in a community.

Village life: the myth of community

GENERALISATIONS

Communities show great varieties in social life, and it is not possible to generalise from one study to other, similar locations. If generalisations are made, then it is essential to base them on a number of relevant samples, and not just one.

METHODOLOGY

Many community studies are based on acceptable sociological methods, such as sampling, interviewing, and observation. However, there are some community studies which rely on anecdotal evidence and journalistic reporting styles, but do not contain a clear sociological method of investigation. Several examples of classic community studies include the following.

R.Hoggart, 'Uses of Literacy' (1957). Although Hoggart's book is not specifically sociological, but more cultural, it nevertheless provides a significant account of the area of Hunslett in Leeds. Hoggart identifies the central features of the working-class community in this locality, pointing out the small corner shops, back-to-back housing, and sense of commitment to local affairs and social relationships. In addition, self-respect, tolerance and enjoyment of life were attitudes found by Hoggart. He argues that these pockets of traditional working-class culture were changing in the post-war era, with the emergence of mass culture replacing traditional values.

M.Young and P.Willmott, 'Family and Kinship in East London' (1957). Used a range of sociological methods of investigation to study the East End community of Bethnal Green. They used questionnaires and interviews to collect data from a sample of just under 1,000 people in the locality. Their hypothesis was concerned with looking at whether post-war social change had resulted in the breakdown of the extended family in traditional working-class communities. Young and Willmott found that the community in Bethnal Green was still close-knit, with kinship ties especially strong and mothers and daughters having a particularly close relationship. The extended family network remained significant in this area well into the 1950s, providing job contacts and camaraderie for men, and substantial social and emotional support for women. When 47 young married couples moved from Bethnal Green to Greenleigh (twenty miles away) a different type of community emerged. The atmosphere was less intimate and sociable, with no supportive extended family. Loneliness, materialism and isolation characterised Greenleigh, with 'window to window' relationships the norm. The move to **privatised families** was completed with the transition from segregated to joint conjugal roles.

Similar studies on traditional working-class communities which reflect Young and Willmott's findings include J.Tunstall, 'The Fishermen'(1962) and N.Dennis, P.Henriques, and C.Slaughter, 'Coal is Our Life' (1956).

J.Goldthorpe and D.Lockwood, 'The Affluent Worker in the Class Structure' (1969). This study, described in detail in Chapter 15, concentrated on the privatised lifestyles of affluent workers in Luton. Goldthorpe and Lockwood emphasised the home-centred nature of such families, although later studies revealed that privatisation is not a straightforward issue. G.Marshall et al, 'Social Class in Modern Britain' (1989) described three forms of privatisation:

1. **Structural privatisation** refers to the way different areas of life (family, work, leisure) are increasingly separate, and less likely to overlap.
2. **Cultural privatisation** refers to the decline of 'class consciousness' and the concentration of interests on home rather than on work or the community.
3. **Privatised politics** indicates a preference for voting on an individual basis, rather than along class lines.

Marshall et al found that there was little evidence to support any one of the above, as work was still important in people's lives and there did not appear to be a retreat from class interests. Also, the three categories are not mutually exclusive, and may overlap.

A follow-up to Goldthorpe and Lockwood's study by F.Devine in 1994 found that during the 1980s people who moved to Luton from outside the area were often followed by their kin and neighbours. She found that the traditional working-class lifestyles did not seem to change as much as the Luton study had predicted, for social lives outside the home were common, and there were still elements of segregated role relationships.

Most contemporary studies of the community are local case studies, which cannot be used to generalise from. They do, however, offer 'snapshots' of life in towns and villages, but with the same nostalgia for the past as Tonnies and Durkheim had shown. Several of the most renowned include the following:

1. R.S. and H.M.Lynd, 'Middletown' (1929). The authors spent 18 months living in the mid-American town of Muncie, Indiana.
2. C.M. Arensberg and S.T. Kimball, 'Family and Community in Ireland' (1940) concentrated on the village of Luogh, in County Clare, in S. Ireland.

3. A.D. Rees, 'Life in a Welsh Countryside' (1951) includes several studies of Welsh rural villages.
4. H. Gans, 'The Urban Villagers' (1962) found 'village-like' or gemeinschaft ethnic working-class communities in Boston and New York.
5. R. Frankenberg, 'Comunities in Britain' (1966) uses the urban/rural continuum to examine the major differences between city living and rural living.
6. R.E. Pahl, 'Urbs in Rure' ('The City in the Countryside') (1965) describes the 'culture clash' which existed in Hertfordshire commuter villages between the locals and the newcomers. These villages were neither gemeinschaft nor gesellschaft, but contained elements of both types of relationships.

Community studies in the past twenty years have concentrated on examining the concept of '**loss of community**'. M. Bulmer and P. Abrams, 'Neighbours' (1986) argue that traditional working-class communities have declined due to improved material conditions and economic security. However, rather than losing their community nature, they have changed to different forms. Thus, Young and Willmott predicted that Greenleigh would develop the close social networks characteristic of Bethnal Green over a period of thirty years or so. D. Widgery, 'Some Lives' (1991) argues that East End values still persist, binding people into a sense of community.

Another recent focus has been on the '**romanticisation**' of community, or the often presented nostalgic belief that life was better in the past. There is, however, much contemporary evidence to debunk this view. R. Glasser, 'Growing Up in the Gorbals' (1987) points out the harsh realities of living in Glasgow tenements in the 1930s, and G. Pearson, 'Hooligan' (1983) describes how concern over youth problems was just as prevalent in Victorian times as it is now. Other studies, for example G. Beattie, 'We Are the People' (1993), demonstrate how communities have been destroyed by redevelopment, leaving people with no social support systems. R. Williams, 'The Country and the City' (1973) argues that the 'myth of community' is used to help people accept the rigours of capitalism. Hence, alienation and dissatisfaction creates a need for people to envisage an era which was more fulfilling and satisfying.

Community and its effects on gender, race and age

Community may have different meanings for various groups within the population, and create different effects on individuals, according to their gender, race and age.

GENDER

Many community studies, especially those focusing on traditional working-class communities, have concentrated on the effects of living in these areas on males. Some of the early studies, such as Hoggart, and Young and Willmott did, however, examine the extent to which women's lives were affected by their community. The studies of H. Gavron, 'The Captive Wife' (1966) and M. Young and P. Willmott, 'The Symmetrical Family' (1973) both illustrate how women experience community in a different way to men. They found that social contacts and the extended family networks were more significant for women than for men. Gavron described the lonely life of 'captive wives' in London tower blocks, away from the 'woman's world' of their extended family networks. Young and Willmott found that, even with joint conjugal roles, women were still undertaking more of the domestic responsibilities than men, and missed their extended family support.

Because women tend to rely on the community for support more than men do, they are more likely to become involved in 'community activities', such as school PTA, voluntary work, etc. According to J. Bornat et al, 'Community Care' (1993) women are also central in community-based actions concerned with organising, defending, or protesting over education, health, housing, or welfare issues.

There appears then to be a conflict between the way in which community can 'liberate' women and give them greater opportunities to pursue a range of interests and become involved in their locality, and the ways in which certain communities can confine women to traditional roles and responsibilities. It is interesting that the notion of 'community care' often means in practice that female carers are expected to look after their husbands, partners, or ageing parents.

RACE AND ETHNICITY

Racial and ethnic minorities in Britain are concentrated in certain areas of the country, often in cities, such as Manchester or Birmingham, or in particular regions, such as West Yorkshire and South-East London. These areas frequently constitute distinctive communities, with particular lifestyles and values associated with certain ethnic minorities. Research on some of these include the following:

AFRO-CARIBBEANS

K. Pryce, 'Endless Pressure' (1979) is one of the most comprehensive studies of Afro-Caribbeans, based on St Paul's community in Bristol. The composition of the community is predominantly poor and powerless black people, who suffer 'endless pressure' in their lives. Pryce queries the existence of a close-knit, cohesive community, and argues that there are many divisions within the area. In spite of this, he believes that a sense of interdependence and mutual ethnicity binds the people together. He identifies a range of lifestyles in St Paul's, based on age/ocupation/religion, with varying levels of commitment to the community.

S. Hall et al, 'Policing the Crisis' (1978) found that black Afro-Caribbean communities were becoming more cohesive and developing a distinctive cultural identity, leading to a revival of black consciousness. They describe the emergence of Afro-Caribbean shops, markets, music, leisure, etc.

P. Gilroy, 'There Ain't No Black in the Union Jack' (1987) backs up Hall et al in stressing the importance of community to Afro-Caribbeans. Although he found strong cultural links between Afro-Caribbeans in different parts of the country, Gilroy found no evidence to support a distinctive 'black identity'. Instead, he found that they were fragmented by class, occupations, housing, etc. Gilroy suggests that the spate of urban riots in the 1980s in St Paul's in Bristol, Toxteth in Liverpool, and areas of Birmingham and London may in part have been an expression of discontent and frustration by the black community over their marginal position in society, and an attempt to re-assert their black identity in the area. Although it is difficult to identify the real causes of the riots, as whites were involved as well as blacks, and the media focused on the activities of black youths, a desire to 'reclaim their locality' may have been a contributory factor.

ASIANS

Communities comprised largely of Asians tend to reflect the values of many traditional, working-class communities: extended families, close-knit networks, mutual support systems, strong moral consensus. There are also obvious differences, such as the Asian tendency towards arranged marriages, and differences between Asian groups, based on language, customs, caste, and religion. Thus, Hindus, Muslims and Sikhs do not simply represent different religions, but also support different values and lifestyles.

P. Bachu, 'Twice Migrants' (1985) is a detailed ethnographic study of East African Sikhs in Britain. This group of people migrated early this century from the Punjab to East African countries such as Uganda and Kenya. They were then forced, under these countries, 'Africanisation policies', to seek refuge in Britain in the late 1960s and early 1970s. Bachu describes the uniqueness of this group of people, with their fluent command of English, good educational qualifications, and substantial occupational skills. Although they have a strong commitment to their host country, with no desire to return to their country of origin, they have shown little desire to be assimilated into the mainstream British culture. They remain a cohesive, close-knit community, with a strong religious emphasis, and extensive social networks.

The Muslim population is more fragmented than other ethnic minorities, with different communities developing, based on sects, territories, and language. Their shared faith and identity does, however, override their differences, with specific codes of conduct concerning dress, diet, and behaviour, clearly separating them from the non-Muslim population.

AGE

Age may not instantly be associated with the concept of community, but there are particular lifestyles and values which are linked to age, and could therefore be interpreted as just another variation of community. Although age is a biological fact, it is also determined by cultural norms and social factors (it is socially constructed). Thus, each age group tends to be defined in terms of social roles, responsibilities, and expectations.

Adolescence as a concept largely developed this century as a result of the gradual extension of education and training in the post-war era. As described in Chapter 10, the development of a 'teenage market' emerged in the years after the war with a distinctive lifestyle and values. Allied to this, a range of youth sub-cultures developed from the 1950s onwards, for example Teddy Boys, Mods and Rockers, and Punks, all with particular styles of clothing, music tastes, and activities. Youth communities are also class based, whether in terms of sub-cultures, or in relation to their access to education and the labour market.

Old age/retirement may also be seen as a 'subcultural community', with its own set of values and lifestyle, whether it involves living in the community or in residential care. E. Cumming and W. Henry, 'Growing Old' (1961) developed a number of ideas to create a **'disengagement theory'**, which explains how ageing has physical, psychological, and social effects, which change as people grow old. It is characterised by a gradual physical deterioration, lowered levels of interest and concentration, and social withdrawal. However, although disengagement may happen in modern industrial societies, there is little evidence to indicate that it persists in pre-industrial communities where the role of the elderly frequently increases with age. It may be that disengagement is encouraged in industrial societies by the negative media perceptions of old age, and the existence of an official 'retirement age'.

It should be noted that many old people do not succumb to an 'elderly mentality', but continue to have active, healthy and fulfilling lifestyles well into their 70s, 80s, and beyond. There are, however, significant variations in elderly lifestyles according to social class, gender, and ethnicity, influencing access to leisure, education, work, as well as determining family responsibilities.

Urban sociology

Urban sociology is concerned with the discovery and explanation of the economic, political, and social forces that cause urbanisation, and an understanding of the effects of an urban environment on human relationships. The study of cities and city life often reflects one of two views:

In the early twentieth century the city was viewed as a separate, unique entity, with a life of its own. Thus, the city was seen to have a direct effect on human relationships. Although this perspective is not as widely held today, many people still regard the physical aspects of villages and towns as having distinct influences on social relationships.

The 1970s and 1980s saw the emergence of a view of the city based on the external influences which determine the extent and type of urban areas. This view also sees the city as a reflection of the wider society, acting as a focus for social, political, and economic conflicts.

Urbanisation, or the growth and development of towns and cities, varies enormously between countries, and does not necessarily follow or depend on industrialisation. Urbanisation has differed substantially between capitalist, socialist, and 'developing' areas of the world.

Urbanisation in the first (capitalist) world developed from the social and economic revolutions of the seventeenth and eighteenth centuries. It was particularly influenced by the agricultural revolution, the enclosure movement (which pushed the peasants off the land), the industrial revolution (which attracted the displaced labour), developments in transport, and a large increase in population. The second half of the twentieth century has been characterised by a trend towards **urban dispersal**, or **counter-urbanisation**, leading to the growth of satellite towns and commuter villages. Hence, there has been a growth from 'industrial cities' of the Victoria era to the development of the '**metropolis**' or conurbation in the twentieth century, and the recent emergence of the '**megalopolis**' (a sprawling urban area linked by roads and communication networks) in the post-war years. According to some authors, town centres have been transformed in recent years.

K. Worpole, 'Towns for People' (1992) claims that towns are losing their social significance as meeting places and localities for public facilities and services, and their civic identities have diminished. Today, people seek leisure and other services outside the city centre, leaving the towns as purely commercial and shopping centres.

Although Britain had the first industrial revolution, and hence the first urban revolution, similar patterns in urbanisation can be found in other Western European countries, and also in the USA, although the latter has been influenced to a greater extent by mass immigration.

Urbanisation in the second (socialist) world has been similar to Western developments, with the exception that cities in socialist countries are usually **centrally planned**. Urbanisation has generally followed industrialisation, although some Eastern bloc countries with the same levels of industrialisation have substantially different levels of urbanisation. Thus, other factors such as population increase and the movement of peasants from rural areas are significant influences on urbanisation. R.A. French and F.E.I. Hamilton, 'The Socialist City' (1979) emphasise the neighbourhood organisation of socialist cities, which attempt to reduce inequalities and create a balance between urban and rural living. French and Hamilton argue that despite centralised control 'classless' cities do not exist, and they are 'socialised', rather than socialist. Other socialist countries such as China also see the neighbourhood as a community support system, integrated with industry, but with local grass roots support instead of centralised planning.

Urbanisation in the third (developing) world is not closely related to, or caused by, industrialisation. Urban development in Third World countries arises largely through the migration of peasants into towns, followed by a very high birth rate, leading to the creation of some of the most densely populated cities in the world (Mexico City, Sao Paulo). The lack of industry, shortage of housing, and extreme poverty, lead to the creation of shanty towns, which contrast sharply with the opulence of the wealthy in these countries. Whereas urbanisation is seen as a mark of social and economic progress in capitalist and socialist countries, it is often seen as a form of **dependency** in 'developing' countries, a theory which will be further explained in the next section.

URBAN LIVING

The early theories of Tonnies, Durkheim and Simmel on urban and rural life were unified by a group of social scientists at the university of Chicago between 1916 and 1940. The Chicago School was attempting to explain the effects of massive immigration into Chicago, and used the organic analogy to describe the processes of urban life. The ideas of the Chicago School were set out by several of their most famous adherents.

R.E. Park developed a theory of '**human ecology**' to explain how the laws of urban life emerge out of chaos. Thus, people invade territories, struggle for the right to exist, and are often pushed out to invade their neighbour's territory. Using Darwin's theory of 'survival of the fittest', Park explains how the rich are more likely to have the most choice concerning their habitat, while the poor are subject to the desires of the 'fittest'. A state of equilibrium is constantly maintained as the processes of invasion and succession take place in the city.

E. Burgess applied Park's idea of human ecology to the study of the physical and social development of the city. This notion of '**urban ecology**' led Burgess to develop his 'Concentric Zone Theory of City Growth' where cities grow outwards from the centre (central business district), through the zone of transition (slums, crime, immigrants, vice), to the zone of working-class homes, followed by a residential zone of middle-class homes, and finally a commuter zone which is interspersed with rural areas. Many subsequent studies, particularly on crime, have concentrated on the zone of transition or '**twilight zone**', leading to theories about the concentration of deviance in cities. However, many cities do not conform to Burgess's zones, and it is possible to find public housing outside the inner zones, as well as finding young, affluent people living in the city centre: a process known as '**gentrification**'.

L. Wirth, following Durkheim's urban/rural dichotomy, defined the city in terms of population size, density, and heterogeneity. Wirth also used Tonnies' notion of gesellschaft relationships to describe the cultural effects of the city on people, in particular the increase in secondary group contacts at the expense of more permanent and satisfying primary group relationships. Wirth saw the emergence of voluntary associations and corporate organisations as a partial solution to the isolating nature of urban lifestyles, and stated that urbanism was an inevitable way of life of modern society. H. Gans, 'The Levittowners' (1967), in contrast to Wirth, rejects the idea of a distinctive urban way of life, and argues instead that the city offers a choice over lifestyles, even within the confines of class and age. Gans emphasises the diversity within and between the suburbs in the USA, exhibiting a combination of gemeinshcaft- and gesellschaft-type living. H. Raban, 'Soft City' (1975) believes it is misleading to see the city as a fixed or 'hard' environment. He prefers the concept of a 'soft city', which offers people wide opportunities to impose their own meanings on city life.

P. Sennett, 'The Uses of Disorder' (1973) and 'The Fall of Public Man' (1976) has stressed the fear which the the city presents to people, and in particular, fear of the 'stranger'. He says that this leads to the creation of 'like with like' communities, whether they are middle class suburbs or ethnic communities. Sennett describes this as **'destructive gemeinschaft'** because it prevents mixing between different social groups, reduces diversity, and increases disorder and fear of the unknown.

CRITICISMS OF THEORIES ON THE URBAN AND RURAL FRAMEWORK

The **urban/rural dichotomy**, or two-part model (gemeinschaft/gesellschaft, mechanical/organic solidarity) is an ideal-type and an over-simplification. Real communities are more complex and diverse, and the division between city and country is not so clear-cut, as there are many overlapping areas. Wirth describes the existence of 'urban villages' in inner cities, and R. Pahl, 'Whose City?' (1975) argues that places and social relationships do not always coincide. Lifestyles may be determined by factors other than locality, such as social class, age, and ethnicity.

The **urban ecology theory** of the Chicago School is descriptive rather than explanatory. It assumes that residential patterns in a city emerge as a 'natural' event, and ignores the market forces which determine where people live.

Anomalies exist in many of the early theories. Thus, the urban ecology theory does not explain the factors which enable ethnic groups to live in the commuter zone. Wirth's argument that overcrowding leads to high levels of stress is not borne out in many cities: Hong Kong is overcrowded, but death rates and disease are comparatively low.

All of the early theories accept capitalism as 'given', thus disregarding the importance of class conflict and social forces outside the city, which determine which social groups inhabit certain areas.

The existence of 'urban problems' in rural areas make it difficult to sustain the notion of a distinct urban culture. Isolation, anomie, and class divisions were noted by H. Newby in his East Anglian studies, and by R. Williams, 'The Country and the City' (1973). The Report of the Archbishops' Commission on Rural Areas 'Faith in the Countryside' (1990) discovered extensive poverty and social conflict in rural areas, largely as the result of the impact of unemployment, poor services and transport, and inflated property prices caused by outsiders moving into rural localities.

The urban way of life is viewed in a pessimistic or negative light, whereas rural lifestyles are regarded in terms of positive social relationships. This nostalgia for the 'good old days' tends to mask the poverty and repression which is often found in rural communities. H. Newby, 'Country Life' (1987) illustrates how the romantic myths about the countryside as 'rural idylls' do not match the reality, as agricultural developments have dramatically changed the nature of country life. In Victorian times villages were essentially farming oriented, with a class structure of landowner, tenant farmer, and landless labourer. This gradually changed to a two-class system, as landowners became more visible on farms, resulting in owner-occupier farmers and farm workers. The post-war era, according to Newby, has been characterised by the take over of many small farms by large holdings and the extension of intensively mechanised farming methods ('agribusiness'). Many farm workers have become unemployed and displaced, moving into cities to find work, or into local service industries such as tourism.

The division between urban and rural environments has become less apparent as people have increasingly moved from towns and cities into country areas, creating 'commuter' villages, which are linked by motorways and trains to major cities. Urban dwellers have increasingly moved into rural areas, purchasing weekend retreats, raising property values, and forcing locals to move out of the area (for example in Wales and Yorkshire).

A. Cohen, 'Belonging' (1982) argues that it is impossible to generalise about the nature of country life, as rural environments exhibit great variations and cultural differences: Welsh hill farms and Scottish crofts may differ significantly.

Following the spate of community studies in the mid-1960s, the conservative theories of Tonnies, Durkheim, and the Chicago School came under mounting criticism. In particular, their acceptance of inequality in urban environments as somehow 'natural' and 'inevitable' was heavily questioned. Against the background of increasing disorder in cities in America and Western Europe, a view of the city developed based on the effects of external influences on geographical areas. This new '**radical**' approach involved the analysis of urban areas from both a Weberian and a Marxist perspective.

The Weberian perspective on the city originated with the study by J. Rex and J. Moore, 'Race, Community and Conflict' (1967) on the inner-city area of Sparkbrook, Birmingham. Rex and Moore studied the operation of the housing market, and in particular why black immigrants tended to be concentrated in the poorest housing in the twilight zone. They did not accept that racial discrimination alone accounted for the segregation, but that it was merely one aspect of the operation of the rules and regulations of the housing market. Blacks could not obtain mortgages because of low incomes and insecure employment, and did not fulfil residency requirements for council accommodation. This socioeconomic perspective analysed the city in terms of class and conflict, with Rex and Moore identifying seven **housing classes**, corresponding to position in the housing market. This typology, however, could be extended ad infinitum, as no two individuals are in identical positions in the housing market.

R.E. Pahl, 'Whose City?' (1970) used a Weberian approach in his '**managerial thesis**', which explains how 'urban managers' (bankers, building society managers, town planners) control the distribution of housing. The problem with the managerial thesis is that it tends to ignore the decision-makers at the top of the power structure, who ultimately control the allocation of resources. In order to account for the role of the state in the allocation, Pahl developed the '**corporation thesis**'.

The Marxist approach to the study of urbanism is essentially based on the role of the state (or the political economy) in advanced capitalist societies. One of the leading exponents of this view is M. Castells, 'Urban Question' (1977), who argued that that the elements of urban life can only be truly analysed as a product of the capitalist system. Capitalism requires a readily available pool of workers concentrated in city areas, who must be provided with adequate housing, health care, education, transport, etc. Initially, these services were provided at a minimum level to ensure the reproduction of labour power. From the late 1960s onwards, however, increasing pressure on these services has led to 'urban conflict', with various groups campaigning against the lack of facilities and the destrucion of communities caused by mass unemployment. Although Castells' claim to universal applicability can be questioned, he did pave the way for a new perspective on urban studies.

D. Harvey, 'Social Justice and the City' (1973) used a Marxist perspective to analyse problems associated with urban living, such as poverty, crime, housing, etc. Harvey, a social geographer, argued that urban 'problems' were not caused by the city itself, but were a result of the effects of a capitalist socio-economic system on the geographical area of the city. Thus, the problems are **'societal'** rather than **'urban'**, and as such can occur in rural locations as well as urban ones.

The development of **'radical'** perspectives in the 1970s heralded a new era in urban studies, with the replacement of the 'loss of community' and ecological approaches by a **political economy** view. Much of the contemporary research in urban sociology is concerned with explaining the process and effects of policy-making, town planning, inner city conflict, and international relations on individuals and areas. Several texts on these topics include R. Mellor, 'Urban Sociology in an Urbanized Society' (1977), P. Saunders, 'Urban Politics: A Sociological Interpretation' (1979), and I. Szelenyi, 'Urban Inequalities Under State Socialism' (1983).

Theories of development

PROBLEMS OF DEFINITION

The terms 'development' and 'underdevelopment' present problems of definition. They are often used in connection with industrialisation; thus the transition from non-industrial society to industrial society usually marks the movement from 'undeveloped' country to 'developed' country. This definition implies differences in income, modes of production, and frequently family size. Development is defined primarily though in economic terms, measured by a country's per capita GNP (Gross National Product). It is also used to refer to the level of social and political development, although economic growth does not necessarily lead to social and political development. There are what A. Foster-Carter calls 'trade-offs', for example the advantages of industrialisation such as increased life expectancy and improvements in lifestyle are balanced by environmental losses and the decline of traditional communities. Hence, the notion of development as a positive process is not always true; there are many negative aspects to development. Bearing these problems of definition in mind, it is possible to identify three categories of 'development', based on economic and social progress:

Developed countries, with high levels of wealth, heavily industrialised, and a low birth rate, for example USA, Britain, Germany, France.

Developing countries or less developed countries (LDCs), with moderate levels of wealth, increasing industrialisation, and a declining birth rate, for example Brazil, Turkey, Thailand.

Underdeveloped countries, with low levels of wealth, minimal industrialisation, and a high birth rate, for example Ethiopia, Bangladesh, Indonesia.

Following the end of the Second World War, an alternative form of classification emerged based on the idea of two industrialised and developed worlds, and a third world with low levels of industrialisation and poor living standards.

The First World came to be recognised as the capitalist, market economies of North America, Western Europe, Japan and Australasia.

The Second World was defined as the centrally-directed economies of the socialist/communist nations of Eastern Europe.

The Third World consisted of countries which were either underdeveloped or undergoing development, including large parts of Latin America, North Africa, and parts of Asia.

There are, however, a number of anomalies surrounding the idea of three distinct 'worlds'. Since 1989 and the collapse of communism in Eastern and Central Europe the distinction between First and Second Worlds is hard to sustain as these nations are now moving towards free market economics. The political divide which emphasised the First and Second Worlds is diminishing, and it may now be seen as irrelevant to regard them as two distinct zones. The concept of a Third World is also fraught with difficulties, as the past twenty-five years have witnessed a range of variations in countries traditionally thought of as being in the Third World. Some Third World countries have high levels of wealth than are usually associated with this group, for example the so-called 'Newly Industrialised Countries' (NICs) such as the 'Four Tigers of Asia' (Hong Kong, Singapore, Taiwan, South Korea), as well as Mexico, Israel, Brazil, and Middle Eastern states such as Saudi Arabia. There are also Third World countries, such as Vietnam and Sri Lanka, which have low wealth, but score high on indicators of social development. Distinctions may be made too, between poor countries (for example in Latin America) and very poor countries (Sudan, Ethiopia). Finally, there are countries which do not fit easily into any category, such as China and India.

An alternative classification which has been used to overcome some of these problems is the one used by the Brandt Report (1980), using the concepts of **North and South** to divide the world's nations. There tends to be a North/South geographical distribution of rich and poor countries, with the exception of the wealthy nations of Australia and New Zealand in the South. The Brandt Report also emphasises the way in which nations in the South have a history of dependence upon richer countries in the North, the shared history of colonialism amongst the countries in the South, and the political and economic inequalities between North and South.

There are several different perspectives on how and why countries have made the transition from underdeveloped to developed nations.

MODERNISATION THEORY

This view derives essentially from functionalist ideas of **social evolutionism**, which see societies developing through a defined series of stages. Comte, Spencer, and Parsons all described the process of change from a traditional to a modern society in terms of 'evolutionary adaptation'. Parsons in particular extended this idea to include the concept of 'social equilibrium', where social systems attempt to retain equilibrium during their adaptation to change. Once the change is completed, the equilibrium may settle at a different level, with increased levels of industrialisation and more highly differentiated institutions. These early views concerning the movement of all societies through a set number of stages towards modernisation contain many problems. Some societies might deliberately retain their labour intensive industries rather than develop machine technology. The evolutionary idea ignores outside influences on societies, such as colonisation. Finally, no account is taken of the role of individuals in creating the type of society they desire.

W.W. Rostow, 'The Stages of Economic Growth: a non-communist manifesto' (1960) developed the early ideas of modernisation theory into a distinct perspective on the development process. Rostow's work is based on the idea of a sequential process of self-sustaining economic growth, which he saw as being in direct contrast to Marx's stages of economic development. Rostow proposed the view that all societies pass through five stages of economic development:

Traditional, which includes Stone Age cultures as well as many societies prior to the industrial revolution. Their common features include a basically agrarian economy, a social structure essentially dependent on kinship, and 'pre-Newtonian' science and technology.

The pre-conditions for take-off: the idea that progress is possible develops in this stage, prompted by external forces which Rostow does not clearly specify. He does mention the importance of trade, communications, an increase in scientific develop-ments, greater provision of services, and the emergence of an elite who are prepared to reinvest their wealth in the country.

The take-off: this stage marks the transition from an underdeveloped country to a developed one. Manufacturing industries predominate, and investment as a proportion of national income rise to at least 10%. The range of social and political institutions expands, and develops in a way which complements the pursuit of economic growth. Rostow estimates that this stage takes about twenty years to complete; thus, the take-off for Britain occurred between 1783–1803.

The drive to maturity refers to a state where developed countries consolidate their position, with the extension of science and technology, and investment increased to perhaps 20%. Political and social reforms continue, and the society's economy gains importance internationally.

The age of high mass consumption represents an extension of the previous stage, with the surplus wealth concentrated in individual consumption (for example USA), welfare services (for example Western Europe), or in military arsenals designed for the pursuit of world power (former USSR).

Rostow's theory of socio-economic development can be criticised for a number of reasons, including the following:

1. In common with early ideas on modernisation, Rostow's work is essentially evolutionist, assuming that a fixed set of stages can be identified.
2. Rostow implies that all societies follow identical stages of growth, yet many societies 'miss out' a stage, or remain in an underdeveloped state.
3. Rostow underestimates the extent to which different sections of the same society can be at different stages of development.
4. Although external influences on development are mentioned, Rostow fails to explain the crucial role of other societies on a country's development.
5. According to Rostow, a society's take-off can only be identified after it has occurred,

which means that policy planners cannot be involved in the transition to development.

6. Rostow sees the stages of development as 'automatic', and ignores the active pursuit of development by many capitalist countries. The role of the state in determining a society's development is not pursued.

There are several variations of the modernisation view, reflecting other aspects of functionalist theory.

Development is seen as a dichotomy, or pair of opposites. Thus, in a similar way to the gemeinschaft/gesellschaft continuum, traditional societies and modern societies can be presented as direct opposites. This static view does not, however, reveal anything about the process by which a traditional society becomes a modern one.

The process of development is seen as a diffusion from developed countries to underdeveloped ones. Technology, culture, and social institutions may all be diffused from one society to another, or even between different sections of the same society.

The continued existence of underdeveloped countries can be explained by a form of psychologism, which lays the blame on the cultures of Third World people for their backward position in the world.

A New Right version of modernisation theory emerged in the 1980s as a response to the prominence given to liberal, free market economics. The collapse of the Second World communist states in 1989 increased the emphasis on this model, leading to the view that countries fail to develop because of internal factors such as government interference in the economy. This radical modernisation theory does not accept that cultural factors such as population size, attitudes and values restrict development. From this perspective, any country can develop if it adopts free market economics and restricts government intervention. It is particularly critical of the communist model of state planned economic development, which reduces pluralism and stifles democracy.

A Marxist view of modernisation theory has also been proposed, which differs from evolutionary modernisation theory by emphasising the sharp and revolutionary nature of social change. B. Warren, 'Imperialism: Pioneer of Capitalism' (1980) suggests that capitalism can be a positive means of promoting Third World development, and even supports colonialism for introducing capitalist values into underdeveloped countries. Warren claims that the promotion of capitalism in Third World countries will lead to the creation of an industrial proletariat and hence socialism.

DEPENDENCY THEORY

A.G. Frank, 'Capitalism and Underdevelopment in Latin America' (1969) is the leading exponent of dependency theory, sometimes referred to as the 'neo-Marxist view', or 'underdevelopment theory'. Frank, in direct contrast to Rostow, places the aims and problems of underdeveloped countries first, and sees them, along with developed countries, as part of the 'world embracing system' of capitalism. Frank's main arguments can be summarised as follows:

The internationalist capitalist system, particularly in terms of **imperialism** and **economic exploitation**, is responsible for the gap between the wealth of the developed and underdeveloped countries.

Many Third World countries rely on one crop or commodity for their 'non-aid' income, and are thus **economically dependent** on First and Second World countries.

Developed countries exploit the resources of Third World nations, utilising cheap labour and materials in the production of manufactured goods.

This national economic structure whereby developed countries exploit the Third World and prevent their development can be described as a '**metropolis-satellite relationship**'.

Satellites cannot develop along metropolitan lines because they are retained in their subordinate position by the metropolis (developed) countries. Satellites are therefore underdeveloped.

Satellites can only develop if they sever or drastically weaken their ties with the metropolis.

Frank's model is in direct opposition to the evolutionary view of modernisation theorists. Frank recognises the crucial role of external influences on Third World countries, and does not accept a common or linear mode of development for all countries. Frank's views have, however, been subject to a number of criticisms, including the following:

J.G. Taylor, 'From Modernisation to Modes of Production: a critique of the sociologies of development and underdevelopment' (1979) argues that although Frank explains why underdevelopment occurs, he does not offer a positive theory of development. According to Frank, satellites or Third World countries should avoid dependency, but he does not suggest what positive steps they should take to achieve the status of a developed nation.

The concepts of metropolis and satellite are not easily identifiable. Both are a mixture of geographical and social characteristics. and exist both within and between countries.

Frank believes that no underdeveloped countries can progress under a capitalist world economy, yet some nations, such as Cuba, have managed to move towards development.

B. Moore, 'Social Origins of Dictatorship and democracy: lord and peasant in the making of the modern world' (1966) is a good example of an approach which is neither modernisation theory nor dependency theory. In some respects it manages to combine the modernisation view with a Marxist perspective. Moore uses six case studies (Britain, France, USA, Japan, China, and India) to demonstrate their 'routes to the modern world'. In particular, he concentrates on the type of political regime which resulted from modernisation, and the patterns of class relationships which preceded and followed development. Moore identifies three routes:

Bourgeois revolution, leading to capitalist democracy, for example Britain, France, USA.

Revolution from above, leading (temporarily) to fascism, for example Germany, Japan, Italy.

Peasant revolution, leading to communism, for example China, Russia. (India does not appear to 'fit' into any of the three routes).

Moore's work paved the way for a large number of comparative studies on development which, unlike modernisation and dependency theories, contained firm empirical evidence. Moore is probably closer to modernisation theory than dependency, for he emphasises the internal events of a country, and ignores the extent to which the availability of a route depends on the routes which other countries have already taken.

POPULISM AND NEO-POPULISM

Populism is a social and economic theory which dates from the eighteenth century, when the negative effects of the industrial revolution on people's lives were being observed. Populism argues that the process of development and high levels of technology are costly and damaging to people, and thus rejects modernisation theory as either desirable or sustainable. Populists suggest that material progress can be made by preserving small scale agricultural and industrial production.

Neo-populism rejects large-scale capital-intensive industrialisation as inappropriate for Third World countries which have large populations, and therefore require more labour-intensive methods of production. The use of small-scale agricultural, manufacturing, and service enterprises would also be less alienating and less damaging to the environment. Also, the emergence of large cities in underdeveloped countries destroys the peasant base and dehumanises the people.

POSTMODERNISM

In the 1990s development issues have increasingly focused on the problems which are associated with development, such as poverty, the collapse of communism, and the presence of Third World elites. Postmodernists do not focus on the 'grand theories' of modernisation and dependency theories, but are concerned to emphasise how development affects local and regional areas. Recent examples include the ethnic tension in the former Yugoslavia, and the problems of the emerging politically independent but economically backward states of the former Soviet Union.

GLOBALISATION

Although postmodernism rejects the 'grand theories' of development, it does accept that there is evidence of a general process of globalisation. Globalisation focuses on the increasing economic interdependence of countries, which is determined to a large extent by the significance of '**transnational companies**' (TNCs). These are international companies which plan, produce and market their products on a global scale, using labour from different countries. Examples include Coca Cola, Nestlé and McDonalds. In addition to global production and marketing, these companies also create cultural levels of globalisation, with the extension of the product into films, books, magazines, computer games, etc. Many fundamentalist groups, such as the Islamics, have opposed such invasion into their own culture, particularly as globalisation is also associated with the creation of social problems.

The relationship between developed and less developed societies

Modernisation theorists and dependency theorists view the relationship between developed and less developed countries in very different ways, depending on whether they see the First World as aiding the Third to progress, or whether they see Third World dependency as a consequence of First World development. There are two main areas where the relationship between the First and Third Worlds can be interpreted in these two ways.

THE IMPACT OF TRANSNATIONAL COMPANIES

Transnational companies (TNCs) are companies with subsidiaries (offices, plants, etc.) in two or more countries, and are usually owned by Western organisations. The number and extent of TNCs have expanded this century, and in particular since the Second World War. They are extremely wealthy organisations, with foreign investment in other industrialised countries, 25% of which is in the Third World. There are often large investments in agriculture, frequently contracting peasants and agricultural labourers to produce the raw materials for the TNCs. A certain level of political stability and a certain standard of industrialisation and infrastructure are a requirement of investment, with most TNCs found in Latin America, Newly Industrialised Countries, and Eastern Europe.

Modernisation theorists argue that TNCs have particular benefits for the Third World, for example investment of foreign capital, introduction of new technology, training of local workers, higher disposable income, and access to world markets. They emphasise the importance of the integration of Third World nations into the global arena.

Dependency theorists would, however, suggest that TNCs exploit Third World countries by utilising their cheap labour, and forcing them to produce crops which benefit the TNCs (cash crops) rather than subsistence crops which feed the people. They argue that TNCs do not benefit the Third World, but perpetuate the dependency of these nations on the First World. The technology which is introduced to the Third World is often specific to the particular industry's process, and cannot be used for any other purpose. TNCs can also benefit by 'transfer pricing', where they transfer back to the parent company some of the profits, thus minimising taxes payable to the host country and to their own country.

THE CONSEQUENCES OF WESTERN AID

P. Harrison, 'Inside the Third World: An Anatomy of Poverty' (1979) argues that the rich countries in the North take extensively from the poor ones in the South, and return a small amount in the form of 'aid'. This aid primarily consists of official government grants and loans to Third World countries, and assistance from charities. Although the United Nations recommends that governments give a minimum of 0.7% of their Gross National Product as aid, most countries fall substantially below even this small amount.

Most of the government aid is in the form of **'tied aid'**, given on condition that the recipient country buys specified goods and services from the donor country. Other ways in which First World countries benefit from aid is by using the aid budget to provide subsidies to companies to enable them to secure Third World contracts, thus undercutting Third World competitors. Aid can also be used for geo-political reasons: money may be given to Third World regimes which are anti-communist (for example Chile, Philippines) or to bolster security in a particular region, such as the Middle East.

Countries in the South may lose their land, as it is sold or rented for the development of **'aid industries'** and projects, which frequently involve the employment of Western 'experts' rather than using local people. Ecological damage may ensue as a result of pollution and lack of knowledge of the local environment and culture.

Recently, attempts have been made by several Third World nations to gain control of their aid. Hence, a number of **non-governmental organisations** (NGOs) have

Third world poverty

developed in the Third World, which consist of locally-based charities, employing indigenous workers, and selling their goods to the First World, for example 'Traidcraft.'

Western aid also involves **giving loans** to Third World countries, which in the past twenty years have increased poverty as interest repayments become unmanageable for many nations. In order to repay the debts, many countries are forced to use their land to produce cash crops which can be sold to the West, such as cotton, rather than food. If countries in the South wish to attract further loans they must satisfy the demands of the International Monetary Fund and implement a Structural Adjustment Programme. This programme includes cutting public expenditure in health, education, and transport, so that the loan can be repaid. **Spiralling debt** is often a consequence of these further loans, with an increasingly impoverished population.

The main features of first and third world countries

The sociology of development is not just confined to theories of development and underdevelopment, but is also concerned with examining the key differences in First and Third World lifestyles. Some of the main features which differentiate the two worlds follow.

THE PROCESS OF INDUSTRIALISATION AND THE GROWTH OF URBAN AREAS

Modernisation and dependency theorists both argue that large-scale industrialisation is essential for long-term economic growth. In the post-war era, Third World countries have realised that, in order to progress, they can no longer rely on being suppliers of primary produce (agriculture, farming, fishing, etc.) to the First World, but they must develop their own programmes of industrialisation. Industrialisation is therefore seen as a necessary requirement for increasing the living standards of the population in Third World nations. There are a number of difficulties with developing industrialisation in the South, including '**internal obstacles**' (poor foreign exchange, lack of technology, poor transport, inadequate education and training) and '**external obstacles**' such as dependence on foreign loans and aid, and lack of 'hard' (Western) currencies.

In spite of the problems of introducing industrialisation into the Third World, there have been some notable successes, especially in the so called 'Four Tigers of Asia' (Hong Kong, Singapore, Taiwan, South Korea). However, the process of industrialisation in these countries has been different to that which occurred in the West, with the development of **import substitution industries**, where goods are produced locally for the home market in order to reduce imports. Where TNCs have threatened these industries, countries such as the 'Four Tigers' have turned to **export-oriented industries** where a range of light industrial products (textiles, electronic goods, etc.) are produced for home and abroad. The consequences of industrialisation are often different for the two worlds, with the West benefiting from higher living standards and political democracy, with the Third World often suffering economic, social, cultural, and ecological effects as they struggle to emulate the West.

Urbanisation is the process whereby an increasing proportion of the population are living in towns and cities. In the First World approximately 75% of the population are urbanised, compared to about 65% in Latin America, and 30% in each of Asia and Africa. However, the process of urbanisation in the First and Third Worlds is very different. In the West, urbanisation occurred as a result of industrialisation and the need for a constant, easily available supply of workers. In the Third World, though, industry is more capital intensive, and there is little demand for local labour, especially when many TNCs employ workers from the parent country. Many workers in Third World nations are employed in the informal sector of the economy, either self-employed or within a family business. Thus, a **dual-sector economy** is common in many of these countries. Much Third World urbanisation derives from high birth rates within city areas, in contrast to the First World, where the expanding towns and cities drew in migrants from the countryside. Finally, urbanisation in the South frequently leads to the creation of a **'primate city'**, which dominates the country (for example Mexico City and Cairo), leaving other towns as **satellites**, mainly because Third World development is too fast to plan for services and infrastructure.

DEMOGRAPHIC TRENDS, INCLUDING POPULATION DISTRIBUTION, AND POPULATION POLICIES DESIGNED TO REDUCE THE BIRTH RATE

Changes in birth rates, death rates, and migration all affect the size of populations, as well as influencing their composition by age, sex, and ethnicity. The current world population stands at almost six billion, and is projected to rise to ten billion by 2050. It is estimated that three-quarters of the world population live in the Third World, over 90% of whom are infants, with Third World populations currently doubling every 35 years. There are regional differences in these populations, with the numbers stabilising in Asia and Latin America, but continuing to rise in Africa.

The **population explosion** in the Third World is primarily caused by the poverty and inequalities between the countries in the North and the South, for although Western hygiene and medicine has reduced the death rates, little impact has been made on the high birth rates, and with no increase in the food supply or improved job opportunities, coupled with a lack of welfare services, large families are still considered essential. In contrast, Western nations have undergone a **'demographic transition'**, initially having a stable population in terms of size and structure, with high birth and death rates. This was followed by a period of change, involving high birth rates and decreasing death rates, and then from the 1870s onwards, a return to a stable state, characterised by decreasing birth and death rates. The Third World has not experienced these stages because the same factors leading to the changes have not been present in these countries, such as a large quantity of and high quality food, public health systems, advances in medical science, reduced child mortality, reliable and easily available contraception, welfare services, and extended schooling and investment in education. Countries in the South are still in the second stage, with decreasing death rates, but still high birth rates.

Population policies involve a range of measures designed to encourage people to reduce their reproductive rates. One example is **'land reform programmes'**, where land is redistributed from a few large landowners to peasant farmer families to improve family income, and by utilising modern technology, to reduce the need for large numbers of children to work on the land. Other methods include the provision of economic security by implementing **welfare benefits** such as old age pensions and sick pay, although the cost of these measures is prohibitive for many Third World countries. Another method involves **birth control policies**, which are generally unsuccessful unless they are accompanied by an improvement in economic security.

Two countries which have introduced birth control policies on a national, widespread scale, underpinned by government policy, are India and China. In the late 1960s India introduced extensive state programmes of birth control, which mushroomed out of control, resulting in a large number of compulsory sterilisations and vasectomies. Although the policies were toned down, they are still ongoing, and have had some success in reducing the birth rate, although rather slowly. China's approach was much more draconian, introducing in the late 1970s a 'one child' policy, with organisational and cultural resources allocated to enforce such an unpopular policy. Financial inducements were offered to those who conformed to the policy, and stiff financial and social penalties were imposed on those who had more than one child. Although the policy does appear to be working in reducing the birth rate, there are many negative consequences, such as high levels of female infanticide (a son is preferable) and destruction of the natural family relationships. The policy has been relaxed in some rural areas where large families are still required for farming and welfare support.

Cultural factors are significant when designing birth control programmes, for in many countries, such as Latin America, large numbers of children are seen as a sign of virility. In Asian countries there is a preference for male children, as they attract dowries and can contribute more to the workforce in farming communities. Religion also discourages smaller families, for example Roman Catholicism in Latin America, and Muslim countries stretching from North Africa to Pakistan and Bangladesh.

HEALTH AND HEALTHCARE SYSTEMS

Health differences can be measured using life expectancy, infant mortality rates, and death rates. These measurements tend to vary in accordance with a country's per capita Gross National Product, with the lowest levels of GNP and poorest health in African countries, correspondingly, middle levels in Asia, and relatively high levels in Latin America. There are also differences between countries in the same band, but there is generally a correlation between poverty and ill-health. There are significant differences in the types and nature of the diseases experienced by people living in the First and Third Worlds. Nations in the North have generally eradicated or controlled infectious diseases with improved sanitation, better hygiene, mass immunisation programmes, and better socioeconomic conditions. The First World is now primarily affected by non-infectious diseases, degenerative diseases, and 'diseases of affluence', such as coronary heart disease, cancers, strokes, and road accidents. In contrast, countries in the South are still overwhelmed by communicable diseases (such as measles, dysentery, tuberculosis) which are spread by impure water and poor sanitation, and exacerbated by malnutrition and generally poor socioeconomic conditions. Colonialism and contact with the West have increased ill-health in the Third World, through the replacement of subsistence crops with cash crops, the development of TNCs and the promotion of Western products such as baby milk. The WHO Report (1997) described the way in which rich industrialised nations such as Britain are exporting deadly diseases along with the Western lifestyle to the developing nations. New cases of heart disease, strokes, diabetes, and some cancers increase dramatically in the Third World as Western habits such as smoking and fat-rich diets are adopted. In newly industrialised countries such as China and in Central America, cancers, cardiovascular disease, and diabetes are increasing at a phenomenal rate. A change in exposure in lifestyle has been accompanied by a change in the disease pattern in many Third World nations.

The Western model of a healthcare system has been introduced into the Third World, resulting in hospital-based care, an urban focus for medicine, a high level of technology, and a small number of health professionals. Rural areas have limited healthcare services, and the emphasis on Western medicine and treatments has devalued traditional methods and alternative approaches. In most Third World countries primary healthcare remains severely underfunded, yet remains the most effective way of improving healthcare in these countries by focusing on diet, family planning, immunisation, and general health education – in other words, concentrating on preventative medicine, rather than the Western emphasis on curative medicine.

THE ROLE OF EDUCATION IN A COUNTRY'S DEVELOPMENT

Modernisation theorists argue that education is the major means of achieving development, at both societal and individual levels. Education serves economic, political, and cultural functions, by training people, encouraging diverse groups to mix, and creating a modern outlook. The individual can also develop by using education to escape poverty and improve their occupational prospects, leading to social mobility.

Dependency theory has an opposite view of the role of education in the Third World, arguing that it is a forum for the diffusion of Western values and institutions, and that the elites in these countries have access to secondary and tertiary education, with the masses given only primary schooling. This ties in with the colonial origins of Third World countries, where it was politically advantageous to have a well-educated indigenous elite as an auxiliary to the main colonial power. Cultural dependence on the parent country is then used to develop a 'colonised personality', where individuals are socialised into, and tied to Western culture and language.

In contrast to the extensive education enjoyed by children in the First World, UNESCO estimate that at any given time over half of Third World children are still not attending school. It is difficult to obtain reliable figures on school enrolments and on literacy rates, but in the 1980s the World Bank revealed that 60% of such children do receive at least some schooling. However, only a small number of children in Third World countries progress through secondary education and on to higher education in comparison with children in the First World.

THE POSITION OF WOMEN

The position of women in terms of education, employment, health, marriage, and the family varies significantly between the First and Third Worlds. Inequality between men and women is widespread in all areas of the world, for although women form 50% of the world's population, they work two-thirds of all work hours in the world, yet receive only 10% of world income, and own a mere one percent of world property (A. Foster-Carter). These inequalities are magnified in Third World nations, where there is often no legislation to protect or enhance women's rights, as there is in Western countries. Levels of illiteracy are higher amongst women in the Third World, with three out of five illiterates being female. Progress for women in education has, however, been made in the last thirty years, with as few as 15% of girls receiving any education in the 1960s, compared to 80% in the 1990s. For the first time a generation of Third World women will see education as a norm, and subsequently demand more rights in other areas, such as the law, employment, family life, reproductive control, and health.

In terms of employment there is a gender imbalance in the Third World, with women often comprising as much as 75% of all agricultural workers and as many as 90% of workers in food processing. In particular, factory-produced goods have forced women to work outside the home, replacing indigenous crafts which enabled women to more easily combine work and family life. The lack of equal opportunities legislation in the workplace means that women continue to work long hours for little pay, and with no childcare provision.

Standards of healthcare and sexual/reproductive control are significantly low in the Third World, where women suffer low mortality rates, but high morbidity rates, with childbirth a high risk procedure, and a lack of access to, or cultural constraints on, contraception.

In many Latin American countries there is a 'machismo' ideology, which encourages the socialisation of women into the roles of wives and mothers, and women's employment is seen as peripheral to men's work. In many Asian cultures male dominance is legally and cultural enforced, with no equality and no divorce for women. Marriage and family life is greatly affected in the Third World by the concept of migrant labour, where males may work away for months or years at a time, leaving women to run farms and bring up children. In some countries, such as the Philippines, the converse occurs, where women gain employment outside their country and leave their husbands and children behind.

Modernisation theorists would argue that development has improved women's position in society and increased their range of opportunities. Urban living, educational access, and opportunities in manufacturing industry are all seen as enhancing women's lives.

Dependency theorists argue that this fails to recognise the continuing dual nature of women's roles as wives/mothers and workers, and ignores the dependence of women on male-dominated institutions. In response to these inequalities, many Third World countries have developed various kinds of women's movements. These movements are more likely than Western feminist groups to emphasise the need to transform the total process of development, rather than isolate women's inequalities from the wider issues. They are therefore more inclined to fight with men against the oppression of all people in Third World nations.

CHECK YOUR UNDERSTANDING

On completion of this chapter the student should now be able to define the following terms.

1   Gemeinschaft
2   Gesellschaft
3   Social network
4   Communitarianism
5   'Spirit of community'
6   Romanticisation of community
7   Disengagement theory
8   Urban sociology
9   Urbanisation
10   Urban dispersal
11   Metropolis
12   Megalopolis
13   Urban ecology
14   Concentric zone theory of city growth
15   Twilight zone

16 Gentrification
17 Destructive gemeinschaft
18 Developed countries
19 Less developed countries
20 Underdeveloped countries
21 First World
22 Second World
23 Third World
24 Newly Industrialised Countries
25 Modernisation theory
26 Dependency theory
27 Populism
28 Globalisation
29 Transnational companies
30 Import substitution industries
31 Export-oriented industries
32 Dual-sector economy
33 Demographic transition
34 Population policies

SELF-ASSESSMENT QUESTIONS

1 Describe **three** ways in which the term 'community' can be used.
2 Summarise the evidence against the 'loss of community' approach.
3 Briefly explain the relationship between community and gender.
4 What criticisms can be made of urban/rural theories?
5 What problems are associated with defining development and underdevelopment?
6 Give **three** criticisms of modernisation theory and **three** criticisms of dependency theory.
7 How have TNCs and Western aid affected North/South relationships?
8 Briefly summarise the key differences between First and Third World nations.

'A' LEVEL SOCIOLOGY ESSAY QUESTIONS

1 Assess the different ways in which sociologists have attempted to explain the apparent loss of community in modern society. (AEB, Nov, 1992)
2 Outline and evaluate sociological contributions to an understanding of the development of urbanization and urbanism in modern society. (AEB, Summer, 1994)

3 Compare and contrast funtionalist and conflict explanations of the ways in which societies change and develop. (AEB, Nov, 1992)

4 Asses the argument that the concept of underdevelopment is more useful than the concept of development in explaining global inequalities. (AEB, Summer, 1994)

5 Critically discuss the view that economic growth is only one aspect of development (Summer, 1996).

LEARNING OBJECTIVES

ON COMPLETION OF THIS CHAPTER THE STUDENT SHOULD BE ABLE
TO:

1 UNDERSTAND THE SOCIAL CONSTRUCTION OF HEALTH AND
   ILLNESS
2 DESCRIBE AND EXPLAIN THE RELATIONSHIP BETWEEN SOCIAL
   CLASS AND HEALTH
3 DESCRIBE AND EXPLAIN GENDER AND ETHNIC DIFFERENCES IN
   HEALTH
4 DESCRIBE THE RELATIONSHIP BETWEEN MEDICINE AND SOCIAL
   CONTROL

The social construction of health and illness

The concept of health can be difficult to define because it often implies a **subjective** element (people can feel healthy or ill in different degrees) and as such it cannot be quantified. The World Health Organisation (WHO) defines health as 'not merely the absence of disease and infirmity, but complete mental and social well-being.' (WHO, 1955). This definition has been criticised by R. Dubos and M. Pines, 'Health and Disease' (1980) as being too idealistic or Utopian. They also point out that the WHO definition is an absolute term, whereas health must be seen as a **relative concept**. Thus, the meaning of health varies, with people regarding the terms 'sick' or 'ill' in different ways. In addition, health is dependent on factors such as age, sex, status, physical activity, diet, and lifestyle. Many of the terms associated with health are problematical, and raise issues concerning their definition.

Disease is a general concept, which is used to refer to a medical diagnosis of pathological abnormality, which is indicated by a set of signs and symptoms, for example heart disease. It may a physical or mental condition, and may be caused by illness, injury, or accident. Disease may also be measured **objectively**, by searching for specific pathological conditions such as viruses, for example measles.

Illness implies a deviation from a normal 'healthy' state, and refers to a person's subjective feelings of 'ill-health' through pain, discomfort, etc. Thus, people can feel ill, but not have a disease, and people can have a disease (such as high blood pressure), but not feel ill.

The definition of illness is not based simply on biological changes, but also on social conditions. It is possible to interpret illness as deviant behaviour in some situations: obesity, frigidity, fear of strangers have all been regarded as deviant at various times. The reverse of this is more common, where deviant or undesirable behaviour is interpreted or labelled as an illness or even as a disease as the following cases show:

1. In 1851 Dr. Samuel Cartwright, chair of the Louisiana Medical Association, described a disease called 'drapetomania'. Drapetomania only affected Negro slaves, and its main symptom was running away. Thus, 'healthy' slaves were ones who did not run away from their masters – a useful form of social control.
2. Disruptive or anti-social school pupils are often labelled as 'hyperactive' or 'maladjusted'.
3. Reading and writing problems have become a 'neurological' disease called dyslexia.
4. Political dissenters in the Eastern bloc countries were frequently diagnosed as suffering from mental illness.

Examples of illness and disease which are socially defined reflect the culture within which the medical profession diagnose. Obviously, not all illness is culturally defined, and people do suffer from genuine pain and disease. However, in some circumstances the ability of people to feel pain may depend on culture. R. Melzak, 'The Puzzle of Pain' (1973) describes a hook-hanging ritual practised in parts of India, where men swing freely supported by hooks embedded in their backs. During the ritual there is no evidence that the men are in pain, and afterwards the wounds heal remarkably quickly. Fire-walking practices also illustrate cultural variations in the ability of people to experience pain (Although this observed lack of pain may be a case of technique over supposed pain).

The social and cultural environment may be responsible for the emergence of certain diseases: 'cultural diets' high in smoked food lead to high rates of stomach cancer. Similarly, cultural patterns concerning alcohol, smoking, and sexual behaviour can influence the level of certain diseases. The structure and organisation of work relationships can also lead to stress, heart disease, ulcers, and depression. Both Durkheim and Marx described how psychological damage such as alienation can occur in a capitalist society dominated by exploitive work relationships. The social implications of ill-health are illustrated by several other examples:

The process of **'becoming a patient'** involves a complex sequence of events, whereby 'Needs have to be felt as such, perceived, then expressed in demand' (J.N. Morris, 1967). The conditions under which individuals take their symptoms to a doctor vary according to their ability to withstand pain and discomfort, as well as the degree to which they perceive their symptoms as a problem. The recognition of symptoms and the particular action taken to deal with them are **social processes** involving interaction between the individual and the medical profession.

T. Parsons, 'The Social System' (1951) presents a view of society based on a system of interlocking social roles which maintain social stability. If people have to withdraw from their role obligations through sickness, then certain rules must regulate the procedure to ensure that individuals do not use sickness as a means of opting out of their roles. Parsons argues that the medical profession act as agents of social control by creating the conditions for the officially defined **'sick role'**. Thus, the individual is obliged to consult a doctor, and in return for officially sanctioned 'time off' from role obligations must submit to medical intervention. This **functionalist** interpretation of the role of the medical profession in maintaining social stability has been criticised for its assumption that the medical profession are committed to serving society and keeping social control.

Mental illness, in contrast to physical illness, presents particular problems of definition, interpretation, and action. There is even debate as to whether 'illness' should be applied to a range of conditions including anxiety, depression, psychoses, and psychosomatic states. Implicit in all forms of mental illness is the inability of a person to meet social expectations, and in some cases to be unaware that these expectations are not being fulfilled. T.J. Scheff, 'Being Mentally Ill' (1966) argues that the label 'mental illness' may be applied to people in order to explain their violation of society's accepted behaviour. Scheff describes this as **'residual rule breaking'**, rather than mental illness.

Labelling theory can be used to explain how negative stereotypes of mental illness are learned in childhood, and constantly reinforced by their usage in the mass media. T. Scheff, 'Labelling Madness' (1975) argues that labels such as 'dangerous', 'lunatic', 'mental instability', are used to describe behaviour which is at variance with the

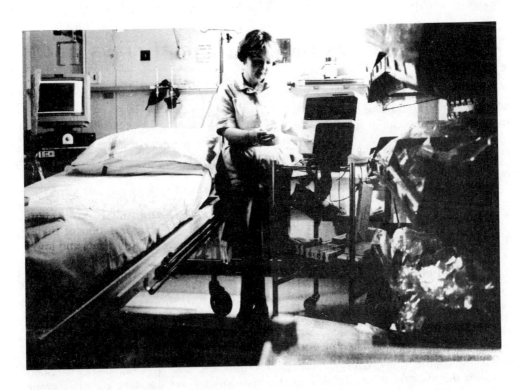

The growth of technology in medicine

norm. The stigma of mental illness in society may help to explain why many doctors are reluctant to diagnose emotionally disturbed patients.

Another perspective on mental illness is provided by T. Szasz, 'The Myth of Mental Illness' (1961), who argues that the word 'illness' can only properly be applied to physical conditions, where disease exists. As no such disease is apparent in mental illness, it cannot be called an illness, but is a myth which is used as a way of labelling society's misfits. Although mental illness can be viewed as a social product, Szasz fails to see that physical illness may also depend on value judgements by the medical profession. Therefore, there is no reason why the term 'illness' should not be applied equally to physical and mental states which are perceived as normatively different. In other words, 'illness' is not an objective 'thing', but refers to a particular status given to people with certain conditions.

It is therefore impossible to devise a reliable and valid definition of health, but it is obviously important to attempt to measure the amount of 'health' within a country, and also to be able to compare levels of health between countries. In order to do this, two **indicators of health** are used: **morbidity** and **mortality**.

Morbidity measures the amount of sickness in society, calculated from statistics on time off work or by self-reported illness in health surveys. Morbidity is really measuring the absence of health, or negative health, and is not a very reliable measure because its definition is based on subjective judgement, which makes it difficult to compare figures within and between societies.

Mortality measures death rates in societies, using official mortality statistics. Information concerning rates of death for different age groups and from particular causes can be obtained. Compared to morbidity it is an objective measure, but is limited because it only provides information on ill-health which is ultimately fatal.

The relationship between social class and health

Medical historians, such as T. McKeown, 'The Role of Medicine' (1976) have suggested that medical intervention has been far less important in promoting health than have other social and economic changes. Therefore, the decrease in death rates and the eradication of ill-health have resulted from the following changes:

1. Improved nutrition and diet due to the introduction of new crops and improved farming techniques.
2. Improvements in public hygiene, such as better food and water purification, improved sewage disposal, better sterilisation and quicker transportation of milk.
3. Improved environmental conditions, such as better working environments and lower levels of pollution.
4. A reduced birth rate which restricted the size of families, improving health for both mothers and children.

Although the changes in social conditions described above led to a general improvement in health, there always have been, and there continues to be, disparities between the health of people from different social classes. Thus, studies of epidemics in the nineteenth century (the origins of epidemiology) indicated that epidemic diseases tended to cause the greatest mortality among the very young and the very old, the lower working class, and the inhabitants of slums.

Evidence from mortality statistics indicates that at all life stages, the higher the social class the greater the chance of survival. Thus, child mortality figures show that the risk of dying before reaching the age of five is more than twice as great for a child born into an unskilled manual workers family than for a child born into a professional home (The Court Report, 1976). For adult males, the risk of death before the age of 65 is much greater for unskilled manual workers, and even diseases most popularly associated with stressed executives (such as ulcers, heart disease) are in fact the cause of greater mortality among unskilled manual workers. P. Townsend and N. Davidson, 'The Black Report' in P. Townsend and N. Davidson and M. Whitehead (eds.) 'Inequalities in Health' (1992) showed how mortality rates for lower-class males were higher in 65 out of 78 disease categories, and 62 out of 82 for lower-class females. The only exception to this are the rates for malignant melanoma for both males and females, and breast and brain cancer for females which are higher in social classes 1 and 2. They also found that accidental death is more common in the lower classes, with children in social classes 4 and 5 between five and seven times more likely to die from accidental death by fire, falling, drowning, or being hit by a car than children from social class 1.

Similarly, morbidity rates between the classes illustrate large differences. Evidence from the OPCS and the British Heart Survey indicate that the lower classes experience more sickness and ill-health than the higher classes. Children from the working class have lower birth weight, experience more sickness, have longer periods off school, and have worse teeth. In adulthood, the working class are more likely to suffer from acute diseases, with the gap between the classes greatest for chronic conditions such as bronchitis, rheumatism, backache and hypertension. It also appears that 'diseases of poverty' such as tuberculosis, bronchitis, and cancer of the cervix are more concentrated among the poorer sections of society. Further evidence on social class differences in healthcare include the following studies:

The General Household Survey (1972) found that the rate of long standing illness was almost three times greater for social class 5 than for social class 1. Also, the rate of reported absence from work was almost five times greater in social class 5 than in social class 1. A combination of material (housing, diet, etc.) and cultural (alienation, attitudes to healthcare, etc.) reasons may explain these differences.

A. Howlett and J. Ashley, 'Selective Care' (1979) found that the 'best' teaching hospitals tended to admit a substantially larger proportion of middle-class men for treatment of an enlarged prostate gland. No reasons are offered for this fact, and the implied superior treatment is not proved. Howlett and Ashley do show that the middle class make better use of the preventive health services, such as cervical smears. They also suggest that the working class may get more out of the NHS **quantitatively**, but they get less out of it **qualitatively.**

The Report of the Working Party on Inequalities in Health (The Black Report) (1980) also revealed that the middle class benefits more from the NHS than the working class, for although the working class use the NHS more frequently, they do not use it as much as might be expected **relative to need.**

The Black Report (1980) used the Registrar-General's 1 to 5 occupational classification to show that health differences between the social classes can be traced through all stages of life. Some of these differences, in which the middle class have more advantages than the working class, include the following examples:

– Infant and child mortality rates: boys born into class 5 families are ten times more likely to die by fire, falls, or drowning, than sons of class 1 parents.
– Use of health services by children under seven: 16% of children in class 1 had never visited a dentist, compared to 31% of children in class 5.

- Preventive services: class 4 and 5 women are less likely to be screened for cervical cancer.
- Adult death rates show that working-class people are more likely to die younger than middle-class people, although the difference diminishes as people get older, as the risk of death for both groups is then high.
- Deprived areas, such as the East Midlands and North have the highest death rates, whereas the South East and South West have the lowest death rates.

The Black Report examines four kinds of explanation to account for health inequality:

The 'artefact' or social constructionist explanation. This argues that inequalities in health are artificial because they are an effect produced when attempts are made to measure something which cannot be accurately measured. Thus, changes in occupational classification make it difficult to compare class and health over a period of time. However, P. Townsend, N. Davidson and M. Whitehead (eds.), 'Inequalities in Health' (1992) argue that class differences in health are real, and should be regarded as such. In the area of mental illness, though, definitions of mental health are subject to wide variations in classification. Thus, T. Scheff, 'Labelling Madness' (1975) describes how those people with the least power and the fewest resources are most likely to be labelled as mentally ill. In addition, he argues that symptoms displayed by the working class are more likely to be interpreted as mental illness.

'Natural'/ 'social' selection explanation. This approach argues that inequalities in health reflect a process of social mobility based on health, with the 'healthy poor' moving up the social hierarchy and the 'unhealthy rich' moving down the scale. According to J. Stern the statistician, this exchange of people increases inequality as the poor lose all their healthy people and receive in return the unhealthy people from the higher social classes. Stern sees health as a fixed, genetic property, independent of social and economic circumstances. He therefore assumes that health itself can lead to social mobility, with the 'healthy poor' able to overcome their material disadvantage and move up the social ladder. The validity of this explanation depends on the extent to which health can be isolated from material factors.

This view also assumes that poor working class health is a cause of social class membership, with the concentration of ill-health in the working class reflecting processes of social selection. Thus, sickly babies move on to become ill children, with time off school, leading to low achievement and low-status jobs. Conversely, healthy babies and children achieve high levels of success, and subsequently move into high-status jobs.

'Cultural-behaviourist' explanation. This view sees inequalities in health as a result of the inadequate culture of the working class in matters relating to healthcare, for example late ante-natal care, poor diet, heavy smoking. This explanation argues that there is a **'poverty of health'** culture, which has been illustrated by M. Blaxter, 'Health and Lifestyles' (1990) and other epidemiological studies, where it has been shown that excessive smoking and drinking and inadequate diet and exercise are associated with lower socioeconomic classes. Blaxter also points out, however, that there are geographical differences in health behaviour: in London and other middle-class owner-occupied non-industrial areas, non-manual men are more likely to be heavy drinkers. Similarly, exercise is related to socioeconomic group and age/sex/geographical location, with a higher proportion of non-manual females than manual ones having higher levels of exercise whatever their age or geographical location. Two main criticisms of the cultural-behaviourist explanation can be made:

1. Even when smoking, drinking, diet and exercise are controlled, differences in mortality rates of the different social classes remain.
2. People's behaviour cannot be separated from the social context in which it occurs. Poor working and housing conditions lead to poor health, and stressful circumstances may promote smoking and drinking.

'Materialist' or structural explanation. This argues that inequalities in health are due to a lack of adequate resources to maintain subsistence levels. Health inequalities are seen as a product of the fundamental inequalties in the distribution of income and wealth between the social classes. This is the explanation favoured by the Black Report, and has been summarised by J.T. Hart (1975) in the 'Inverse Care Law', which states that the availability of good medical care tends to vary inversely with the need for it in the population served. The materialist approach stresses the importance of 'life circumstances' (material and social), and suggests links between material deprivation and poor health and mortality. Hence, the condition of the local environment (housing, play areas, pollution) is significant in health levels. Low income can result in reduced access to healthcare (lack or unavailability of transport, time off work, etc.). Unemployment may lead to poor diet and stress-induced 'cultural behaviours', such as smoking and drinking. Social factors such as family support, neighbours, integration or isolation within the community, may also be relevant in health levels. There is evidence, too, to support a **'delayed effects' thesis**, which argues that poor material and social conditions in the early years of life can lead to high levels of adult morbidity and premature mortality: D.J.P. Barker, 'Mothers, Babies and Disease in Later Life' (1994).

The Black Report gives a list of recommendations designed to reduce health inequalities. These are based on a broad anti-poverty strategy, and include a fairer distribution of resources, increased benefit levels, more facilities for the under-fives, etc. The government's reaction to the Report was to delay publication of it by four months, then to issue it at the end of the Bank Holiday weekend when Parliament was not sitting. A foreward by the then DHSS Minister Patrick Jenkin stated that the research had not been particularly helpful, the conclusions were unclear, and the recommendations 'quite unrealistic in the present economic circumstances'.

Since the Black Report the disparity in death and morbidity rates between the social classes appears to be widening, and as changes in income distribution continue to occur, such disparities can be expected to increase. Recent research on the relationship between health and social class includes the following:

C. Blackburn, 'Poverty and Health: Working with Families' (1991) found that in 1986 babies in the lower social classes had lower birth weights and higher mortality rates than babies in higher social classes. Young children from working-class backgrounds were also more likely to suffer from poorer teeth and increased rates of respiratory diseases.

National Children's Home (1991) Report included a survey on the eating habits of low income families in Britain. Results showed that one in five parents denied themselves food because of lack of money, and one in ten children under the age of five did not have enough to eat at least once a month.

Department of Health, 'Health of the Nation: Variations in Health' (1995) Report showed that the poor continue to experience more ill-health than the more affluent in society. The report claimed that life expectancy at birth is seven years longer in social class 1 than in social class 5. It found that children in class 5 were four times more likely to suffer accidental death than children in class 1. With regard to adults, the report found that of the 66 major causes of death in men, 62 were more common among those in social classes 4 and 5 combined than in all other social classes. Similarly, of the 70 major causes of death in women, 64 were more common in women married to men in social classes 4 and 5. The report underlined the fact that other government departments had to be involved in reversing health inequalities, and warned that lifestyle factors alone could not account for the differences between social classes.

Gender and ethnic differences in health

There is substantial evidence to indicate that, in addition to the health inequalities which exist between the social classes, there are also significant morbidity and mortality differentials based on both gender and race.

GENDER

Statistics from the Office of Population Censuses and Surveys indicate that premature death rates in all age groups are greater for men than for women, with male death rates almost twice that of females in every social class. However, the sex differential in mortality risk increases with age, unlike class differences which become less significant in old age. On the basis of the figures, it appears that women are healthier than men, but the picture becomes more complicated when morbidity rates are examined. Evidence from self-report studies and medical records indicate that men suffer mostly from heart disease, lung cancer, and respiratory diseases, whereas illnesses which most affect women are heart disease, breast cancer, and cervical and uterine cancer. In self-report studies, results show that men do not seem to experience as much ill-health as women, although they tend to die earlier. Although sickness and ill-health can be used as alternative indicators of health, they are dependent to some extent on subjective judgements as well as the availability of medical records and access to treatment.

Explanations for the gender differences outlined above can be summarised using the headings taken from the Black Report:

1. Social constructionist/artefact explanation

This view is concerned that the definitions and statistics on illness are socially constructed, and therefore do not represent 'true' measurements of ill-health. Gender socialisation may explain why female illness is more likely to be recorded than male illness, with females more likely to be hospitalised, and females more frequently diagnosed as suffering from psychiatric disorders. Females may be socialised to accept and admit illness and pain, and to seek treatment because children are dependent on them. Doctors may be more likely to label women as 'sick', especially for mental illness, because of society's attitudes towards women and ill-health. Thus, morbidity rates for women are higher than those for men, but this may be because they are 'artificially constructed', rather than being 'real figures'.

2. Natural selection explanation

This approach would argue that there is a genetic or biological explanation for the sex differences in morbidity and mortality. Available evidence for a genetic basis is limited, for example female hormones may offer some protection from certain diseases, and female foetuses have a greater survival rate than male ones. Greater numbers of male babies suffer from malformations and genetically transmitted disorders, and are more vulnerable to illness and injury. This could be nature's way of evening up the numbers of each sex, as more male babies are born than female ones. The extent of variation in morbidity and mortality rates between the sexes and across countries would, however, indicate that social and cultural factors are more important than genetic ones in determining levels of health.

3. **Cultural-behavioural explanation**

This explanation focuses on the differences in attitudes, norms and behaviour of the sexes, which may lead to increased levels of ill-health and premature death. Thus, males are more likely than women to smoke, drink alcohol, drive, and are at greater risk of suicide and murder. However, since 1970 the gap between the sexes in smoking, drinking, and driving has decreased, indicating that changes in female socialisation patterns may lead to an increase in morbidity for some women.

It is also possible that female socialisation into 'helplessness' may increase women's passivity and acceptance of sickness, and at the same time make women more prone to depressive illnesses. On the other hand, female expression of emotion enables women to cope more successfully than men with stress.

4. **Materialist-structuralist explanation**

This view suggests that differences in social positions and experiences within the social structure affect the quality of health between the sexes. In particular male and female occupational roles may have a significant effect on morbidity and mortality. Thus, male mortality is higher in physically hazardous occupations such as mining, construction work, diving, the armed services. For women, increased morbidity is found in clerical work, where heart disease, stress, and low status combine with the pressure of domestic duties to affect their health. Whereas unemployment and early retirement lead to an increase in premature death amongst men, women appear to suffer more illness as a consequence of their dual role as housewife-mother/worker. The 1988 Report of the government's advisory Women's National Commission found that women are twice as likely to suffer stress as men, largely as a result of combining multiple roles. For working-class women there may be greater dependence on the reproductive role for achievement and status, which may account for their higher levels of post-natal and menopausal depression, caused by the achievement and cessation of their reproductive role. (G.W. Brown and T. Harris, 'The Social Origins of Depression' (1979)).

ETHNICITY

Data concerning ethnic differences in morbidity and mortality is generally inadequate, and prior to the 1991 census (which asked for the ethnic group of respondents) the only available information was that held on birth and death certificates, which simply record an individual's country of birth. However, the ethnic origins of people born in this country are not included in death certificates. Also, people of European origin born outside Europe are not clearly identified in death certificates. Data on morbidity is even more difficult to obtain and may not necessarily be valid.

However, despite these methodological problems, there are a number of studies which have indicated that groups originally from India, Pakistan, Bangladesh, Africa and the Caribbean are more likely to suffer from certain diseases than members of the white population. Thus, people from India, Pakistan, and Bangladesh are more inclined to suffer from heart disease, whereas strokes and hypertension are more common in Africans and Afro-Caribbeans. All of the above groups are at greater risk of tuberculosis, diabetes, and maternal mortality, with Asian and Caribbean communities suffering more from deaths due to accidents, violence, and poisoning. Conversely, many types of cancer, in particular lung cancer, appear less frequently as a cause of death among the above ethnic minorities. Certain ethnic minority groups are at greater risk for particular conditions: Asians are more prone to rickets, and the Caribbean community has the highest rates for sickle-cell anaemia. Mental illness also appears disproportionately in particular groups: Afro-Caribbeans are more likely to be admitted to mental hospitals and to be committed on a compulsory admission than any other group within the population. Possible explanations for the differences in morbidity and mortality between ethnic groups can be explained in a number of ways.

Natural selection explanation. This view assumes that genetic differences between ethnic groups may be significant in causing certain diseases, or predisposing some sections of the population towards particular conditions. Very few disorders have a direct genetic link, as does sickle cell anaemia which mainly affects the Afro-Caribbean population. There is no substantial evidence to indicate that genetic factors are a critical factor in ethnic differences in morbidity and mortality. It is likely that social and economic conditions are more important.

Cultural-behavioural explanation. This approach focuses on the ways in which different cultural lifestyles and behaviour between ethnic groups can influence morbidity and mortality rates. High rates of coronary heart disease and diabetes amongst Asians may be due to their use of certain cooking fats and high carbohydrate foods: heart disease rates amongst Asians living in the Indian sub-continent are lower, suggesting that traditional Asian vegetarian diets confer better health. The behaviour of certain ethnic groups in relation to healthcare may also explain their higher morbidity/ mortality rates. Low levels of attendance at ante-natal clinics, poor take-up of screening tests, and a reluctance to visit GPs may all lead to increased ill-health.

Materialist-structural explanation. This view argues that it is the position of ethnic minorities within the class structure which affects their morbidity and mortality. In particular, their role within the occupational structure can have a significant effect on their health. Thus, many male Asians and Caribbeans are employed in low-paid manual occupations, such as textiles and footwear, which involve long working hours and poor conditions, with a high risk of injury. A large number of female Asians work at home as 'outworkers' on piece-work rates of pay, where long hours, job insecurity, and sometimes faulty equipment can lead to poor health.

Racism. It is difficult to evaluate the contribution which racism makes to the ill-health and mortality rates of ethnic groups. It appears that the low social and occupational status of ethnic minorities is compounded by racist attitudes. High levels of unemployment, excessive shift work, difficult working conditions, and low pay are often linked to racism rather than to social class position. A good example is the NHS, which employs a large number of ethnic minorities. However, black people within the NHS are disproportionately found in the lower ranks ancillary work, such as cleaning and catering, and even within the nursing/medical staff they tend to occupy the low-status positions in the less prestigious areas, such as geriatrics and mental illness.

Racism may also contribute to poor housing conditions, which in turn can create a significant health risk. Racist attitudes within the medical profession may alienate many ethnic minorities, where a lack 'of respect for cultural and religious beliefs and practices can lead some groups to view those who provide health services as offensive and unapproachable.

The relationship between medicine and social control

The power and influence which medicine wields in society can be explained in a number of ways. For many functionalists such as T. Parsons, the prestige and power of medicine derives from the possession of scarce knowledge and skills which are essential to the continuance of society. The high rewards commanded by many medical professionals is justified on the grounds that they have sacrificed substantial years of training to gain their skills and knowledge, and only they have the ability to promote good health and save lives. However, there is evidence to show that the medical profession attempted to increase their status and power years before they significantly affected the incidence of disease (N. Hart, 'The Sociology of Health and Medicine' (1985)).

Recent threats to medical autonomy and the ability to cure people have arisen as a result of the shift in morbidity rates from infectious to degenerative diseases. According to M. Morgan, M. Calnan, and N. Manning, 'Sociological Approaches to Health and Medicine' (1985), the emphasis on curative medicine is declining, whilst there has been a pronounced emphasis on preventive and rehabilitative medicine. This has given greater power and status to paramedical occupations such as physiotherapy and occupational therapy, which can make greater contributions to the care of people suffering from long-term conditions. Another attack on the medical profession's power has come from the NHS and Community Care Act, 1990, which led to the creation of more management administrators in hospitals, whose control over budgets can influence power relationships within the health service.

The organisation of health services has also been seen as a means by which the medical profession have retained their privileged position. M. Weber argued that the hierarchical structure of the medical profession, and its control over training and registration, have perpetuated its high status and rewards. E. Freidson, 'The Profession of Medicine' (1970) suggests that the power and privilege of the medical profession is a consequence of their struggles with other competing groups in the health field. This led to the medical profession being granted two exclusive rights by the state: firstly, the right to determine who can perform the work and secondly, how it should be done. This has meant that the medical profession's definitions of health, illness, and treatment are accepted as the only legitimate ones, in contrast to the nursing profession who lack the same level of autonomy.

Another perspective on the link between medicine and social control is the view that medicine operates as an institution of the superstructure, and protects the interests of the capitalist class. I.K. Zola, 'Medicine as an institution of social control' (1972) argues that medicine is becoming a major institution of social control, incorporating the traditional institutions of religion and law. The expansion of the 'medical model' to account for a range of phenomena, often unconnected with disease, has been described by Zola as the **'medicalizing'** of society. Thus, a range of behaviour, including homosexuality, smoking, over-eating, drinking, etc. have become regarded as 'unhealthy' life activities. Virtually any activity can be labelled as a 'medical problem', or, as Zola comments, 'Living is injurious to health'.

This Marxist analysis can also be used to illustrate the profit-making, commodity production process of capitalism. The NHS, in common with other large organisational structures, produces vested interests, such as the British Medical Association and the drug companies. Alternatives to large-scale organisational health services, such as community-based healthcare (recommended by the Black Report), would threaten these interests, and reduce the autonomy of the medical profession. V. Navarro, and J. McKinley, have argued that the high rewards of the medical profession reflect the profession's usefulness to the capitalist class by maintaining the health of the workforce and reducing absenteeism.

The view above has also been expressed by I. Illich, 'Medical Nemesis' (1976), who argues that doctors play the role of 'experts' within the larger 'health machine' or bureaucratic structure. Doctors remove the responsibility for health from the individual, and decide what 'label' to apply to the person. The individual is then passed 'down the line' to the pharmacy, clinic, or hospital. Illich further argues that 'the medical establishment has become a major threat to health', calling for the dismantling of existing Western healthcare, and its replacement by community-based medicine. Illich identifies **'iatragenic'** diseases – disease and disability caused by medical intervention, such as the side effects of drugs, unnecessary surgery, etc. Illich uses the term **'cultural iatrogenesis'** to describe the process whereby pain, sickness, and death itself are removed from the control of the individual and **'institutionally managed'** by the medical profession.

Finally, social control is also apparent in doctor-patient relationships. F.F. Cartwright, 'A Social History of Medicine' (1977), P.S. Byrne and B.E. Long, 'Doctors Talking to Patients' (1976) and T. Johnson, 'Professions and Power' (1972) describe the extent to which doctors control their consultations with patients, and exercise their autonomy and control in deciding a patient's treatment. Social control of patients also occurs in situations where they are hospitalised or institutionalised (E. Goffman, 'Asylums' (1961).

CHECK YOUR UNDERSTANDING

After reading this chapter you should now be able to define the following terms.

1 Health
2 Disease
3 Illness
4 Sick role
5 Residual rule breaking
6 Morbidity
7 Mortality
8 Inverse care law
9 'Delayed effects' thesis
10 'Medicalizing' of society
11 Iatragenic diseases
12 Cultural iatrogenesis

SELF-ASSESSMENT QUESTIONS

1 Distinguish between health and disease.
2 Why is mental illness sometimes considered to be a 'myth'?
3 What is epidemiology?
4 In what ways do gender and ethnicity affect the level of health?
5 What explanations can be given for inequalities in health between the social classes?
6 How does the medical profession maintain its status and power?

'A' LEVEL SOCIOLOGY QUESTIONS

1 Assess the view that improvements in the health of the population in modern society are the result of better health care. (AEB, summer 1996).
2 'The Welfare State has still not significantly redistributed health resources in favour of the most needy'.
   Critically examine the sociological arguments for and against this view (AEB, summer, 1992).
3 Critically examine the relationship between social class background and the nature and distribution of different types of illness (AEB, summer, 1994).

CHAPTER EIGHTEEN

MASS MEDIA

LEARNING OBJECTIVES

ON COMPLETION OF THIS CHAPTER THE STUDENT SHOULD BE ABLE TO:

1 DEFINE THE MASS MEDIA AND DESCRIBE ITS STRUCTURE
2 DISCUSS THEORIES OF THE MASS MEDIA
3 DESCRIBE AND EXPLAIN THE INFLUENCE OF THE MEDIA ON POLITICS AND THE PRESENTATION OF NEWS
4 DISCUSS MEDIA REPRESENTATIONS OF WOMEN AND ETHNIC MINORITIES
5 DESCRIBE AND EXPLAIN THE RELATIONSHIP BETWEEN THE MASS MEDIA AND VIOLENT BEHAVIOUR

The mass media

The mass media consists of the various forms of mass communication:

– printed matter, for example books, magazines, newspapers;
– audio communication, for example radio, records, cassettes, CDs;
– audio-visual systems, for example television, cinema, video, cable, satellite;
– computer aided communication, for example e-mail, internet.

Since the nineteenth century the range of media, particularly in the field of audio-visual communication, has expanded dramatically. The audiences for these various forms of cummunication are huge, with people able to simply absorb the information, or, if they desire, to participate in the media process, through radio 'phone-ins, TV talk shows, letters to magazines and newspapers, charity fund-raising (Comic Relief). Participation in the media is, however, restricted, with calls screened before they go on air, and letters edited for newspapers. The controllers of the media are therefore very powerful, yet the audience retains the power to reject aspects of the media. Many people on Merseyside refused to buy the *Sun* newspaper after its news coverage of the Hillsborough disaster was seen by many to be biased against Liverpool supporters.

The mass media is, for the majority of the population, their major source of information and entertainment, with 20 million people watching the TV news each day, and adults watching approximately 26 hours of TV per week. Newspapers do not enjoy the same level of consumption, with circulation declining since the 1940s as TV ownership has increased. The introduction of cable and satellite viewing, and the creation of Channel 5 in 1997, have expanded the opportunities for this form of mass media.

STRUCTURE OF THE MASS MEDIA

The structure of the mass media must be viewed within an historical context, which locates these changes in the general pattern of industrialisation. The industrialisation of mass communications has followed a number of stages, leading to changes in the ownership, and ultimately the control, of the media.

Differentiation refers to the process whereby the expansion of small-scale or personalised media organisations resulted in the separation of ownership and distribution. The introduction of new technology in the nineteenth century encouraged further differentiation, with consumption becoming large-scale and impersonal.

Concentration resulted from the growth of monopoly capitalism in the second half of the nineteenth century, with a handful of large companies gaining ownership of most of the media. P. Baran and P. Sweezy 'Monopoly Capital' (1966) describe this trend towards concentration in some detail. Coupled with this concentration of ownership was the trend towards joint-stock companies or corporations, where shares are sold to outside investors. The decline of the owner-entrepreneur and the increasing size of corporations led to the emergence of a new group of professional managers, heralding the '**managerial revolution**' in which managers were becoming a new ruling elite. This 'managerial revolution' thesis has been developed by A. Berle and G. Means, 'The Modern Corporation and Private Property' (1968).

A good example of the historical development of ownership in the media can be found in the newspaper industry. Prior to the Second World War, wealthy individuals and families owned and controlled individual newspapers. These 'press barons', such as Lord Beaverbrook of the *Daily Express*, and Lords Northcliffe and Rothermere of the *Daily Mail*, influenced the content and style of the newspapers, often reflecting a particular political bias. In the post-war era a series of mergers and takeovers resulted in the creation of transnational companies involved in the press, broadcasting, and other interests. The concentration of media industries in the hands of a small number of owners or corporations was shown by the Royal Commission of the Press (1974–77), indicating that five major companies were responsible for over 80% of national morning newspapers and Sunday newspapers. There are still, however, examples of modern-day barons, such as Rupert Murdoch, the owner of News International plc, which has a 30% share of the newspaper market, as well as media interests in other countries such as Australia and the USA. The late Robert Maxwell headed the Mirror Group Newspapers Ltd, which, since his death in 1991, has been taken over by a consortium of banks and financial institutions. Out of the national dailies, only the *Guardian* and the *Independent* have remained apart from the huge conglomerations which now own and control the press and other media interests. The huge costs of running a newspaper make it very prohibitive individual ownership – Eddy Shah's attempts via the *Today* newspaper in the 1980s cost him over £20 million before he sold out to News International.

Diversification is the process whereby media or non-media organisations extend

Satellite television: the expanding mass media

their interests beyond their immediate concerns, creating even larger organisations by takeovers and mergers. General conglomerations result from the takeover of a company specialising in one or more branches of the media by a company with non-media interests, for example the £6 million takeover of the *The Observer* by the Lonrho Group in 1981. Another example is the property and shipping conglomerate Trafalgar House, who took over Express Newspapers in 1977, successfully launched the *Daily Star*, and subsequently sold all press holdings in 1986 to United Newspapers. Multi-media or communications conglomerates are companies with diversity of interests in the media or leisure industries only. Richard Branson's Virgin Group is involved in music, videos, hotels, airlines, soft drinks, and railways.

Theories of the mass media

The extent to which the mass media influence attitudes and behaviour may depend on a number of factors, including the following:

1. The source of the information – a credible person or institution is more likely to influence people's opinions than an individual or organisation with no social acceptability.
2. The form and content of the information – the clarity of the information and the level of change expected will affect how influential the information is.
3. The situation in which the information is received. Information conveyed in private (at home) may be less influential than publicly received information, where there may be social pressure to conform to certain attitudes.

A number of theories have developed concerning the way in which the media affects its audience. These are outlined below:

The hypodermic syringe model is based on the idea that the media 'injects' its effects into the veins of the audience, and therefore influences behaviour. This model dates back to the nineteenth century when cheap shows and theatres were believed to corrupt the young and lead to juvenile crime. They are largely psychological theories, involving various forms of laboratory experiments in an attempt to measure the effects of the media. The advent of cinema, and later television and video, increased support for the 'hypodermic' model, yet studies do not indicate a direct causal link between film-watching and delinquency. The 'hypodermic' model has been criticised by E. Katz and P. Lazarsfeld, 'Personal Influence' (1955) for its assumption that the audience are passive recipients of the media, with no control over its influences.

The two-step flow model is developed from the work of Katz and Lazarsfeld, who used research on voting behaviour to demonstrate that people are influenced by 'opinion leaders', who are found in all social groups such as family, friends, work. Opinion leaders experience greater exposure to the media, and because of their high-status position in the community, they transmit media effects to the wider audience. The two-step flow is therefore from the media to opinion leaders, and from the opinion leaders to the rest of the population. Katz and Lazarsfeld did acknowledge that opinion leaders were also subject to influences besides the media, thus complicating the simple two-step flow. Critics have pointed out that the distinction between leaders and followers is debatable, and it is possible to conceive of a three-, four-, or five-step flow of communication: D. Howitt, 'Mass Media and Social Problems' (1982).

The uses and gratifications approach is based on the belief that people use the media to fulfil certain social and emotional needs. Thus, soap operas centred around every day life, such as *Eastenders* and *Brookside*, provide social companionship for some people (D. McQuail, 'Sociology of Mass Communications' (1972)). Different aspects of the media satisfy different needs for a range of people. Social prestige may be gained from reading a particular newspaper, entertainment may be derived from a music programme, or knowledge may be sought from a documentary. This theory is, however, in danger of over-emphasising the psychological influences of the media, while neglecting the social context in which people experience the media.

The cultural effects theory argues that the media has long-term, cumulative effects on people, which over a period of time may affect people's views and understanding of the social world. In particular, the cultural stereotypes which are perpetuated by the media, such as the presentation of women or ethnic minorities, may be influential over time. These images are, however, received by different groups of people (age, gender, ethnicity, class), so that the media effects are related to the social situation within which they are encountered, affecting people in different ways. The biggest problem with the cultural effects theory is how to measure these effects, and how to separate them from the other influences which affect people's lives.

Pluralist theories are a result of the expansion of various forms of media in capitalist democracies. The 'market liberal' or pluralist perspective considers that the media is 'free', since it provides access to a wide range of opinion. This view is based on a number of arguments:

1. Anyone is free to set up a newspaper, magazine, or other publication (providing they have the money), which ensures the representation of a wide range of public opinion.
2. Editors and journalists, not proprietors, decide the content of newspapers.
3. The media represent the opinions of all the major groups in society, therefore expressing a balanced opinion. Minority groups may be represented, provided they are 'within the law'.
4. The public can influence the media by refusing to buy its products, switching off programmes, complaining via letters to newspapers, or by forming pressure groups (for example National Viewers' and Listeners' Association).

The pluralist view outlined above argues that 'people get what they want' from the media. This attitude, expressed by writers such as J. Whale, 'The Politics of the Media' (1978), has been strongly criticised by supporters of the Marxist perspective, who argue that the media acts as an agency of social control by reproducing and reinforcing the inequalities in society.

Marxist theories stress the power of the media to control people in society. These views argue that the media acts as an agency of social control by reproducing and reinforcing the inequalities in society. The media reflects the established attitudes and values, promoting a conservative view of society. The wealthy capitalist class who own and control the media can therefore use it in their own interest to produce profit and to maintain the status quo.

The process by which the media legitimate an unequal society has been described by R. Miliband, 'The State in Capitalist Society' (1973), L. Althusser, 'Legitimation Crisis' (1976). These accounts reject the pluralist view, and argue instead that the state (government, police, justice system, military) exercise power in favour of the ruling class, using the media, as an 'agency of conservative indoctrination' (R. Miliband). Ideological control is achieved by filtering the messages which people receive, via censorship, editing, and selecting only certain items for inclusion in the news. In this way a state of 'false consciousness' is induced, whereby people are persuaded to accept the inequalities and status quo within society. A state of contentment is further encouraged by the use of the media for entertainment. Thus, soap operas, quiz shows, and game shows are used to give consumers the impression of satisfaction, and divert attention away from the real issue of inequality in society.

Postmodernist theories of the media are related to the idea that people's style and images are largely derived from media sources. Thus, TV programmes, actors, musicians, and advertising all influence the consumer choices which people make concerning clothes, hairstyles, decor, etc. The bombardment of media images and culture can, however, create confusion in the audience. D. Strinati argues that world-wide news and images, and variations in time and space (from past to sci-fi future) lead to a distortion and disorganisation in people's lives. Stability and security are threatened when people can no longer identify their culture within a specific time zone. Strinati believes that this distortion of reality constantly changes and challenges our perceptions of what was, is, and could be in the future.

Media influences on politics, and on the presentation of news

POLITICS AND THE MEDIA

The government directly controls the media through a number of laws which restrict the content of the media. Libel laws encourage newspapers to prevent erroneous reporting, the Official Secrets Act restricts politically sensitive information, and advertising regulations monitor standards. In addition, the government collects a licence fee for the BBC, and can influence BBC policy by its choice of appointees on the board of governors. Therefore political appointments can be used to achieve influence and control. There may be pressure from the government to control the content and transmission of certain programmes if sensitive issues are involved, as was the case during the Falklands War and the Gulf War. The media may also be used by the government to promote its own interests. Privatisation issues in the 1980s (the selling-off of public utilities) were heavily advertised in the press and on television. It is debatable whether this was purely for informative purposes. In a similar way, public information may also be disseminated via the media by the government, including health issues, information on education and social security benefits.

Political parties may use the media as a vehicle for their views and policies. With the exception of the *Daily Mirror*, the *Guardian*, and the *Independent*, the other national dailies promote a pro-Conservative approach in their news reporting and key articles. Until the *Sun* recently announced its support for the Labour Party in the 1997 general election (a surprising *volte face*), the *Daily Mirror* was the only pro-Labour national newspaper. Election campaigns offer a clear opportunity for political parties to infiltrate the media. Every party has a '**spin doctor**', or someone who turns the news around (spins it) so that the bad news is seen in a positive light. Their aim is news management – to raise the impact of good news, and limit the damage of bad news. Press releases are written for the media, and political broadcasts are limited to the main parties, and to those with sufficient funds to publicise their cause. In the 1997 election, Sir James Goldsmith spent £20 million of his own money to promote the Referendum Party.

THE PRESENTATION OF NEWS IN THE MEDIA

The ways in which the media control the production of news is determined both by the ownership and the actual operation of the particular medium itself. R. Pahl and J. Winkler, 'The Coming of Corporatism (1974) describe these two methods of control as **'allocative'** and **'operational'**.

Allocative control is concerned with the way in which the structure of the organisation affects the output of the particular enterprise. The scope and scale of the activities, and the overall allocation of resources within the organisation, are essentially determined by the owners. The owners have the power to merge with other groups or to close part of their enterprise. They are also able to influence the views which are projected by the organisation through their employees.

Operational control is directly affected by allocative control, and is concerned with the routine day-to-day production of the news. Agenda-setting is the process by which journalists and broadcasters select news, and choose to include some items rather than others. 'Organisational factors' will often determine the selection, for example the space available, deadlines, competing events, photographs or film, and cultural relevance. As B. Dutton, 'The Media' (1986) states, editorial staff and journalists thus act as **'gatekeepers'** of the news by choosing certain items to include (opening the gate), and those which to exclude (closing the gate). News agencies (for example Reuters) also have a role to play in 'gatekeeping', for they produce 'pre-packed news' for papers to buy and use. Local papers in particular will often use these sources as they are cheaper than sending a reporter to the location.

Operational control does not, however, take account of the social constraints under which journalists operate. As H. Gans, 'Deciding What's News' (1980) argues, the news is not merely 'out there' to be collected, but must be actively constructed by reporters and editors. In a study of the BBC, P. Schlesinger, 'Putting Reality Together' (1978) found that about 70% of the 'news diary' (the dates of forthcoming important visits, statistical data, etc.) was used in news bulletins. Another example of how journalists construct the news is provided by S. Chibnall, 'Law and Order News: An Analysis of Crime Reporting in the British Press' (1977). Chibnall examines the process by which some crime news receives more sensationalist coverage than other crime stories, with the consequence that the media has an important role to play in the labelling process. Crime reporters are often dependent on official sources and statistics, with the result that the police act as 'gatekeepers' by restricting access to certain information. Chibnall does not accept the Marxist view that journalists are contained by their owners or editors, but argues that they have to construct the news within the constraints of owners, editors, colleagues, and the audience.

S. Cohen and J. Young (eds.), 'The Manufacture of News' (1973) argue that news does not just 'happen', but it is a socially manufactured product. In addition to allocative and operational controls, journalists carry their own beliefs and values which influence their selection of 'newsworthy items'. These 'news values' often reflect consensual social and political values, with dissenting views presented as representative of a deviant minority. The socially produced nature of media news can be examined with reference to a number of areas, including crime and industrial relations.

The presentation of certain items of crime news in preference to others has already been mentioned with reference to the work of S. Chibnall. An example of how inaccurate media information about crime actually is, can be found in the study by J.

Ditton and J. Duffy, 'Bias in the Newspaper Reporting of Crime News' (1983). Ditton and Duffy studied the reporting of crime in six Scottish newspapers during March, 1981, and concentrated on the Strathclyde region, as this area has the highest number of reported crimes committed in Scotland. They found that the crime news reported was highly selective, with less than one percent of known crimes or prosecutions actually appearing in the press. Furthermore, the crimes reported were overwhelmingly biased towards those which involved sex or violence.

An interactionist approach to the presentation of deviance is provided by S. Cohen, 'Folk Devils and Moral Panics' (1972). Cohen used **'labelling theory'** (see Chapter 10) to explain how various activities are identified as 'problems' and subsequently result in censorious action. The media have an important role to play in developing and reinforcing the deviant labels, creating what Cohen calls 'folk devils'. Cohen used the example of the Mods and Rockers in the mid-1960s to show how the media used a selective choice of material to present the teenagers as folk devils. Cohen recognised three main methods by which the 'amplification of deviance' occurred in the media. These were: exaggeration of actual events, accompanied by emotive language; the prediction that similar incidences would occur in the future; and the symbolization of words, clothing and hairstyles with delinquent behaviour. Using these three processes together, the media are able to create the conditions for a 'moral panic', where the labelled individuals are presented as a threat to the stability and values of society.

A similar moral panic over football hooliganism was created in the 1980s, despite the fact that the problem existed for many years prior to that. The response of the media to primary deviance such as spectator misbehaviour at domestic matches was to exacerbate the problem by labelling the people involved as 'savages' or 'morons'. The stigmatisation of this group by the media leads to a call for 'action', resulting in media campaigns calling for stronger police action and the restoration of moral values. The police response to control hooliganism may involve separating rival groups of fans, using closed circuit television to monitor matches, and the use of identity card schemes. The result of this action may be increased levels of violence, as the spectators resent the interference in 'their' game, thus increasing hooliganism and justifying the media identification of a moral panic. More detailed accounts of football hooliganism may be found in J. Williams et al, 'Hooligans Abroad' (1989) and J. Kerr, 'Understanding Soccer Hooliganism' (1994).

A Marxist perspective is applied to the idea of a moral panic in S. Hall, et al, 'Policing the Crisis: Mugging, the State, and Law and Order' (1978). Hall et al examined the moral panic which emerged in the early 1970s over the crime of 'mugging'. They use Gramsci's term **'hegemony'**, or the process by which the ruling class maintains power by convincing other classes that ruling-class views are the 'right' ones, to show how in the late 1960s the ruling class experienced a crisis of hegemony. Thus, economic problems made it difficult for the ruling class to gain the support of the wider population. Industrial disputes and increased levels of crime in the early 1970s meant that law and order became a central issue. In order to legitimate the strengthening of the law, police and courts, the ruling class had to convince the public that certain crimes, in particular mugging, necessitated stronger state action. Hall et al argue that mugging (which does not exist in strict legal terms) became the focus of the moral panic because it combined the public concern over youth and race, with the media often presenting the stereotype of the 'young, black mugger'. Hall and his co-authors use statistics relating to robberies and assaults to show how the press over-reported the level of street crime, creating a moral panic which served to legitimate a more authoritarian approach to law and order. Hall et al do not, however, explain why mugging in particular emerged as the focus for the moral panic, nor do they explore the possibility that urban deprivation and racial conflict may have led to the increased coerciveness of the police rather than media amplification.

The presentation of industrial relations in the media generally reflects the ruling class ideology that trade unions and industrial action are disruptive and operate against the national interest. P. Beharrel and G. Philo (eds). 'Trade Unions and the Media' (1977) examine how union demands and action are presented in the media in a way which distorts their real position. For instance, inflation is often linked in the media to increased wages, when there is no conclusive evidence to support this connection. The most renowned studies of media representations of industrial relations are those which have been conducted by the Glasgow University Media Group: 'Bad News' (1976), 'More Bad News' (1980), and 'Really Bad News' (1982). The first book contains an analysis of television news presentation of industrial relations between January and April, 1975. The Group found that there was a consistent over-reporting of disputes in certain industries, such as car manufacturing, transport, and communications, yet industrial action in other industries was not reported, despite accounting for 37% of all stoppages, according to the Department of Employment statistics. There was also no direct relationship between the amount of television coverage and the severity of the stoppages: 24.9% of the total number of days lost through stoppages occurred in the engineering industry, but only 5.3% of the total number of disputes reported were from the engineering industry. Selective editing of interviews was used by television to present the view that the workforce were to blame for industrial disputes. The choice of interviewees was heavily slanted, for example in the Glasgow garbage collectors' strike, council representatives and not strikers were interviewed on television. The second and third books continue the same theme, with a series of case studies to support the Group's arguments. The overwhelming view is that the media distorts events by selective emphasis, and helps to perpetuate the notion that industrial conflict is disruptive and irrational. The underlying issues, such as lack of investment and management problems, are rarely reported.

Recent studies by the Group have moved towards studying the reporting of world issues, 'War and Peace News' (1985) and 'Getting the Message – News, Truth, and Power' (1993). Here, it is assumed that the agenda-setting as seen by journalists and broadcasters concurs with what the general public regard to be newsworthy. These studies also examine the way in which Western audiences receive information about the Third World, and how Third World issues are regarded as relatively unimportant by Western media standards.

Although extremely useful, the work of the Glasgow Media Group has been criticised for its over reliance on a limited number of case studies. Although the Group reject the pluralist model of the media, they fail to explain why television reflects the dominant ideology, and whether the broadcasters consciously present a biased picture or simply reflect the 'due impartiality' of the status quo.

Media representations of women and ethnic minorities

Media representations of certain groups within the population have received particular attention because of the way in which negative, stereotypical images of these groups are portrayed in the press and on TV, reinforcing their minority position within society. Two groups which have been the subject of research into the presentation of such images are women and ethnic minorities.

WOMEN AND THE MEDIA

As described in Chapter 6, representations of women in the media reflect a **patriarchal ideology**, which supports the vested interests of men and maintains the subordination of women. Since the 1970s and the growth of **feminism**, a number of studies have attempted to analyse the presentation of women in various forms of media. In particular, the huge market for 'female' magazines has attracted significant interest, for they present a range of contradictory images, on the one hand promoting careers, advice and information for women, and on the other reinforcing traditional roles through advertising and 'domestic' articles. B. Fowler suggests that women's magazines in the 1920s and 1930s took on the role of moral agent previously held by the church and the extended family, and largely included articles supporting marriage and family life, with divorce presented as most unacceptable. The assumption that women are 'taken in' by these stereotypes of 'good' and 'bad' women is challenged by C. Adams and R. Laurikietis, 'The Gender Trap, Book 3: Messages and Images' (1976) who argue that women readers are not as gullible as this, and are capable of questioning the articles and images presented.

The most comprehensive account of women's magazines is provided by M. Ferguson, 'Forever Feminine' (1983), who analysed the shared values underpinning *Woman*, *Woman's Own*, and *Woman's Weekly* between 1949 and 1974. She found that there was a distinctive '**cult of femininity**' permeating all the magazines, which equated women with childrearing, housework, cooking, and beautification. Ferguson found that love and marriage were the main themes in all three magazines, with self-improvement the second major topic covered. In a follow-up study in 1979–80, Ferguson found that these themes were reversed, with self-improvement the chief message of the cult of femininity, and the conflict between women's dual roles played down. With the decline in magazine readership between 1958 and 1981 estimated at approximately 50%, Ferguson argues that the women's magazines have been victims of their own success, for once women achieved self-improvement the role of the magazines became superfluous. The movement of 'women's issues' to newspapers, with women's pages, and to radio, with *Woman's Hour*, further reduced the role of the magazine culture, yet also served to emphasise the fact that women should be treated as a minority group within society.

Women are often portrayed in television in **stereotypical roles** which as J. Tunstall, 'The Media in Britain' (1983) argues, tends to emphasise women's domestic, sexual, consumer, and marital activities. Thus, they are frequently presented as having low-paid, low-status jobs, as lone parents, and as victims of one sort or another. There is correspondingly less emphasis on men's family and domestic situations, with careers being the focus for men's roles in soap operas and dramas.

ETHNIC MINORITIES AND THE MEDIA

As in the case of women, it is difficult to assess the effects of the media on people's perceptions of ethnic minorities compared with other influences in social life. There is certainly evidence to indicate that the media may have a role to play in reinforcing racist attitudes.

P. Hartmann and C. Husband, 'Racism and the Mass Media' (1974) argue that the media help to perpetuate **negative perceptions** of black people, and define race relations in terms of inter-group conflict. They identify two inter-related components of the presentation of race in the media:

The cultural legacy refers to the existence in Britain of an ideology which is derogatory to foreigners, and in particular to black people. Jokes, stereotypes, and images of blacks based largely on colonial associations are reinforced in the media and help to perpetuate a negative approach to race relations. News reporting in the press can often reinforce this cultural legacy (T. Van Dijk, 'Racism and the Press' (1991)). Van Dijk studied the reporting of ethnic affairs in a sample of British newspapers (*Times, Guardian, Daily Telegraph, Daily Mail, Sun, Independent*) over two six-month periods during 1985 and 1989. He found that most editorials in the papers supported a 'criminal' explanation for the disturbances (labelled riots by the press) occurring in several areas of London in 1985, whilst neglecting the existence of any 'social' explanations. The latter were explanations based on deprivation, inadequate housing, etc., and although they were alluded to, they were not regarded as serious reasons. Van Dijk provided a discourse analysis of the newspaper reports, where he studied the style and ideology surrounding coverage of ethnic affairs. He found that the articles used certain words to present a positive view of British white citizens and a negative picture of blacks and ethnic minorities. The newspapers also reflected the underlying British ideology concerned with the British 'opening doors' for immigrants, welcoming them into 'our homeland', and then castigating them for abusing 'our hospitality'.

The concept of 'news values', whereby journalists and broadcasters choose particular information, applies to the selection of newsworthy events concerning race relations. The news-reporting of race is usually framed around concepts of conflict or deviance, and is easily identifiable within existing cultural stereotypes. Hartmann and Husband show how the presence of ethnic minorities is frequently represented in the media as a problem for society. In a study of the handling of race in the British national press from 1963 to 1970. P. Hartmann et al, 'Race as News' (1974) found that newspapers focused on racial conflict, immigration control, and population increase amongst ethnic groups. There was no attempt by the press to examine the problems of access which black people have to education, employment, and housing. The notion that the media operate from a 'white' perspective has been developed in several studies. C. Husband, 'White Media, Black Britons' (1973) argues that racist beliefs are endemic amongst the white native population in Britain, and since the media are owned and staffed mainly by whites, with a predominantly white audience, there will be a tendency for the media to reinforce existing prejudices. B. Troyna, 'Public Awareness and the Media: a Study of Reporting Race' (1981), in a study of local and national press and local radio between 1976–78, found that black people were commonly presented as 'the outsider within'. The marginalisation of ethnic minorities was the main topic in press reporting of race, with immigration second (despite declining immigration from the New Commonwealth). Troyna surveyed public attitudes to see if they coincided with public opinion as represented in the media. His results supported Hartmann et al in finding that the media had encouraged an ideological belief that blacks were a source of trouble in society.

The main problem with all the above studies, however, is the extent to which the media actually promote racial prejudice, or whether they simply reinforce racist attitudes. P. Braham argues that the media may reflect racist attitudes rather than create them. D. Howitt acknowledges the problems which exist in attempting to separate media influences from other influences in people's lives. He also suggests that there are two possible consequences resulting from the unfavourable presentation of ethnic minorities in the media, firstly, whites will accept the negative images, which will reinforce their prejudices, and secondly, blacks will be encouraged to accept the images and the prejudice which goes with them.

The relationship between the mass media and violent behaviour

There is no evidence to suggest that there is any more violence in society today than there was in the past. However, through the mass media, different types and levels of violent behaviour are more visible to a much wider audience than ever before. A lot of attention has therefore focussed on the possible effects of media violence on people's behaviour, and on children's behaviour in particular.

Violence and violent behaviour are, however, difficult to measure, especially as viewers perceive and evaluate violence in different ways. Thus, B. Gunter, 'Dimensions of Television Violence' (1985) argues that cartoon violence such as *Tom and Jerry* is considerably less threatening and disturbing than watching people being killed. The context in which the violence occurs, news or fiction, can also influence the degree to which it is perceived. A violent society may replicate its violence in the media.

Much of the empirical research on the relationship between violence and the media is contradictory and inconclusive. One reason for this is the variation in methods used to study the effects. Thus, three sources of data are used to investigate the effects of the portrayal of violence on the screen: clinical case studies, laboratory experiments, and field studies. Some of the research from the three areas is summarised below:

Case studies of individuals who have imitated violence on the screen in real life are often very plausible. They also provide the public with an easily understood explanation for the violent behaviour. A good example is the case of the two eleven year old boys who murdered two year old James Bulger in Merseyside in 1993. The favoured explanation for their behaviour was that they had repeatedly watched a video entitled 'Child's Play 3' in which scenes resembled their own activities. In fact, there was no conclusive evidence to indicate that the children had even seen the film, yet alone imitated it.

One of the main problems with the case study approach is that it is unscentific, as it is impossible to compare similar individuals to find out why some are more prone to violence than others. Also, analysis or a series of isolated cases are questionable, as there may be underlying motives which might explain an individual's violent behaviour.

Laboratory experiments of groups of individuals and their reactions to violent material have been used mainly by psychologists. H.J.Eysenck and D.K.B.Nias, 'Sex, Violence and the Media' (1980) conducted laboratory research into the effects of the television portrayal of sex and violence on both adults and children. Eysenck and Nias found that exposure to high levels of televised violence led to consistently more aggressive behaviour than was found in the control groups. If these results were duplicated outside the laboratory then the case for censorship of media violence (advocated by Eysenck and Nias) would be proved. However, by their very nature, laboratory experiments on people cannot be conducted over long periods of time, so short-term effects might not be indicative of long-term exposure to violence. Also, cross-cultural research indicates that in some societies, such as Japan, a high level of violence on television is not reflected in the actual rates of violence in the country. In Japan, the explanation for this is that the society emphasises the suffering caused by violence, and not the aggression that caused it.

Field studies include the use of questionnaires, interviews, and observation to measure the effects of violence in the media on individuals. Some elements of the experimental method may be included, such as holding certain factors constant, to obtain a 'scientific analysis'. W.Belson, 'Television Violence and the Adolescent Boy' (1978) used this rigorous approach in his interviews with 1,565 London boys aged 12 to 17, to test the hypothesis that exposure to television violence increases the likelihood of committing violent acts. Belson found evidence to support his hypothesis, although critics such as D.Howitt, 'Mass Media and Social Problems' (1982) argue that his results indicate that there is a link between all types of television viewing and violent acts. Belson's work is also suspect because of the reliance he placed on the boys' remembered viewing experiences as well as their self-reported acts of violence. Belson also appears to be insensitive to the realities of contemporary youth culture, and the impact that sub-cultures and class may have on violent behaviour.

The issue of female violence is often ignored in field studies, yet D.Robins and P.Cohen, Knuckle Sandwich' (1978) illustrates how the influence of 'king fu' movies in the 1970s raised interest in the martial arts for both boys and girls, with social background and experience being more relevant to violent behaviour than their sex.

Field studies cannot prove that violence on television is a greater causal factor of violent acts than other influences, such as family, friends, or physical environment. However, television and video are easy subjects to blame, and provide convenient scapegoats for violent behaviour when there are no other visible causes.

CHECK YOUR UNDERSTANDING

After reading this chapter you should now be able to define the following terms.

1 Mass media
2 Differentiation of media
3 Concentration of media
4 Diversification of media
5 Multi-media conglomerates
6 Hypodermic-syringe model
7 Two-step flow model
8 Opinion leaders
9 Cultural effects theory
10 Pluralist view
11 Agency of conservative indoctrination
12 Postmodernist theory
13 Spin doctors
14 Allocative control
15 Operational control
16 Agenda-setting
17 Gatekeepers of news
18 Socially manufactured news
19 Moral panic
20 Hegemony
21 Cult of femininity
22 News values

SELF-ASSESSMENT QUESTIONS

1   Describe the three stages in the industrialisation of mass communications.
2   What is the main difference between the hypodermic-syringe theory and the two-step flow model?
3   How does the pluralist view of the media differ from the Marxist interpretation of media influences?
4   Describe the differences between allocative control and operational control.
5   How do 'news values' influence the presentation of industrial relations in the media?
6   How can the choice of methodology affect the study of media effects?

'A' LEVEL SOCIOLOGY ESSAY QUESTIONS

1   Evaluate the sociological arguments surrounding the claim that the mass media have created a mass culture in society (AEB, summer, 1992).
2   Evaluate the contributions of Pluralist and Marxist theories to an understanding of the role of the mass media in modern society (AEB, summer, 1995).
3   'The selection and presentation of the news depends more on practical issues than on cultural influences'. Discuss (AEB, summer, 1996).